CHILD PROTECTION IN AMERICA

Child Protection in America

Past, Present, and Future

JOHN E. B. MYERS

OXFORD

UNIVERSITY PRESS

2006

OXFORD

UNIVERSITY PRESS

Oxford University Press, Inc., publishes works that further
Oxford University's objective of excellence
in research, scholarship, and education.

Oxford   New York

Auckland   Cape Town   Dar es Salaam   Hong Kong   Karachi
Kuala Lumpur   Madrid   Melbourne   Mexico City   Nairobi
New Delhi   Shanghai   Taipei   Toronto

With offices in

Argentina   Austria   Brazil   Chile   Czech Republic   France   Greece
Guatemala   Hungary   Italy   Japan   Poland   Portugal   Singapore
South Korea   Switzerland   Thailand   Turkey   Ukraine   Vietnam

Published by Oxford University Press, Inc.
198 Madison Avenuse, New York, New York 10016

www.oup.com

Oxford is a registered trademark of Oxford University Press

Library of Congress Cataloging-in-Publication Data

Myers, John E. B.
Child protection in America : past, present, and future / John E. B. Myers.
p.   cm.
ISBN 0-19-516935-2
ISBN 13 978-0-19-516935-5
1. Child welfare—United States.   2. Child welfare—United States—History.   3. Child abuse—
United States—Prevention.   4. Child abuse—Law and legislation—United States.
5. Children—Legal status, laws, etc.—United States.   I. Title.

HV741.M928   2006
362.760973—dc22   2005024921

1   3   5   7   9   8   6   4   2

Printed in the United States of America
on acid-free paper

*This book is dedicated to
child protection social workers
past, present, and future*

PREFACE

Protecting children from abuse and neglect is a worthy goal. The purpose of this book is to advance this goal in two ways. First, the book offers recommendations to reduce the amount of abuse and neglect. Second, because it is not possible to eliminate maltreatment entirely, the book suggests reforms to the child protection system.

To fully understand the strengths and weaknesses of today's child protection system, it is useful to study the historical development of child protection. Part I traces the history of child protection in America. With the history in place, part II shifts the focus from past to present and begins by analyzing the principal causes of child abuse and neglect. Once the causes of maltreatment are outlined, part II describes broad societal changes that hold promise for reducing child abuse and neglect. Unfortunately, we will never prevent all maltreatment, and the book ends with proposals to strengthen the child protection system.

Historians and social commentators do more than report "facts." No matter how diligently we try to be objective, we interpret. I have endeavored in these pages to remain conscious of my viewpoint. In the final analysis, however, my twenty years' work in child protection undoubtedly influences my writing. My "bias" is to see the best in the motives of the people engaged in child protection. Thus, I'm an optimist. I believe the reformers who labored to protect children in the past acted foremost out of genuine concern for children. The same is true for professionals in child protection today.

Every writer views the world from their unique perspective. Some writers on childhood, child maltreatment, and child protection paint a gloomy picture. Lloyd deMause, for example, in his book *The History of Childhood* (New York: Psychohistory Press, 1974), set the tone in these words, "The history of childhood is a nightmare from which we have only recently begun to awaken. The further back in history one goes, the lower the level of child care, the more likely children are to be killed, abandoned, beaten, terrorized, and sexually abused" (p. 1). Although portions of deMause's book are positive, the overall impression is pessimistic. By contrast, John Boswell wrote an entire volume on abandonment of children and somehow managed to leave the reader uplifted rather than depressed. Boswell's more hopeful approach begins with his title, *The Kindness of*

Strangers: The Abandonment of Children in Western Europe from Late Antiquity to the Renaissance (New York: Pantheon, 1988). Throughout *The Kindness of Strangers*, Boswell connects the reader with the love that runs from parent to child, even when that parent abandons the child. I am closer to Boswell than deMause.

Although an optimist, I'm not naïve. I understand that the child protection system has major faults, and that the professionals in the system share the weaknesses and prejudices of their fellow creatures. In the final analysis, however, I believe the story of child protection in America is a story of steady progress. The goal in these pages is to contribute to that progress.

ACKNOWLEDGMENTS

Many people helped with this project.

As the manuscript neared completion, my friend Fawn Alvarez edited the text, adding enormously to readability. Fawn also provided many ideas that can be found in the text.

Thanks to Philip O. Alderson, M.D., Chair of Radiology, Columbia-Presbyterian Medical Center, New York, for the picture of John Caffey; Robyn Alsop, M.S., former Information Specialist at the Children's Division of the American Humane Association; Sister Joan Marie Aycock, Archivist of the Ursuline Convent Archives and Museum in New Orleans for her help in my research of the Ursuline orphanage in New Orleans; Lucy Berliner, M.S.W., for her wisdom and advice over the years; Debra Daro, Ph.D., Chapin Hall, University of Chicago, for her guidance on a number of issues; Diane DePanfilis, Ph.D., Assistant Dean for Research, University of Maryland School of Social Work, for discussing with me the role of social work education in improving child protection; Don Duquette, J.D., for reading an early version of the manuscript and for many good ideas; Barbara Feaster, for sharing her story; David Finkelhor, Ph.D., for his wisdom and ideas; Ruth Kempe, M.D., for discussing with me the work of her late husband C. Henry Kempe, and for the photograph of Dr. Kempe; Claire McCurdy, Archivist for the Union Theological Seminary for information on Charles Loring Brace; Nancy McDaniel, M.P.A., Director of Program and Planning and Operations of the Children's Division of the American Humane Association; Gary Melton, Ph.D., for keeping me honest; Victor Remer, Archivist of the New York Children's Aid Society, for providing the photograph of Charles Loring Brace.

I owe a particular debt of gratitude to the librarians at my university, without whose efforts, ideas, skill, and creativity this book would have been impossible: Skip Allums, Kelly Anders, Stephanie Braunstein, Kim Clarke, Michele Finerty, Evelyn Posamentier, Louise Roysdon, Susan VanSyckel, Sue Welsh, and Harriet Zook.

Nothing gets done in academia without secretarial support, and I have the best: Denai Burbank, Paul Fuller, Sharleen Jackson, Cathleen Reis, and Sally Snyder.

CONTENTS

CHILD PROTECTION IN AMERICA

Part I

THE ROAD TRAVELED

The History of Child Protection in America

The progress of a state may be measured by the extent to which it safeguards the rights of its children.
GRACE ABBOTT, *The Child and the State*

Every day across America, child protection agencies receive thousands of telephone calls reporting abuse and neglect. Before you finish this sentence, a phone will ring to report a child at death's door, a sexually abused child, a neglected child, or some other variant of the misery of child maltreatment.

Once child protection social workers sift through the daily avalanche of calls and separate the abused and neglected children from the children who are not maltreated, the sad reality comes into focus: More than 2,500 children are abused or neglected every day in America. That is nearly a million children a year. Each day, four children die because of abuse or neglect.[1] To make matters worse, official statistics underreport the true scope of child abuse and neglect.

Many abused and neglected children cannot live safely at home, and for that reason more than 500,000 children reside in foster care. The average stay in foster care is two years, but thousands of children languish in care much longer. Fortunately, with help from social workers, many abusive or neglectful parents resolve the problems that necessitated removal of their children, and families are reunited. Increasingly, children who cannot return to parents find permanent homes through adoption. Yet, the depressing fact remains that half a million children live away from their parents.

America's child protection system is staffed by social workers, police officers, juvenile court judges, attorneys, mental health workers, nurses, and physicians. These professionals work hard and care deeply about children and families, yet they labor under heavy caseloads. Some social workers are responsible for nearly 100 children. Children's attorneys in some communities have caseloads above 300. Try as they might, professionals cannot keep up. As a result, children who could be protected fall through the cracks, parents who could be helped go without services, and foster children who could return home or be adopted wait years for permanence.

The work of child protection is extremely stressful, particularly for social workers. Child protection social workers make agonizingly difficult decisions, often with inadequate information and little time for reflection. Thus, at two in the morning a social worker visits a home and must decide whether to remove a child or leave the child at home. If the social worker leaves the child at home and the child is injured or killed, the social worker is blamed and feels enormous guilt. If the worker removes the child, the worker may be criticized for needlessly breaking up the family. Given the high caseloads and constant stress, it is not surprising that turnover among social workers is high. The average tenure of social workers in child protection is a mere two years.

There are no simple answers to the problem of child abuse and neglect. More money for child protection is part of the solution, but federal, state, and local governments already spend millions on child welfare. Throwing more money at child abuse and neglect will help, but money will not solve the problem. To stem the tide of maltreatment, America's child protection system needs reform, and with reform in mind, this book has two objectives. First, the book makes recommendations to reduce the prevalence of child abuse and neglect. Second, because it is not possible to prevent all maltreatment, the book recommends improvements to the existing child protection system.

To understand the strengths and weaknesses of today's child protection system, it is useful to examine the history of child protection. To that end, part I of the book traces the history of child protection in the United States from colonial times to the twenty-first century. With the historical background in place, part II tackles the issues of prevention and reform. Chapter 6 analyzes the causes of child abuse and neglect, as well as impediments to improving child protection. Chapter 7 discusses broad reforms intended to reduce child abuse and neglect. Finally, chapter 8 describes specific improvements of today's child protection system.

Before delving into the history of child protection, consider four cases. In the first case, a little boy named Eli Creekmore was failed miserably by the child protection system. In the other cases, children were rescued. These cases are emblematic of the challenges of child protection.

Eli Creekmore

Late at night, an ambulance races to the small, ramshackle house in Everett, Washington, where three-year-old Eli Creekmore lies dying. Paramedics rush Eli to the emergency room, where doctors and nurses work feverishly to save him. It's too late. Eli dies because his father, Darren Creekmore, kicked him in the stomach, ripping his intestines.

On the night Eli died, he was sitting at the dinner table with his parents, Darren and Mary Creekmore. Eli started crying, and Darren sent him to his room. Darren followed Eli to his room, and Mary heard a noise, a gasping noise, followed by a thud as Eli hit the floor. Eli emerged from his room, sobbing, and said, "I pooped my pants." Darren asked, "Why did you poop your pants, boy?" Eli responded, "Because you kicked me." When Mary said, "Don't kick him," Darren threatened her with violence. Darren ordered Eli to the bathroom to clean himself. In the bathroom, Eli peed in his pants and threw up on himself. Darren beat Eli with a belt for soiling himself and ordered him to bed. In terrible pain, Eli lay crying. Mary pleaded to take her son to the hospital, but Darren refused. Later that night, Eli stopped breathing.

The tragedy of this senseless murder is compounded by the fact that Eli was well known to child protective services (CPS). Months earlier, the then two-year-old Eli and his mother visited Eli's maternal grandmother, Myrna Strachen. Myrna noticed that Eli had lost weight and was covered with bruises. Eli's leg hurt, and he had trouble walking. Myrna asked her daughter to take Eli to the hospital, but Mary refused. Myrna called CPS, and a social worker and a police officer went to Eli's home and took him to the hospital, where he was examined by doctor Peter Millican. Dr. Millican diagnosed child abuse and filed a report with CPS. Eli was placed in foster care but was soon returned to his parents.

CPS referred the Creekmores to Homebuilders, a family preservation service designed to help abusive parents. A Homebuilders case worker visited the Creekmores for four weeks and recommended the family stay together. CPS arranged for Eli to attend a family day care operated by Ken and Joanne Lechner. On numerous occasions, the Lechners noted bruises on Eli and telephoned CPS, but CPS did not return calls or said they believed the Creekmore's explanations.

Social workers concluded the Creekmores were making progress, and CPS withdrew from the family. But the social workers were wrong. A few months later, Eli was again covered with bruises. Darren admitted using a ruler to discipline Eli. Darren was charged by the police with assault. CPS reopened the case and required Darren to move out, but he soon returned to the home. Mary did not inform CPS that Darren was back and the violence continued.

On his third birthday, Eli had a party. When Eli's grandmother, Myrna, arrived for the party, she was shocked at the bruises on Eli's face and around his eyes.

Desperate to get Eli out of the house, Myrna offered to take him for ice cream. At the restaurant, Eli put a spoonful of ice cream in his mouth, winced, and said, "Ow grandma." He pulled the spoon out of his mouth and it was covered with blood. The inside of his mouth was raw and inflamed. A few hours later, two police officers were having coffee at the restaurant. The waitress who served Eli told them about the ice cream and the bloody spoon. The officers went to Eli's home and took him to the hospital. The same doctor, Peter Millican, was on duty, and this time he was seriously worried. The bruises around Eli's eyes indicated that he might have a skull fracture. Dr. Millican filed another report with CPS, this time warning that if something was not done, Eli could be seriously injured or killed. In a decision that seems incomprehensible, CPS decided that if the Creekmores would submit to a psychological evaluation, Eli could go home. The evaluation was never performed, and two months later, Eli was dead. Darren was convicted of homicide.

The Creekmore case is described in a powerful documentary film *The Unquiet Death of Eli Creekmore* by David Davis.[2] In the film, Dr. Millican, the emergency room physician who twice warned CPS of Eli's danger, summed up the dilemma so often faced by child protective services. "They are supposed to protect children from injury and harm and neglect. And on the other hand they are supposed to mobilize the resources of society to keep families together. I'm sure almost every case they see, those two jobs are on a collision course." In the same documentary, CPS social worker Lee Doran, who was responsible for forty cases at once, described the difficulties he faced every day. "It's just not that clear cut, usually. And we just do the best we can, and it's hard to know whether you are doing the right thing for the child and the family. So many aspects of what we do are controversial. If I leave the child in the home, I run the possibility of being wrong and having the child hurt. It's impossible to do it all well. We feel like there's a real potential for a child to turn up dead or seriously injured because we *can't* do it all. It's inevitable, unfortunately, that even with the best child protective services, even with the best laws, kids are going to continue to be at risk in their homes and are probably going to die. We can't guarantee that kids won't die in the future."

Barbara Feaster

Barbara Feaster was born in Salt Lake City, Utah. From the time she was a baby, her father sexually abused her. When Barbara was six, her father confessed to the leader of the Mormon church he attended. In the Mormon Church—the Church of Jesus Christ of Latter Day Saints—neighborhood congregations are led by a lay bishop rather than a professional minister. The bishop discussed the illegality and immorality of the conduct and Barbara's father promised to reform. He didn't. Before long, he was molesting Barbara again and threatening her to keep her silent.

The sexual abuse continued for years. Like many victims, Barbara was powerless to stop it. When you are a child—completely dependent—and the most powerful person in your world, your father, is violating you, you feel powerless and trapped. It is drilled into your head, "This is a secret." You try to make the best of your dilemma; you accommodate. You live for the good times when your dad isn't molesting you, but you fear the bad times. Deep down you know it isn't over. But what can you do? You're just a powerless kid. Many victims *never* disclose their abuse. Others delay reporting for months or years.

Barbara's abuse continued into her teenage years. Finally, when Barbara was sixteen, her father went again to the bishop, a new man. The bishop listened and delivered an ultimatum, "What you are doing is going to stop. It is not only a sin, it is a crime. Either you go to the police or I will." Finally, someone took a stand. Barbara's father knew it was over. To his credit, he told Barbara that she would be interviewed by the police, and that she should tell the truth. Barbara's father confessed to the police, but he was free on bail awaiting a decision about his punishment. Barbara's mother refused to believe her husband was guilty and wanted him to return home so Barbara had to get out. Child protective services got involved and arranged for the seventeen-year-old Barbara to move into an apartment.

A young CPS social worker was assigned to Barbara's case; a social worker who helped Barbara change her life. Like so many victims of sexual and psychological abuse, Barbara was depressed and lacking self-confidence. She viewed herself as worthless, as damaged goods. But her social worker would have none of it. She told Barbara, "You are as important as the child of a king. You deserve the best. You're smart, and you can do anything you want." And she didn't say it once, or twice, or a dozen times; she said it over and over again until Barbara started to believe it. The social worker helped Barbara get into counseling and finish high school. Then it was off to college. Years later, Barbara said, "My social worker saved my life." Today, Barbara Feaster is happily married with children of her own.[3]

Jamal

Jamal's mother, Ruby, living near the California coast, was a devoted adherent of a macrobiotic diet.[4] She ate only grains, beans, and vegetables, and avoided meat, fish, milk products, and fruit. Ruby had two children, two-year-old Barron and eight-month-old Jamal. Ruby imposed her macrobiotic diet on the children despite the objections of Barron's father and the repeated advice of her physician, Gilbert Carter, who warned her that the diet was unhealthy for young children. Dr. Carter specifically warned Ruby that breastfeeding Jamal while she was on a macrobiotic diet was hazardous for the baby.

Barron's father sought help from CPS, and social worker Donald Allegri met with Ruby and the children. Allegri urged Ruby to contact Dr. Loretta Rao, a pediatrician who Allegri knew was a vegetarian. Allegri thought Ruby might be able to relate to Dr. Rao. Ruby took Barron to Dr. Rao, but not Jamal. When Allegri learned Ruby did not take Jamal to Dr. Rao, Allegri phoned Dr. Carter and expressed his concern over Jamal's condition.

Soon thereafter, Dr. Carter spent two hours with Ruby and the children. The doctor was shocked when he observed Jamal. Dr. Carter said, "Ruby, how could you do this? How could you not take care of your baby?" Dr. Carter reiterated the dangers of breastfeeding Jamal while Ruby was on a macrobiotic diet and urged Ruby to modify her diet and increase the calories and protein she provided Jamal. Like social worker Allegri, Dr. Carter urged Ruby to consult Dr. Rao about her diet.

Two days later, Dr. Carter saw Jamal again and observed that the baby remained malnourished and significantly underdeveloped. Carter again pressed Ruby to visit Dr. Rao. During a telephone conversation two weeks later, Dr. Carter repeated his warning about the severity of Jamal's condition and urged Ruby to visit Dr. Rao or take Jamal to the hospital emergency room. Ruby said she would "take care of things."

Finally, Ruby took Jamal to Dr. Rao's office. The nurse led Ruby and the baby into an examination room; Dr. Rao noticed that the nurse stayed in the room longer than usual. Finally, Dr. Rao opened the door and the nurse said, "Thank God you are here. I was afraid to leave the room because the baby might die." Dr. Rao glanced at the baby and confirmed the nurse's concern. Jamal was dying of starvation. Dr. Rao told Ruby that the baby had to be hospitalized immediately, but Ruby declined and prepared to leave. Dr. Rao called the police and told Ruby to stay right where she was. The police arrived and took Jamal into protective custody. He was rushed to the hospital where emergency procedures saved his life.

While Jamal was in the hospital, Ruby surreptitiously brought him macrobiotic food despite warnings not to do so. She continued breastfeeding him after she was told that her milk contained dangerous levels of sodium.

When Jamal was well enough to leave the hospital he was placed in a foster home. On a visit to the foster home, Ruby abducted Jamal and fled to Puerto Rico. An FBI agent located Ruby in Puerto Rico, where she and her children were living in squalor. The only food was beans, millet, and noodles. Ruby told the FBI agent she took Jamal from the foster home because "the foster mother fed Jamal eggs and sugar. He was getting fat." The children were returned to California and placed in foster homes. Ruby ended up in a mental hospital.

In Jamal's case, the coordinated efforts of a social worker, two doctors, the FBI, local police, the juvenile court, and the foster care system protected a baby from a well intended but mentally ill mother, saving the child's life.

Olivia Waggner—Social Worker

Olivia Waggner was born and raised in Springfield, Illinois.[5] She graduated from college in 1940, and got a job as a social worker in rural Illinois. Olivia was the only child welfare worker for several counties. In the 1940s, child welfare workers were generalists, providing foster home studies, adoption services, intervention when married couples had problems with their kids or each other, child protection, and anything else that came up.

Late one night, Olivia was at home when a deputy sheriff called. Would she go with him to a home out in the country where a family was having problems? Olivia and the deputy went to the house, actually a shack. When the sheriff knocked, the woman hesitated to let him in, but Olivia assured her they were there to help. The dirt floor was littered with trash and the place was utterly filthy. Seven hungry children were milling about in rags. There was no food. A sick puppy died while they were there. Olivia said, "Children can't live this way." The mother replied, "I know, but we have no money." Olivia placed the children in foster care where they got food and medical care. She helped the parents get on their feet.

Most of the parents Olivia worked with were poor. In one case, however, the parents were well-to-do. They had a son who was a deaf mute. The boy's mother insisted, however, that he was mentally retarded. Olivia knew he was nothing of the sort. Olivia spoke with the boy's father and told him, "Your son is not retarded. He's a smart young man and he needs to be in school." Seeing his son in a new light, the father overrode his wife's decision to keep the boy at home. Not only did the boy finish high school, but he also went to Gallaudet University, America's premier university for deaf students, and became a teacher.

Years later, Olivia's own son was teaching at the local community college. After class one day, a man approached him and asked, "Are you related to Olivia Waggner?" Olivia's son replied, "Yes, she's my mother." The man said, "Would you thank her for me? A long time ago, when I was a boy, she had a talk with my dad. Your mom saved my life."

Critics of child protection might characterize Olivia Waggner as an officious intermeddler, who was too quick to inject her own values into other people's private family matters. To me she's a heroine. The perfect tough-minded, no-nonsense person we need helping children and parents.

$$\cdot \quad \cdot \quad \cdot$$

These stories illustrate the fundamental issues that have shaped America's response to child abuse and neglect. How can child abuse and neglect be prevented? When should government intervene in families to protect children? When intervention is necessary, should it be voluntary or involuntary? When involuntary intervention is necessary, who should take the lead: law enforcement or social work? When abuse or neglect occurs in a family, some children can remain safely at home, while others must be removed. In doubtful cases, should the preference be to leave children at home or to err on the side of safety and remove them? When children are removed because their home is unsafe, where should they live? With relatives? With foster parents? In an institution? When children are placed in out-of-home care due to abuse or neglect, how long should they stay there? What should maltreating parents be required to do to regain custody of their children? How long should maltreating parents be given to overcome addiction, learn to control anger, or gain basic parenting skills? When is it appropriate to give up on parents and terminate the parent-child relationship so children can be adopted?

Part I examines how Americans struggled with these questions in the past. Part II builds on this history to recommend improvements in today's child protection system.

I

CHILD PROTECTION FROM
THE COLONIAL PERIOD TO 1875

The saga of child protection in America begins in colonial times. In early America, cities were few in number and small. In 1700, for example, New York City had only 7,000 people. In 1720, Boston's population reached 12,000. In 1770, the colonial population was just over two million. Most colonists lived on farms or in small villages.

When rural families were poor, or when children were orphaned, neglected, or abused, help often came from family, friends, neighbors, or the church. The same informal resources were frequently available in cities. When informal resources were exhausted or unavailable, local officials stepped in and employed time-tested principles of English Poor Law, including outdoor relief, apprenticeship, and indenture.

Outdoor relief was financial assistance provided to the "deserving" poor in their own homes.[1] Decisions about outdoor relief were made by town officials. Stipends were small but enough to keep body and soul together. Over the years, significant numbers of poor children were supported at home with outdoor relief.

Apprenticeship has roots in ancient Egypt and Babylon. In England, apprenticeship had a long history, and the institution crossed the Atlantic with the colonists. Public education did not exist in the colonies, and apprenticeship was a sensible way to teach young people a trade and prepare them for adulthood.

Apprenticeships were voluntary or involuntary. With voluntary apprenticeship, a master agreed to teach an apprentice a trade as well as provide food, clothing, shelter, religious instruction, and a modicum of "book learning." Children were apprenticed at various ages, but generally not before they were old enough to work. The period of apprenticeship was often seven years. Involuntary apprenticeship was used for substantial numbers of poor children and orphans. Local officials had authority to remove dependent children from their parents and place the children with masters.

An indentured servant was a person, often a young adult, who agreed to serve a number of years without pay in exchange for bed and board, and, perhaps, some instruction in a trade. After 1630, many immigrants arrived in the colonies as indentured servants. Poor children could be "bound out" by local officials as indentured servants. Robert Bremner observed, "Although the law defined servitude and apprenticeship as two separate institutions, apprenticeship in practice was often merely a specialized form of servitude. The main distinction between apprenticeship and servitude was in the master's obligation to teach the former a specific trade. Even this difference disappeared, however, in the case of poor and dependent children, who were bound out as 'apprentices,' but actually worked as servants."[2]

For much of our history, clear distinctions were not drawn between children who were poor and children who were maltreated. The term "dependent child" applied to both groups, and the Poor Law remedies of outdoor relief, apprenticeship, and indenture were prescribed for children who were poor, as well as for children who were neglected or abused. It was not until the third quarter of the twentieth century that social policy and law drew relatively clear distinctions between poverty and maltreatment.[3] Even now, the distinction is blurred because poverty and maltreatment overlap.

Legal documents creating apprenticeship or indenture often contained provisions against cruelty. Additionally, some communities had laws requiring authorities to intervene in cases of mistreatment of apprentices or servants. A Massachusetts law of 1781 authorized overseers of the poor to apprentice children of poor parents who "shall in their Opinion be unable to maintain them." The law provided, "It shall be the duty of the Overseers or Selectmen, to make enquiry into the treatment of Children . . . and if they find them at any time injured, to seek a redress thereof." A New York City ordinance from 1800 authorized the directors of the almshouse to bind out poor children to "suitable trades or occupations," and required that "if any of those who shall have been so bound out, shall be injured or ill-treated, the superintendent shall consider it as his duty to procure them redress."[4] Needless to say, the extent to which laws protecting apprentices and servants were enforced varied from place to place. Nevertheless, the fact that protective laws existed indicates awareness of maltreatment.

Further evidence of concern about abuse is scattered across the historical record. As early as 1642, Massachusetts had a law authorizing magistrates to remove children from parents who did not "train up" their children properly.[5] In 1655, a tradesman from Plymouth was convicted for causing the death of his young servant.[6] In 1735, an orphan girl in Georgia was sexually abused in several homes until she was finally rescued and "placed with a reliable woman."[7] In 1809, a New York City shopkeeper was prosecuted for brutality against a slave and her three-year-old daughter.[8] In 1810, a woman was prosecuted for murdering her baby shortly following birth, although the woman was found not guilty because she was insane.[9]

Homer Folks wrote, "From about 1825 there came a more and more general recognition and practical application of the principle that it is the right and duty of the public authorities to intervene in cases of parental cruelty, or gross neglect seriously endangering the health, morals, or elementary education of children, and to remove the children by force if necessary, and place them under surroundings more favorable for their development." Murray and Aleline Levine added, "As early as 1825, as the cities grew and people lived in closer proximity, statutes began to appear emphasizing the right and the duty of the public to intervene in cases of parental cruelty or gross neglect."[10]

Almshouses

By 1700, the colonial population reached 250,000, and as the population expanded, so did the number of people unable to fend for themselves, including the infirm elderly, the mentally ill, the retarded, the poor, the seriously and terminally ill, and dependent children. Traditional methods of providing for the poor (outdoor relief, apprenticeship) proved inadequate. Turning to England for solutions, colonists erected almshouses, also called the poor house, the workhouse, or the county farm. Care in an almshouse was called "indoor relief." One of the first American almshouses was built in New York State in 1653.[11] Most almshouses were erected after 1700, and the pace of construction was brisk during the nineteenth century. The almshouse was America's first institution to provide for large numbers of dependent children. In 1823, one New York City almshouse housed more than five hundred children.[12]

At first, the almshouse was considered an advance over earlier methods.[13] Some residents worked or learned a trade. Others were cared for by staff and by each other. Grace Abbott observed, "Almshouse care, particularly when a work program was provided, was regarded as greatly superior to outdoor relief."[14]

Any notion that the almshouse was a suitable place for children faded quickly. In 1856, a New York Senate committee reported that almshouses were "the most disgraceful memorials of public charity. . . . Filth, nakedness, licentiousness, general bad morals . . . gross neglect of the most ordinary comforts and decencies of life" were rampant. The committee concluded that for children, almshouses were "the worst possible nurseries." Similar views were expressed in 1897 by Henry Williams, who wrote, "If the intention and desire were to make sure that these dependent children should grow up to be paupers, vagabonds, and criminals, then this throwing them in with the human wreckage of the almshouse would be an ideal method of disposal. But if it be desired to make useful citizens instead of vagabonds, then the almshouse, considered as a home for dependent children, is simply an abomination."[15] In 1894, Homer Folks wrote a stinging critique of the almshouse: "Everywhere men have instinctively spoken of 'going to the poor-house' as the last and bitterest of earthy misfortunes. If the vital statistics of poor-houses could be accurately kept, the percentage of deaths from a broken heart would be surprising."[16] By the late 1800s, an increasing drumbeat of criticism called for removal of children from almshouses.

Orphanages

For children who were orphaned or who had living parents but could not remain at home or who had no home, the orphanage was a significant improvement over the almshouse. America's first orphanage was established in New Orleans in 1728 by Ursuline nuns.[17] The first public orphanage opened in Charleston, South Carolina in 1790. By 1800, there were just five orphanages, and most dependent children were cared for with outdoor relief, apprenticeship, indenture, or the almshouse.[18]

FIGURE 1.1
Pupils at the Ursuline Orphanage in New Orleans singing roundelays. From Mother Therese Wolfe, *The Ursulines and Our Lady of Prompt Succur: A Record of Two Centuries—1727 to 1925*. 1925. New York: P.J. Kennedy & Sons.

FIGURE 1.2

Boys of the Sacramento Children's Home are joined by the superintendent in 1927.
Photograph provided by and reproduced with permission of the Sacramento
Children's Home.

The number of orphanages grew steadily during the nineteenth century, fueled by immigration, economic downturns, disease, and growing urban poverty.[19] The New York Orphan Asylum Society was founded in 1806. The nation's second public orphanage opened in Philadelphia in 1820. In 1822, the Society of Friends opened the first orphanage for African American children, which was a necessity because children of color were often excluded from orphanage care. By 1850, there were more than seventy orphan asylums, many of them affiliated with religious denominations and nondenominational charities. The Civil War created thousands of orphans and half-orphans (a child with one living parent), and by 1880, some six hundred orphanages dotted the national map, and in 1900, the number of children living in orphanages topped 100,000.[20]

Charles Loring Brace and the New York Children's Aid Society

Charles Loring Brace is a towering figure in American child welfare. Brace was born June 9, 1826, at Litchfield, Connecticut.[21] At sixteen, Brace entered Yale, where he studied religion and moral philosophy. Brace decided on the ministry,

FIGURE 1.3
Charles Loring Brace at
age twenty-nine.
Photograph provided by
and reproduced with
permission of the New
York Children's Aid
Society.

and upon graduation from Yale, he attended Union Theological Seminary during
1848 and 1849.

College and seminary behind him, Brace was faced with a choice between the
comfortable life of a preacher or the arduous existence of a missionary to the
poor. He settled on the latter, joining a long tradition of religiously inspired assistance to New York City's poor. Brace took up his duties in the notorious slum
known as Five Points.[22] In 1842, Charles Dickens visited America and toured Five
Points, describing it in these words: "This is the place: these narrow ways, diverg-
ing to the right and left, and reeking everywhere with dirt and filth. . . . Debauchery has made the very houses prematurely old. See how the rotten beams are
tumbling down, and how the patched and broken windows seem to scowl dimly,
like eyes that have been hurt in drunken frays. . . . Ascend these pitch-dark stairs,
heedful of a false footing on the trembling boards, and grope your way with me
into this wolfish den, where neither ray of light nor breath of air, appears to
come. . . . Where dogs would howl to lie, women, and men, and boys slink off to
sleep, forcing the dislodged rats to move away in quest of better lodgings."[23]

John Griscom, City Inspector for New York City, campaigned against conditions in slums like Five Points, especially the airless cellars, which he described as
"living graves for human beings."[24] Brace poured his heart into Five Points, writing

to his father in 1852, "If I am only a city missionary with two hundred dollars a year, or anything else mean, but really doing good, you should be contented. I don't care a straw for a city pastor's place. I want to raise up the outcast and homeless, to go down among those who have no friend or helper, and do something for them of what Christ has done for me."[25]

While thousands of New York's poor children lived in rundown, unsanitary, rat-infested tenements, thousands more had no home at all. Living on the street, homeless children survived by their wits. In 1852, New York's police chief warned that more than 3,000 children lived on city streets. Some homeless children were orphans. Others had one or both parents living, but preferred the streets to conditions at home. Confronted by harsh New York winters, droves of street urchins huddled in doorways or struggled for a measure of warmth in old boxes and under piles of rags. A majority of crime reports were against children, and a quarter of the inmates in city jails were children.[26]

Why was poverty such a problem in New York City? By 1850, the city's population reached 515,000, outstripping employment, housing, and services.[27] New York's expanding population resulted largely from immigration, and immigrants were among New York's poorest inhabitants.[28] Although many immigrants moved

FIGURE 1.4
Street children in New York City photographed by Jacob Riis. Jacob A. Riis, *How the Other Half Lives.* 1890. New York: Charles Scribner's Sons.

beyond New York to start new lives in the West, thousands more were trapped in the City because they lacked the resources to leave or because they hoped to make a go of it in New York.[29]

Disease took a terrible toll. Outbreaks of cholera in 1849 and 1852 killed thousands, leaving corpses stacked in the street. Typhus and consumption (tuberculosis) were ubiquitous. Edwin Burrows and Mike Wallace reported, "Between 1850 and 1860 more than half of those under the age of five died each year—seven of every ten under the age of two."[30] Dairy milk for babies was often tainted.[31] Burrows and Wallace wrote, "Foul milk, like foul water, proved durable and deadly . . . , felling infants by the thousands."[32]

By the 1850s, the Industrial Revolution was at full steam. Industry required large numbers of low-wage, unskilled, or marginally skilled laborers. Despite long hours of grueling labor, a week's wages seldom made ends meet. Disabling and fatal industrial accidents were regular occurrences, yet disability pay, workers compensation, and health insurance lay in the future. Families that were "just making it" on a father's wages fell into poverty when the breadwinner was laid off, fired, disabled, or killed on the job.

With adults earning so little, child labor was needed to keep body and soul together. Of course, there was nothing new about child labor. From colonial times forward, children worked on family farms and as apprentices and servants. Robert Bremner noted, "The labor of children was a social fact, not a social problem."[33] Industrialization, however, changed the conditions of children's labor. The centuries-old apprentice system, in which a single child spent years learning a trade from a single craftsman, broke down. LeRoy Ashby wrote, "Industrialization and surging population devastated the apprentice system, which had long provided a way of caring for dependent children as well as a source of training in skilled labor."[34] Factories did not need children with skills, they needed little hands to perform repetitive and often dangerous tasks hours-on-end for very little money. In New York City and its environs, more than 100,000 children worked ten to sixteen-hour days, often in poorly ventilated, unsafe, and unwholesome conditions.

Education promised escape from poverty. The well-to-do sent their children to private schools. For the poor, however, the promise of education lay in public schools. Massachusetts was a pioneer in public education. In 1837, Massachusetts established a state board of education, and in 1852, the legislature passed the nation's first compulsory attendance law. Other states, including New York, followed suit. By 1918, all states had compulsory attendance laws. Unfortunately, as public schools became available, many nineteenth- and early twentieth-century poor children worked rather than studied.

Thus, midway through the nineteenth century, New York City faced a chronic crisis of poverty. It was this crisis, with its particular impact on children, that brought the youthful Charles Loring Brace together with more senior colleagues to create an organization focused specifically on poor children. Following an initial planning meeting, Brace received a letter dated January 9, 1853, inviting him to lead the new "mission to the children." As Brace struggled to make up his mind, he wrote to his father, "I have just about decided on an important step for me; that is, to be city missionary for vagrant boys during the year, with office and salary ($1,000). I have hesitated a good deal, as it interrupts my regular study and training, but this is a new and very important enterprise. The duties are to organize a system of boys' meetings, vagrant schools, etc., which shall reach the whole city; to communicate with press and clergy; to draw in boys, find them places in the country, get them to schools, help them to help themselves; to write and preach, etc. A new and rather expanded thing at present, but to become clearer as we go on. Mornings in office, afternoons in visiting. It suits my sympathies, has variety, and is or can be of infinite use. Still it will keep me here, even in hottest weather, and it binds me down for a year. What do you say? Is it the best field for my talents? Can I do more elsewhere for humanity?"[35] The invitation Brace thought he might accept for a year became the work of a lifetime, and gave rise in 1853 to the New York Children's Aid Society.

Brace described the challenge before him, "What soon struck all engaged in these labors was the immense number of boys and girls floating and drifting about our streets, with hardly any assignable home or occupation, who continually swelled the multitude of criminals, prostitutes, and vagrants. . . . It was clear that whatever was done, must be done in the source and origin of the evil—in prevention, not cure." Brace was painfully aware of the harm inflicted on children by extreme poverty and overcrowding. He wrote, "The influence of *overcrowding* has been incredibly debasing. When we find half a dozen families—as we frequently do—occupying one room, the old and young, men and women, boys and girls of all ages sleeping near each other, the result is inevitable. The older persons commit unnatural crimes; the younger grow up with hardly a sense of personal integrity or purity; the girls are corrupted even in childhood; and the boys become naturally thieves, vagrants, and vicious characters."[36] Brace's reference to child sexual abuse was repeated elsewhere in his writing. In 1854 he wrote, "Of the young girls in the city, driven to dishonest means of living, it is most sad to speak. Privation, crime, and old debasement in the pure and sunny years of childhood."[37] Like others of his time, Brace was aware of child sexual abuse, but felt constrained to hint at it rather than describe it forthrightly. Brace was equally aware of physical abuse and neglect.[38] The New York Children's Aid Society (CAS) was not a child protection agency as we understand child protection today. Its mission was broader, to help "the poor children of the city."[39] Yet, CAS saved thousands of children from maltreatment.[40]

In his "mission to the children," Brace created "industrial schools, where the children of the working classes are taught habits of industry, order, and cleanliness, together with common school lessons." By 1890, the Children's Aid Society operated twenty-two industrial schools instructing nearly 10,000 children.[41]

In addition to industrial schools, Brace and his colleagues established night schools so children who worked during the day could obtain an education. Brace wrote, "The eagerness of these hard-working youths after a day of severe toil to obtain the rudiments of education is one of the most pathetic experiences in the field of the society's work. In one school, the Park School, near Sixty-eighth Street, young girls and lads, who have been working from seven o'clock till six, have been known to go without their supper in order not to miss the evening lessons. The stormiest weather and the worst walking do not keep them from these schools. In various night schools of the Children's Aid Society will be found hundreds of little ones from six to thirteen who have been working very hard the whole day, and who are now just as eager to learn their little tasks."[42]

In 1854, Brace opened The Newsboys' Lodging-House, which provided lodging, food, a bath, night-school, and guidance for homeless lads.[43] Brace felt the boys learned something from paying for their stay. A bed was ten cents. A meal seven cents. By 1890, the CAS operated five lodging-houses for homeless boys and one for homeless girls.[44]

In addition to lodging-houses, night schools, and industrial schools, the Children's Aid Society operated kindergartens, free reading rooms, Sunday schools, baths, gymnasiums, and homes for sick children. To give poor city children a taste of the country, Brace created farms and seaside vacation homes, where groups of poor children enjoyed week-long romps.

The Children's Aid Society was a private charity, and it raised most of its budget through donations. In addition to his organizational and administrative responsibilities, Charles Loring Brace was a tireless fundraiser. "He went about

FIGURE 1.5
The Newsboys' Lodging House, established in 1854.

lecturing and preaching, sometimes every evening in the week and the Sunday in delivering sermons and addresses, both in New York City, and in other parts of the Eastern States."[45]

Although Brace worked on many fronts, he is best remembered for the so-called orphan trains that relocated—placed out—nearly 100,000 New York City children to new homes in the Midwest between 1854 and 1929.[46] Brace did not invent placing out of poor children.[47] Colonial officials used the technique. Brace, however, put placing out on a grand scale. Why did Brace favor sending dependent children to the Midwest? As a boy in Connecticut, Brace had daily access to pure, fresh air. At Yale, Brace enjoyed fishing, hiking, and other outdoor activities. In fact, Brace so loved the outdoors that when he could afford a home of his own, he built it a healthy distance from New York City.[48] Brace's youth in the open air stood in stark contrast to his years in New York City's festering tenements, where he saw the results of poverty and overcrowding, and where he longed for a breath of country air while he inhaled the stench of the slum. Brace believed that for many children, particularly the homeless, the abused, and the neglected, the only hope lay in a fresh start, almost a rebirth, in the wholesome environs of midwestern farms and villages. Brace wrote glowingly of "the happy changes seen in the boys and girls of our dangerous classes when placed in kind Western homes. The change of circumstances, the improved food, the daily moral and mental influences, the effect of regular labor and discipline, and above all, the power of Religion, awaken these hidden tendencies to good."[49]

Brace's advocacy for placing dependent children with families was based on several factors. First, he believed in the restorative powers of rural living and religion. Second, Brace believed in the need for a clean break from the degrading influences of the city. Finally, Brace's passion for placing out was fueled by his rejection of institutional care for children. Brace was one of the nineteenth-century's most forceful critics of institutional care for dependent children.[50] In 1879, Brace made a presentation at a meeting of the American Social Science Association and outlined the advantages of placing out. He wrote, "The best influence on a poor child must come from family life, and no asylum, however well managed, can approach in healthful natural influences an average farmer's family. . . . All pauper children should be removed as soon as possible from Almshouses, and placed, if possible, at once in families, subject to a careful visitation and inspection by officials or local committees. The poor-house is no place for a child."[51]

The New York Children's Aid Society's placing out efforts began shortly after the CAS opened its doors in 1853. Initially, children were not sent great distances from New York. Early efforts placed children in rural areas of Pennsylvania, Connecticut, New York, and other eastern states. The first orphan train to the Midwest departed in September 1854. Brace described one of his earliest placements, "In visiting, during May last, near the docks at the foot of Twenty-third Street,

FIGURE 1.6
An orphan train in Kansas. Photograph provided by and reproduced with permission of the Kansas State Historical Society.

I found a boy, about twelve years of age, sitting on the wharf, very ragged and wretched-looking. I asked him where he lived, and he made the answer one hears so often from these children; 'I don't live nowhere.' On further inquiry, it appeared that his parents had died a few years before—that his aunt took him for a while, but, being a drunken woman, had at length turned him away; and for some time he had slept in a box in Twenty-second Street, and the boys fed him, he occasionally making a sixpence with holding horses or doing an errand. He had eaten nothing that day, though it was afternoon. I gave him something to eat, and he promised to come up the next day to the office."[52] The lad was placed in a good home in Maryland.

Some of the children sent west on orphan trains were indeed orphans. Other children had one or both parents living. These children could not be placed without parental consent, and employees of the Society visited parents to obtain the necessary permission.[53] Some parents agreed, hoping to improve their child's prospects. Others withheld consent.

Small groups of orphan train children were gathered, fed, bathed—some for the first time, many for the first time in months—given decent clothes to replace their rags, and sent to the train station with an agent of the society.[54] The agent accompanied the children on the journey to one or more preselected destinations, where local citizens' committees, which were established in advance for the purpose, were ready to receive them. Weeks prior to the children's arrival, circulars were distributed informing farmers and townsfolk of the date and time of the children's arrival. A crowd welcomed the train, and everyone walked to the town hall or other public meeting place for the big event. The children were introduced one by one, and adults selected a child of their liking. If the committee approved, the child went home that very day with new "foster parents."[55]

If this procedure seems informal, remember, these were small communities where people knew their neighbors. The committee responsible for placing children was usually made up of the local minister and perhaps a judge, lawyer, doctor, or leading merchant. These individuals, with input from other residents, were in a good position to block most inappropriate placements. Ill-considered placements occurred, of course, and some orphan train children were abused. In the main, however, placements worked well.[56]

The society did not use indenture or apprenticeship for orphan train riders.[57] The CAS remained the child's guardian unless the child was formally adopted. Older children could leave their placement and quite a few did. The adults who took a child could return the child to the society. Agents of the society visited children periodically, and the office in New York corresponded with children and their foster parents.[58]

Although many applauded the orphan trains, Brace had no shortage of critics.[59] Since the parents of many orphan train riders were Catholic, Brace was accused of trying to convert Catholic children by sending them to Protestant homes in the Midwest.[60] Brace was also criticized by those who believed in the superiority of institutional care. Some criticized the informality of Brace's placement procedures and lack of follow-up to make sure children were well cared for. Finally, some accused Brace of ridding the city of "bad seeds," who grew up to populate midwestern prisons.

Criticism continued into the twentieth century. Perhaps the most strident, and in my view, least accurate modern critic is Richard Wexler, who ascribed to Brace "an abiding hatred of urban Catholic immigrants."[61] Wexler accused Brace of shipping "tens of thousands of children around the country on 'orphan trains,' although many were not orphans. Once taken, the children were handed out to farmers looking for cheap labor." Wexler is far off target. Brace's placing out system had faults, but anyone who studies Brace's work with an open mind understands that Brace was motivated by devotion to children, not "hatred."

Four independent assessments lend support to the overall success of the orphan trains.[62] In 1884, Hastings Hart, conducted an evaluation of children placed in Minnesota. Hart suggested that the Society improve its placement and supervision procedures, and Hart found a 16 percent "failure" rate.[63] Most children in Hart's study did well. Hart concluded, "Our examination shows, with reference to the children under thirteen years old, that nine-tenths remain, four-fifths are doing well, and all incorrigibles are cared for by the society. If properly placed and faithfully supervised, we are willing to take our full share of these younger children in Minnesota."[64]

Francis White described a study of two groups of orphan train children placed in Kansas. The first group arrived in 1867 and was made up mostly of teenage boys. The second group arrived in 1884 and consisted primarily of young girls and boys. In 1891, White contacted as many of the children as he could find. White agreed with Hastings Hart that younger children fared better than teenagers. White wrote, "Eighty-four per cent. of the children under eight years do well. Of the party placed in 1867, composed of boys between the age of fourteen and seventeen, by far the larger part drifted away or turned out badly; while just the reverse is true of the party placed in 1884, composed of children for the most part twelve years old or under. . . . It seems clear that the earlier children are placed, the more likely are the results to be satisfactory."[65]

Georgia Ralph studied records of the Children's Aid Society created at various times from 1865 to 1905. Most orphan train children succeeded.[66]

Finally, in 1985, Kristine Nelson compared the outcomes of late nineteenth-century placements in Iowa by the New York Children's Aid Society and the Iowa Children's Home Society. Nelson wrote, "It is surprising to find that an in-state placement agency had no more success in spite of the considerable advantage of placing younger children in a much smaller geographic area. The New York program did not differ from the Iowa program on the two central issues of adequacy of placement and supervision procedures, and placement of undesirable children."[67]

In 1872, Brace wrote a lengthy reply to his critics, and it seems appropriate to allow him to defend himself in his own words:

> This most sound and practical of charities always met with an intense opposition here from a certain class, for bigoted reasons. The poor were early taught, even from the alter, that the whole scheme of emigration was one of "proselytizing," and that every child thus taken forth was made a "Protestant." Stories were spread, too, that these unfortunate children were re-named in the West, and that thus even brothers and sisters might meet and perhaps marry! Others scattered the pleasant information that the little ones "were sold as slaves," and that the agents enriched themselves from the transaction.
>
> These were the obstacles and objections among the poor themselves. So powerful were these, that it would often happen that a poor woman, seeing her child becoming ruined in the streets, and soon plainly to come forth as a criminal, would prefer this to a good home in the West; and we would have the discouragement of beholding the lad a thief behind prison-bars, when a journey to the country would have saved him. Most distressing of all was, when a drunken mother or father followed a half-starved boy, already scarred and sore with their

brutality, and snatched him from one of our parties of little emigrants, all joyful with their new prospects, only to beat him and leave him on the streets.

With a small number of the better classes there was also a determined opposition to this humane remedy. What may be called the "Asylum-interest" set itself in stiff repugnance to our emigration-scheme. They claimed—and I presume the most obstinate among them still claim—that we were scattering poison over the country, and that we benefitted neither the farmers nor the children. They urged that a restraint of a few years in an Asylum or House of Detention rendered these children of poverty much more fit for practical life, and purified them to be good members of society.

We, on the other hand, took the ground that, as our children were not criminals, but simply destitute and homeless boys and girls, usually with some ostensible occupation, they could not easily, on any legal grounds, be inclosed within Asylums; that, if they were, the expense of the maintenance would be enormous, while the cost of a temporary care of them in our Schools and Lodging-houses, and their transference to the West, was only trifling—in the proportion of fifteen dollars to one hundred and fifty dollars, reckoning the latter as a year's cost for a child's support in an Asylum. Furthermore, we held and stoutly maintained that an asylum-life is a bad preparation for practical life. The child, most of all, needs individual care and sympathy. In an Asylum, he is "Letter B, of Class 3," or "No. 2, of Cell 426," and that is all that is known of him. As a poor boy, who must live in a small house, he ought to learn to draw his own water, to split his wood, kindle his fires, and light his candle; as an "institutional child," he is lighted, warmed, and watered by machinery. . . .

One test, which I used often to administer to myself, as to our different systems, was to ask—and I request any Asylum advocate to do the same—"If your son were suddenly, by the death of his parents and relatives, to be thrown out on the streets, poor and homeless—as these children are—where would you prefer him to be placed—in an Asylum, or in a good farmer's home in the West? The plainest farmer's home rather than the best Asylum—a thousand times!" was always my sincere answer. . . .

The effort to reform and improve these young outcasts has become a mission-work there. Their labor, it is true, is needed. But many a time a bountiful and Christian home is opened to the miserable little stranger, his habits are patiently corrected, faults without number are borne with, time and money are expended on him, solely and entirely from the highest religious motive of a noble self-sacrifice for an unfortunate fellow-creature. The peculiar warm heartedness of the Western people, and the equality of all classes, give them an especial adaptation to this work, and account for their success.

Wherever we went we found the children sitting at the same table with the families, going to the school with the children, and every way treated as well as any other children. Some whom we had seen once in the most extreme misery, we beheld sitting, clothed and clean, at hospitable tables, calling the employer "father," loved by the happy circle, and apparently growing up with as good hopes and prospects as any children in the country. Others who had been in the city on the very line between virtue and vice, and who at any time might have fallen into crime, we saw pursuing industrial occupations, and gaining a good name for themselves in their village.[68]

Toward the end of the nineteenth century, midwestern states produced enough homegrown dependent children of their own to strain services, adding to rising sentiments against orphan trains.[69] In 1895, Michigan passed a law limiting placement of children from other states, and other states followed suit.[70] The last New York Children's Aid Society orphan train headed west on May 31, 1929.[71]

The New York Children's Aid Society was not the only organization to employ orphan trains. The New England Home for Little Wanderers in Massachusetts sent children to farms; the Boston Children's Aid Society sent girls and boys "out west"; and the New York Foundling Home had orphan trains.[72]

Charles Loring Brace was a remarkable individual and deserves to be remembered as one of childhood's greatest friends and protectors. His tireless efforts to save children, his antipathy toward institutional care, and his pioneering efforts to place unfortunate children in good homes helped shape the child welfare system of the twentieth century.

Conclusion

There was never a time when children in America were completely bereft of protection from abuse and neglect. Although organized child protection did not begin until the creation of the New York Society for the Prevention of Cruelty to Children in 1875, children were protected from the earliest colonial days. Egregious abuse was prosecuted criminally. Early laws authorized intervention in the family. Local officials dispensed outdoor relief to poor parents. Orphanages gave refuge to abused, neglected, and abandoned children as well as orphans. Charities like the New York Children's Aid Society rescued thousands of children.

Following the Civil War, America was ready for a more focused approach to child protection, and the birth in 1863 of a little girl named Mary Ellen set the stage for a momentous step forward. Mary Ellen's story unfolds in chapter 2.

2

SOCIETIES FOR THE PREVENTION
OF CRUELTY TO CHILDREN

Organized child protection began in 1875, the year in which the New York Society for the Prevention of Cruelty to Children (NYSPCC) was incorporated. This chapter describes the NYSPCC and the spread of similar nongovernmental child protection societies across America. From 1875 through the early decades of the twentieth century—more than half a century—privately funded child protection societies pulled the laboring oar in child protection. It was not until the second half of the twentieth century that government agencies assumed the leadership in child protection.

Rescue of Mary Ellen Wilson

The New York Society for the Prevention of Cruelty to Children resulted from the rescue of a little girl named Mary Ellen Wilson, and no telling of American child protection is complete without this dramatic case.[1] Mary Ellen's mother, Francis Conner, arrived in New York City from London in 1858. Frances married Thomas Wilson, who died fighting in the Civil War. Now a poor pregnant widow, Frances struggled to survive. After Mary Ellen's birth in 1863, Frances found work as a hotel maid, and she boarded Mary Ellen with a woman named Score, paying Score eight dollars a month for Mary Ellen's care.

In 1864, Mary Ellen's mother disappeared, and the money for the baby's care dried up. Score took Mary Ellen to the Department of Charities, where the child lived until 1866 when, at eighteen months of age, she was indentured to Thomas McCormack and his wife Mary. Soon thereafter, Mr. McCormack died, and Mary took a new husband, Francis Connolly.

FIGURE 2.1
Etta Angell Wheeler.
Photograph provided by
and reproduced with
permission of the George
Sim Johnston Archives of
the New York Society for
the Prevention of Cruelty
to Children.

Mary Ellen spent eight long years with Mary and Francis Connolly, years filled with neglect and cruelty. Mary Ellen was not permitted to play with other children. Nor was she allowed outside, except occasionally at night. She was beaten routinely. When the Connollys went out, Mary Ellen was locked in. She had only one item of clothing, a threadbare dress over an undergarment. She slept on a piece of carpet on the floor.

In late 1873, a religious missionary to the poor named Etta Angell Wheeler was visiting a woman in the tenements of Hell's Kitchen, one of New York's worst slums. The woman told Wheeler that a little girl who used to live nearby "was often cruelly whipped and very frequently left alone the entire day with the windows darkened."[2] The girl's family had recently moved a few blocks away. Wheeler investigated, but when she knocked at the door, no one answered. She inquired next door, where she encountered a young woman recently arrived from Germany and very ill. The young woman told Wheeler she often heard a child being beaten and crying, "Oh, mamma! mamma!" Wheeler returned to the apartment and knocked again. This time the door opened slightly and a woman's voice asked, "What do you want?" Wheeler cajoled her way into the apartment, where, in Wheeler's own words, she

FIGURE 2.2
Henry Bergh, founder of the American Society for the Prevention of Cruelty to Animals.
Photograph provided by and reproduced with permission of the George Sim Johnston
Archives of the New York Society for the Prevention of Cruelty to Children.

"saw a pale, thin child, barefooted, in a thin, scanty dress, so tattered that I could see
she wore but one garment besides. It was December and the weather was bitterly
cold. She was a tiny mite, the size of five years, though as afterward appeared, she
was then nine. Across the table lay a brutal whip of twisted leather strands and the
child's meager arms and legs bore many marks of its use. But the saddest part of her
story was written on her face, in its look of suppression and misery, the face of a
child unloved, of a child that had seen only the fearsome side of life."[3]

Etta Wheeler was determined to rescue Mary Ellen. She went to the police, but
they said there was nothing they could do without more evidence of assault.
Wheeler visited several child-helping charities, but they declined because they
lacked authority to intervene in the family. In April 1874, after four months of fu-

FIGURE 2.3
Elbridge Gerry, founder
and longtime president of
the New York Society for
the Prevention of Cruelty
to Children. Photograph
provided by and
reproduced with
permission of the George
Sim Johnston Archives of
the New York Society for
the Prevention of Cruelty
to Children.

tile efforts, Wheeler was running out of ideas. She had thought several times of asking help from Henry Bergh, the influential founder of the American Society for the Prevention of Cruelty to Animals, "but had lacked courage to do what seemed absurd."[4] Wheeler's niece encouraged her to contact Bergh, saying, "You are so troubled over that abused child, why not go to Mr. Bergh? She is a little animal, surely." Wheeler plucked up the courage and went to Bergh's office, where he listened courteously. The next day, Wheeler visited the sick woman living next door to Mary Ellen, where she encountered an investigator sent by Henry Bergh.

Bergh contacted the lawyer for the animal protection society, Elbridge Gerry, and asked Gerry to find a legal means to rescue Mary Ellen from the Connollys. Gerry located a little-used law that fit the bill. The law was a variation on the ancient writ of habeas corpus.[5] Gerry drew up the necessary papers and asked Judge Abraham Lawrence to issue a warrant authorizing the police to take Mary Ellen into custody. The judge obliged, and on April 9, 1874, New York City police officer Christian McDougal, assisted by Alanzo Evans from the animal protection society, went to the Connolly's apartment and whisked Mary Ellen to safety. Outside, it was chilly, and the two men wrapped Mary Ellen in a carriage blanket to keep her warm. The child was taken to police headquarters where the matron took

FIGURE 2.4

Mary Ellen Wilson immediately following her rescue. Photograph provided by and reproduced with permission of the George Sim Johnston Archives of the New York Society for the Prevention of Cruelty to Children.

a scrub brush to her. Mary Ellen was filthy; her hair matted and filled with vermin. It took several tubs of hot water to remove the dirt caked on her body.

Later that morning, Officer McDougal carried Mary Ellen into Judge Lawrence's courtroom bundled in the carriage blanket. When the blanket was removed, the judge was shocked at the sight of the little girl, clad in her tattered dress and

FIGURE 2.5

Mary Ellen one year following her rescue. Photograph provided by and reproduced with permission of the George Sim Johnston Archives of the New York Society for the Prevention of Cruelty to Children.

covered with cuts and bruises, including a fresh gash on her face where Mrs. Connolly cut her with scissors. Etta Wheeler recalled, "The child was sobbing bitterly when brought in but there was a touch of the ludicrous with it all. While one of the officers had held the infuriated [Mrs. Connolly at the tenement], the other had taken away the terrified child. She was still shrieking as they drove away and they called a halt at the first candy shop, so that she came into court weeping and terrified but waving as a weapon of defense a huge stick of peppermint candy. Poor child! It was her one earthly possession."[6]

Elbridge Gerry informed the judge of the case while Henry Berg and Etta Wheeler listened. In the judge's chambers, Mary Ellen told her sad story. She said she could not remember ever "having been kissed by any one—have never been kissed by mamma. I do not want to go back to live with mamma, because she beats me so."[7]

The next day, everyone was back in court, and by this time, Mary Ellen's story was front-page news. Etta Wheeler's husband was a newspaper man, and he may have played a role in generating media interest. Reporters and curious onlookers filled the courtroom and crowded the hallway. Mrs. Connolly was present and was cross-examined by Gerry. After several days of testimony from various witnesses, Judge Lawrence removed Mary Ellen from the Connolly's custody.

Later in 1874, Mrs. Connolly was prosecuted before a different judge for assaulting Mary Ellen with scissors. Etta Wheeler testified, as did Mary Ellen. Although it was very difficult for Mary Ellen to speak in the courtroom, she managed to describe how Mrs. Connolly cut her face while they worked on a quilt. Mrs. Connolly was convicted and sent to prison for a year.

A legend grew up around the rescue of Mary Ellen. According to legend, when Etta Wheeler informed Henry Bergh of the animal protection society of Mary Ellen's plight, Bergh said, "The child is an animal. If there is no justice for it as a human being, it shall at least have the right of the cur lost in the street. It shall not be abused."[8] Thus was born the idea that Mary Ellen was rescued under animal protection laws. What a powerful irony! A charitable society existed to protect animals, but not children. It is a good story, but it is not what happened. Henry Bergh did indeed facilitate the rescue of Mary Ellen, but not under animal protection laws or the auspices of the Society for the Prevention of Cruelty to Animals.[9] Bergh acted as a private citizen.

What became of Mary Ellen? No relatives could be found, so Judge Lawrence placed her in the Sheltering Arms, an institution for homeless children.[10] Etta Wheeler did not believe an institution was the place for Mary Ellen, so Wheeler asked the judge if Mary Ellen could live with Wheeler's own mother on a farm near Rochester, New York. Judge Lawrence approved, and in June 1875, Mary Ellen was trundled off to the farm. Etta Wheeler's mother died shortly thereafter, but Etta's sister stepped in and raised Mary Ellen as a daughter.

Following her rescue, Mary Ellen enjoyed a happy childhood. At twenty-four, she married Lewis Schutt, who worked for the railroad. In 1897, Mary Ellen gave birth to her first child, Etta—named, of course, for Mary Ellen's guardian angel, Etta Angell Wheeler. A second child, Florence, was born four years later. Both of Mary Ellen's daughters attended college and became teachers. Mary Ellen died October 30, 1956, at age ninety-two.

Helping abused and neglected children can be depressing. Cases turn out badly. Children die, and many survivors carry psychological scars throughout life. It is

FIGURE 2.6
Mary Ellen and her daughters
Etta and Florence.

heartening to know that Mary Ellen's case—the case that started the child protection movement—had a happy ending. Thanks to the efforts of neighbors, Etta
Wheeler, Henry Bergh, Elbridge Gerry, Officer McDougal, Judge Lawrence, and
others, Mary Ellen was rescued from torment and given a fresh start. Cases like
Mary Ellen's make the hard work of child protection worthwhile.

Creation of the New York Society for the Prevention of Cruelty to Children

With Mary Ellen safe, Elbridge Gerry and Henry Bergh discussed the need for an
organization to protect children. Laws were on the books to begin the work, but
no government agency or private organization had specific responsibility for
child protection. Charles Loring Brace's Children's Aid Society and other charities
helped many abused and neglected children, but they did not view themselves as
child protection agencies. The police often stepped in, but child protection was
not the focus of police work. Special courts for children lay twenty-five years in
the future.

As Gerry and Bergh discussed the problem, they drew on their experience protecting animals. Bergh had founded the American Society for the Prevention of Cruelty to Animals (ASPCA) in 1866, and Gerry was the society's lawyer. Both men believed animal protection was best accomplished through private organizations rather than government agencies. Bergh and Gerry took a law enforcement approach to animal protection. Although ASPCA agents were not police officers in the full sense of the word, they had limited police power delegated by the City. ASPCA agents received reports of animal cruelty, conducted investigations, wore badges, made arrests, and prosecuted abusers in court. Gerry and Bergh incorporated the law enforcement-prosecution model into child protection.

Gerry took the lead in planning a child protection society. He contacted influential New Yorkers, and on December 15, 1874, eleven men gathered to launch the New York Society for the Prevention of Cruelty to Children (NYSPCC). A retired merchant named John Wright was elected president, with Gerry serving as secretary and attorney. The NYSPCC was officially incorporated in April 1875 and took up temporary quarters at the offices of the Society for the Prevention of Cruelty to Animals.

John Wright died in 1879, and Elbridge Gerry assumed the presidency.[11] Gerry remained president until his retirement in 1901. Following retirement, Gerry stayed on as the Society's attorney until his death in 1927. As president of the NYSPCC, Elbridge Gerry was well known about town. Many New Yorkers referred to the NYSPCC as the "Gerry Society" and employees of the Society were sometimes called Gerry agents. In 1919, a New Yorker asked a young shoe shine boy how old he was. Casting a suspicious eye on the adult, the lad replied, "Say, Mister, you ain't one of them Gerry agents, is you?"

Elbridge Gerry viewed the New York Society for the Prevention of Cruelty to Children as a law enforcement agency, not a social service agency. The 1875 law authorizing incorporation of the NYSPCC reinforced the law enforcement approach, stating, "Any society so incorporated may prefer a complaint before any court or magistrate having jurisdiction for the violation of any law relating to or affecting children, and may aid in bringing the facts before such court or magistrate in any proceedings taken." Not surprisingly, Elbridge Gerry wrote the law. Agents of the NYSPCC, like their counterparts in animal protection, received complaints of child abuse and neglect, investigated, and brought prosecutions in court.[12] NYSPCC employees worked closely with police and sometimes wore badges. After a judge took action, the society's job was done, and social agencies took over the child's long-term placement and care.

Although agents of the NYSPCC viewed their primary mission as enforcing criminal laws against cruelty, the society did more than prosecute.[13] Often, prosecution was unnecessary, and agents helped families connect with social and financial resources. Agents used the threat of prosecution to coerce better parenting. The society pioneered the provision of temporary shelter care and medical care for children removed from their parents and for children suspected of crime who would otherwise be sent to jail. The society brought court actions on behalf of "children found in a state of destitution." Elbridge Gerry obtained legislation to address a broad range of problems, including street begging by children and children in houses of prostitution and saloons. The NYSPCC assumed responsibility for collecting court-ordered child support and prosecuted parents who failed to pay.

Although the NYSPCC was more than a prosecution office, it remained true to its core mission of law enforcement. At the 1908 convention of New York State societies for the prevention of cruelty to children, Gerry did not mince words when he asserted that child protection societies should remain aloof from child welfare agencies:

> Year after year there are added to the ranks of philanthropy those who are anxious to benefit the helpless, to devote their time to works of charity and mercy, to aid in the education of the growing children of the great republic and to promote the spread of religion and learning throughout the country; but they draw no practical distinctions in their work. The ancient axiom that it is better to do one thing well than half a dozen imperfectly does not enter their mind.
>
> If child-rescue is the object, stick to that and that alone. If general philanthropy is the object, leave child-rescue work to those who by devotion to it and exclusion of other subjects have become experts in that work. . . . There is nothing to-day which scientific charity does not seek to appropriate to itself, and when it cannot absorb collateral work it endeavors to obtain possession of the subject of that work and utilize it for its own ends. Our workers should be careful to remember the copy book axiom and mind their own business, politely suggesting the like course to outsiders who endeavor to improve upon it.[14]

In 1910, Roswell McCrea extolled the virtues of the law enforcement approach to child protection, writing, "The work has to be done in cold blood, so to speak, with a deaf ear to the pleadings and entreaties of mothers and fathers whose love for their children is never so strong as when they think their children will be taken from them. The best interests of the children, and not the feelings of those closely connected with them, have to be considered, and a trained charity worker is seldom qualified by his or her training to absolutely banish the spirit of 'love for fellow-man' from his or her work. The SPCC worker, on the other hand, looks at the matter from a colder (a legal) viewpoint, and therefore the only training he should receive is such that will enable him to detect cruelty and apply the remedy, regardless of how the application affects those who are responsible for the cruelty. In short, SPCC is not, never has been and never will be charitable."[15]

Spread of Nongovernmental Child Protection Societies

News of the New York SPCC spread, and reformers in other cities created nongovernmental child protection societies. In many communities, child protection was accomplished by expanding the role of existing animal protection societies. Other cities established societies devoted exclusively to child protection. By 1880, there were thirty-seven child protection societies in the United States. In 1902, the number was 161, and by 1910, some 250 nongovernmental societies were protecting children or children and animals. At the high watermark, 1922, the number exceeded 300. Although 300 is impressive, many cities and nearly all rural areas had little or no access to a SPCC. In 1933, Theodore Lothrop wrote, "Viewing the country as a whole, organized child protective service is woefully inadequate to meet the needs. Large areas, especially in rural sections where it is frequently most needed, are without child protective service of any kind. And in many places where it exists, the work is frequently poorly done and without proper standards of service or trained personnel."[16]

SPCCs were nongovernmental charities, dependent for survival on contributions. Although many SPCCs received government subsidies, SPCC administrators and boards of directors were constantly raising funds. To tug at the heartstrings of the public, and to open pocketbooks, SPCCs publicized the plight of abused and neglected children. Their most potent fundraising tool was the "before and after" photograph of an abused child. The "before" photo shows a sad-faced, dirty, battered urchin immediately following rescue, while the "after" photo depicts the smiling, plump, well-dressed result of intervention. The most famous "before and after" photos are of Mary Ellen herself. Before and after images from California and New York appear below.

In an interesting twist on the "before" and "after" scenario, in 1917, the superintendent of the SPCC in Yonkers, New York, described the difficulty the society encountered getting a particular judge to believe that children needed to be removed from neglectful homes:

> Not long ago it seemed very hard for us to present certain cases of improper guardianship before a certain court. So one day when we had a case referred to us in which four children were really about as neglected as any we have ever had, we loaded them into the automobile and took them, just as they were, dirty and ragged, with their hair matted and full of soil, etc., right before the judge. He said he had never seen such a condition in his life. Then we took them to the shelter and the matron went to work and by the next morning when we took them to court he said: "These are not the same children." We go to the home and take these children out and bring them to the shelter and wash and dress them up and put nice ribbons on them and when we take them to court it really needs almost an apology for being there.[17]

The judge saw the light.

FIGURE 2.7

Nellie Brady as she was discovered by the New York Society for the Prevention of Cruelty to Children and after a short stay in the care of the Society. From Helen Campbell, *Darkness and Daylight.* 1892. Hartford, Conn.: A.D. Worthington.

Differing Approaches to Child Protection— The Day-to-Day Work of SPCCs

The law enforcement approach to child protection, exemplified by the New York SPCC, was popular. Before long, however, a competing perspective emerged that was based as much on social work as on prosecution. In 1881, for example, Henry Jones, the president of the Brooklyn SPCC wrote, "We have no wish to sever the sacred bond between parent and child, but rather to strengthen it by kind advice and counsel—and yet prevent cruelty at all hazards." In 1917 the SPCC stated, "Only as a last resort do we remove children or institute adult prosecutions."[18] The Massachusetts SPCC pioneered the social work approach to child protection. In his report to the society, General Agent Frank Fay wrote:

> One of our methods of relieving children is to reform the parents. Many cases occur where the proof of neglect may not be sufficient to enable us to take the children, and where, if the parents will abandon the habit of drinking, it is better for them to remain. In these cases, with persuasion and warning, the parents are put on probation, recognizing always the parental rights, and the fact that institution life is not the natural life for children, and does not fit them for the best manhood and womanhood. When the home life is not degraded, or can be essentially improved, it is better not to separate parent and child.[19]

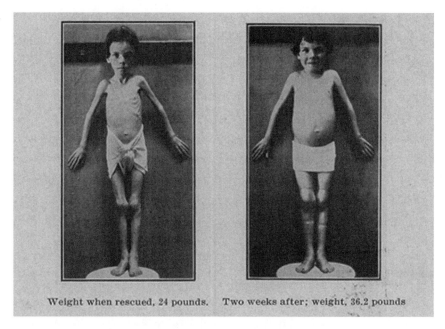

Weight when rescued, 24 pounds.   Two weeks after; weight, 36.2 pounds

FIGURE 2.8

Nine-year-old girl rescued by the California Society for the Prevention of Cruelty to Children in San Francisco. This photograph was included in an annual report of the society. Photograph provided by and reproduced with permission of the Bancroft Library of the University of California, Berkeley.

At the 1906 meeting of the MSPCC, its president described the shortcomings of the law enforcement approach, "There is no attempt to discover the cause of the conditions which make actions by the [protection society] necessary, and therefore no endeavor to prevent a recurrence of these conditions." In 1907, Carl Carstens became general secretary of the MSPCC and vigorously pursued the social work approach.[20] Vincent De Francis observed, "In the early 1900's a growing public consciousness that *prevention is a better cure than punishment* turned the emphasis away from prosecution and toward the application of remedial measures."[21]

In addition to the Brooklyn and Massachusetts SPCCs, other organizations favoring the social work approach included societies in Cleveland, Detroit, Minneapolis, Newark, and Philadelphia.[22] The American Humane Association eventually embraced the social work function of protective work. Standard III(d), provided in part:

Today we do not necessarily cite parental failure to provide adequate care as willful neglect. We recognize neglect (or negligence) as a result, usually of the parents' immaturity, maladjustment or physical or mental illness, and not infrequently as a result also of economic or social change over which the parent has not control. Protective service is a service to parents on behalf of their children and is directed not so much at rescuing the child from the home, as preserving, where possible, the home for the child.[23]

By the 1940s, social work was in the driver's seat of child protection.[24]

The Massachusetts SPCC—always among the leaders in child protection— drew on a plethora of laws to accomplish its goals of prevention, child protection, and family preservation. In 1893, Frank Fay, lead agent of the MSPCC, summarized the laws at his disposal. The neglect law authorized rescue of children under fourteen. Guardianship law allowed courts to transfer custody of children from unfit parents to proper guardians. The nonsupport law punished parents who failed to support their children. In 1851, Massachusetts passed the nation's first comprehensive adoption law, and the MSPCC occasionally used the law to create new families for children. A law punished abandonment of infants. Laws also prohibited the sale of liquor, tobacco, dangerous toys, firearms, and obscene literature to children. Another law forbade exhibition of deformed children. Children under fifteen were not allowed to sing, play musical instruments, dance, or perform as acrobats on stage. Children were not to be employed in dangerous occupations, nor were children under thirteen to work in factories when school was in session. Factories where children worked were to have fire escapes and sanitary facilities. Children were not allowed to peddle goods on the street without a license. The law prohibited children begging. It was a crime to abduct a girl for "vicious purposes." Boys serving as messengers were not to be sent to "disorderly houses." A statute prohibited children in bars. Children had to have a note from their parents to enter billiard rooms and bowling alleys. Children under thirteen were banished from licensed shows and amusements after sunset unless accompanied by a parent. Court cases involving juvenile offenders, truants, and neglected children were conducted in a separate courtroom from adult criminals. Children under twelve were not to be confined in prisons, and older children were not to be in the same jail cell with adult criminals. Children over four years of age were generally not allowed in almshouses. A license was required to operate a child care facility.

In addition to drawing on this wide range of laws, the Massachusetts SPCC worked to improve sanitary conditions, especially in tenement basements where the death rate was extremely high. Agents of the Society kept an eye on "dime museums and cheap shows of all kinds; dance-houses, gambling rooms, and liquor saloons, where children may be employed unlawfully; street peddling by children, especially by girls; [and] the enforcement of school laws."[25]

Although not all states had the breadth of laws available in Massachusetts, it is clear that by the late nineteenth century, protective societies had quite a legal toolbox at their disposal. The remainder of this section describes additional problems tackled by child protection societies, ranging from baby farms to child actors.

Baby Farms

Quality child care is a perennial concern for working parents. For millennia, relatives and neighbors took care of children while parents worked. Sonya Michel traced the history of American child care, noting, "Child care began in creches, day nurseries, and day care centers; in institutions designed for other purposes, including nursery schools and kindergartens, orphanages, shelters, refuges, workhouses, and houses of industry; and was as informal as care by neighbors, relatives, and other children. . . . The practice of child care had multiple and staggered origins, going back to colonial America and before that to early modern Europe."[26]

As American industrialization progressed, droves of impoverished immigrants arrived. Cities grew rapidly, and thousands of women entered the labor force to supplement their spouse's wages or as sole breadwinners. Many mothers labored

FIGURE 2.9
A "little mother" taking care of her younger siblings. From Ernest K. Coulter, *The Children in the Shadow*. 1913. New York: Nast & Co.

at home and tended their children while they worked. Thousands more went out to work, making child care necessary. When a daughter was old enough to tend younger siblings, she might join the ranks of "little mothers," some as young as five. Needless to say, few little mothers went to school.

Many poor single parents placed their children in orphanages. "Parents' use of orphanages for child-caring purposes became so widespread that by the second half of the nineteenth century, 'half-orphans' (children with one living parent) outnumbered full orphans in most asylums."[27] Some working parents let their children fend for themselves, either locked indoors or free to roam the streets. Child care of good quality was available, but not in anything approaching adequate supply. Moreover, high quality child care was too expensive for most working class parents.

Despite the expense, parents struggled to find day care for their children, and a veritable child care industry sprang up. Women took in one or two children to supplement family income. Wet-nurses cared for infants. Small institutions were established to care for babies and young children. Overcrowding was a problem, and contagious diseases, unsanitary conditions, and contaminated milk claimed many young lives.

During the nineteenth century, government regulation of child care was spotty. Although most child care providers undoubtedly did their best, the number of horror stories was shocking. "Baby farmer" was the epithet affixed to incompetent or unscrupulous child care providers. Some providers starved children purposely or through gross neglect. Edward Cowley, for example, operated a child care facility in New York City called Shepherd's Fold. In January 1878, three-year-old Louis Victor was admitted to Shepherd's Fold by his father. Upon admission, Louis "appeared to be in a perfect state of health—very plump, lively, happy and stout."[28] Two years later, Cowley's wife rushed Louis to St. Luke's Hospital, where his condition shocked the doctors. He was skin and bones. He would not talk except to plead for food. With assistance from the New York Society for the Prevention of Cruelty to Children, Edward Cowley was prosecuted for starving Louis. It took the jury just eighteen minutes to return a guilty verdict. Cowley was sent to prison and Louis recovered.

With some baby farms, the implicit agreement was that the baby, often born out of wedlock, was left to die. The Massachusetts Society for the Prevention of Cruelty to Children investigated a baby farm that took infants for twenty-five dollars. The parent could give a false name and was not expected to visit. The parent was told that if the infant lived, it would be adopted. If the baby died, a burial was promised, "but the fact that the bodies of many infants were found unburied in that vicinity threw a doubt upon the case."[29] Through efforts of the MSPCC, the baby farm was denied a license.

Elbridge Gerry of the New York SPCC lobbied for legislation requiring licensure of child care providers. A law passed in 1883 authorized the Health Department and the NYSPCC to inspect premises where children were boarded. Similar laws were enacted in Massachusetts and other states. Unfortunately, "better regulation of baby-boarding homes in the cities pushed baby farming into the countryside: as late as 1910 there were exposés of baby farms in New Hampshire that took scores of Boston infants."[30]

Padrones

A padrone was a man who brought Italian children to America as indentured servants and forced them to work, often playing musical instruments on the street or selling trinkets. In Italy, parents were paid a small fee and promised their child's safe return a few years hence. Once in America, the padrone kept all the money earned by the child. Some padrones were abusive. Charles Loring Brace of the New York Children's Aid Society warred against padrones and was joined by child protection societies. In 1879, the president of the California Society for the Prevention of Cruelty to Children in San Francisco reported to members of the Society, "You have broken up the infamous Italian padrone system existing in our midst, which turned children into the chattels of the mercenary masters, and made them the instruments of their unhallowed gain."[31] In 1874, Congress passed a law aimed at padrones, and prosecutions under the federal law helped curtail the practice.

Italians were not the only nationality exploiting child labor. In 1893, Oscar Dudley reported on the work of the Chicago Humane Society, stating, "Good work was done in breaking up the padrone system, and the similar arrangement under which Belgian and other foreign children were forced to beg for the support of their so-called guardians, who thrashed them unmercifully and half-starved them if they failed to bring in a certain sum every night."[32]

Children Begging on the Streets

In the late 1800s, large numbers of children begged on the streets of American cities. Child protection societies devoted considerable energy to street begging, and legislation against the practice was obtained across the country. An 1877 New York statute provided, "Every person having the custody of any child under the age of fourteen years shall restrain such child from begging, whether actually begging or under the pretext of peddling."[33]

Children on Stage and in "Moving Pictures"

Many early child protection workers viewed "show business" as a form of child abuse, and protective societies obtained laws limiting children in exhibits, plays, and circuses. In 1879, the president of the California Society for the Prevention of

Cruelty to Children congratulated the Society on its stand against children on stage. "This practice is intensely vicious. Its effect upon the health, resulting from exposure, and denial of repose, is the least of the evils it entails. Intoxicated by the glare and excitement, the weak, untutored, mind of infancy is trained to impressions, and desires, which cannot but end in the subversion of purity and virtue."[34] With the advent of motion pictures, child protection workers expanded their concerns. Children now acted in dangerous scenes, had their eyes damaged by harsh artificial lighting, learned unwholesome lessons, and missed school.

Medical Neglect

Parents have a legal duty to provide their children food, clothing, and shelter. Additionally, parents must provide necessary medical care, and when they fail to do so, the state may step in. In the 1880 case of *Heinemann's Appeal*,[35] a man refused to call a physician when his wife and three of his five children were stricken with diphtheria. Tragically, the mother and the three children died. The maternal grandmother pleaded with her son-in-law to summon a doctor for the surviving children, but he refused. Undaunted, the grandmother went to court, and the judge gave custody of the surviving children to her. The father appealed to the Pennsylvania Supreme Court, but the court rebuked him, writing that he had "shamefully neglected" the medical needs of his children.[36]

Societies for the prevention of cruelty to children occasionally intervened when parents failed to obtain necessary medical care for their children. Alfred Kerchley, assistant secretary of the NYSPCC, wrote in 1920, "The Society seeks out and investigates all specific complaints to interfere on behalf of every child in need of medical attention which parents refuse to provide. Children, crippled and in need of appliances, or verging into blindness for the need of corrective glasses, the improper care of babies in boarding homes, and children stunted in body by the imposition of household duties too burdensome for their frail and tender bodies, are all included in this category."[37]

Ubiquitous Role of Alcohol and Drugs

Child protection workers have always understood the role of alcohol and drugs in neglect and abuse.[38] Charles Loring Brace, for example, was acutely aware that intemperance was a major culprit. In Massachusetts, the *First Annual Report* of the MSPCC stated in 1881, "Our records show that the larger part of the cases brought to our notice have their origin in the use and abuse of intoxicating drinks."[39] A year later, the MSPCC lamented, "So long as men and women drink to excess, parents will be brutal, children will be neglected and will suffer, and so long there will be a necessity for an organization like ours."[40] In 1935, Jacob and

Rosamond Goldberg published their study of 1,400 New York City girls victimized by sexual abuse. Discussing the role of alcohol in incest, the Goldbergs wrote, "The problem centers about the man who, under the influence and stimulation of alcohol, seizes upon his young daughter as a readily accessible female to give vent to his overstimulated senses."[41]

Potpourri of Child Protection Laws

In 1910, Roswell McCrea conducted a state-by-state inventory of child protection laws.[42] All states had laws against sexual abuse. Nearly all states had criminal statutes against abandonment, desertion, and nonsupport. Quite a few states had statutes establishing juvenile courts, and these statutes specified that the court had authority over neglected and dependent children as well as delinquent children. Only a few states had laws regarding licensing and inspection of child care facilities. A majority of states limited children's performance in circuses and other public exhibitions. Louisiana, Michigan, New York, Pennsylvania, and Virginia specified that agents of societies for the prevention of cruelty to children had limited police authority. A New York law provided that mothers in prison could retain custody of their babies until age two.

Most states had laws protecting children from obscene literature. Some interesting variations on the obscenity theme were an Arizona law that punished "indecent language" in the presence of children; an Iowa statute that outlawed use of a phonograph to play indecent songs; a Kansas statute that required children to be excluded from trials where "vulgar" evidence was produced; and Missouri, Montana, and Nebraska had laws that made it illegal to expose children to news of crime.

Practically every state had laws against children visiting billiard and ten-pin parlors, gambling and card rooms, houses of prostitution, saloons, or dance halls. A few states added skating rinks to the forbidden zone. Massachusetts legislators found it in their hearts to allow children to enter dance halls when the dance was sponsored by a school or a church.

Nearly all states made it a crime to sell tobacco to children, and Kansas threw in opium for good measure. Most states prohibited the sale of dangerous weapons to minors. New Hampshire said firecrackers were okay provided they were less than six inches long. Rhode Island allowed firecrackers, but only if they *were* made of gun powder.

A Year in the Life of a Small City SPCC

Sacramento County, California in 2005 was home to more than one million people. In 1907, however, the county's population was just over 60,000. Early in the twentieth century, Sacramento was a small city—the state capital—surrounded by farms and ranches interspersed with little towns. Sacramento had an SPCC staffed by one agent, Daniel Healy. Mr. Healy's yearly salary was $215, with the proviso that he provide his own horse and buggy.

The *Sacramento Union* newspaper covered the work of Sacramento's SPCC, and *Union* articles from 1906 and 1907 provide insight into day-to-day operations of a typical SPCC.[43] From June 1906 to June 1907, Daniel Healy handled more than 400 cases. Healy responded to a wide range of situations. Interestingly, relatively little of his work involved physical abuse. Runaways were returned to their parents. Fathers were forced to support their families. Healy issued hundreds of "cautions and warnings against cruelty and injustice to children [which] resulted in betterment of conditions in several cases."[44] Numerous parents asked the Society for help with their children. For example, "a dying father besought the Society to place his 9-year-old half-orphan boy in an institutional school, and it was done."[45] Alcohol played a major role in neglect. Healy helped children secure work permits. "Three tramp boys were given good places to work." Healy urged better school programs in the manual arts for boys, and home economics for girls. "Several wayward boys were put into the right path."[46] The parents of two small boys were hauled into juvenile court because the parents required the boys to sell newspapers "at late hours of night on the streets and enter saloons and public places for that purpose, while the mother watches outside to see that the lads prosecute the vocation diligently."[47]

The Sacramento SPCC endeavored to protect teenage girls. In January 1907, the *Sacramento Union* reported, "Improper associations by girls were broken up in two cases and the children saved from becoming criminals. The deportation of girls in two cases to Tonopah [a mining town] to enter alleged amusement joints was prevented, and the girls saved to decent lives."[48] Healy intervened with five "wayward girls"—two were returned to their parents, two were sent to institutions. In 1906, "the mother of a wayward girl sought the aid of the Society to save her, and it was extended."[49]

Then as now, juvenile crime and mischief were common. Healy served as unpaid probation officer to the juvenile court. On August 16, 1907, the *Sacramento Union* reported, "There is growing up in this city a numerous brood of boys who seem to have been taught nothing regarding the meum and tuum [mine and yours] of property. The records of the children's society reveal a surprisingly large number of small boys are given to the taking of the goods and chattels of others with apparent unconcern as to ownership."[50] Two boys, nine and eleven, took a grocer's "fine sorrel mare and new top buggy and harness" from the grocery store for a joy ride. The grocer managed to capture the culprits and "brought the young thieves to the county jail and asked that they be locked up for a time and then be sent home. They were jailed to inspire in them a wholesome fear of the law. But it was a failure. Though Jailer Cook turned the bolts on them in a still dark cell and told them they would have to stay there indefinitely, they kicked up their heels in contempt and laughed and jeered at the officer." The district attorney looked into the case and asked Dan Healy to find a solution.

In an episode eerily similar to Fagan's nest of young thieves and pickpockets in *Oliver Twist*, Dan Healy and police officer Logue responded to reports of a "vile dive in the basement of a building. Robert Thompson was occupying the place for the purpose of ruining boys and girls and teaching them to steal. A raid was made on the den last Thursday night by Officer Healy and patrolman Logue, but Thompson broke through a window screen and jumping from the window escaped into the alley. Enough evidence was secured to gain a conviction should he be arrested. Thompson had been masquerading as a sign-painter, but instead of working he has been directing boys to steal for him. The theft of a diamond ring brought the case to the attention of the officers and the breaking up of the den resulted."[51]

Healy responded to allegations of child sexual abuse. In his 1907 annual report, Healy mentioned nine cases of "unnatural acts" and seven of "seduction." In June, the *Sacramento Union* reported:

> The police and Special Officer Dan Healy of the Society for the Prevention of Cruelty to Children, are investigating a number of cases of human monsters who are alleged to have committed felonious assaults on young boys and who have led their innocent victims into vice and crime. One of these, Harry Collins, was arrested last Tuesday, and if half the admissions of his boy accusers are true, he is the lowest of moral degenerates and a menace to society.
>
> Collins makes a sweeping denial of the accusations, but the police are in possession of notes and letters and other damaging evidence to show that he has been guilty of inhuman practices. He has not only enticed small boys to his room, but offered money to the urchins to persuade other boys to visit his den of vice. He is about 50 years old, and the attention of Special Officer Healy was first directed to the case by the landlady of the lodging-house where Collins roomed. She noticed that many boys visited Collins' room and her suspicions were aroused that all was not right. The investigations of the special officer and the police proved these suspicions to be well founded and Collins will be prosecuted.[52]

Dan Healy was quite a jack-of-all-trades—part social worker, part policeman, part probation officer, part truant officer, part counselor, and part community problem solver for children. Healy typified agents of SPCCs.

What Was the Role of the Government during This Period?

Early child protection societies were nongovernmental. Why did child protection fall to private organizations rather than public officials as it does today? There are several explanations. Apart from their traditional responsibility for poor relief, cities and counties in the nineteenth century played a limited role in social welfare. State governments were even less involved. It was not until the late nineteenth and early twentieth centuries that most states created state-level departments of social services. In the nineteenth century, social work as a profession did not exist. What we think of today as social work was carried out primarily by private citizens like Charles Loring Brace, Etta Wheeler, and Elbridge Gerry. Most nineteenth-century child protection workers believed private organizations could do a better job of child protection than government, a view shared by most politicians.

Conclusion

The rescue of Mary Ellen Wilson in 1874 gave rise to organized child protection. Nongovernmental societies for the prevention of cruelty to children saved thousands of children and established the foundation for child protection in the twentieth century. The next chapter examines how a loose patchwork of nongovernmental SPCCs was gradually transformed into the nationwide system of child protection in place today.

One of the perennial debates in child protection is whether to take a punitive or a therapeutic approach to parents who abuse or neglect their children. The law enforcement approach was pioneered by the New York Society for the Prevention of Cruelty to Children and similar nineteenth-century protective societies. Yet, from the earliest days of organized child protection, some professionals rejected the law enforcement approach in favor of nonpunitive social work intervention to help struggling parents. The debate seesawed back and forth across the twentieth century and continues today. Recently, several authorities on child welfare recommended a partial return to the law enforcement approach. (Their proposals are discussed in chapter 7.) In the final analysis, neither side of the debate over a law enforcement versus a social work approach to child protection can claim victory because there is merit in both positions. The real challenge is finding the proper balance between the punitive and the therapeutic. Our nineteenth-century forebears searched for the proper balance, and we continue the quest today.

3

CHILD PROTECTION FROM
1900 TO 1962

Child protection in the twentieth century can be divided into two periods, one before 1962, and one following. This chapter chronicles developments prior to 1962, while the next chapter describes the post-1962 era. The principal topics discussed in the present chapter are the juvenile court, protection of teenage girls, the gradual transition from nongovernmental child protection societies to government child protection, race in American child welfare, the decline of the orphanage, the rise of foster family care, and the relative obscurity of child protection from roughly 1929 to 1962.

Progressive Era

Late nineteenth- and early twentieth-century child protection overlapped the Progressive Era, a period of agitation on numerous social fronts, including efforts to help children, women, the poor, and working class people. Historians differ on when the Progressive Era began. Some say 1890, others 1901. As for the end of the Progressive Era, many scholars point to 1917, the year America entered World War I.

The Progressive Era was a response to several factors, including dramatically increased population. In 1860, the population was 33 million. By 1900, the population soared to nearly 76 million. In the late nineteenth century, the Industrial Revolution was at full steam, creating wealth for industrialists but low wages, unsafe working conditions, and long hours for workers, including children. The Progressive Era was a reaction against exploitive industrial labor, urban poverty, and other social injustices.

Emergence of Social Work, Pediatrics,
Psychology, and Psychiatry

Today, child protection is the domain of social work, with supporting roles for police, mental health, medicine, nursing, and law. When organized child protection began in 1875, however, social work had not emerged as a profession. This is not to say social work was not practiced. Colonial officials arranged for orphans, protected abused children, and provided for the poor. The nineteenth century saw a proliferation of private charitable organizations such as the New York Children's Aid Society and associations to improve the condition of the poor. Employees and volunteers of these societies were not called social workers, but many of them did wonderful social work.

In 1877, the first Charity Organization Society (COS) was established in Buffalo, New York. Eventually, more than one hundred COSs were scattered across the country. The COSs improved the administration of poor relief by coordinating voluntary and public efforts. Gradually, COSs hired full-time workers to replace volunteers. Of course, full-time workers need training. Early training was informal and on-the-job. Eventually, however, more formal training was needed. Nathan Cohen wrote that in 1898, the "New York Charity Organization Society expanded its in-service training program into a more organized effort and established the first school for training social workers. It was called the New York School for Philanthropy."[1] Today, the school is the influential School of Social Work at Columbia University. With increasingly full-time staffs, COSs contributed to the professionalization of social work.

Another contributor to the professionalization of social work was the settlement movement, briefly described in the next subsection. Like their colleagues in COSs, settlement workers also needed training. Ralph and Muriel Pumphrey wrote, "The COS and the settlement movements were the primary places where an interest in method and education moved workers and the emerging field of social work toward professionalization. . . . In the forty years between the [economic] panic of the [1890s] and the depression of the [1930s], social work became a recognized profession."[2] In 1919, there were seventeen social work schools; by 1930, the number exceeded thirty.

Pediatrics emerged as a specialty in the second half of the nineteenth century. One of the fathers of pediatrics was Abraham Jacobi. In 1860, Jacobi established a clinic for children at the New York Medical College, where he was professor of infantile pathology and therapeutics. Along with other doctors, Jacobi founded the pediatric section of the American Medical Association (AMA). In 1930, the American Academy of Pediatrics was formed by pediatricians, who were upset with the AMA's opposition to the federal Sheppard-Towner Act, a law that provided money to assist states in the promotion of maternal and infant health.

Psychology developed during the last quarter of the nineteenth century, with clinical psychology emerging during the early twentieth century. Psychiatry came to the fore in the first decades of the twentieth century. With the professions of social work, pediatrics, psychology, and psychiatry in place, the cast of characters was set for the emergence of child protection as we know it today.

Settlement Movement

The first settlement house was established in 1885 in London's East End slums. This experiment in assisting the poor was created by Oxford and Cambridge students working under the guidance of Samuel Barnett, a young clergyman of the Church of England. The first settlement was christened Toynbee Hall to honor historian Arnold Toynbee, an advocate for the poor who chose to live in humble surroundings.

Stanton Coit of New York City visited Toynbee Hall and came home inspired to create a settlement. Along with Charles Stover, Coit established the Neighborhood Guild of New York City in 1886, America's first settlement. America's most famous settlement, Hull House in Chicago, was started in 1889 by Ellen Starr and Jane

FIGURE 3.1
Jane Addams reading with a nephew. Photograph provided by and reproduced with permission of the University Library at the University of Illinois, Chicago, Jane Addams Memorial Collection.

Addams following Addams' visit to Toynbee Hall. By 1920, more than four hundred settlements operated in the United States.

Jane Addams was an extraordinary leader. In 1931, she was awarded the Nobel Peace Prize for her efforts to avert World War I. During the early twentieth century, Addams had an enormous impact on social policy in general and child welfare in particular. Addams's Hull House was home to many leading social workers, and Addams was their inspiration. Thus, Julia Lathrop of Hull House was the first director of the U.S. Children's Bureau, and the first woman to lead a federal agency. Grace Abbott succeeded Lathrop at the Children's Bureau.[3] Edith Abbott, Grace's sister, was one of social work's leading intellectuals. Sophonisba Breckenridge (Nisba to her friends) was involved in a host of social issues. Edith Abbott and Sophinisba Breckenridge played key roles in creating the University of Chicago's influential School of Social Service Administration. Florence Kelley was at the forefront of the child labor movement.[4] These remarkable individuals were deeply involved in women's suffrage, child labor, working conditions in industry, public health and sanitation, and other issues. Settlements created "kindergartens, child-welfare clinics, homemaking programs, handicrafts, play groups, and the involvement of workers in preschool education, juvenile courts, and child and labor legislation. . . . American settlers were at the forefront of the demands for labor legislation, especially for women and children, and they were as much responsible for its passage as any group in the Progressive Period."[5]

Child Guidance Movement

From the beginning of the juvenile court movement in 1899, judges relied on advice from social workers and mental health professionals. Judge Merritt Pinckney of the Chicago juvenile court was frustrated with the number of delinquent boys who appeared before him again and again. In 1908, Judge Pinckney formed a committee to advise him on recidivism. The committee included Ethel Dummer, a wealthy and energetic advocate for children, Julia Lathrop of Hull House, and William Healy, a psychiatrist. Together, they conceived the idea of an institute to conduct psychological and physical examinations of children and to advise the judge. Thus was born Chicago's Juvenile Psychopathic Institute, with Healy as director.[6]

In 1915, Healy published *The Individual Delinquent*, an in-depth study of 800 delinquent children. This book established Healy as an authority on criminology and delinquency. Healy rejected the popular idea that certain children are "born criminals." His research convinced him delinquency is learned. Healy believed in a thorough psychological, physical, and social assessment of each child. The social workers, psychologists, and psychiatrists at the Juvenile Psychopathic Institute studied not only the child but also the child's family and community.

Clockwise from top left: Grace Abbott, Edith Abbott, Sophonisba Breckenridge, and Julia Lathrop. Photographs provided by and reproduced with permission of the University Library at the University of Illinois, Chicago, Jane Addams Memorial Collection.

In 1917, Healy moved to Boston where he created a clinic associated with Boston's juvenile court. The clinic was called the Judge Baker Foundation, after Boston's first juvenile court judge, Harvey Baker. Under Healy's leadership, the Judge Baker Foundation "quickly became a model for others interested in improving juvenile justice through psychological testing and mental analysis."[7] Healy and his colleagues evaluated children referred to the clinic by the juvenile court and by community agencies. In addition to evaluations, clinicians at the foundation provided treatment.

The Juvenile Psychopathic Institute in Chicago and the Judge Baker Foundation in Boston laid the groundwork that was capitalized on by the Commonwealth Fund, an important charity that was determined to reduce delinquency. Efforts by the Commonwealth Fund and others culminated in the child guidance movement. In her book on the movement, Margo Horn wrote that the movement "established community facilities called child guidance clinics for treating mild behavior or emotional problems in school-age children of normal intelligence. . . . Child guidance clinics employed clinical teams made up of a psychiatrist, a psychologist, and a psychiatric social worker, who pooled their different perspectives to provide treatment sensitive to all aspects of each child's situation. Established as facilities to treat *all* maladjusted children in a community, the new clinics cooperated with existing social welfare, educational, and medical services to reach the widest range of children."[8]

By the 1930s, child guidance was an established area of mental health practice. In the middle of the twentieth century, many child guidance clinics merged with mental health centers serving clients of all ages. In 1946, Congress passed the National Mental Health Act, which provided money for mental health clinics for adults and children. In 1963, Congress passed the Community Mental Health Centers Act to expand community-based mental health services for children and adults. Child guidance clinics were assimilated into the larger mental health system.

Child Labor Movement

Throughout American history, children worked on family farms and in small shops. The wisdom of apprenticeship as a means to learn a trade was not questioned until late in the nineteenth century. Thus, it was not work per se that sparked the movement to curtail child labor. Rather, the child labor movement was triggered by work in the factories, mills, and mines of the Industrial Revolution. The first law regulating child labor was passed in England in 1802. Massachusetts passed the first American child labor law in 1836. Little progress was made during the nineteenth century, however, and opponents of child labor did not prevail until the 1930s.

The child labor movement is sometimes simplistically portrayed as a battle against evil capitalists and greedy, uncaring parents ready to sacrifice their children for a few dollars. Reality is more complex. To be sure, many business owners turned a blind eye to the harm of industrial child labor. As for parents, the children of the wealthy and middle class did not labor in factories. It was working class and poor parents who sent their children to work, and who often needed the child's meager earnings to pay the rent and put food on the table.[9] Poor parents love their children as much as privileged parents, but sending a child to work often determined whether there was milk for the baby. Many working class parents opposed laws limiting child labor, not out of callousness, but out of concern for their families. Although the triumph of child labor laws was a great victory, it is a mistake to condemn all poor parents who sent their children to work.

Orphanage Care versus Foster Family Care

During the second half of the nineteenth century and the first half of the twentieth, there was debate over the relative merits of institutional care versus foster family care for dependent children. In the nineteenth century, two types of foster family care predominated: free homes and board homes. In free homes, foster parents were not compensated; thus, such homes were "free." In most free homes, children were expected to work, popularizing this arrangement in farming communities. Occasionally, children in free homes were formally indentured to the family, although most were placed without indenture. In 1920, Lawrence Royster wrote, "The choice of a home is of vast importance. Too many children have been taken out of institutions and given apparently good homes, only to become servants. Not that such children should be reared in indolence, but they should be given education, religious training and recreation, and their activities not limited to drudgery. To accomplish this best, a trained observer should investigate every home."[10]

In board homes, foster parents were compensated. Children too young to work were more easily placed in board homes, as were troubled or disabled youngsters. As child labor diminished in the twentieth century, free homes where children worked decreased. By the middle of the twentieth century, some 300,000 children were in foster care, most of it compensated, and toward the end of the twentieth century, compensation was the norm.

During the nineteenth century, orphanages grew rapidly. In 1825, New York State had two orphanages; by 1866, it had sixty. "Between 1830 and 1850 alone, private charitable groups established fifty-six children's institutions in the United States."[11] As the nineteenth century progressed, many state, city, and county governments provided financial support for private orphanages. California and New York, in particular, provided government subsidies to private orphanages. By 1904, there were more than 1,000 orphanages and children's homes in the United States.

In some states, governments operated their own children's institutions. Thus, in 1866, the Ohio legislature authorized counties to establish county children's homes. County homes cared for orphans and dependent and neglected children and removed children from almshouses. By 1901, Ohio had fifty-one county children's homes. Connecticut and to a limited extent Indiana adopted Ohio's county children's home model. Although workers in county homes placed many children with families, the foster care aspect of the work did not always proceed according to plan, and many children languished in county homes. Eventually, the county home model was abandoned.

Several states, primarily in the Midwest, examined California's and New York's public subsidies to private institutions, as well as Ohio's system of county children's homes, and chose a different path. Minnesota, Michigan, Wisconsin, Kansas, and Rhode Island each built a single state institution called a State Public School. Dependent children from across the state were sent to the State Public School, where they were cared for until they could be returned to their parents or placed with families. In addition to State Public Schools, these states had private, church-sponsored orphanages.

Pennsylvania sought to avoid institutional care by placing dependent children directly in foster care. Homer Folks wrote in 1894, "Most of the counties have accepted the co-operation of a private organization, the Children's Aid Society of Pennsylvania. Under their plan all children are sent directly to families, who are paid a reasonable sum for their care and maintenance. From these boarding homes they may be transferred to free homes, as in other States they are transferred from a central institution to free homes, or, as often happens, they are kept permanently and without payment for board after a few months or a year or two by the family which received them as boarders."[12]

Turning from Pennsylvania to Massachusetts, Folks described the Bay State as "a combination of the Pennsylvania boarding system and the State system of Michigan. There is a central State institution, the State Primary School, from which children are placed out in families, in free homes if approved free homes can be secured, in boarding homes if free homes are not available. Foundlings and other infants are boarded in families, from which many of them are adopted."[13]

The quality of care in orphanages varied. In 1910, Hastings Hart observed:

> There still survive orphan asylums where children are kept in uniform, with shaved heads; where they do not have individual clothing, but have clothing distributed to them promiscuously from week to week; where lice and bedbugs prevail; where food is meager and of inferior quality; where good and willing girls are kept scrubbing floors month after month because they do not complain; where sleeping rooms are insanitary; where thin straw beds let the tender bodies down upon hard wooden slats; where cuffs and abuse are more freely distributed than kind words.

But on the other hand there are children's homes and orphan asylums where tenderness and love prevail; where mirth and jollity are contagious; where weary heads find a pillow on gentle bosoms; where generous diet is prescribed by medical advice and served with liberal hands; where foster homes are constantly sought as a better haven than even the good and homelike shelter of such an institution.[14]

Supporters of orphanage care highlighted the order, cleanliness, and discipline of institutional life. Children were educated, fed, clothed, and instructed in morality and piety. As the nineteenth century wore on, however, criticism of orphanage care grew. Opponents argued that the most humble home was better than the finest institution. Institutional life deprived children of love and lessons only families could provide. Charles Birtwell of the Boston Children's Aid Society put it this way, "I know what I should want for my little boy if my wife and I were blotted from his life. If he should fall into the hands of charity I should pray God to guide him to an agency that would open for him at once the door to family life."[15] Charles Loring Brace of the New York Children's Aid Society was a tireless campaigner against institutional care for children. With Brace at the forefront, efforts strengthened to place dependent children in foster homes rather than orphanages. "Placing out" societies were established across the United States.

Few supporters of the orphanage were absolutists. Advocates of orphanage care favored foster homes for selected children, and many orphanages had programs to place children with families. For example, Murray Shipley, a Quaker minister and merchant, founded the Cincinnati Children's Home. From the outset, the Cincinnati Home emphasized placing dependent children with families rather than raising them in the institution. For their part, opponents of institutional care acknowledged that some children require services only institutions can provide. By the time of the influential 1909 White House Conference on the Care of Dependent Children (described below), a consensus was emerging that "the carefully selected foster home is for the normal child the best substitute for the natural home."[16] Orphanage administrators increasingly opted for the cottage plan—still in use today—in which small numbers of children live in the family-like environment of a cottage, supervised by house parents.[17]

Supporters and opponents of orphanage care agreed on one thing, children should be removed from almshouses. In 1873, Michigan passed the first law against children in almshouses. In 1875, New York passed similar legislation, as did Massachusetts in 1879. Other states followed. Efforts to get children out of almshouses did not succeed overnight. In 1909, more than 8,000 children bided their time in almshouses. Attendees at the 1909 White House Conference on the Care of Dependent Children remarked, "The sending of children of any age or class to almshouses is an unqualified evil, and should be forbidden everywhere by law, with suitable penalty for its violation."[18] In 1930, attendees at the third White

House Conference on Child Health and Protection lamented, "Almshouses, condemned a hundred years ago, for the care of children, are still used for this purpose, in certain localities."[19]

Increasing Role of Government in Social Services

The role of government in social services in general and child welfare in particular changed substantially over time. From the colonial period until the Civil War, care of dependent children was the responsibility of local officials, assisted by the increasing number of private charitable organizations such as the New York Children's Aid Society. By the twentieth century, the number of nongovernmental child-helping organizations reached the point that Lillian Wald quipped, "The air is murky with many organizations."[20] Although state legislatures had long appropriated funds to support private charities and the efforts of local officials, it was not until the 1860s that state governments began assuming leadership roles.

Massachusetts created the first State Board of Charities in 1863 to coordinate the work of various charities. Other states followed suit, creating state-level departments with oversight of public and private charities receiving state funds. In 1869, Massachusetts created the first state department of health. State-level oversight of social services, child welfare, and health took years to develop and was not complete until the middle of the twentieth century.

White House Conference on the Care of Dependent Children, 1909

There have been thousands of conferences on child welfare, but none more important than the 1909 White House Conference on the Care of Dependent Children.[21] The conference was convened in January 1909 by President Theodore Roosevelt at the behest of leading child welfare authorities of the day, including Homer Folks, Hastings Hart, Julian Mack, and Charles Birtwell.[22] Folks and his colleagues emphasized the urgent need to respond more effectively to children who were poor, orphaned, abandoned, abused, or neglected.

More than two hundred experts attended the conference, including Jane Addams of Hull House, Charles Loring Brace, Jr. of the New York Children's Aid Society, Carl Carstens of the Massachusetts Society for the Prevention of Cruelty to Children, Julia Lathrop of Hull House, Timothy Hurley of the Chicago Visitation and Aid Society, Ben Lindsey of the Denver Juvenile Court, Jacob Riis the documentary photographer and author, and Lillian Wald of the Henry Street Settlement in New York City. These luminaries and the other experts in attendance joined voices to proclaim, "Home life is the highest and finest product of civilization. It is the great molding force of mind and of character. Children should not be deprived of it except for urgent and compelling reasons."[23] With this fundamental precept in mind, the conferees made thirteen recommendations that helped shape child welfare policy in the twentieth century. First, "children of worthy parents or deserving mothers should, as a rule, be kept with their parents at home." To this end, the conferees endorsed "mothers' pensions," a form of outdoor relief for poor parents so they could care for their children at home. Second, the conferees agreed, "Society should endeavor to eradicate causes of dependency like disease and to substitute compensation and insurance for relief." Third, "homeless and neglected children, if normal, should be cared for in families, when practicable." The conferees devoted considerable attention to institutional care versus foster care and agreed that most children who could not live at home should be cared for in a family setting rather than an institution. Why did the conferees limit their preference for foster care to "normal" children? In 1909, most experts believed it was appropriate to care for mentally retarded, blind, and deaf children in specialized institutions. The movement to deinstitutionalize the mentally retarded and the mentally ill lay some fifty-five years in the future. The reform of America's education system to "mainstream" disabled children did not occur until the 1975 passage by Congress of the Education for All Handicapped Children Act, now called the Individuals with Disabilities Education Act.

The fourth 1909 White House recommendation was that "institutions should be on the cottage plan with small units, as far as possible." The conferees' fifth, sixth, and seventh recommendations stated that institutions caring for dependent children should be subject to state supervision and inspection. The eighth recommendation sought improvements in recordkeeping on dependent children. Ninth, the conferees stated that every needy child should receive medical care and instruction in health. Tenth, the conferees stressed the importance of cooperation between agencies. The eleventh recommendation focused on interstate placement of children by organizations like the New York Children's Aid Society. By the turn of the twentieth century, a number of midwestern states restricted interstate placement. The conferees, including Charles Loring Brace, Jr., did not object to reasonable restrictions. What the conferees opposed were laws that effectively eliminated interstate placement. The conferees stated that legislation prohibiting the transfer of dependent children between states should be repealed. The twelfth recommendation was for a permanent organization to work along the lines of these resolutions. This recommendation led to the creation in 1920 of the Child Welfare League of America. Last, but certainly not least, the conferees recommended that a federal children's bureau be established. There was enthusiastic applause when President Theodore Roosevelt informed the conference that he would send a special message to Congress, recommending the establishment of a federal children's bureau.

Mothers' Pensions

Financial assistance to the poor in their own homes, or outdoor relief, was available in colonial times. Yet, outdoor relief was never popular. Then as now, many people blamed the poor for their condition and believed outdoor relief perpetuated poverty by making people dependent. In the early 1900s, reformers trying to help widowed mothers of young children mounted a limited challenge to the antipathy for outdoor relief. The reformers argued that giving financial assistance to mothers allowed them to raise their children at home, and that this was preferable to placing children in institutions while their mothers worked. The reformers realized, however, that if financial help to mothers was called outdoor relief, it would garner opposition, so Homer Folks coined the clever term "mothers' pensions."

As mentioned above, the child welfare experts attending the 1909 White House Conference endorsed mothers' pensions. The conferees wrote, "Children of parents of worthy character, suffering from temporary misfortune and children of reasonably efficient and deserving mothers who are without the support of the normal breadwinner, should, as a rule, be kept with their parents, such aid being given as may be necessary to maintain suitable homes for the rearing of the children."[24] The moral fitness requirement reflected the time-honored belief that relief should be limited to "worthy" poor. The conferees recommended that mothers' pensions come from private funds rather than tax dollars. It soon became apparent, however, that private charity was not up to the task, and local and state governments assumed financial responsibility for mothers' pensions.

The first statewide laws authorizing mothers' pensions were passed in 1911 in Missouri and Illinois. Much of the groundwork for the Illinois law was laid by Julia Lathrop, Edith Abbott, and Sophonisba Breckenridge of Hull House. By 1920, forty states had mothers' pension laws, and by 1935, nearly all states had such laws. In the early days of mothers' pensions, juvenile courts were often given administrative responsibility for the program, although the trend was toward administration by county welfare agencies.

In 1930, "some 253,000 needy children [were] living in their own homes, cared for by their own mothers through the operation of mothers' aid laws." The report of the 1930 White House Conference on Child Health and Protection stated, "It is difficult fully to comprehend the significance of so great a change. Many thousands of children, except for this aid, would have been taken from their homes" and placed in orphanages.[25]

Not all communities offered mothers' pensions. Moreover, allowances were often miserly, and women of color were often excluded. What is more, "in many localities, people imbued with the punitive assumptions of poor relief or private charity were in charge of granting mothers' pensions."[26] Too often, a child's need was obscured by questions about her mother's character.

The decade long Great Depression, which began in 1929, vastly increased the number of poor families, outstripping the capacity of mothers' pension programs. In December 1933, for example, there were 2,700 mothers waiting for pensions in Ohio. In 1935, Congress passed the Social Security Act, which included the Aid to Dependent Children (ADC) program, the successor to mothers' pensions. ADC quickly spread across the nation, becoming the nation's primary "welfare" program supporting children. In 1962, the name Aid to Dependent Children was changed to Aid to Families with Dependent Children (AFDC). In 1996, AFDC was replaced with the Temporary Assistance to Needy Families program.

Children's Bureau

The idea of a federal agency devoted to children originated in the early 1900s with Lillian Wald and Florence Kelley. Lillian Wald was a nurse who worked with the poor in New York City.[27] Wald and her nursing school classmate, Mary Brewster, established the Nurses' Settlement, later known as the Henry Street Settlement. Wald played a key role in establishing public health nursing and school nursing.

Florence Kelley entered Chicago's Hull House in 1892 and resided there thirteen years. Kelley was deeply involved in the child labor movement. She was Illinois' chief inspector of factories from 1893 to 1897. In 1899, Kelley became secretary of the National Consumers' League, and in 1900 "gave a series of lectures in various parts of the country in which she proposed a 'United States Commission for Children.' "[28] In her 1905 book *Some Ethical Gains Through Legislation*, Kelley "suggested that there be constituted a Commission for Children, whose functions should be to correlate, make available, and interpret the facts concerning the physical, mental and moral condition and prospects of the children of the United States, native and immigrant." Kelley believed a children's commission could assist states, cities, and rural areas with up-to-date information on infant mortality, "registration of births, orphanage, desertion, illegitimacy, degeneracy (subnormal childhood), delinquency, offenses against children, illiteracy, and child labor."[29]

Wald and Kelley hatched a plan for legislation to create a federal children's bureau, and in 1906 a bill was introduced in Congress. The bill languished. Eventually, however, momentum grew, supported by "the National Child Labor Committee, women's organizations, the National Consumers' League, the National Conference of Charities and Correction" and the 1909 White House Conference on the Care of Dependent Children.[30] Congress finally acted, and the law establishing the Children's Bureau was signed by President William Howard Taft on April 9, 1912. The law stated the bureau's duties: "Investigate and report . . . upon all matters pertaining to the welfare of children and child life among all classes of our people, and . . . especially investigate the questions of infant mortality, the birth rate, orphanage, juvenile courts, desertion, dangerous occupations, accidents and diseases of children, employment, [and] legislation affecting children in the several states and territories."[31]

Julia Lathrop of Hull House was appointed the first director of the Children's Bureau. The staff of the Children's Bureau published groundbreaking studies of infant mortality. The bureau also documented maternal death during childbirth. The bureau's research on infant and maternal mortality contributed to the first federally funded child welfare program, the Sheppard-Towner Act. Sheppard-Towner operated from 1921 to 1929, and provided funds to states to promote maternal and infant health.

The Children's Bureau issued reports on the need for birth registration, lack of sanitary conditions for children, the need for proper prenatal care for pregnant women, the juvenile court, and other topics. The bureau was an ally of the child guidance movement and a strong supporter of mothers' pensions. Until the 1960s, the Children's Bureau focused little attention on child abuse and neglect, leaving this work to others.

The bureau produced publications for parents, including *Infant Care* and *Your Child from One to Six*. These short, easy-to-read pamphlets found their way into millions of homes. Thousands of mothers wrote to the bureau for advice, and professionals at the bureau, including the director herself, wrote personal letters in reply.

In August 1921, Grace Abbott became the second director of the Children's Bureau. Abbott described the challenge of lobbying for children in the hurly-burly of Washington politics:

> Sometimes when I get home at night in Washington I feel as though I had been in a great traffic jam. The jam is moving toward the Hill where Congress sits in judgment on all the administrative agencies of the Government. In that traffic jam there are all kinds of vehicles moving up toward the Capital. . . . For example, the Army can put into the street tanks, gun carriages, trucks. . . . There are the hayricks and the binders and the ploughs and all the other things that the Department of Agriculture manages to put into the streets, . . . the handsome limousines in which the Department of Commerce rides, . . . the barouches in which the Department of State rides in such dignity. It seems so to me as I stand on the sidewalk watching it become more congested and more difficult, and then because the responsibility is mine and I must, I take a very firm hold on the handles of the baby carriage and I wheel it into the traffic.[32]

Social Security Act of 1935

Prior to 1935, the federal government played an insignificant role in child welfare policy and funding.[33] Creation of the Children's Bureau in 1912 broke the ice, followed by the Sheppard-Towner Act in 1921. It was the Great Depression of the 1930s, however, that stimulated a sea change in the federal government's role in social programs. With the economy in shambles, bold action was required. Franklin Delano Roosevelt brought the necessary leadership to the White House when he took office on March 4, 1933. Roosevelt assembled a cadre of advisors to formulate rescue plans for the nation. Calling his vision for economic recovery the "New Deal," Roosevelt asked and received Congress's help. Meeting in special session from March 9, 1933 to June 16, 1933—the so-called Hundred Days— Congress passed a broad array of economic laws to cope with the depression.

Building on the first wave of legislative reform, in June 1934, President Roosevelt created the Committee on Economic Security to "study problems relating to the economic security of individuals."[34] Edwin Witte was appointed executive director of the committee.[35] Witte worked with hundreds of individuals, including Grace Abbott and Katherine Lenroot of the Children's Bureau, to draft the Social Security Act. The act became law in 1935.

The Social Security Act "marked the beginning of the federal government's participation in a broad range of social-insurance and public-welfare programs. This act has had implications for almost every American family and for many of our social institutions."[36] In addition to old-age pensions, unemployment insurance, and vocational and rehabilitation services, the Social Security Act created the Aid to Dependent Children program (ADC), which replaced and expanded mothers' pensions.

To be eligible for federal ADC funds, states had to abide by conditions set forth by Congress in the Social Security Act. Each state desiring ADC funds was required to submit a plan to the federal government describing its ADC program and promising to comply with the conditions attached to the money. The technique of attaching conditions to federal money gives Congress tremendous leverage to shape public policy in the states. Congress passes laws making billions of federal dollars available to states that are willing to abide by the conditions attached to the money. Since states cannot afford to forego federal largess, Congress exerts wide-ranging influence over state policy and practice.

In addition to ADC, the Social Security Act revived the Sheppard-Towner Act, providing funds for maternal and child health.[37] Katherine Lenroot and Grace Abbott of the Children's Bureau worked to secure the legislation reviving the Sheppard-Towner law, benefits for handicapped children, and the provision regarding dependent and neglected children. The Children's Bureau urged adoption of ADC to expand mothers' pensions. The bureau also suggested an appropriation of $1,500,000 a year to assist state welfare departments in promoting better care and protection of children and to strengthen local public services. The Social Security Act also provided funds for "crippled children." Finally, and directly relevant to child welfare and protection, the Social Security Act authorized the Children's Bureau "to cooperate with State public-welfare agencies in establishing, extending, and strengthening, especially in predominantly rural areas, [child welfare services] for the protection and care of homeless, dependent, and neglected children, and children in danger of becoming delinquent."[38] This provision of the

Social Security Act was an important shot in the arm for the nascent field of child welfare, and a modest step toward what, in the 1970s, became a central role for the federal government in child protection policy and funding. By 1939, every state had a child welfare plan approved by the Children's Bureau. The preference for rural areas dropped away in 1958.

Summary of Progressive Era Reforms

Progressive Era reforms had a direct impact on children. The emergence of social work, pediatrics, psychology, and psychiatry created the workforce needed to advance the fields of child welfare and children's mental and physical health. Efforts to limit child labor dovetailed with the spread of compulsory public education, and children put down factory tools and picked up school books. The debate over orphanage care versus foster care tipped in favor of the latter. State governments slowly assumed leadership in the provision of social services. The 1909 White House Conference on the Care of Dependent Children set standards that shaped child welfare throughout the twentieth century, especially the overarching premise that the best place for children—including poor children—is their own home. The White House conferees agreed that mothers' pensions should be available so that poverty did not break up families. Finally, the Progressive Era saw an end to the long-held tradition that the federal government has no role to play in social issues.

For the most part, the reforms discussed above were not focused directly on abused and neglected children. Child protection proceeded on a parallel track, contributing to progressive reforms and benefiting from them.

Juvenile Court

Every state has a juvenile court. In several states (e.g., Hawaii, Nevada, New York), the juvenile court is called family court. The juvenile court has authority over three groups of children: abused and neglected children, juvenile delinquents, and status offenders. A status offense is misbehavior that is not delinquency, but that nevertheless brings a child under the authority of the juvenile court. The traditional status offenses are truancy, smoking and drinking under age, running away, curfew violations, and so-called ungovernable behavior.

America's first juvenile court was established in 1899. The Progressive Era reformers who created the juvenile court were concerned primarily about the criminal justice system's harsh treatment of delinquent children. Prior to the juvenile court, children who broke the law were arrested, jailed, brought to trial, and punished similarly to adults. Children as young as six occasionally languished in jail with adult criminals. Ernest Coulter wrote in 1913, "Five hundred children ranging in age from six to sixteen years had been confined in the Philadelphia County Prison in the enlightened year of our Lord 1900."[39]

The earliest legal reforms for young lawbreakers did not involve a new court. In 1869, a Massachusetts law provided that when a child under sixteen was charged in criminal court, notice was to be given to the State Board of Charities so that a representative of the Board could attend the trial and advise the judge what to do with the young malefactor. An 1870 Massachusetts law required separate hearings for children in Boston's criminal courts. A Massachusetts "law of 1877 not only authorized separate trial of children's cases but also used, perhaps for the first time, the term 'session for juvenile offenders.' "[40] Massachusetts also pioneered the use of probation for youthful offenders, as did Michigan.

Like Massachusetts, New York was at the forefront of reform. In 1825, New York City established America's first "reform school," the House of Refuge. Other states followed suit. In 1877, New York passed a law disallowing children under sixteen "in any prison or place of confinement, or in any court room or in any vehicle in company with adults charged or convicted with crime, except in the presence of proper officers." A New York law of 1884 established probation as an alternative to incarceration, and an 1892 law authorized separate trials for juveniles. Ernest Coulter wrote, "There were a number of humane and sensible magistrates and judges who, without the authority of any special statute, but guided solely by their sense of the fitness of things, held the hearings of children brought before them separate from adults at least ten years before the first separate courts for children were established by law."[41]

The first true juvenile court was established in Chicago. Legislation authorizing the court was approved April 21, 1899, and the court opened for business July 1, 1899. What stood the Chicago juvenile court apart from earlier reforms was that it removed youthful offenders *altogether* from the criminal justice system. Rather than subject children to trial, conviction, and punishment as criminals, proceedings in juvenile court were civil. The juvenile court adjudicated the youngster a delinquent rather than a criminal and provided individualized treatment rather than punishment. The goal in juvenile court was to save the child from a downward spiral leading to a life of crime. The reformers who created the juvenile court believed rehabilitation was superior to the retribution meted out by criminal law. Julian Mack, a judge of the early Chicago juvenile court, and an influential spokesperson for the juvenile court movement, put it this way in 1909, "Why is it not just and proper to treat these juvenile offenders . . . as a wise and merciful father handles his own child whose errors are not discovered by the authorities? Why is it not the duty of the state, instead of asking merely whether a boy or girl has committed a specific offense, to find out what he is, physically, mentally, morally, and then if it learns that he is treading the path that leads to criminality, to take him in charge, not so much to punish as to reform, not to degrade but to uplift, not to crush but to develop, not to make him a criminal but a worthy citizen."[42]

In addition to delinquency, the Chicago juvenile court had authority over neglected and dependent children, which the 1899 law defined as any child under sixteen, "who for any reason is destitute or homeless or abandoned; or dependent upon the public for support; or has no proper parental care or guardianship; or who habitually begs or receives alms; or who is found living in any house of ill fame or with any vicious or disreputable person; or whose home, by reason of neglect, cruelty or depravity on the part of its parents, guardian or other person in whose care it may be, is an unfit place for such child."[43] This definition became a model for juvenile court laws across the United States.

The original Illinois Juvenile Court Act did not clearly distinguish poverty from neglect. According to Paul Anderson this was because

> Drafters of the Juvenile Court Act realized that a court of equity had to examine the condition of a child very carefully to make the right decision or disposition. With years of practical experience, both Julia Lathrop and Timothy Hurley knew that there was an important difference between a child in need and a child in jeopardy. Notwithstanding, for very different reasons, these two reformers did not try to differentiate between *dependent child* and *neglected child* in the Juvenile Court Act.
>
> Julia Lathrop was visionary, but also an opportunist. Juvenile courts were essential to modernization of the state's child welfare system, but so was a state board of guardians with authority to place children in, or remove children from, licensed institutions or foster homes. Lathrop knew that any attempt to differentiate between *dependent child* and *neglected child* in the Juvenile Court Act would stir controversy. It was for this reason alone that the 1897 bill to establish a state board of guardians did not even attempt, as had the 1895 bill, to make that distinction. Trusting in the prudence of circuit and county court judges, Lathrop allowed juvenile court judges wide discretion in discriminating between dependency and neglect.[44]

Thus, the first juvenile court was established at Chicago. Or was it? Not according to Benjamin Lindsey, the crusading Colorado judge who molded Denver's juvenile court. Lindsey pointed out that the law authorizing Chicago's juvenile court was approved on April 21, 1899. Ten days earlier, on April 12, 1899, the Colorado legislature passed a law that, according to Lindsey, authorized a juvenile court. Although the Colorado law was part of the education code and did not mention a "juvenile court," Lindsey argued that made no difference. According to Lindsey, Colorado's law preceded the date Chicago claimed as the origin of their first juvenile court, and this Colorado legislation permitted even more to be done for the care of delinquent juveniles.

So, who really had the first juvenile court? There is little doubt that the Chicago court, which opened its doors in 1899, was operational before the Denver court. Ben Lindsey did not become a judge until 1900, and he is acknowledged

FIGURE 3.3
Judge Ben Lindsey.
Photograph provided by
and reproduced with
permission of the Denver
City Public Library,
Denver, Colorado.

as Denver's first juvenile court judge. Moreover, Colorado's law specifically creating a juvenile court was not passed until 1903. Chicago has the stronger argument. In the final analysis, however, it doesn't matter. Both courts served as catalysts for the rapid expansion of juvenile courts across the United States and in other countries.

Judge Lindsey was a colorful character of the old west and a tireless campaigner for social justice. Born in Tennessee in 1869, Lindsey's parents moved to Denver when Ben was ten. Lindsey decided to become a lawyer, but in those days law schools were few and far between, so Ben followed the traditional path of studying in a lawyer's office. To put bread on the table, Lindsey sold newspapers and did janitorial work at night. He was admitted to the bar in 1894, at age twenty-five.

Throughout his long career as a lawyer and judge, Lindsey helped the "little guy." He took on the rich and powerful, exposing politicians he viewed as corrupt. He criticized political parties, the Colorado Supreme Court, civic groups, the criminal justice system, the police, social workers (whom he called "scientific robots"), the Ku Klux Klan, churches, and anyone else he believed stood in the way of progress. Needless to say, Lindsey made enemies, and his opponents eventually had him disbarred by the Colorado Supreme Court. Lindsey moved to California and continued his legal career. Eventually, the Colorado Supreme Court offered to reinstate him if he would apologize for the things he said about the court. In typical fashion, Lindsey refused. A few years later, he was reinstated without the desired apology.

Lindsey was devoted to children. As a young lawyer practicing in Denver, he was appointed to represent two defendants accused of burglary. When he met his clients, he was surprised to find boys of twelve. Later in life, Lindsey wrote, "I think it must have been some of the impressions, conscious or subconscious, that came to me in that experience of defending young criminals that really enlisted my interest in what afterwards was to become the Juvenile Court."[45]

Lindsey was keenly aware of the relationship between poverty and delinquency. In a speech to the 1909 White House Conference on the Care of Dependent Children, Lindsey reminded his audience, "We must go down deep into the causes of poverty and ignorance which is responsible for most of our dependency and crime."[46]

Lindsey advocated tirelessly for children's interests, including, among other projects, the creation of public baths in Denver. Many of Denver's poor had no

FIGURE 3.4

Ben Lindsey presiding in his early twentieth-century juvenile court. Photograph provided by and reproduced with permission of the Denver City Public Library, Denver, Colorado.

place to bathe. When his pleas to city officials for public baths fell on deaf ears, Lindsey organized a group of boys to go swimming in the ornate fountain in front of the courthouse. When the police arrived to chase the boys away, they ran dripping wet into Lindsey's courtroom, where Lindsey had newspaper reporters waiting to record the whole thing. The stunt made the papers and persuaded embarrassed city officials that if there was money for fountains in front of public buildings, perhaps a few dollars could be spared for public baths.

Juvenile courts spread across the United States. By 1919, all states but three had juvenile courts, and eventually all states fell in line. The early juvenile court was as much social agency as law court. For that reason, the formal procedures of the courtroom were relaxed in favor of informality. In many juvenile courts, the judge sat at a desk rather than on an elevated bench. The child and adults sat at the desk with the judge. Most of the time, attorneys were not present. Everyone provided input, and the judge decided what was needed to turn the young offender away from crime. Most delinquents were placed on probation. Some were sent to reform schools or other institutions. In cases of abuse or neglect, the judge could remove children from home or leave them at home under the supervision of the court's probation officers.

Protecting and Controlling Teenage Girls

Prior to the 1960s, and to a lesser extent today, many adults had different expectations for adolescent girls and boys. Boys were expected to sow a few wild oats. After all, "boys will be boys." Girls, on the other hand, were supposed to act like, well, like *girls*! In *The Real Mother Goose*, published in 1916, we see this attitude reflected in the oft-repeated rhyme, "What Are Little Boys Made Of?"

> What are little boys made of, made of?
> What are little boys made of?
> "Snaps and snails, and puppy-dogs' tails;
> And that's what little boys are made of."

> What are little girls made of, made of?
> What are little girls made of?
> "Sugar and spice, and all that's nice;
> And that's what little girls are made of."[47]

It was a different world for adolescent girls and boys. Adolescent shenanigans that were winked at from boys were shocking in girls. In particular, sexual experimentation by teenage boys was frowned on but largely ignored—those wild oats again—whereas similar behavior from girls was cause for alarm.

Child protection societies intervened on behalf of teenage girls. In 1918, the secretary of the Columbus, Ohio Humane Society urged adults to "go out on the streets and note the young girls in their teens parading up and down the streets with their camouflaged complexions, unaccompanied by parents or other elder persons looking for the opportunity to meet strange young fellows or to take an automobile ride. And later, much later in the evening, you will note, and if you are inclined to be old-fashioned, you will be shocked that these same young children are still on the streets, although any intelligent human being ought to know the place for such children is at home. How long, oh Lord, how long, are we going to continue to throw temptation in the way of the children of our cities, and then hold up our hands in holy horror and pretend to be shocked when they go wrong?"[48]

In some cities, specialized societies sprang up to help adolescent girls in trouble, particularly girls treading close to sin. In 1935, Douglas Falconer described such societies:

> The problems presented in girls' protective work are varied and are frequently concerned with the intangible values of life. They range from minor personal situations, where advice and guidance are sufficient, to serious behavior difficulties, mental or emotional disturbances, or conditions resulting from physical or mental handicaps. They include defiance of authority, disobedience, untruthfulness, associating with undesirable companions, family friction, truancy, running away from home, and sexual misbehaviors. Efforts are made to deal with these situations without the aid of a court, relying upon intensive case work service and the assistance of interested agencies, such as child guidance clinics, schools, vocational guidance service, and recreational agencies.
>
> In 1925 the Girls' Protective Council was organized. It is now known as the National Girls' Work Council. Its over 200 member agencies include not only those dealing exclusively with girls but a variety of other social agencies having contact with girls' problems.[49]

Although Falconer noted that professionals working with teenage girls generally avoided juvenile court, the court was used on a regular basis.[50] As mentioned earlier, juvenile courts have authority over three categories of children: abused and neglected, juvenile delinquents, and status offenders. Unruly adolescent girls were hauled before juvenile courts as status offenders or sex delinquents.[51] Boys, on the other hand, were seldom controlled this way.[52] When teenage boys appeared in juvenile court it was for delinquency.

Delinquent boys were usually placed on probation. Teenage girls who were adjudged status offenders or "sex delinquents," however, were frequently institutionalized to keep them out of harm's way. In 1910, Hastings Hart discussed the benefits of institutionalizing troublesome teenage girls. Hart described girls already in foster care:

A girl may be well placed in a family home, and may do well for years. When she reaches the age of fourteen or fifteen years she becomes restless, uneasy, discontented. She chafes under restraint, desires more liberty, wants to choose her own associates and her own recreations. She wants to go out at night. She craves pretty clothes and admiration. Perhaps she is the recipient of flattering and dangerous attentions from some young man. The situation is often complicated by the disturbing suggestions of meddlesome neighbors or thoughtless young people, who stimulate her discontent by criticizing her foster parents. The girl is not vicious, she does not want to do anything wrong, but she is in a critical and dangerous situation. She is giddy, headstrong, easily influenced. She needs to be kept safe for a year or two, until she comes to herself, and in the meantime she ought to receive such training as will either enable her to support herself or will make her a more efficient housewife and mother. It is for this class of girls that industrial schools are now demanded.[53]

My research on the Sacramento, California juvenile court of the early twentieth century confirms the use of the court to control "naughty girls." Every year, small numbers of teenage girls were brought to the Sacramento juvenile court for noncriminal misbehavior. In many cases, the judge committed the girl to an institution as a kind of "shock treatment." Most commitments lasted less than a year, and the girl was returned to her parents. I found almost no cases in which teenage boys were controlled this way.

Transition from Nongovernmental SPCCs to Government Child Protection

During the early twentieth century, calls arose to shift child protection from nongovernmental SPCCs to government agencies. Carl Carstens of the Massachusetts SPCC led the movement toward public child protective services. Carstens believed protective work should be in the hands of counties overseen by state agencies.[54] It was not Carstens' goal to put nongovernmental child protection societies out of business. According to Carstens, basic child protection was the bailiwick of government, with private organizations providing prevention programs, treatment, and research.

Writing in 1929, Ray Hubbard stated, "Leaders in the field of child protection now generally agree that such work should become a public function and be made a part of a statewide program with county units under state supervision or control."[55] In 1935, Douglas Falconer wrote, "For many years responsibility for child protection was left almost entirely to private agencies. . . . They were generally independent, autonomous, local units, only loosely gathered into national federations, if indeed they had any such national relationship. Great sections of child population were untouched by them and in many other places the service rendered was perfunctory and of poor standard. The brilliant exceptions to this general picture have been few in number. These few have made great contributions to the understanding of the problem of neglected children and have blazed the trial for a wider and more generally effective service, but the belief has become increasingly accepted that if children are to be protected from neglect the service must be performed by public agencies."[56]

The call for government child protection coincided with the increasing role of state governments in social services. As discussed earlier, prior to the twentieth century, there were relatively few state-level departments of social services. What government services there were, primarily outdoor relief, were the province of local government, that is, towns, cities, and counties. During the first half of the twentieth century, however, states created or strengthened state departments of welfare, social services, health, and labor.

By 1935, half the states had child welfare divisions within the state department of welfare or social services. At the county level, counties developed welfare departments and slowly added child welfare workers.[57] In 1935, Douglas Falconer stated that hope for improved services to abused and neglected children "lies in the establishment of child welfare bureaus within county welfare departments, staffed by workers trained in the child welfare field. In 1932 there were 16 states which had such departments more or less generally organized, but full-time workers were employed in less than a fifth of the 1,537 counties in these states."[58] In 1959, half the counties in the United States had no social workers providing full-time child welfare services.[59]

The Great Depression, which began with the stock market crash of 1929, and persisted through the 1930s, hastened the demise of nongovernmental SPCCs. The charitable contributions that were the lifeblood of SPCCs dried up with the economy, and only the heartiest SPCCs weathered the economic drought. In the 1930s and 1940s, many SPCCs merged with children's aid societies or family social work agencies or went out of business altogether. In some communities, child protection was assumed by the juvenile court or the police department, while in other communities organized protective work ceased.

In 1939, Herschel Alt sent questionnaires to social service councils in thirty-six cities with populations over 250,000.[60] Thirty councils responded. Alt's questionnaire asked about the role of private agencies in meeting the needs of children, including foster care, aid to dependent children, institutional care, and protective services. Half the responding communities reported that private children's agencies had some responsibility for child protection. In three cities, public welfare departments had "recently assumed primary responsibility for protective service to children as part of a general case work service to children in their own homes."

Carl Carstens discussed the disorganized state of child protection in the 1930s, "The lack of systematic children's protective work is still a serious gap in the

FIGURE 3.5
Vincent De Francis in his office at the Children's Division of the American Humane
Association. Photograph provided by and reproduced with permission of Pat De Francis.

children's work of many cities and states. . . . At present a large part of the country
is without skilled child protection and in great need of it.[61]

World War II, from 1941 to 1945, caused major dislocations in American life, as
thousands of fathers went off to war, and thousands of mothers entered the labor
force. Neglect and delinquency increased, but the number of foster homes remained stagnant or, in some places, declined. In some communities, the war increased pressure to merge social agencies. Child welfare services, including child
protection, were stretched thin.

Vincent De Francis was the director of the Children's Division of the American
Humane Association from 1954 to 1977. In 1956, De Francis conducted a national
inventory of child protective services.[62] Before discussing De Francis's inventory,
however, it is important to introduce this pioneer of child protection. De Francis
was born in New York City on Christmas Eve, 1907. He graduated from City College of New York in 1929, and studied law at Fordham, graduating in 1932. De
Francis practiced law in New York until 1941, when he accepted a position with
the Brooklyn Society for the Prevention of Cruelty to Children, doing casework
with families and prosecuting abuse cases in court. The Brooklyn SPCC had long
favored a social work approach to child protection, and this approach rubbed off

on the young lawyer. De Francis realized his legal training did not adequately equip him to help children and families, so he took social work classes at the New York School of Social Work. In 1946, De Francis became executive director of the Queensboro Society for the Prevention of Cruelty to Children, a position he held until 1954, when he was appointed director of the Children's Division of the American Humane Association in Denver, Colorado. Under De Francis, AHA's Children's Division became one of America's most influential organizations addressing child protection.[63]

Although his initial training was in law, Vincent De Francis was a social worker at heart. He clearly understood the intergenerational nature of child maltreatment, writing, "What makes their situation more pathetic is the fact that much of this pathology, if it remains untreated, tends to perpetuate itself, with yesterday's neglected children becoming today's neglecting parents; thus creating a cycle of neglect, delinquency and emotional disturbance which begets more neglect, delinquency and emotional disturbance."[64] De Francis understood the destructiveness of psychological neglect, writing, "Most damaging is the failure to give a child the love and affection, and the sense of belonging and the security which is so important to a proper personality development."[65] Like Grace Abbott, Charles Loring Brace, Elbridge Gerry, and others before him, De Francis believed child maltreatment leads to delinquency. In testimony before Congress, De Francis stated, "Perhaps our thinking can best be epitomized by such catch-all phrases as 'the neglected child of today is the delinquent of tomorrow' or 'Scratch a delinquent and you will find a neglected child underneath,' or again, 'Stop neglect—Prevent delinquency.' "[66] De Francis was convinced that most maltreating parents want to do better and can be helped. Although he knew court action was necessary in some cases, De Francis believed the solution to child maltreatment lay in prevention and social casework. He described his approach:

> No understanding of the value, need, and importance of child protective services is complete without a recognition of the basic philosophy upon which the entire structure of child protection is built. Over the past twenty-five years or more practitioners in this field have thought of their work as a helping process, and not a punitive, law enforcement or prosecuting service. To punish parents who neglect children brings no real help to the children. To remove them from the care and custody of such parents will impose upon the children all the emotional conflicts and guilt feelings which ordinarily follow such separation and will without question seriously impair their normal emotional life as adults. The only way we can truly protect these children is to give to their parents the kind of help which will assist in bringing about the change necessary to eliminate the neglect.[67]

In 1956, De Francis wrote letters to child welfare professionals throughout the United States, asking them to describe child protection in their state, county, city, or town. In his letters, De Francis defined protective services as "a specialized casework service to neglected, abused, exploited, or rejected children. The focus of the service is preventive and non-punitive, and is geared toward a rehabilitation of the home and a treatment of the motivating factors which underlie neglect."[68]

The responses to De Francis's letters provide valuable insight into child protection midway through the twentieth century. De Francis found eighty-four non-governmental SPCCs, down from the high of three hundred early in the century. The eighty-four SPCCs were located in sixteen states: Connecticut, Illinois, Indiana, Kentucky, Maryland, Massachusetts, Minnesota, Missouri, Nebraska, New Jersey, New York, Ohio, Pennsylvania, Rhode Island, Tennessee, and Texas. Only four states—Connecticut, Massachusetts, Maryland, and Rhode Island—approached statewide coverage by SPCCs. Other states had limited SPCC coverage. Texas, for example, had only two SPCCs, Minnesota one. Thirty-two states had no SPCC. In these states, and in states with only partial SPCC coverage, government agencies were gradually assuming responsibility for child protection.

De Francis found fifteen states where the law did not clearly impose responsibility for child protection on a state agency. Lack of a specific state law did not mean, of course, that children were unprotected. De Francis's finding, however, provides insight into the unfinished business of government child protective services in the mid-twentieth century.

In the 1950s, many communities had no agency clearly in charge of child protection. Responding to De Francis's letter, a New Jersey official wrote, "Protective casework services for children in this metropolitan community of about 35,000 inhabitants are most conspicuous by their absence." From Oklahoma, an official from a midsized city wrote, "When I read your original letter I laid it aside because we have practically no services for neglected, abused, exploited, or rejected children in our community." De Francis wrote, "An appalling number of communities, many of them large cities, have not made provision for bringing help to neglected children."[69]

Many communities relied on the police or the juvenile court for child protection. A Florida official wrote to De Francis, "We have no protective service for children organized as such. The Juvenile Court is the agency called when authoritative action with respect to child welfare is required. The police departments of our major municipalities have juvenile aid bureaus which are frequently called upon also." In a similar vein, a Georgia official wrote, "We do not have in this area a child protective agency with functions as you describe in your letter. The only services available for neglected, abused, or exploited children [are] through the Juvenile Court, where some attempt is made on the part of probation officers to correct conditions in the home." An Idaho official wrote, "Any services that can be technically defined as protective services in Idaho would be provided under the supervision of the Probate Courts which function as Juvenile Courts in Idaho."[70]

As government gradually assumed responsibility for child protection, the usual practice was to assign the task to the county department of welfare or social services. Until the 1960s and 1970s, many departments lacked social workers trained in child welfare, let alone specialized units focused on child protection.[71] Protective work was typically part of an undifferentiated social work caseload.[72] In 1949, the Children's Bureau reported, "A few States give 'protective' service through special case workers assigned to this field."[73] In the 1950s, a number of large cities and a smattering of smaller communities established separate child protection units.[74]

A decade after his 1956 research, De Francis again took the pulse of American child protection. By 1967, the number of states with SPCCs was down to ten. The handful of SPCCs still active in 1967 was a far cry from the 300 in the early decades of the century. De Francis wrote, "Responsibility for provision of Child Protective Services under voluntary agency auspices, like the old soldier it is, is slowly fading away."[75]

In his 1967 report, De Francis wrote, "Protective Services under public welfare auspices [were] reported to exist in 47 states." Yet, De Francis complained, "No state and no community has developed a Child Protective Service program adequate in size to meet the service needs of all reported cases of child neglect, abuse and exploitation."[76] A few years before De Francis's 1967 report, Elizabeth Glover and Joseph Reid wrote, "In hundreds of counties in the United States, there is no protective service for children, other than police services, and, in many of the nation's largest cities, the only protective service is provided by voluntary agencies that are not sufficiently financed to give total community coverage."[77] California in 1965 did not have a county system of child protective service.[78] Child protection was provided by the police and the probation staff of the juvenile court. In other states, protective services were not available statewide. Fewer than five states had complete geographic coverage. Moreover, most communities lacked twenty-four hour service. After regular working hours, reports went to police or juvenile court probation officers. Specialized child protection units, separate caseloads, and trained workers were the exception.[79]

Thus, for the first six decades of the twentieth century, protective services in most communities were inadequate and in some places nonexistent.[80] Yet, despite obstacles, professionals protected children.[81] In 1958, Claire Hancock described the dedication common among child protection workers then and now. "Day after day, the staff, under great pressure, were faced with staggering problems. They were attempting to make suitable plans for children whose lives were all tangled up, whose needs were desperate, often beyond the resources available to meet them. Their endurance, their consistent effort to do the very best they could under the circumstances, commands one's admiration as well as sympathy for the strain and discouragement that was common experience."[82]

Race in American Child Welfare

Prior to the 1960s, America had a dismal civil rights record. Indeed, the struggle for equality is not over. Child welfare workers of earlier times partook of the racial climate of their day, and children of color were often treated insensitively or excluded altogether from child welfare services.[83] It did not dawn on many nineteenth- and early twentieth-century professionals that it was wrong to treat children of color differently.[84] Yet, throughout our history, enlightened professionals cared for children across color lines.[85] Charles Loring Brace, for example, abhorred slavery, writing, "If I can do something to lessen on American soil that curse of slavery, I shall be satisfied." Brace's New York Children's Aid Society helped children of all races.[86]

The 1930 White House Conference on Child Health and Protection devoted considerable attention to inequities tied to race. Ira Reid, on behalf of the White House Subcommittee on the Negro in the United States, wrote, "Though constituting but 10 per cent of the total population of the United States, the Negro forms a much larger percentage of the dependent population. The problems of such a situation are both created and augmented by the prevailing racial situation in which the Negro suffers grave economic and social injustices. In many communities efforts are made to ameliorate these conditions, but such efforts are often based upon racial distinction which tends to perpetuate rather than to eliminate the problems of dependency."[87] The subcommittee asserted, "It is the responsibility of every community to see that full resources for care be available for Negro children as well as for white children. . . . Lower standards of care for Negro children than those available for white children in the same community can in no way be condoned."

Decline of the Orphanage

The number of children in orphanages peaked during the Great Depression at roughly 144,000. Following World War II, orphanages declined, and by 1980, Americans viewed the orphanage as a relic of the past. Marshall Jones attributed the demise of orphanages to the Social Security Act of 1935, skyrocketing costs, and the deinstitutionalization movement of the 1970s.[88]

The Social Security Act created Aid to Dependent Children (ADC), which provided financial assistance to millions of low-income parents, vastly expanding mothers' pensions, and allowing many children to remain at home. Prior to ADC, thousands of poor parents placed their children in orphanages.

Rising costs contributed to the demise of orphanages. In the typical nineteenth-century orphanage, children lived together in large buildings where they were fed, clothed, sheltered, educated, and prepared for work. This arrangement was not

FIGURE 3.6

Patrick (Pops) Mulloy and his children in 1933 at Columbus College Orphanage in Sioux Falls, South Dakota. Mr. Mulloy was a widower. At the height of the Great Depression he was so poor that he had to place his children in the orphanage. Mulloy could not tolerate being separated from his children, so he took a job as a maintenance man at the orphanage. The orphanage children called him "Pops." Photograph provided by and reproduced with permission of Cathleen Reis, granddaughter of Pops. Cathleen's father is standing at the far right.

cheap but neither was it expensive. Beginning in the 1920s, several factors conspired to drive up costs. First, professionals were increasingly sensitive to the mental health needs of children in orphanages, and treatment programs were initiated. Obviously, it is more expensive to employ social workers, psychologists, and psychiatrists than lay attendants. Second, the proportion of orphanage children with serious mental health problems rose because "normal" children were increasingly supported at home with ADC, or placed in foster homes, or adopted. With the children in orphanages increasingly disturbed, costs rose. Third, to make institutional life less homogenized and more family-like, orphanages adopted the cottage plan, incurring capital expenditures and increased staffing costs. A fourth factor driving up costs was increased regulation of children's institutions by state governments and accrediting agencies like the Child Welfare League of America. State regulatory bodies and CWLA imposed increasing programatic, staffing, and institutional requirements. Eventually, it became less expensive to find foster homes for children—including difficult-to-place children—than to maintain orphanages. Matthew Crenson observed that foster care "was another of the arrangements that helped to dissolve the regime of the orphanage. Weekly rates for boarding children in family homes became standards of comparison for evaluating the operating costs of orphan asylums. The orphanage almost always fared badly in such comparisons, especially when capital expenditures for institutional buildings and equipment were figured into the tally, and the results looked even worse for orphanages that took on the increased expenses associated with the cottage plan."[89]

A further factor contributing to the demise of large orphanages was the deinstitutionalization movement of the 1970s, which dramatically decreased the number of people living in state mental hospitals, state training schools for the mentally retarded, and orphanages. In addition, by the middle of the twentieth century, there were fewer orphans to go around. Dramatic advances in public health, workplace safety, and medicine led to greater life expectancies not only for children but also for moms and dads.

As orphanages slowly disappeared, foster care grew. In 1933, 47 percent of children who could not live at home were in foster homes, while 53 percent lived in institutions. By 1972, 80 percent of children needing out-of-home care lived in foster homes or group homes, and 20 percent lived in institutions.[90]

Relative Obscurity of Child Protection
from 1929 to 1962

From Mary Ellen's rescue in 1874 until the Great Depression of the 1930s, impressive achievements occurred in child protection. Societies to prevent cruelty to children made no secret of their work, publicizing heartrending cases in the press and in fund-raising appeals. Child protection was out in the open for all to see. Then came the stock market crash of 1929 and the Great Depression. SPCCs declined. Attention shifted from the reforms of the Progressive Era to economic survival. Overseas, a plethora of issues, dominated by the rise of fascism, preoccupied government and public alike. America, it seemed, was headed again for war, less than twenty years after World War I, "the war to end all wars." In this climate, child protection did not cease, but it retreated into relative obscurity.

The end of Progressive reforms, the Great Depression, World War II, Korea, and the Cold War, with its omnipresent threat of nuclear annihilation, were not the only reasons for the relative obscurity of child protection from the 1930s to the 1960s. As child protection shifted to government agencies, the highly specialized and visible SPCCs disappeared. Child protection became one of the many functions of government social workers. Few communities had special units responding to child maltreatment, and child abuse disappeared into an undifferentiated child welfare caseload. Moreover, many social workers disliked abuse and neglect cases, involving as they often do confrontation and courts. In 1943, Dorothy Berkowitz wrote candidly in *The Family*, "The private agency has continued through the years to carry some portion of the burden of protective cases, consisting usually of those coming to its attention through the complaint by a member of the community of parental neglect or abuse of children. But protective case work has been far from a major interest of the private family field. May we not honestly admit that most family case workers have considered it more of an unavoidable inheritance from the past than a rightful function of the present? Perhaps we have used protective cases as a training ground for students, but scarcely have we given them the benefit of conscious study toward more expert techniques. We may even have viewed them as the drudgery, if not the downright dregs, of our case loads."[91]

From the Great Depression to the 1960s, there was little professional writing about child protection. In 1955, Vincent De Francis of the American Humane Association wrote, "For at least a decade the writer has been concerned over the fact that aside from a number of excellent conference papers on special interest areas in the field there has been no great wealth of literature on protective services and none attempting to cover the subject as a whole."[92]

Loss of a specialized identity was not the only by-product of the transformation from private SPCCs to government child protection. Unlike SPCCs, which *sought* public attention to raise money, government agencies such as departments of social services and juvenile courts eschew public attention and are shrouded in confidentiality. Under government auspices, child protection "officially" disappeared from public view.

Additional factors contributed to the relative obscurity of child protection from the 1930s to the 1960s. Except in cases of obvious brutality, physicians and nurses were not particularly adept at differentiating accidental from nonaccidental injuries, particularly in young children and babies.[93] Medical professionals were apt to accept a parent's explanation for a child's injuries. Regarding sexual abuse, professionals were aware of the problem. Yet, it was not until the late 1970s that America opened its eyes to the reality of child sexual abuse.

Conclusion

During the thirty years from 1930 to 1960, thousands of children were protected, but many went without help. Professionals working in the trenches knew the stark reality of child abuse and neglect. For the outside world, however, child abuse faded from view. Yet, even during this period of relative obscurity, seeds were planted that ushered in a new era of child protection, an era of remarkable and lasting change.

4

CHILD PROTECTION FROM 1962
TO THE PRESENT

From 1900 through the 1960s, child protection was an incomplete patchwork of government agencies and nongovernmental societies to prevent cruelty to children. Many communities lacked organized child protection. Apart from occasional headlines recounting horrendous abuse, the public was blissfully ignorant. The 1960s and 1970s, however, witnessed an explosion of interest in child abuse. This explosion was triggered in major part by physicians who alerted the medical profession to physical abuse of young children. Discoveries by doctors attracted media attention and increased media and professional interest spurred passage of laws, requiring professionals to report abuse to authorities. The first reporting laws appeared in 1963 and quickly spread across the country. In 1974, Congress assumed a leadership role with passage of the Child Abuse Prevention and Treatment Act (CAPTA). Through CAPTA and other laws, Washington financed and shaped child protection policy from the 1970s to the present.

Medical Profession "Discovers" Child Physical Abuse

The medical profession played a key role in kindling interest in child physical abuse. Of course, physicians have always known of child abuse.[1] Prior to the 1960s, however, medical schools provided little or no training on the topic. There was also a dearth of medical literature on physical abuse, little or no information on the subject was available in pediatric or medical texts.[2]

In 1946, pediatrician and radiologist John Caffey published a groundbreaking article titled "Multiple Fractures in the Long Bones of Infants Suffering from Chronic Subdural Hematoma."[3] Caffey's article created a spark that smoldered for sixteen years, slowly building heat until it ignited in 1962.

FIGURE 4.1
John Caffey, M.D., in 1948.
Photograph provided by
and reproduced with
permission of Philip O.
Anderson, M.D.,
Columbia-Presbyterian
Medical Center,
New York.

John Caffey practiced general pediatrics in New York City from 1925 to 1929, when he joined the faculty at New York's Babies Hospital. Caffey had no formal training in radiology, which, in the 1920s, was just coming into its own. According to Caffey, his interest in radiology resulted from an offhand remark following a radiology meeting at Babies Hospital. Frustrated by what he perceived to be the lack of expertise in pediatric radiology, Caffey quipped to a colleague, "Well, that was another hour wasted." Caffey did not realize the chairman of his department was walking close behind. Caffey's boss said, "Do you think you could do any better, Jack?" Caffey, replied, "I could try." The chair fired back, "All right, you are now our radiologist." Caffey took his assignment to heart and became one of the world's foremost pediatric radiologists. His 1945 book *Pediatric X-ray Diagnosis* is a classic.[4] Caffey retired from Babies Hospital in 1960 and relocated to the University of Pittsburgh School of Medicine, where he published two landmark articles describing shaken baby syndrome.[5] John Caffey died in 1978 at the age of eighty-three.

In his groundbreaking 1946 article, Caffey described six young children with subdural hematoma (bleeding inside the skull) and twenty-three fractures of the legs or arms. Although Caffey did not expressly state that any of the children were abused, he hinted at it.[6] He commented, "In not a single case was there a history of injury to which the skeletal lesions could reasonably be attributed." Caffey wrote that for two of the children, "fresh fractures appeared shortly after the patient had arrived home after discharge from the hospital. In one of these cases the infant was clearly unwanted by both parents and this raised the question of intentional ill-treatment of the infant; the evidence was inadequate to prove or disprove this point." Following his 1946 article, Caffey often called attention to the traumatic origin of fractures and subdural hematoma in infants.[7]

Following Caffey's 1946 paper, a series of articles in the medical literature pointed with increasing clarity to child abuse as an explanation for certain injuries in young children. In 1953, radiologist Frederic Silverman wrote, "It is not often appreciated that many individuals responsible for the care of infants and children . . . may permit trauma and be unaware of it, may recognize trauma but forget or be reluctant to admit it, or may deliberately injure the child and deny it."[8]

In 1955, pediatrician Paul Woolley, Jr. and radiologist William Evans, Jr. described three injury-causing situations for young children. First, some children are hurt accidentally. "Experience both as physicians and parents leads us to doubt whether a child ever reaches his second birthday without at least one tumble of sufficient force, potentially, to injure a bone." Second, some children live in "unprotective environments" that increase the likelihood of injury. Third, some children are deliberately abused. Woolley and Evans wrote, "Immaturity, manifested by uncontrolled aggression on the part of either parent or other custodian, and overt psychotic or psychoneurotic behavior by the same group of persons played a much larger role than we initially had assumed."[9]

In 1958, radiologist Samuel Fisher called "attention to the need of suspecting willful mistreatment of children by parents."[10] In 1960, radiologists Donald Altman and Richard Smith observed that the problem of traumatic injury to young children "is being recognized with increasing frequency."[11] In 1961, radiologists John Gwinn, Kenneth Lewin, and Herbert Peterson stated, "Unsuspected or unrecognized trauma in infancy is a clinical entity resulting from episodes of willful trauma." Gwinn and his colleagues urged physicians "to be aware of the danger that exists for the child in a home situation where such trauma has occurred in the past. Repeated injuries are the rule rather than the exception. Serious injury and even death are not at all uncommon after these infants have been returned to the home environment. . . . The only certain method of safeguarding the infant is to remove him from the environment where the trauma has occurred." Gwinn and colleagues pointed out that willful trauma is little appreciated by practicing physicians. They maintained that any one physician in private practice would not encounter a sufficient number of cases to make him fully cognizant of willful trauma. Gwinn et al. noted that "the medical history . . . is almost always misleading, since the trauma may be unsuspected by the informant or deliberately concealed. Consequently, local infection or systemic disease are commonly the mistaken initial diagnosis, and the true traumatic nature of the condition may go completely undetected, particularly since the parents are likely to go from one physician to another for the care of individual episodes." The authors emphasized that multiple bone involvement is the rule: "*The presence of traumatic changes in several locations and in different stages of healing is indicative of repeated episodes of trauma and is a sine qua non for the roentgenographic diagnosis.* . . . In questions of accidental versus willful trauma, a bone survey will often show multiple injuries of different ages in the latter."[12]

Also in 1961, pathologist Lester Adelson noted, "It is relatively simple to destroy the life of a child in almost absolute secrecy without the necessity of taking any elaborate precautions to ensure that secrecy."[13] Adelson noted the unreliability of the history given by caretakers who kill their children: "When it has been established that death was the result of injury, and the responsible adults are questioned, a variety of explanations may be offered for the trauma . . . Further questioning by the police for exact details of the circumstances and time of these fatal incidents often results in fabrications that are completely rebutted by the nature, degree and age of the traumatic lesions."

Physicians were not the only ones coming to grips with physical abuse of young children. Social workers Elizabeth Elmer and Helen Broadman published groundbreaking papers in 1960 and 1962. Elmer wrote:

> Hospital social workers, along with their colleagues in other professions, appear strangely unaware of a rare hospital phenomenon that cries dramatically for attention—evidence of unbelievably primitive transactions that take place beyond our gaze, safe from our curious questions, and thus an index of social pathology which would seem to merit more attention. This is the fact that a small number of infants and children are hospitalized every year with injuries sustained through the ignorance, gross negligence, or deliberate abuse of the parents or other responsible adults. . . . It can now safely be said that very little is known about any facet of the problem and that methods for dealing with it are random and inadequate.[14]

Helen Boardman described a program created in 1959 at Children's Hospital of Los Angeles to respond to abuse of young children. Boardman wrote, "The incidence of inflicted trauma is startling."[15]

In 1946, John Caffey started a march toward greater understanding of maltreated young children and infants. Sixteen years later, in 1962, Drs. Henry Kempe, Frederic Silverman, Brandt Steele, William Droegemueller, and Henry Silver advanced the journey with their article, "The Battered-Child Syndrome." Kempe and his colleagues reported the results of a year-long survey of hospitals and prosecuting attorneys. The hospitals reported 302 cases of physical abuse of young children. Thirty-three of the children reported by hospitals died, and eighty-five suffered permanent damage. Prosecutors reported 447 cases. Among the cases reported by prosecutors, forty-five children died of their abuse, and twenty-nine suffered brain damage. Kempe and his colleagues described battered child syndrome:

> The battered-child syndrome may occur at any age, but, in general, the affected children are younger than 3 years. In some instances the clinical manifestations

FIGURE 4.2
C. Henry Kempe, M.D.
Photograph provided by
and reproduced with
permission of Ruth
Kempe, M.D.

are limited to those resulting from a single episode of trauma, but more often the child's general health is below par, and he shows evidence of neglect including poor skin hygiene, multiple soft tissue injuries, and malnutrition. One often obtains a history of previous episodes suggestive of parental neglect or trauma. A marked discrepancy between clinical findings and historical data as supplied by the parents is a major diagnostic feature of the battered-child syndrome. . . . Subdural hematoma, with or without fracture of the skull, is, in our experience, an extremely frequent finding even in the absence of fractures of the long bones. . . . The characteristic distribution of these multiple fractures and the observation that the lesions are in different stages of healing are of additional value in making the diagnosis.[16]

The first author of the term "battered child syndrome," Henry Kempe, played a leading role in bringing child abuse to national attention during the 1960s and 1970s. Kempe was born in Breslau, Germany in 1922. In 1937, his family left Germany to escape the Nazis. Henry's parents went to South America; Henry to England. Following a year in England, a refugee organization placed Henry in San Francisco, where he worked his way through the University of California at Berkeley. Kempe attended the University of California School of Medicine at San Francisco, graduating in 1945. Following an internship in pediatrics at San Francisco, the young doctor donned a uniform for two years' service as an army virologist. During his early career, Kempe was interested primarily in infectious diseases. Upon discharge from the army, Kempe completed a residency in pediatrics at Yale and returned home to San Francisco accompanied by his new wife, psychiatrist Ruth Kempe. Henry joined the medical faculty at the University of California.

In 1956, Kempe was appointed chair of the Department of Pediatrics at the University of Colorado School of Medicine in Denver. As chair of pediatrics, Kempe was responsible for pediatric services at four Denver hospitals. He grew increasingly disturbed at the number of children with unexplained injuries. Kempe lost patience with the false excuses offered to explain fractures, bruises, burns, head trauma, and other injuries. Thus, it was in Denver that Henry Kempe focused on child abuse.[17]

In 1963, pediatricians Vincent Fontana, Denis Donovan, and Raymond Wong followed up on the battered child syndrome with their article titled, "The 'Maltreatment Syndrome' in Children." Fontana and his colleagues wrote, "Only recently has there been an apparent increased incidence of 'battered' children reported in the medical literature and noted by child-protective agencies. Before these reports, this pediatric syndrome of the maltreated child has for the most part been unsuspected and has gone unrecognized by the medical profession."[18]

John Caffey, Henry Kempe, Vincent Fontana and other physicians alerted the medical profession to physical abuse of young children. The growing medical literature—particularly on battered child syndrome—joined forces with the factors described below to stir national interest in child abuse and neglect.

Amendments to the Child Welfare Provisions of the Social Security Act, 1962

The 1935 Social Security Act provided limited funds for child welfare services, which the Act defined as services "for the protection and care of homeless, dependent, and neglected children, and children in danger of becoming delinquent." In 1959, an Advisory Council on Child Welfare Services recommended expanding the definition,[19] and in 1962, Congress obliged, redefining child welfare services under the Social Security Act as "public social services which supplement, or substitute for, parental care and supervision for the purpose of (1) preventing or remedying, or assisting in the solution of problems which may result in, the neglect, abuse, exploitation, or delinquency of children, (2) protecting and caring for homeless, dependent, or neglected children, (3) protecting and promoting the welfare of children of working mothers, and (4) otherwise protecting and promoting the welfare of children, including the strengthening of their own homes where possible or, where needed, the provision of adequate care of children away from their homes in foster family homes or day-care or other child-care facilities."[20] The 1962 definition focused squarely on abuse and neglect. Vincent De

Francis remarked that the 1962 amendments "for the first time, identified Child Protective Services as part of all public child welfare." But De Francis also noted that "While this mandate is clear, it has not proven to be specific enough. Nor, has it stressed with sufficient force the obligation of each state to implement its responsibility for full services to protect children. . . . With varying degrees of competency, the public departments of social service, and the remaining private protective agencies, are the backbone of present-day efforts to bring help and protection to our country's neglected and abused children."[21]

In addition to clarifying the definition of child welfare services, the 1962 amendments required states seeking child welfare funds under the Social Security Act to pledge that by 1975, they would make child welfare services available statewide.[22] This requirement fueled the expansion of child welfare services, including protective services.

Growing Public Awareness of Abuse

The 1960s witnessed increased media attention on child abuse and neglect.[23] Although local media had always covered noteworthy cases, as when a child died or was horribly mistreated, coverage of physical abuse and neglect in national media outlets was uncommon prior to the 1960s. During the 1960s, however, national media coverage grew. In August 1960, for example, *Newsweek* described three Canadian children who "spent eleven years in prison—at home," confined for the most part to a single room. The children were drastically underweight and short in stature. Fourteen-year-old Gordon weighed 44 pounds and stood less than four feet tall. His sisters were similarly afflicted. *Newsweek* reported, "Their tearful mother, Mrs. Shirley Leach, 38, tried to explain. She has six children from her first marriage. She hid three of them 'when we moved from Windsor to Detroit [in 1949] because no one would rent to a couple with six kids. . . . When we bought our own home [in Tecumseh, Ontario, in 1953] we still kept the children inside. . . . But then it was because . . . they were not like other children.' "[24]

In April 1962, *Newsweek* published an article titled, "When They're Angry . . ." Quoting Katherine Oettinger, chief of the Children's Bureau, the article stated, " 'Since 1959, [the Bureau has] been receiving an increasing number of reports from pediatricians and hospitals about physical abuse of children by their parents. We're now giving the problem of the battered child top priority.' " The article described battered child syndrome and quoted Henry Kempe saying, " 'One day last November, we had four battered children in our pediatrics ward. Two died in the hospital and one died at home four weeks later. For every child who enters the hospital this badly beaten, there must be hundreds treated by unsuspecting doctors. The battered child syndrome isn't a reportable disease, but it damn well ought to be.' "[25]

In July 1962, *Time* magazine reported, "To many doctors, the incident is becoming distressingly familiar. A child, usually under three, is brought to the office with multiple fractures—often including a fractured skull. The parents express appropriate concern, report that the baby fell out of bed, or tumbled down the stairs, or was injured by a playmate. But X rays and experience lead the doctor to a different conclusion: the child has been beaten by his parents."[26]

In June 1963, *Life* published a story titled, "Cry Rises from Beaten Babies." The article contained disturbing photographs. The text stated, "The atrociously battered little boy at left bears wounds inflicted by his own father. Suddenly, across the U.S. . . . there is an upsurge in discoveries of brutal cases of child beating. Beyond doubt many cases never come to the attention of doctors. Of those that do, the cause of injury is often written off as accidental. Even if the truth is suspected, it may be ignored because the doctors are unwilling either to believe the evidence or to get involved in legal complications."[27]

In March 1964, *Good Housekeeping* published a powerful description of abuse. Four-year-old Christopher was playing outside in his new sandbox. He carried a pail of sand into the house and accidentally spilled it on his mother's freshly waxed floor. "Chris' body suddenly became rigid as he stared at the disaster before him. Suddenly a heavy blow caught him across the upper part of his back and knocked him ten feet across the kitchen floor. The boy looked up to see his mother advancing upon him with the handle of the dust mop. He stiffened his body as more blows were rained upon his arms, legs and back. Not once did he utter a sound, although his mother screamed all the time she was hitting him that he was a 'horrible child' and 'bad clear through.' Minutes later, her arms exhausted, Kate stopped the beating and stormed from the kitchen. Chris lay on the floor, his body quivering, his large eyes staring."[28]

In January 1965, *Time* magazine reported,

> Each year hundreds of U.S. children are brutally assaulted and even killed by their own parents. . . . If all such cases were reported, say some experts, the total would reach 10,000 a year. Many doctors suspect that more U.S. children are killed by their parents than by auto accidents leukemia or muscular dystrophy. But the problem is more than medical, 'Battered-Child Syndrome'—the telltale symptoms of child beating—has become the law's latest headache. . . . Doctors fear being sued for slander if they tip off the police and the charge turns out to be false. In a head-on attack on the problem, the Children's Bureau has drawn up a model state law requiring all doctors and hospitals to report suspected child beatings immediately to the police. . . . Already 21 states have enacted some form of the law.[29]

Thus, a steady stream of news stories on child abuse—often mentioning battered child syndrome and Henry Kempe—brought the issue to the fore in American society.[30] Child abuse was a hot topic.

Growth in Professional Literature

Prior to 1962, there was little professional research and writing on physical abuse. In 1963, Elizabeth Elmer wrote, "The amount of systematic research on the problem of child abuse and neglect is conspicuously scant."[31] Following publication of the "Battered Child Syndrome" in 1962, however, a trickle of writing became a torrent. In 1964, pediatrician Vincent Fontana published the first American medical text on abuse, *The Maltreated Child*. Fontana wrote, "In discussing this problem with other physicians, it became apparent that a blind spot existed concerning the importance or frequency of [child abuse]. . . . The maltreatment of children has not been considered important enough to be included in the curricula of medical schools; it has not been given notice in any of the major pediatric textbooks, and it has been ignored by both society and physicians for many years."[32]

Turning from books to journals, numerous articles on abuse appeared during the 1960s. In 1969, the Children's Bureau published a *Bibliography on the Battered Child*, listing 262 articles or books on abuse.[33] Publication continues at a brisk pace in the twenty-first century.

Child Abuse Reporting Laws

In January 1962, the U.S. Children's Bureau sponsored a small meeting of child abuse experts.[34] Henry Kempe was there, as was Vincent De Francis of the American Humane Association. According to De Francis, the purpose of the meeting was "to look into the medical aspects of the abuse of children."[35] The experts discussed the complexity of diagnosing physical abuse and steps the Children's Bureau could take to better inform professionals. At a follow-up meeting in May 1962, experts discussed the need for laws encouraging doctors to report physical abuse to child protection or police agencies.

Out of the Children's Bureau meetings and similar gatherings, pressure mounted for laws requiring physicians to report suspected abuse. Four organizations suggested wording for reporting laws: the Children's Bureau, the American Humane Association, the American Medical Association, and the Council of State Governments.[36] In 1963, ten states passed reporting laws, and by 1967, every state had reporting legislation on the books.

Most first-generation reporting laws focused on physical abuse. With the emphasis primarily on physical abuse, many early reporting laws limited the reporting duty to medical professionals, especially physicians. The American Medical Association opposed singling out doctors, stating, "Is reporting by only one group the answer? . . . This is a social problem in which the physician plays but a part.

Visiting nurses, social workers, school teachers and authorities, lawyers, marriage and guidance counselors, and others frequently learn of cases before medical care is demanded or received. To wait until the child requires medical attention is too late. To compel reporting by the physician alone may single him out unwisely. Knowing of this requirement, the parent or guardian may, for his own protection, put off seeking medical care."[37] Before long, the reporting duty reached all professionals working with children.

From the outset, most reporting laws made reporting mandatory rather than optional. A few states left the reporting decision to the doctor, a position favored by the American Medical Association, which asserted, "No evidence has been presented, and none is known to exist, which establishes that mandatory reporting in and of itself will eradicate undesirable social conduct." On the other hand, Vincent De Francis asserted, "Only if the reporting law is made mandatory can we be sure that no child, identified as needing protection, is left unaided."[38] Eventually, all states adopted mandatory reporting.

Prior to the reporting laws, little was known about the prevalence of abuse and neglect. In 1962, Vincent De Francis attempted to estimate the scope of physical abuse, but there were no national data to draw from, so De Francis was forced to resort to newspaper stories. He wrote, "There were a total of 662 cases of child abuse during 1962 in newspapers in all but two of the fifty states and the District of Columbia."[39] Beginning in 1965, David Gil conducted a series of nationwide surveys of physical abuse for the Children's Bureau. Gil estimated there were between 6,000 and 7,000 incidents of serious physical abuse each year.[40]

It was the reporting laws that uncovered the frightening dimensions of abuse and neglect. By 1974, some 60,000 cases were reported. In 1980, the number exceeded one million. By 1990, reports topped two million, and in 2000, reports hovered around three million. At the close of the twentieth century, reports declined but remained high.

Neglect

This section discusses the most common form of maltreatment, neglect. Although not as dramatic as physical and sexual abuse, neglect can be extremely damaging.

Neglect Defined

Neglect occurs when a parent or caretaker fails, intentionally or unintentionally, to provide a child with essential food, clothing, shelter, medical care, or love.

James Garbarino and Cyleste Collins describe neglect as "a pattern of behavior or a social context that has a hole in the middle where we should find the meeting of basic developmental needs." The Utah Supreme Court observed, "Children are entitled to the care of an adult who cares enough to provide the child with the opportunity to form psychological bonds, in addition to the physical necessities of life. . . . An unfit or incompetent parent is one who substantially and repeatedly refuses or fails to render proper parental care and protection."[41] At its core, neglect occurs when the "care" is missing from "caretaker."

The "Neglect of Neglect"

From colonial times forward, neglect was a concern of child protection workers. For example, most of the children assisted by Charles Loring Brace and his Children's Aid Society were neglected rather than physically or sexually abused. Despite the dominance of neglect in child welfare case records, this form of maltreatment was the last to emerge from relative obscurity in the late twentieth century. As discussed above, physical abuse became the subject of great interest in the 1960s. Sexual abuse emerged from obscurity in the late 1970s and the 1980s. Neglect, however, remained in the background as these more newsworthy forms of maltreatment shared the spotlight. In a classic article published in 1984, Isabel Wolock and Bernard Horowitz coined the term "the neglect of neglect." Wolock and Horowitz wrote:

> Child maltreatment as a social problem has come to be defined predominantly as child abuse, with child neglect having received relatively little attention and having been dealt with generally as an appendage to the problem of abuse. . . . The focus of the media has been predominantly on abuse. . . . Political debate is another area in which it is apparent that child maltreatment is defined primarily as physical abuse. . . . The overshadowing of child neglect by child abuse is also apparent in the research and practice literature. . . .
>
> Neglect was virtually excluded from the initial phase in which child maltreatment as a contemporary social problem was recognized, from the second phase in which the problem was legitimized, and from the third in which support for the problem was mobilized. . . .
>
> The low priority accorded to neglect may be understood in terms of the link between neglect and poverty, reflecting in essence the low priority accorded to the alleviation of poverty.[42]

Today, neglect continues to simmer while sexual and physical abuse boil. Fortunately, there is more research and writing today on neglect than when Wolock and Horowitz wrote in 1984.[43] Yet, neglect, with its inextricable ties to poverty, remains low on the agenda.

Prevalence and Harmful Effects of Neglect

Neglect is the most common form of child maltreatment. The U.S. Children's Bureau reported that in 2003, slightly more than 60 percent of maltreatment cases involved neglect. Physical abuse made up 20 percent of cases, sexual abuse 10 percent, and psychological maltreatment 5 percent. Margaret Smith and Rowena Fong wrote, "Studies have shown that the ratio of neglect to abuse reports ranges from 3:1 to 10:1." Martha Erickson and Byron Egeland observed, "It is likely that the actual incidence of neglect is much higher than reporting statistics indicate. Because neglect (particularly emotional neglect) often leaves no visible scars, it is likely to go undetected."[44]

Some children who are neglected are also physically or sexually abused. Jay Belsky wrote, "Many parents both abuse and neglect their offspring." In a study of 160 maltreated adolescents, Robin McGee and colleagues reported that 90 percent of the adolescents experienced more than one form of maltreatment.[45]

Neglect can have devastating consequences. Children suffer serious injury or die as often from neglect as from abuse. Smith and Fong wrote, "Most child deaths resulting from identifiable events involve some type of neglect." The U.S. Children's Bureau reports that neglected children are more likely to suffer recurrent maltreatment than physically abused children.[46]

Chronic neglect exacts a heavy toll on psychological development. Smith and Fong wrote,

> Neglected children also experience more problems with academic achievement and discipline in school than their nonneglected peers. In addition, neglected children suffer more health problems including malnutrition, failure to thrive, handicaps and impaired visual and motor skills. . . .
> . . . Neglected children, also, do not do well socially. They suffer more out-of-home placements; poorer peer relationships; more impaired socialization and higher rates of aggressiveness, acting-out/noncompliant behavior, juvenile delinquency, and criminal behavior than their nonneglected peers."[47]

James Garbarino and Cyleste Collins observed, "The effects of neglect are most devastating at early ages when children are developing most quickly. Children who have been neglected early in life showed dramatic declines 'in cognitive and social-emotional functioning and their behavior was of great concern.' " Martha Farrell Erickson and Byron Egeland add, "In some cases, neglect slowly and persistently eats away at children's spirits until they have little will to connect with others or explore the world." James Garbarino and John Eckenrode conclude, "For children, neglect is probably a greater social threat than active abuse."[48]

Psychological abuse and neglect are poisonous to healthy development. Binggeli and colleagues describe six types of psychological maltreatment by caregivers:

1. Spurning (hostile rejecting/degrading) includes verbal and nonverbal acts that reject and degrade the child.
2. Terrorizing includes behavior that threatens to physically hurt, kill, abandon, or place the child or child's loved ones in dangerous situations.
3. Isolating includes acts that consistently deny the child opportunities to meet social and interpersonal needs inside or outside the home.
4. Exploiting/corrupting includes acts that encourage the child to develop inappropriate behaviors (self-destructive, antisocial, criminal, deviant, or other maladaptive behaviors).
5. Denying emotional responsiveness (ignoring) includes acts that ignore the child's attempts to interact (failing to express affection, caring, and love for the child) and that are characterized by an absence of emotion in interactions with the child.
6. Mental health, medical, and educational neglect includes acts that ignore, refuse to allow, or fail to provide the necessary treatment for the mental health, medical needs, and educational problems or needs for the child.[49]

Stuart Hart and his colleagues wrote, "Several studies have indicated that emotional abuse or neglect, occurring alone, is associated with negative effects of a severity equal to or greater than other forms of abuse." Nelson Binggeli and his colleagues wrote, "There is an increasing consensus among researchers that psychological maltreatment is a core component, possibly *the* core component in child abuse and neglect."[50]

Multiple Forms of Maltreatment

A single type of maltreatment is bad enough. Yet, if there is one type of maltreatment in a home, there are often others. Physical abuse and neglect frequently occur together. Sexual abuse and psychological abuse coexist. Many sexually abused children are also physically abused. Neglect is often embedded in a context of physical abuse, domestic violence, substance abuse, and material deprivation. Robin McGee and her colleagues concluded, " 'Pure' maltreatment types do not exist in reality."[51]

Research by Vincent Felitti and his colleagues demonstrates the harm of growing up in a family where children are exposed to multiple traumas. Felitti analyzed questionnaires from 8,506 San Diego adults who belonged to the Kaiser Permanente health maintenance organization. The mean age of respondents was fifty-six. Respondents were asked whether they had experienced any of seven childhood traumas: psychological abuse (11 percent), physical abuse (11 percent), sexual abuse (22 percent), abuse of drugs or alcohol by a household member (26 percent), domestic violence (12 percent), mental illness of a household member (19 percent), and whether a household member went to prison (3 percent). Just over half of the respondents experienced one or more of these childhood traumas. Six percent experienced four or more of the traumas.[52] If a respondent experienced one of the traumas, there was a good chance they experienced others.

Dube and colleagues examined the relationship between childhood traumas and the following behaviors related to disease and death in adults: smoking, severe obesity, physical inactivity, depressed mood, suicide attempts,[53] alcoholism, drug abuse, high number of sexual partners, and having a sexually transmitted disease. There was a strong dose–response relationship between childhood traumas and the number of risky behaviors. That is, the greater the variety of traumas experienced in childhood, the greater the prevalence in adulthood of risky health behaviors and the greater the amount of heart disease, cancer, chronic bronchitis, emphysema, hepatitis, fracture, and poor self-rated health. Felitti and his colleagues also found an association between childhood abuse or household dysfunction and unintended first pregnancy.[54]

Why does childhood trauma lead to smoking, substance abuse, overeating, and other behaviors that cause disease and death? Felitti and his colleagues believe the impact of childhood trauma leads people to self-medicate with cigarettes, alcohol, drugs, food, or sex. As for smoking, "persons exposed to adverse childhood experiences may benefit from using drugs such as nicotine to regulate their mood. . . . Thus, smoking, which is medically and socially viewed as a "problem' may, from the perspective of the user, represent an effective immediate solution that leads to chronic use." Among Felitti's respondents, 25 percent who were sexually abused as children started smoking early, whereas only 9 percent of nonsexually abused children that responded took up smoking at an early age.[55]

Child abuse and neglect have cumulative synergistic effects on children. The harm caused by maltreatment can last a lifetime, undermining an individual's chances of happiness and productivity.

Federal Leadership in Child Protection

Prior to the 1970s, the federal government played a useful but minor role in child welfare. The Children's Bureau was created in 1912, although the bureau devoted little attention to maltreatment until the 1960s. From 1921 to 1929, the federal Sheppard-Towner Act provided funds for mothers and infants. The Social Security Act of 1935 created Aid to Dependent Children, revived Sheppard-Towner, and authorized the Children's Bureau "to cooperate with State public-welfare agencies in establishing, extending, and strengthening, especially in predominantly rural areas, [child welfare services] for the protection and care of homeless, dependent, and neglected children, and children in danger of becoming delinquent."[56] Yet, as late as 1973, U.S. Senator Walter Mondale wrote, "Nowhere in the Federal Government could we find one official assigned full time to the prevention, identification and treatment of child abuse and neglect."[57] It was not until 1974 and passage by Congress of the Child Abuse Prevention and Treatment Act that the federal government assumed a leadership role in responding to child abuse and neglect. Since 1974, the federal government has played an increasingly important role in funding child protection and shaping public policy. The remainder of this chapter describes the principal federal laws on child protection.

Child Abuse Prevention and Treatment Act, 1974

In 1973, hearings were conducted in the U.S. Senate and House of Representatives on bills to create the Child Abuse Prevention and Treatment Act (CAPTA).[58] CAPTA's principal sponsors were Walter Mondale in the Senate and Patricia Schroeder in the House.[59] Numerous experts testified at the hearings, including Vincent De Francis, Elizabeth Elmer, Vincent Fontana, David Gil, and Henry Kempe. In his testimony, Dr. Kempe riveted the Subcommittee's attention with "before and after" photographs of a little girl rescued from cruelty.[60]

Kempe told the legislators that 90 percent of maltreating parents could be helped with appropriate treatment. Kempe pointed out the intergenerational nature of maltreatment, noting, that the majority of abusive parents are severely deprived individuals who had little nurturing love from their parents. Kempe noted the social isolation of abusive families, stating that abusive parents generally they have no close friends, relatives, or neighbors whom they can readily ask for help. Kempe wrote in his report that

> In a study of over 1,000 abusive or seriously neglecting families, we have come to learn that deliberate, premeditated and willful abuse, the old fashioned "cruelty to children," accounts for only 5% of the entire group. These injuries are caused by aggressive sociopaths who are sufficiently pathological to make it unlikely that a change in their personality would be produced through psychiatric intervention. In another 5%, one or the other of the parents is suffering from delusional schizophrenia, and the child is often part of the delusional system to its great peril. The prognosis for ever establishing a reasonable parent/child relationship is again very poor.
>
> The remaining 90% of abusive parents would appear to belong to a great variety of personality types and no one psychiatric definition fits them all. They resemble others in their personality make-up except as it related to their own childhood experiences. . . .
>
> There is little evidence that parent therapy is helpful in the 10% of abusive parents who belong to the categories of aggressive sociopaths or delusional

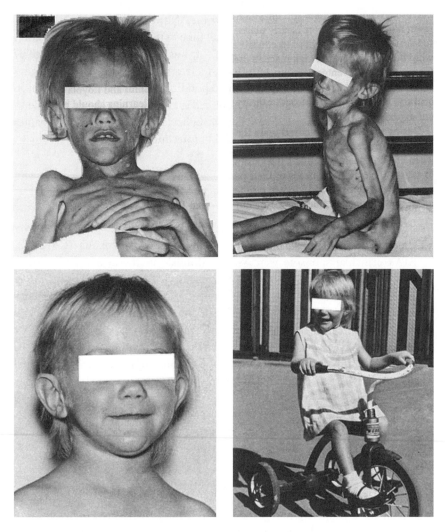

FIGURE 4.3

Photographs of "Jody," shown by C. Henry Kempe as part of his 1973 Congressional testimony in the proceedings of the hearings on the Child Abuse Prevention and Treatment Act. *Top*: Jody on admission to the hospital. *Bottom*: Jody five weeks later.

schizophrenics and in those who scapegoat a single child, particularly if the child remains in the family, and many disasters have occurred when these kinds of parents have been treated while the child has been left in the home. In these cases, we tend to urge early termination of parental rights and adoption of these children is then possible. The other 90% of abusive parents are readily treatable by reconstituting their sense of trust and by giving them considerable minute-to-minute support over a crucial period of eight to nine months. There are four treatment modalities used by us: (1) lay therapists, (2) Families Anonymous, (3) a crisis nursery, and (4) a therapeutic day care center.[61]

Kempe made the following recommendations for a national response to child maltreatment:

> Fundamental to all of our recommendations is the concept that the child belongs to himself and is only in the care of his parents; that he is entitled to the full protection of the Constitution and its amendments; and that the citizenry at large has a substantive involvement with the nurturing of all our children. There are four sayings which interfere with progress in this difficult field. They are: "Spare the Rod and Spoil the Child" (he that spareth the rod hateth his son; Old Testament, Proverbs xiii, 24), "Blood is Thicker than Water" (John Ray, English Proverbs, 1670), "A Man's House is His Castle" (Sir Edward Coke, Institutes Pt. iii, p. 162, 1690), "Mid Pleasures and Palaces though We May Roam, Be it Ever so Humble, There is No Place Like Home" (John Woward Payne, 1832). In one way or another community concepts and, therefore judicial concepts, have been blighted by these homilies since they tend to sanctify the home even when it is an undesirable environment for the child. In order to insure each child's basic rights, society must have *access* to the child from birth until school age, the most critical time of child development. This is best done, in our opinion, through implementation of the concept of universal health supervision in the broadest sense. This is best done through well baby care by the family physician. But 20% of our children fail to receive such care.
> We suggest that a health visitor call at intervals during the first months of life upon *each* young family and that she become, as it were, the guardian who would see to it that each infant is receiving his basic health rights. . . . The system must be equalitarian rather than being directed just towards the poor.[62]

Kempe's call for home visitors was prescient. In 2005, home visiting programs were flourishing around the United States.

In addition to health visitors, Kempe recommended improved child protective services and courts, including a lawyer to represent children in juvenile court, better training for judges and lawyers, a computerized national registry of child abuse reports, more foster homes to keep children safe while parents receive treatment, implementation of innovative treatment modalities, crisis nurseries, and therapeutic day care centers. Kempe also suggested family life education, of which he wrote, "Widespread public campaigns on television and radio are needed to acquaint all young parents with the ups and downs of family life, that love and hate can go together, that children are not unmixed blessings; and that some of the rage and anger felt towards small children is universal to all parents and that help can be had."

Vincent De Francis used his testimony to remind Congress that child abuse includes more than physical injury. De Francis stated, "We are concerned about the abused child, but children are abused in many ways, not purely the battered child, we have children who are sexually abused, we have children who are psychologically abused, we have children who are neglected in a host of ways. If we are going to address ourselves to the problems of children who need help we must address ourselves to the entire problem.... We estimate there must be somewhere between 30,000 and perhaps 40,000 at the outside of truly battered children but there must be at least 100,000 children each year who are sexually abused and probably two or three times that number of children who are psychologically damaged."[63]

Like Henry Kempe, the other experts emphasized the intergenerational nature of maltreatment.[64] Pediatrician Vincent Fontana stated, "This generation's battered children, if they survive, will become the next generation's battering parents, the disturbed and troubled adolescents, the drug addicts, the hardcore criminals, and murderers responsible for the violence in our cities today.... This disease is perpetuated from generation to generation with violence breeding violence."[65]

The experts favored preventive and therapeutic measures rather than a punitive response to maltreatment.[66] Dr. Fontana stated, "We have found that treating and protecting the child is totally inadequate unless it is coupled with a simultaneous concern for the parent who neglects, batters, or kills a child."[67] Vincent De Francis had long advocated help rather than prosecution for most maltreating parents. Henry Kempe stated, Most parents who injure their children want help, and if sympathetic help is offered without resorting to threats or accusations, the parents are usually co-operative.... We have come to feel that criminal penalties for battering parents are absolutely worthless.... Parents do not wish to hurt their child even though they do so repeatedly. If you intervene so that they cannot hurt their child, by temporary or prolonged separation, and initiation of treatment with or without the use of the courts, you do something *for* rather than, as is often believed, *against* them."[68]

The Nixon administration initially opposed CAPTA. As political momentum grew, however, the administration withdrew its opposition, and in January 1974, President Nixon signed CAPTA into law.[69] CAPTA authorized federal funds to improve the response to physical abuse, neglect, and sexual abuse. CAPTA provided money to train professionals, funds for multidisciplinary centers on child abuse and neglect, and financial support for demonstration projects. Responsibility for administering CAPTA was placed in the newly created National Center on Child Abuse and Neglect (NCCAN).

To obtain CAPTA funds, states had to comply with regulations promulgated by NCCAN. Among other things, the regulations strengthened child abuse reporting laws. The regulations also required "child protective services to provide non-criminal investigations for the verification of reports, to provide immediate protection of children through such means as protective custody, and to provide rehabilitative and ameliorative services."[70] When the regulations were adopted, many communities lacked a coherent system of child protection. Douglas Besharov, the first director of NCCAN, wrote that in 1973, only three states met all the requirements of the CAPTA regulations.[71] Within a few years, however, nearly all states met the requirements. CAPTA and its regulations played a major role in shaping the nationwide system of child protection that was falling into place in the 1970s.

Indian Child Welfare Act, 1978

Prior to 1978, as many as 25 to 35 percent of Native American children were removed from their parents for alleged abuse or neglect. The majority of these children were placed in non-Indian foster homes, adoptive homes, and institutions. In 1978, Congress passed the Indian Child Welfare Act (ICWA) to reduce the number of Native American children removed from their homes. Congress recognized,

> The purpose of the bill (H.R. 12533) . . . is to protect the best interests of Indian children and to promote the stability and security of Indian tribes and families by establishing minimum Federal standards for the removal of Indian children from their families and the placement of such children in foster or adoptive homes or institutions which will reflect the unique values of Indian culture. . . .
>
> . . . The wholesale separation of Indian children from their families is perhaps the most tragic and destructive aspect of American Indian life today.
>
> Surveys of States with large Indian populations conducted by the Association on American Indian Affairs (AAIA) in 1969 and again in 1974 indicate that approximately 25–35 percent of all Indian children are separated from their families and placed in foster homes, adoptive homes, or institutions. . . .
>
> The disparity in placement rates for Indians and non-Indians is shocking. In Minnesota, Indian children are placed in foster care or in adoptive homes at a per capita rate five times greater than non-Indian children. . . .
>
> . . . In 16 States surveyed in 1969, approximately 85 percent of all Indian children in foster care were living in non-Indian homes. . . .
>
> It is clear that the Indian child welfare crisis is of massive proportions and that Indian families face vastly greater risks of involuntary separation than are typical of our society as a whole.[72]

To reduce inappropriate removal of Indian children from their homes, ICWA provides that only tribal courts can decide abuse and neglect cases, involving children whose permanent residence is a reservation. For Indian children who do not live on a reservation, state juvenile courts can make decisions about removal, but the child's tribe must be notified, and the tribe has the right to intervene in the case.

Adoption Assistance and Child Welfare Act, 1980

Child abuse reporting laws and enhanced awareness of abuse produced an increase in intervention. By the mid-1970s, a rising number of children in foster care set off alarm bells in Congress, resulting in passage of the Adoption Assistance and Child Welfare Act of 1980.[73] The Act required states seeking federal foster care funds (i.e., all states) to make "reasonable efforts" to avoid removing children from maltreating parents. When removal was necessary, reasonable efforts were required to reunite families. Every child in foster care had to have a "permanency plan" to return the child home or move toward termination of parental rights. For children who could not go home, Congress provided financial incentives for adoption. Finally, the Act provided financial support for adoptive parents who adopted children with special needs.

The effort to preserve families was a key component of the Adoption Assistance and Child Welfare Act, and "family preservation" was the dominant paradigm of child welfare in the 1980s.[74] Of the many family preservation programs scattered across the country, one of the most well known was Homebuilders, which originated in 1974 in Tacoma, Washington. Homebuilders was an intensive, short-term social work intervention. Homebuilders workers carried small case loads and spent a great deal of time in the child's home helping the family overcome difficulties.

Family preservation programs worked well for many families. In the 1990s, however, critics argued that overreliance on family preservation sometimes led to tragedy. One forceful critic of family preservation was Richard Gelles, who challenged the effectiveness of family preservation in his 1996 book, *The Book of David: How Preserving Families Can Cost Children's Lives.*[75] Gelles criticized the research supporting programs like Homebuilders and argued for a shift in policy toward what he called "A New Child-Centered Policy." Gelles wrote,

> The essential first step in creating a safe world for children is to abandon the fantasy that child welfare agencies can balance the goals of protecting children and preserving families, adopting instead a child-centered policy of family services. This is not a new policy, but rather a return to the policy of the early 1960s that established child safety as the overriding goal of the child welfare system. It is time to abandon the myth that "the best foster family is not as good as a marginal biological family." The ability to make a baby does not ensure that a couple have, or ever will have, the ability to be adequate parents. The policy of family reunification and family preservation fails because it assumes that *all* biological parents can become fit and acceptable parents if only appropriate and sufficient support is provided.[76]

Criticism of the Adoption Assistance and Child Welfare Act's emphasis on family preservation set the stage for enactment in 1997 of the Adoption and Safe Families Act, described later.

Multiethnic Placement Act, 1994

Before the civil rights movement of the 1960s, interracial adoption was uncommon. Several states, including Louisiana and Texas, had outright bans on interracial adoption. Social workers generally believed it was important to place children with adoptive parents of the same ethnic background. During the 1960s, however, courts struck down laws against interracial adoption, and increasing numbers of white parents adopted children of color.[77]

During the 1970s, critics of interracial adoption mounted a spirited campaign against the practice, led by the National Association of Black Social Workers. In 1972, the association issued a position paper based on the premise that America is a racist society. The position paper stated,

> Black children should be placed only with Black families in foster care or for adoption. Black children belong, physically, psychologically and culturally in Black families in order that they receive the total sense of themselves and develop a sound projection of their future. Human beings are products of their environment and develop their sense of values, attitudes and self concept within their family structures. Black children in white homes are cut off from the healthy development of themselves as Black people.[78]

Elizabeth Bartholet wrote that the association's position "found a receptive audience. The establishment forces readily conceded that the black and Native American communities had a right to hold onto 'their own.' . . . The new orthodoxy was quickly established, making the 1960s period of transracial placements seem a brief anomaly in the larger picture." Cynthia Hawkins-Leon and Carla Bradley add, "In an attempt to adhere to the tenets of the [association's] position paper, adoption agencies began to enact and enforce same-race placement policies. As a result, the number of transracial adoptions dropped drastically nationwide."[79]

Unfortunately, children of color, particularly African-American children, are overrepresented in foster care, and African-American foster children tend to wait longer for adoption than white children. The antagonism of the 1970s toward interracial adoption exacerbated the problem of overrepresentation by dissuading whites from adopting African-American children. During the 1980s and 1990s, pressure mounted to lower racial barriers to adoption, and in 1994, Congress passed the Multiethnic Placement Act (MEPA). The 1994 MEPA prohibited child welfare agencies from delaying or denying adoptive placements on the basis of race. Yet, the 1994 MEPA allowed race as a factor in placement decisions. Critics argued that allowing race as a factor perpetuated the status quo against interracial adoption. In 1996, Congress amended MEPA to narrow the circumstances in which race may be considered. Under the 1996 amendment, a child's race must normally be considered irrelevant in determining the best placement for the child. Only in narrow circumstances, where the needs of a specific child make race important, can social workers consider race as a factor.[80]

In 1997, the National Association of Black Social Workers issued a revised policy statement on interracial adoption. The revised statement provides in part:

> Placement decisions should reflect a child's need for continuity safeguarding the child's right to consistent care and to service arrangements. Agencies must recognize each child's need to retain a significant engagement with his or her parents and extended family and respect the integrity of each child's ethnicity and cultural heritage. The social worker's profession stresses this importance of ethnic and cultural sensitivity. An effort to maintain a child's identity and her or his ethnic heritage should prevail in all services and placement actions that involve children in foster care and adoption programs, including adherence to the principles articulated in the Indian Child Welfare Act.[81]

Adoption and Safe Families Act, 1997

The 1980 Adoption Assistance and Child Welfare Act helped many children and parents. Yet, the number of children in foster care did not decline. Too many children languished for years in out-of-home care. Moreover, Richard Gelles and others charged that the reasonable efforts and family preservation requirements of the Adoption Assistance and Child Welfare Act caused social workers to leave children in dangerous homes. Congress responded with the Adoption and Safe Families Act of 1997 (ASFA).[82] Although ASFA did not abandon family preservation, it made child safety the top priority. When children were placed in foster care, ASFA established strict time lines to return them to their parents or terminate parental rights so children could be adopted. In cases of sexual abuse and chronic physical abuse, ASFA authorized states to dispense with efforts to reunify the family and move directly to termination of parental rights.

One of the fundamental debates in child protection focuses on respect for family privacy versus intervention in the family to protect children. This debate is reflected in the federal laws described above. The Child Abuse Prevention and Treatment Act of 1974 contained fairly broad definitions of maltreatment, encouraging greater intervention. By contrast, the Adoption Assistance and Child Welfare Act of 1980, with its emphasis on family preservation, pushed the pendulum away from intervention. In 1997, the Adoption and Safe Families Act placed top priority on child safety, once again shifting the emphasis toward intervention. The intervention pendulum thus swings back and forth, never reaching the extremes, and never standing still.

Conclusion

The period from 1962 to 2000 witnessed remarkable progress. For the first time, child protective services were available across America—in small towns, rural areas, reservations, and cities. The growth of child protection was a boon to thousands of children. Ironically, however, the expansion of the child protection system, particularly the rapid deployment of laws requiring professionals to report suspected abuse and neglect, carried the seeds of crisis. The reporting laws unleashed a flood of cases that overwhelmed the child protection system, and by the 1980s, the system was in trouble. The scope of the modern crisis in child protection, and what can be done to repair the system, are the subjects of part II.

5

CHILD SEXUAL ABUSE

Historically, society's response to sexual abuse has differed somewhat from the response to physical abuse and neglect. For this reason, sexual abuse is treated in a separate chapter.

Prevalence and Effects of Child Sexual Abuse

The true prevalence of sexual abuse is unknown because the abuse occurs in secret.[1] David Finkelhor observed, "Because sexual abuse is usually a hidden offense, there are no statistics on how many cases actually occur each year." Research suggests that as many as 500,000 new child sexual abuse incidents occur in the United States every year.[2]

Approximately 20 percent of girls experience some type of sexually inappropriate experience during childhood, from minor touching to brutal rape. The rate of sexual abuse of boys appears to be lower than of girls. Five to 15 percent of boys are sexually abused. For both genders, sexual abuse occurs at any age, from infancy through adolescence.[3]

Most sexual abuse victims know the perpetrator.[4] Finkelhor wrote, "Sexual abuse is committed primarily by individuals known to the child, unlike the child molester stereotype that prevailed until the 1970s. In adult retrospective surveys, victims of abuse indicate that no more than 10% to 30% of offenders were strangers, with the remainder being either family members or acquaintances."[5]

Turning to the effects of sexual abuse, not all victims exhibit outward manifestations of trauma. For children who are symptomatic, symptoms vary from child to child.[6] Generally, the more severe the abuse, the more likely the child is to be symptomatic. As Kathleen Kendall-Tackett, Linda Meyer Williams, and David Finkelhor wrote, "Molestations that included a close perpetrator; a high frequency of sexual contact; a long duration; the use of force; and sexual acts that included oral, anal, or vaginal penetration lead to a greater number of symptoms for victims."[7]

Many sexually abused children experience anxiety-related symptoms, including Posttraumatic Stress Disorder. John Briere and Diana Elliott wrote, "Child abuse is, by its nature, threatening and disruptive, and may interfere with the child's developing sense of security and belief in a safe, just world. Thus, it should not be surprising that victims of such maltreatment are prone to chronic feelings of fearfulness or anxiety."[8] Some sexually abused children have nightmares. Other children have stomachaches or headaches. Some children misbehave at home and at school. The academic performance of some abuse victims may suffer. Among young children, toileting accidents are relatively common.[9] Some adolescents run away, use drugs or alcohol, experience sexual behavior problems, or engage in illegal conduct.[10] While some abused children act out, others withdraw emotionally and socially.[11] Many sexually abused children have a poor self-concept. Abused children often think the abuse was their fault, and that they are bad, dirty, worthless, or "damaged goods." Not surprisingly, depression is common among sexually abused children and adolescents.[12] Quite a few victims think about suicide.

Shifting the focus from the short-term effects of sexual abuse to long-term harm, many adult survivors suffer for years, and some never fully recover. The more severe the abuse, the more likely the victim will experience long-term adjustment problems.[13] A high percentage of adult psychiatric patients were sexually abused during childhood. Adult survivors have increased levels of somatic symptoms, low self-esteem, depression, anxiety disorders, posttraumatic stress disorder, substance abuse, sexual dysfunction, including high-risk sexual behavior, conversion reaction, suicidal tendencies, self-mutilation, dissociation, multiple personality disorder, borderline personality, and eating disorders. Childhood sexual abuse is found in a large percentage of prostitutes.[14]

Despite what Anna Salter called "footprints on the heart" left by child sexual abuse, most survivors lead productive lives. Patricia Coffey and her colleagues reassure us, "Childhood sexual abuse does not inevitably lead to adult disorders." Joseph Chandy and his colleagues add, "One of the remarkably positive aspects of populations that are vulnerable due to a variety of risk factors is that, in spite of their vulnerability, a large majority of them grow up normally and do well in life."[15]

Given the harm caused by sexual abuse, psychotherapy is often helpful. Fortunately, psychological treatment is effective at alleviating the suffering of many children and adult survivors.[16] David Finkelhor and Lucy Berliner reviewed the treatment literature and wrote, "Taken as a whole, the studies of sexually abused children in treatment show improvements that are consistent with the belief that therapeutic intervention facilitates children's recovery."[17]

Tendency to Ignore Child Sexual Abuse

Public and professional acknowledgment of sexual abuse lagged behind recognition of physical abuse, which came to prominence in the 1960s. Charles Loring Brace, whose nineteenth-century career with the Children's Aid Society was described earlier in chapter 1, was well aware of sexual abuse. Yet, Brace and his contemporaries seldom spoke openly about this "hidden pediatric problem." In 1977, Henry Kempe gave a lecture in which he described "sexual abuse of children and adolescents as another hidden pediatric problem and a neglected area." Indeed, sexual abuse of children is so unpleasant that many prefer to ignore it. Erna Olafson, David Corwin, and Roland Summit note, "Sexual abuse of children has repeatedly surfaced into public and professional awareness in the past . . . only to be resuppressed by the negative reaction it elicits." In a similar vein, Judith Herman and Lisa Hirschman wrote that incest "has been repeatedly unearthed in the past hundred years, and just as repeatedly buried."[18]

Child protection societies in the nineteenth and early twentieth centuries intervened in sexual abuse cases. In her study of the Massachusetts Society for the Prevention of Cruelty to Children, Linda Gordon observed that during the early twentieth century, "Sexual abuse of children in the family—incest—figured prominently in family-violence case records, constituting about 10 percent of the caseload." Yet, Gordon noted that the Massachusetts society considered incest cases "too revolting to publish." In the MSPCC's Annual Report for 1890, we find the following: "Felonious Assault. Several cases of this criminal assault by fathers upon their daughters have been acted upon during the year, the particulars of which cannot be recorded." A nineteenth-century California newspaper described the trial of a man accused of raping a thirteen-year-old girl. The newspaper stated that the details were, "Too revolting for publication."[19] Thus, the unpleasantness of child sexual abuse causes many to turn a blind eye.

Skepticism about Victims: Professional Writing on Child Sexual Abuse Prior to 1970

To understand society's reluctance to acknowledge sexual abuse, it is helpful to examine professional writing on the subject. Prior to 1970, what little writing there was on sexual abuse tended to be skeptical of victims. This section reviews pre-1970 psychiatric, psychological, and legal writing on child sexual abuse.

Tardieu's Early Insights

In 1873, French physician Ambrose Tardieu published a book titled *A Medico-Legal Study of Assaults on Decency*, in which Tardieu described French rape cases from 1859 to 1869. Of the more than eleven thousand victims, nearly 80 percent were children. Roland Summit wrote, "Tardieu generated an oasis of concern for children in a generally indifferent, adult-preoccupied society. Challenging the tradition that children typically lied about sexual assault, a few clinicians dared to argue for the truth and reality of these complaints."[20]

Although Tardieu was influential, his successors largely ignored his concerns about child sexual abuse. In 1880, for example, Alfred Fournier gave a speech titled, "Simulation of Sexual Attacks on Young Children," in which he warned that respectable men are targeted for blackmail by depraved children and their lower-class parents. Another successor to Tardieu, Paul Brouardel, remarked, "Girls accuse their fathers of imaginary assaults on them or on other children in order to obtain their freedom to give themselves over to debauchery." Brouardel continued, "The child comforts herself by telling herself fantasies which she knows are false on every point. . . . This child, to whom one ordinarily paid only the most minor attention, finds for herself an audience that is willing to listen to her with a certain solemnity and to take cognizance of the creations of her imagination. She grows in her own esteem, she herself becomes a personage, and nothing will ever get her to admit that she deceived her family and the first people who questioned her."[21] Tardieu's effort to open society's eyes to sexual abuse was largely forgotten.[22]

Freud's Turnabout

In 1896, Sigmund Freud was rising to prominence in psychiatry. In April of that year, Freud presented a groundbreaking explanation for the etiology of hysteria in adults. Freud theorized that the symptoms he observed in his adult patients were caused by sexual abuse during childhood, often at the hands of fathers. Freud called this the "seduction theory" of hysteria.

Freud's theory received a chilly response from his psychiatric colleagues. Jeffrey Masson noted, "Freud's announcement of his new discoveries in the 1896 address on the etiology of hysteria met with no reasoned refutation or scientific discussion, only disgust and disavowal. The idea of sexual violence in the family was so emotionally charged that the only response it received was irrational distaste."[23] Soon thereafter, Freud wrote, "I am as isolated as you could wish me to be: the word has been given out to abandon me, and a void is forming around me."[24] Within a year, Freud abandoned the seduction theory and replaced it with the Oedipus complex, in which girls fantasize sexually about their father. With the Oedipus complex, Freud concluded that hysteria results from sexual fantasy, not sexual abuse.

Throughout his career, Freud acknowledged that some children are sexually abused. Yet, by suppressing the seduction theory and replacing it with the Oedipus complex, Freud contributed to skepticism about women and girls. Judith Herman and Lisa Hirschman studied the literature and observed "a vastly elaborated intellectual tradition which served the purpose of suppressing the truth about incest, a tradition which, like so many others, originates in the works of Freud. . . . The legacy of Freud's inquiry into the subject of incest was a tenacious prejudice, still shared by professionals and laymen alike, that children lie about sexual abuse. This belief is by now so deeply ingrained in the culture that children who dare to report sexual assaults are more likely to have their complaints dismissed as fantasy."[25]

Common Themes in Pre-1970 Psychiatric
and Psychological Writing

Prior to the 1970s, much of the psychiatric and psychological literature about child sexual abuse reflected four themes. First, children are responsible for their own molestation. Second, mothers are to blame. Third, child sexual abuse is rare. Fourth, sexual abuse does little harm.

Children Are Responsible for Their Molestation.   An oft-repeated theme in pre-1970 writing on child sexual abuse, particularly incest, was that children were responsible for their molestation.[26] In 1937, Lauretta Bender and Abram Blau described their work with five- to twelve-year-old incest victims:

> The few studies that have been made of this subject have been contented to consider it an example of adult sex perversion from which innocent children must be protected by proper legal measures. Although this attitude may be correct in some cases, certain features in our material indicate that the children may not resist and often play an active or even initializing role. . . . The history of the relationship in our cases usually suggested at least some cooperation of the child in the activity, and in some cases the child assumed an active role in initiating the relationship. . . . It is true that the child often rationalized with excuses of fear of physical harm or the enticement of gifts, but these were obviously secondary reasons. Even in the cases in which physical force may have been applied by the adult, this did not wholly account for the frequent repetition of the practice.[27]

In 1927, Karl Abraham announced, "In a great number of cases the trauma was desired by the child unconsciously." Abraham continued that in all cases of sexual abuse, "the trauma could have been prevented. The children could have called for help, run away, or offered resistance instead of yielding to the seduction."[28] In 1953, Alfred Kinsey and his colleagues wrote, "In many instances, [sexual experiences with relatives] were repeated because the children had become interested in the sexual activity and had more or less actively sought repetitions of their experience."[29] In 1975, James Henderson wrote, "The daughters collude in the incestuous liaison and play an active and even initiating role in establishing the pattern." Thus, in pre-1970 writing, the victim was to blame. David Finkelhor noted, "The idea that children are responsible for their own seduction has been at the center of almost all writing on sexual abuse since the topic was first broached."[30]

The most notable exception to the blame-the-victim mentality was a book-length study published in 1935 by Jacob and Rosamond Goldberg for the American Social Hygiene Association. The Goldbergs studied 1,400 New York City girls whose experiences ranged from consensual teenage sex to terrible rape. The Goldbergs wrote, "It is apparent that young girls need protection, and that concerted and serious thought must be given by representative men and women to the problems involved. An attitude of silence in the face of these unpleasant facts will only serve to engender repetitions of the same deplorable experiences for young girls."[31] The Goldbergs believed society owed a "debt to growing girls" to create an environment that minimized sexual exploitation. Unfortunately, the Goldbergs' book was an island of belief in a sea of skepticism.

Mothers Are to Blame.   In pre-1970 writing on incest, mothers often shared the blame with daughters. In 1988, Anna Salter wrote, "The literature on child sexual abuse in the twentieth century has often held victims and their mothers responsible for the sexual abuse, particularly in cases of incest, frequently with little mention of the role of the offender." Theresa Reid reviewed the early literature and concluded, "Mother-blaming is as common as victim-blaming in the psychological and sociological literature. Mothers of incest victims are routinely referred to as frigid, hostile, unloving women. As women who are so cold and rejecting that they cause their husbands to seek sexual satisfaction elsewhere."[32] Judith Herman and Lisa Hirschman wrote,

> If it must be conceded, first, that father-daughter incest occurs commonly, and second, that it is not a harmless pastime, then apologists for the incestuous father are thrown back upon their third and final excuse: he is not responsible for his actions. Most commonly, they blame his daughter, his wife, or both. Thus we make the acquaintance of the two major culprits in the incest romance, the Seductive Daughter and the Collusive Mother. Ensnared by the charms of a small temptress, or driven to her arms by a frigid, unloving wife, Poor Father can hardly help himself, or so his defenders would have us believe. Often he believes it himself. . . . On the subject of the mother's responsibility or complicity, there is a similar concordance of opinion among authors who might ordinarily shun each other's company. The doctor, the man of letters, and the pornographer, each in his accustomed language, render similar judgments of the incestuous father's mate.[33]

Child Sexual Abuse Is Rare. A number of early writers claimed that child sexual abuse is rare. A sociologist wrote, "The problem of incest is peculiar in several respects. Statistically its occurrence is negligible. Because of this infrequency the extent of its disruptive effect on human group life is minor." In 1972, Franco Fer-racuti wrote that incest "has low incidence in all types of societies."[34]

Sexual Abuse Does Little Harm.   In addition to claiming that sexual abuse is rare, contributors to the pre-1970 literature frequently asserted that abuse does little harm. Ferracuti wrote:

> According to Weiner [I.B. Weiner, Father-Daughter Incest: A Clinical Report, 26(4) *Psychiatric Quarterly* 607 (1962)], the daughters who are objects of incest are characteristically precocious in their learning and are anxious to assume the adult role. They are especially gratified by parental attention, and they use the in-cestuous relationship to express their hostility toward the mother. Rarely do they resist the sexual act or feel guilty about it. Frequently they become sexually promiscuous after the end of the incestuous conduct. Nevertheless, it is hardly proved that participation in incest, particularly before the onset of puberty, re-sults in psychological disturbances.[35]

Anna Salter wrote, "The belief that child sexual abuse was not traumatic was entwined with the belief that it was, in actuality, not a trauma visited on the child but a form of acting out by the child."[36]

In 1952, Lauretta Bender and Alvin Grugett wrote, "In contrast to the harsh so-cial taboos surrounding such relationships, there exists no scientific proof that there are any resulting deleterious effects." In 1964, Heinz Brunhold asserted, "Lasting psychological injury as a result of sexual assaults suffered in infancy is not very common." Referring to incest, Judith Herman and Lisa Hirschman noted in 1981, "The argument that incest is harmless has been promoted aggressively in recent years by the publishers of men's sex magazines. It is also advanced by a cer-tain school of sociologists and sex researchers."[37]

In their 1953 study titled *Sexual Behavior in the Human Female*, Alfred Kinsey and his colleagues described data on 4,441 women. Kinsey recognized that early sexual experience was common. Twenty-four percent of the women in Kinsey's study reported that prior to adolescence, they were approached sexually at least once. Under the heading, "Significance of Adult Contacts," Kinsey and his col-leagues wrote:

> There are as yet insufficient data, either in our own or in other studies, for reach-ing general conclusions on the significance of sexual contact between children and adults. The females in our sample who had had pre-adolescent contacts with adults had been variously interested, curious, pleased, embarrassed, frightened, terrified, or disturbed with feelings of guilt. . . .
> . . . It is difficult to understand why a child, except for its cultural condi-tioning, should be disturbed at having its genitalia touched, or disturbed at see-ing the genitalia of other persons, or disturbed at even more specific sexual contacts. . . . Some of the more experienced students of juvenile problems have

come to believe that the emotional reactions of parents, police officers, and other adults who discover that a child has had such a contact, may disturb the child more seriously than the sexual contacts themselves.[38]

Summary.   Much of the pre-1970 psychiatric and psychological literature viewed child sexual abuse as a relatively uncommon problem with few lasting adverse consequences. There were exceptions, of course, such as Jacob and Rosamond Goldberg's 1935 study of New York City girls, many of whom experienced life-changing harm from early sexual experience.[39] On balance, however, the literature downplayed the seriousness of child sexual abuse and viewed victims with skepticism.

Legal Literature Prior to 1970

Law libraries are filled with articles by law professors and law students. These articles are published in journals called law reviews. I examined every law review article I could find on sexual abuse of children and rape of adult women from 1888 to 1975.[40] I included articles about adult rape victims because the attitudes permeating the legal literature were similar whether the victim was a child or an adult. I was struck by the level of skepticism about women and girls. Sexual abuse of boys was rarely mentioned.[41] Three themes dominated pre-1970 law review articles on rape and sexual abuse. First, fear of fabricated allegations. Second, fear of mentally ill women. Third, preoccupation with consent.

Fear of Fabricated Allegations.   The legal profession has always been concerned about fabricated accusations of rape and sexual assault. In his 1736 treatise *The History of the Pleas of the Crown*, English judge Matthew Hale wrote the famous passage, "It must be remembered, that [rape] is an accusation easily to be made and hard to be proved, and harder to be defended by the party accused, though never so innocent."[42] Down through the centuries, countless judges and attorneys intoned Hale's words. In 1997, the South Dakota Supreme Court wrote, "Allegations of sexual misconduct are easy to allege and difficult to disprove."[43]

Law review authors doted on Judge Hale's concern about false allegations. In 1925, for example, Ernst Puttkammer wrote, "In its very nature rape is a crime that is peculiarly open to false accusations and is difficult of defense." Morris Ploscowe cautioned in 1960, "Prosecuting attorneys must continually be on guard for the charge of sex offenses brought by the spurned female that has as its underlying basis a desire for revenge, or a blackmail or shakedown scheme." In 1938, a law student wrote, "The rape statute affords promising fields for extortion and malicious prosecutions."[44] In 1970, a law student wrote, "The incidence of false accusations and the potential for unjust convictions are perhaps greatest with sexual offenses. Women often falsely accuse men of sexual attacks to extort money, to

force marriage, to satisfy a childish desire for notoriety, or to attain personal revenge. Their motives include hatred, a sense of shame after consenting to illicit intercourse, especially when pregnancy results, and delusion." In 1952, a law student
warned, "The sexual nature of the crime is conducive to false accusations." The
student commented, "False reports may also stem from other sources. A rape accusation is so potent a weapon against a man that a woman may deliberately and
maliciously distort her report of the sexual encounter to secure for herself money,
marriage, or revenge."[45]

Fear of Mentally Ill Women and Girls. Fear of false accusations was closely related
to the belief that some women and children are crazy. In 1960, Morris Ploscowe
wrote:

> Complaints of sex offenses are easily made. They spring from a variety of mo-
> tives and reasons. The psychiatrist and the psychoanalyst would have a field day
> were he to examine all complaints of rape, sexual tampering with children, in-
> cest, homosexual behavior with young boys, deviant sex behavior, etc., in any
> given community. He could find that complaints are too often made of sexual
> misbehavior that has occurred only in the overripe fantasies of the so-called vic-
> tims. Frequently, the more or less unconscious wish for the sexual experience is
> converted into the experience itself."[46]

In 1952, a law student wrote, "More serious [than deliberate fabrication] is the
problem of the psychopathic woman. She may completely fabricate a forceful sexual act yet be unaware of the fanciful origin of her complaint." A law student
wrote in 1966, "Masochistic tendencies seem to lead many women to seek men
who will ill-treat them sexually. The problem becomes even greater when one recognizes the existence of a so-called 'riddance mechanism.' This is a phenomenon
where a woman who fears rape unconsciously sets up the rape to rid herself of the
fear and to 'get it over with.' "[47]

During the first half of the twentieth century, John Henry Wigmore was America's most influential scholar regarding the law of evidence in court. In 1904, Wigmore published a twelve-volume treatise on the law of evidence, in which he had
the following to say about sex offense victims:

> Modern psychiatrists have amply studied the behavior of errant young girls and
> women coming before the courts in all sorts of cases. Their psychic complexes
> are multifarious, distorted partly by inherent defects, partly by diseased derange-
> ments or abnormal instincts, partly by bad social environments, partly by
> temporary physiological or emotional conditions. One form taken by these com-
> plexes is that of contriving false charges of sexual offenses by men. The unchaste
> mentally (let us call it) finds incidental but direct expression in the narration of
> imaginary sex incidents of which the narrator is the heroine or the victim. On
> the surface the narration is straight-forward and convincing. The real victim,

however, too often in such cases is the innocent man. . . . No judge should ever let a sex offense charge go to the jury unless the female complainant's social history and mental makeup have been examined and testified to by a qualified physician. It is time that the courts awakened to the sinister possibilities of injustice that lurk in believing such a witness without careful psychiatric scrutiny.[48]

In other words, women and girls are so likely to fantasize or lie that *every one of them* should be examined by a psychiatrist. Wigmore was influential, and his suspicions about women and girls touched generations of judges and attorneys. In 1937, a committee of the American Bar Association wrote, "Today it is unanimously held (and we say 'unanimously' advisedly) by experienced psychiatrists that the complainant woman in a sex offense should always be examined by competent experts to ascertain whether she suffers from some mental or moral delusion or tendency, frequently found especially in young girls, causing distortion of the imagination in sex cases."[49]

Preoccupation with Consent. Rape is defined as sexual intercourse by a man with a woman by force and without consent. In many rape prosecutions, the critical issue is whether the woman consented. Pre-1970 law review articles on rape were preoccupied with consent. Several authors discussed the idea that "no" really means "yes." In 1966, a law student wrote, "Although a woman may desire sexual intercourse, it is customary for her to say, 'no, no, no' (although meaning 'yes, yes, yes') and to expect the male to be the aggressor."[50] Another student wrote,

Many women, for example, require as a part of preliminary "love play" aggressive overtures by the man. Often their erotic pleasure may be enhanced by, or even depend upon, an accompanying physical struggle. A woman's need for sexual satisfaction may lead to the unconscious desire for forceful penetration, the coercion serving neatly to avoid the guilt feelings which might arise after willing participation. The feminine wish to be subjected to a sexual attack may become the subject of an hallucination. Despite the prevalent taboo on aggressive sexuality, many "normal" men and women may unconsciously desire copulation coupled with brute force.[51]

In 1954, a student reported, "Resistance during preliminary love-making greatly increases the sexual pleasure of some women."[52]

Prior to the 1970s, defense attorneys seeking in court to prove consent offered evidence that the woman had consented to sex with *other* men. Lack of "chastity," as it was called, was considered evidence of consent. As one court put it, "The underlying thought here is that it is more probable that an unchaste woman would assent . . . than a virtuous woman." Another court remarked, "Common experience teaches us that the woman who has once departed from the paths of virtue is far more apt to consent to another lapse than is the one who has never stepped aside from that path." A third court wrote, "No impartial mind can resist the conclusion that a female who had been in the recent habit of illicit intercourse with others will not be so likely to resist as one who is spotless and pure." Pre-1970 law review articles supported the strategy of highlighting the woman's lack of chastity. In 1938, a student wrote, "It is everywhere conceded that in a prosecution for rape by force and against the will of a female, her previous unchastity may be shown as rendering it more probable that she consented to the act.[53]

Children are legally incapable of consenting to sex. Yet, even in statutory rape cases, where the victim is a child, and where consent is irrelevant, pre-1970 law review authors favored allowing evidence of unchastity. In 1960, Morris Ploscowe wrote, "It is imperative that the lack of chastity of the young woman be deemed a defense to a charge of statutory rape. It is ridiculous for the police to charge with rape every male who may have had sexual contact with a promiscuous young woman or a young prostitute."[54]

Summary.   During the first six decades of the twentieth century, the legal and mental health literatures contributed to a legacy of skepticism about women and children who alleged rape or sexual abuse. This skepticism supported the tendency of society to close its eyes to this disquieting crime.

Early Efforts to Protect Sexually Abused Children

If the only historical data on sexual abuse prior to 1970 were articles in the legal and mental health literatures, one might assume society was little motivated to protect victims. Not so. Although many academic writers oozed skepticism, professionals in the "real world" knew sexual abuse was a problem and tried to help.[55] The effort was small compared to post-1970 efforts, but children were protected.

Societies for the Prevention of Cruelty to Children

From their inception in 1875, societies for the prevention of cruelty to children responded to sexual abuse. The New York Society for the Prevention of Cruelty to Children (NYSPCC) routinely intervened against sexual abuse. In 1894, the physician for the NYSPCC, Travis Gibb, published what may be the earliest American medical chapter on child sexual abuse. Gibb described the many children he examined for sexual abuse, including a number of brutal rapes of very young girls. As mentioned earlier, Linda Gordon found that in the early twentieth century, about 10 percent of cases handled by the Massachusetts Society for the Prevention of Cruelty to Children involved incest.[56] It is interesting to note that in 2005, sexual abuse continues to make up about 10 percent of maltreatment reports.

Courts

Criminal prosecution of child sexual abuse occurred from the colonial period forward. Although there are no national statistics on the rate of prosecution, several reports shed light on the criminal justice response. In 1939, a citizens committee in New York reported on 1,395 sex offense victims. The average age was thirteen, with an age range from two to sixty-eight. Five percent of the victims were under six. Nineteen percent were between six and ten. Forty-seven percent were between ten and sixteen. In all, 71 percent of the victims were children. In a 1950 study of 250 New York criminal cases, 67 percent of the victims were children, ranging from five to fifteen years of age. From 1945 to 1951 in Kings County, New York, 73 percent of rape indictments leading to conviction were for statutory rape.[57]

A California study disclosed that for the year 1951, "between 1,500 and 1,600 defendants were disposed of on original sex offense charges in California superior courts." The author of the study, Karl Bowman, wrote, "It was found that 31.3 percent of all sex offenders convicted in 1951 were charged with rape. The indications are that these were mostly cases of statutory rather than forcible rape. An additional 27.6 percent of the convictions were on charges of sex crimes against children under the lewd and lascivious conduct felony act, and 24.3 percent of the defendants were convicted for contributing to the delinquency of minors. Together, these three charges accounted for 83.2 percent of all superior court convictions."[58]

My colleagues and I studied 463 randomly selected appeals from child sexual abuse convictions across America between 1900 and 1950. The research disclosed that prosecution increased slowly during this period. The appeals we studied were decided during the heyday of skepticism about the credibility of children, yet appellate court decisions almost never reflected the skepticism so prevalent in professional writing. By and large, appellate court judges handled child sex abuse cases the way they handled other crimes, methodically reviewing the evidence and applying the law. As with other crimes, most child sexual abuse convictions were affirmed on appeal, and when convictions were reversed, it was because the trial judge made mistakes warranting reversal.[59]

Appellate court judges during the first half of the twentieth century were certainly aware of the skepticism concerning allegations of rape and sexual abuse, and more than a few judges undoubtedly shared the skepticism. Why, then, did we find so little skepticism in appellate court decisions? There are several plausible explanations. Judges take their responsibility seriously. The function of an appellate court judge is to review the outcome of a trial to determine whether serious mistakes occurred, not to take sides on divisive social issues. Throughout American history, judges have an admirable, albeit imperfect, record of sticking to the law and avoiding socio-political entanglements. Although quite a few early twentieth-century judges probably shared the skepticism prevalent in the literature, they appear to have held their skepticism in check as they performed their judicial duties. Another plausible explanation for the paucity of skepticism in judicial decisions relates to the strength of the evidence in the cases. Then as now, the prosecution's most important witness was the child, and in many cases, children provide powerful testimony. The famous English judge William Blackstone observed long ago that children "often give the clearest and truest testimony."[60] Judges see the reality of child sexual abuse at close range, and face-to-face experience with the damage inflicted by sexual abuse dampens skepticism.

Turning from criminal to juvenile courts, prior to the 1970s, juvenile courts responded four ways to child sexual abuse. First, juvenile courts protected children from sexual abuse that occurred in their own homes. Although juvenile court action to protect children from intrafamilial sexual abuse became more common after 1970, such intervention occurred throughout the twentieth century. Second, juvenile courts have authority over delinquent children, and when a teenager sexually abused a younger child, the teen could be taken before the juvenile court as a delinquent. Third, teenage girls—whether unwilling victims or willing sex partners—were sometimes labeled status offenders or "sex delinquents" in juvenile court. In 1919, for example, juvenile court judge Victor Arnold wrote, "The cases of delinquent girls who come before the court are in a great majority of instances for immoral conduct."[61] Fourth, in some states, adults were criminally prosecuted in juvenile court for contributing to the delinquency of a minor.

Summary

By today's standards, earlier efforts to protect children from sexual abuse were modest. Yet, our predecessors in child protection and the courts understood the harm inflicted by sexual abuse, took it seriously, and intervened in thousands of cases.

Sexual Psychopath Laws and Their Descendants

The rape or sexual assault of a child by a stranger outrages the public, frightens parents, generates media coverage, and activates politicians.[62] The reaction is particularly intense when a sex offender murders a child. In a newspaper article in 1937, FBI director J. Edgar Hoover warned, "The sex fiend, most loathsome of all the vast army of crime, has become a sinister threat to the safety of American childhood and womanhood."[63] During the 1940s and 1950s, popular magazines discussed the danger of sex offenders and offered advice to protect children.[64] In 1946, *Coronet* magazine warned, "The sexual pervert is lurking right now in the community where you live." *Coronet* offered eight recommendations. First, "vice squads should operate constantly in every community, tirelessly tracking down every instance of perversion, however slight." Second, communities should keep track of sex offenders and should supply the data to the FBI. Third, citizens should be on watch for perverts, and should turn them in. Fourth, many sex offenders are not only criminals, they are crazy and should be locked up. Fifth, states should provide indeterminate commitment for insane sex criminals. Sixth, plea bargaining with sex offenders should be "outlawed immediately." Seventh, research on sex offenders should be funded. Eighth, parents and teachers should provide sex education to children, including information on the dangers of sex offenders.[65]

Beginning in Michigan in 1937, states enacted special laws dealing with sex offenders. By the middle of the twentieth century, fifteen states had such laws. The laws were called "Sexual Psychopath Acts" or "Mentally Disordered Sex Offender Laws." Among other things, the laws authorized involuntary psychiatric hospitalization of dangerous sex offenders. By 1960, twenty-nine states had some form of sexual psychopath law.[66] Karl Bowman described the laws:

> In California and in a considerable number of other states the traditional body of sex crime law has been supplemented by legislation providing specialized procedures for detaining and treating dangerous sex deviates. The basic idea of these new types of law is that numerous sex offenders who are neither insane nor mentally deficient are characterized by personality disorders which predispose them, without regard to consequences, to the commission of sex acts considered dangerous to society. It is felt that imprisonment and other traditional legal penalties will neither deter them or have any rehabilitative effects on them. As an alternative or addition, provisions for treatment and prevention are authorized.[67]

Sexual psychopath laws were little used in most states, and by the 1970s, they had largely disappeared.[68] In the 1990s, however, sexual psychopath laws were resurrected. At the beginning of the twenty-first century, all states have one or more of the following: sex offender registration laws, public notification laws, or involuntary civil commitment laws.

Sex Offender Registration

Today, all states have laws requiring convicted sex offenders to register with designated law enforcement authorities. Failure to register is a crime. Police agencies use registry information to generate lists of suspects in investigations. Many states allow certain employers to inquire whether job applicants are registered sex offenders.

Public Notification of Sex Offenders Living
in the Community

Under registration laws, the police know the whereabouts of sex offenders. The public, however, is generally not privy to registry information. Is it wise to provide information on sex offenders to the public, or, more narrowly, to families living near offenders? On the one hand, parents are in the best position to protect their children from a sex offender living nearby. On the other hand, disclosure of information to the public is a major invasion of privacy, leading to stigma, ostracism, and even vigilantism. The specter of vigilantism is not just theoretical. Washington was the first state to enact a community notification statute. Not long thereafter, a convicted child rapist was about to be released from prison. Five days prior to release, the sheriff distributed fliers containing his picture, a description of his crime, and a statement that he received no treatment while in prison. A crowd gathered where the offender planned to live, and a short time later, the house burned to the ground.

Washington State's community notification statute started a cascade of similar laws, usually called Megan's laws to honor seven-year-old Megan Kanka, who was murdered by a twice-convicted sex offender living across the street from Megan's family. In 1994, the offender lured Megan into his house, where he raped her and strangled her with a belt. If Megan's parents had known a dangerous sex offender lived across the street, perhaps they could have protected her. Megan's tragic death spurred states and the federal government to action, and today, all states have some form of Megan's law.

Public notification laws were challenged in court. The Megan's law in New Jersey, for example, was attacked as a violation of the constitution. In 1995, the New Jersey Supreme Court rejected the challenge, writing, "The Constitution does not prevent society from attempting to protect itself from convicted sex offenders. . . . To rule otherwise is to find that society is unable to protect itself from sexual predators by adopting the simple remedy of informing the public of their presence."[69]

Involuntary Civil Commitment
of Violent Sexual Predators

Some particularly dangerous sex offenders are not safe at large. Yet, when their prison term expires, they are entitled to release. Most such offenders cannot be committed for psychiatric treatment because they do not have the kind of mental illness required for involuntary psychiatric hospitalization. In 1990, Washington State passed a law permitting involuntary civil commitment of "sexually violent predators." Other states followed suit, resurrecting the sexual psychopath laws of the 1950s. In 1997, the U.S. Supreme Court upheld the legality of involuntary civil commitment of dangerous sexual predators.[70]

Sexual Abuse Emerges as
an Important Social Issue

In the 1970s, sexual abuse was still largely invisible to the public, but that was about to change. Two related factors launched sexual abuse onto the national stage and kept it there. First, as discussed in chapter 4, the child protection system expanded significantly in the 1970s. Second, pioneering research in the 1970s and 1980s shed new light on the prevalence and harmful effects of sexual abuse.

Expanded Child Protection System

By the late 1970s, the United States enjoyed for the first time a nationwide system of government administered child protection. The federal Child Abuse Prevention and Treatment Act of 1974 (CAPTA) included sexual abuse in its definition of maltreatment. All states had laws requiring professionals to report maltreatment, including sexual abuse. The reporting laws and CAPTA wrenched sexual abuse from obscurity.

Groundbreaking Research
on Child Sexual Abuse

In 1969, Vincent De Francis completed one of the first empirical studies of child sexual abuse. Supported financially by the U.S. Children's Bureau, De Francis studied 250 sexual abuse cases from the Brooklyn Society for the Prevention of Cruelty to Children. De Francis wrote, "The problem of sexual abuse of children is of unknown national dimensions, but findings strongly point to the probability of an enormous national incidence many times larger than the reported incidence of physical abuse of children." Two-thirds of the children in De Francis's study were emotionally damaged by the abuse. De Francis concluded, "Child victims of adult sex offenders are a community's least protected children. Frequent victims of parental neglect, they are, almost always, also neglected by the community which has consistently failed to recognize the existence of this as a substantial problem."[71]

A decade after De Francis's groundbreaking research, David Finkelhor published *Sexually Victimized Children*. Much had changed since 1969, when De

Francis complained that society ignored sexual abuse. In 1979, Finkelhor wrote, "Child protection workers from all over the country say they are inundated with cases of sexual abuse. . . . Public outrage, which has for several years focused on stories of bruised and tortured children, is shifting to a concern with sexual exploitation. Between 1977 and 1978 almost every national magazine had run a story highlighting the horrors of children's sexual abuse."[72]

In his book, Finkelhor described his research on 796 college students; 530 women and 266 men. Finkelhor found, "19.2 percent of the women and 8.6 percent of the men had been sexually victimized as children."[73] Most of the sexual abuse was committed by someone the child knew, and most was not reported to authorities.

As Finkelhor was finishing his research, Diana Russell was working toward similar results. Russell surveyed 930 randomly selected women. Russell found that "16% of the sample of 930 women reported at least one experience of intrafamilial sexual abuse before the age of 18 years. . . . 31% of the sample of 930 women reported at least one experience of sexual abuse by a non-relative before the age of 18 years."[74] The pioneering research of Diana Russell, David Finkelhor, and Vincent De Francis exploded the old bromide that child sexual abuse is rare.

Late Twentieth-Century Setbacks: Sexual Abuse
in Preschools and Ritual Child Abuse

The 1980s and 1990s witnessed progress against sexual abuse. At the same time, however, two phenomena that baffled experts and excited the public imperiled efforts to understand and respond to sexual abuse: sexual abuse in preschools and allegations of widespread ritual abuse of children.

Preschool Sexual Abuse Cases and Their Aftermath

Beginning in the early 1980s, a number of cases arose involving allegations of sexual abuse in preschools. Although each case was different, they shared common features. Rather than describe them all, the lessons they teach can be gleaned from the most famous—the McMartin Preschool case from Manhattan Beach, California.[75]

Manhattan Beach is an easygoing seaside suburb of Los Angeles. In the 1950s, Virginia McMartin founded her namesake preschool in Manhattan Beach, not far from the ocean. By 1980, McMartin Preschool was a fixture of the community. The director of the preschool was Peggy Buckey, Virginia's daughter. Peggy's twenty-five-year-old son, Raymond, was one of the teachers.

In August 1983, the mother of a two-year-old boy who attended McMartin telephoned the Manhattan Beach Police Department and accused Ray Buckey of sexually abusing her son. Buckey was arrested, but soon released. The police sent a letter to parents of past and present McMartin preschoolers, stating in part, "Dear Parent: This Department is conducting a criminal investigation involving child molestation. Ray Buckey, an employee of Virginia McMartin's Pre-School, was arrested September 7, 1983 by this Department. . . . Please question your child to see if he or she has been a witness to any crime or if he or she has been a victim. Our investigation indicates that possible criminal acts include: oral sex, fondling of genitals, buttock or chest area, and sodomy."[76] The letter set off alarm bells. Parents interrogated their children. Some rushed their youngsters to therapists. Parents talked to each other, sharing what their children told them. Some parents withdrew their children from McMartin; others rallied around the school and its teachers.

As the McMartin saga unfolded, social worker Kee MacFarlane was working on sexual abuse issues at Children's Institute International in Los Angeles. MacFarlane was among the first to videotape interviews of children. A prosecutor asked MacFarlane to interview a few of the youngest McMartin children. Before long, parents were asking MacFarlane to interview children, and within a month more than two hundred children were waiting to be interviewed. Eventually, more than four hundred children were interviewed.

In the early 1980s, interviewers like Kee MacFarlane had little understanding of the dangers of highly suggestive and leading questions. Although training materials on interviewing existed in California in 1983, the materials said little about suggestibility.[77] Suggestibility became an important issue *because of* McMartin, but suggestibility was not on Kee MacFarlane's radar screen when she interviewed the McMartin children. Moreover, MacFarlane was a clinician, not a forensic investigator. As a result, MacFarlane's videotaped interviews contained highly suggestive questions that might be permissible in therapy but were out of line in a criminal investigation.

The investigation dragged on. In January 1984, McMartin preschool closed its doors forever. In February, the case hit the media and remained there for years. In March 1984, Ray Buckey, his mother Peggy, his eighty-year-old grandmother, Virginia, and four female teachers were charged in a 208-count indictment, alleging sexual abuse of forty-two children.

A preliminary hearing in a criminal case is a procedure that allows a judge to listen to witnesses and decide whether the prosecution has enough evidence to justify a trial. If so, the defendant is "bound over for trial." If there is not enough evidence, the case is dismissed. A preliminary hearing typically takes a few hours or, at most, several days. The preliminary hearing for the seven McMartin defendants lasted eighteen months. Fourteen children testified about sexual abuse. Several of the children described witnessing the mutilation and killing of animals, tunnels under the preschool, and being forced to participate in satanic rituals. One ten-year-old was on the witness stand sixteen days, of which fifteen-and-a-half were cross-examination by seven defense attorneys. At the end of this exhausting process, the seven defendants were bound over for trial on 135 counts of child sexual abuse.

In January 1986, a newly elected district attorney dropped all charges against the elderly Virginia and the five female teachers, calling the evidence "incredibly weak." Only two defendants remained, Ray Buckey and his mother Peggy. The trial of Ray and Peggy Buckey began in April 1987, four years after the investigation started. Given how the children had been treated during the preliminary hearing, many parents refused to let their children testify at the trial. Children who did testify described acts of abuse, plus more of the incredible events recounted at the preliminary hearing. For example, children described being taken to meat markets and car washes where they were molested. Children described jumping out of airplanes and digging up corpses.

The defense strategy was to attack the videotaped interviews conducted by Kee MacFarlane, arguing that her suggestive questions caused the children to manufacture accusations of abuse that never happened. Defense attorneys also criticized the letter sent by the Manhattan Beach Police Department to parents at the outset of the investigation. The defense argued that frightened parents grilled their children with highly leading questions and then called each other on the phone to share information, "contaminating" the children's stories.

In January 1990, after a trial lasting two-and-a-half years, the jury acquitted Peggy Buckey of all charges. Ray Buckey was acquitted of most charges, but the jury could not reach a decision on thirteen. In a posttrial news conference, many of the jurors said they believed children had been molested at McMartin, but the evidence did not prove by whom. In May 1990, Ray Buckey was tried a second time on eight counts. Again, the jury deadlocked, and the case finally ended, more than seven years after it started.

What really happened at McMartin Preschool? Were children sexually abused? Many of the jurors thought so, although they could not tell who was responsible. On the other hand, there was not a single conviction in McMartin. And what of the children's claims of molestation in meat markets and car washes? Did secret tunnels exist under the preschool? Did children participate in satanic rituals? Were they were forced to drink blood and watch animals tortured and killed? It seems incredible. The children's testimony about the bizarre and the improbable undermined their credibility in the eyes of the jury.

In the final analysis, we will never know what happened at the McMartin Preschool. From the outset, the case divided people into "true believers" and skeptics. Consider the tunnels. Several McMartin parents, especially the indefatigable Jackie McGauley, hired an archeologist to excavate under the abandoned preschool. The archeologist conducted an excavation and issued an exhaustive report concluding there probably were tunnels. The tunnels had been backfilled with dirt, but McGauley pointed out that the Buckeys had months to fill in the tunnels after the preschool closed. I read the archeologist's report and came away convinced. Yet, I shared the report with a colleague who was just as firmly convinced the report proves nothing.

The primary reason it is impossible to ascertain the truth about McMartin is that the investigation was fatally flawed from the outset. Asking worried parents to interview preschool children about abuse—as the police department's letter did—is like asking an airline passenger to fly the plane. When parents are told to question young children about abuse, highly suggestive questions are virtually guaranteed, making it difficult or impossible to find the truth.

Parents were not the only amateur interviewers in McMartin. Kee MacFarlane, although a competent social worker, had little understanding of the forensic implications of her suggestive questioning style. MacFarlane was not to blame. In 1983, no one was fully aware of the dangers of suggestive questions with young children. Nevertheless, MacFarlane's videotaped interviews, along with the parents' interrogations, were ammunition for the McMartin defense attorneys, and they made good use of it.

McMartin was a tragedy for everyone involved: children, parents, defendants, professionals, and the community. Yet, McMartin, and cases like it across the country, had two important legacies. First, the preschool cases opened people's eyes to the dangers of suggestive questions during forensic interviews. Second, and closely related, the preschool cases stimulated psychological research on children's suggestibility and on effective methods of questioning children.

During the early twentieth century, several European researchers examined children's suggestibility and concluded that children are not to be trusted. In 1910, for example, German physician Dr. Baginsky opined, "Children are the most dangerous of all witnesses." Baginsky argued that children's "testimony should be excluded from the court record whenever possible." In 1911, Belgian psychologist Dr. Varendonck asked, "When are we going to give up, in all civilized nations, listening to children in courts of law?"[78] Freud added to the skepticism with his theory that women and girls fantasize sexual experience. Following this spate of early twentieth-century interest in suggestibility, psychologists dropped the subject until the 1980s, when interviewing children about sexual abuse emerged as an important issue. In the 1980s, psychologists such as Gail Goodman, Karen Saywitz, Stephen Ceci, and Maggie Bruck pioneered a new era of research on suggestibility.

The new research established that although children are suggestible, they are not invariably so.[79] Even preschoolers can be highly accurate. In a Colorado case, for example, a three-year-old was abducted in front of her home by a stranger. The abductor drove to a state park in the nearby Rocky Mountains, where he molested the child and dropped her six feet into raw sewage at the bottom of an outdoor toilet. To escape some of the filth, the child built a little platform from sticks she found in the pit. When standing on the platform, the sewage covered only her feet and ankles. For three long days and nights, she stood on her little platform, all alone. Finally, hikers heard her crying and rushed to her aid. When a hiker asked why she was there, she said, "I'm home. I live here."[80]

Following a hospital stay to treat dehydration, immersion foot, and scratches and bruises, the little girl went home. The police interviewed her and she described her ordeal. From a group of photographs, she picked the man the police suspected of the crime, calling him a "bad man." A few days later, the child sat on her mother's lap and watched a police line up on a television monitor. When the camera focused on the suspect, she said, "That's him, that's the bad man who put me in the hole."

Later, the child was interviewed by psychiatrist David Jones. During the interview, Jones showed the child fourteen photographs, but none of the suspect. The child studied the photos and said, "He's not here." Following a snack, Jones again showed her the photographs, but this time with the suspect's photo included. When she got to the suspect's picture, she gasped and blurted out, "He want to put me in the hole . . . he got a car." When Dr. Jones suggested that the man did not look like a bad man, the child said, "He's a *mean* man." Later in the interview, Jones spread the photos out once more, including one of the defendant. Jones pretended he could not locate the photo of the suspect. Inpatient with the doctor's ineptitude, the child picked up the suspect's photo and showed it to him. Eventually, the suspect made a complete confession, corroborating the child's version of the crime.[81]

Today, significant progress has been made in our understanding of suggestibility and the proper way to question children about abuse. Police officers and social workers who interview children receive training on the dangers of suggestive questions. Overly suggestive interviews still occur, but not on a scale approaching the improper interviewing in McMartin and cases like it.

Ritual and Satanic Abuse

During the 1980s, fear circulated that children were subjected to ritualistic abuse tinged with satanism.[82] Books on ritual and satanic abuse appeared. Workshops on the topic became regular fare at professional gatherings. Yet, investigation after investigation failed to turn up solid evidence. Skepticism grew. The Utah Attorney General's Office concluded:

> Investigators statewide were told stories of bizarre sexual and physical abuse. They listened as victims recalled memories of rapes, torture, animal sacrifice and even murder. Victims spoke of bearing children, only to have them taken away for use in sacrificial ceremonies. Utah's police officers and their departments have dedicated thousands of hours as they followed up on allegations, searched hillsides for

FIGURE 5.1
Little boy escorted into court by police officer.

ritual sites, "staked-out" potential ceremonies, etc. Their combined efforts were unable to uncover any physical evidence to support the claims of the existence of organized cults. Evidence has been uncovered to support the thought that individuals have in the past, and are now committing crime in the name of Satan or other deity. The allegations of organized satanists, even groups of satanists who have permeated every level of government and religion were unsubstantiated.[83]

Believers responded that the satanists were simply too clever for the police, and that cults had infiltrated law enforcement from the local police to the FBI.

In several of the preschool molestation cases of the 1980s, including McMartin, children described bizarre, fantastic, and seemingly impossible events. Several McMartin children claimed they participated in satanic rituals and animal mutilation.

When a young child's otherwise plausible description of abuse contains elements of the fantastic, can anything the child says be believed? Constance Dalenberg studied confirmed cases of severe sexual abuse and found that a small percent of children's descriptions contained elements of the fantastic and bizarre. Dalenberg wrote "It is clear that implausible details are to be expected within some true and [some] false cases."[84]

For many years, Kenneth Lanning was the FBI's leading expert on child sexual abuse. Lanning wrote, "Some of what the victims in these cases allege is physically impossible (victim cut up and put back together, offender took the building apart and then rebuilt it); some is possible but improbable (human sacrifice, cannibalism, vampirism); some is possible and probable (child pornography, clever manipulation of victims); and some is corroborated (medical evidence of vaginal or anal trauma, offender confessions)." When it came to the bizarre, Lanning pointed out that there is "no single, simple answer." Lanning rejected the idea that most bizarre allegations are true. He also rejected the belief that satanic ritual abuse is perpetrated by well-organized conspiracies. Lanning drew on years of work with police across the country to offer seven explanations for bizarre and impossible accusations. First, some allegations may result from "pathological distortion and pseudomemories." Lanning wrote, "The allegations in question may be errors in processing reality influenced by underlying mental disorders such as dissociative disorders, borderline or histrionic personality disorders, or psychosis." Second, fantastic allegations may grow out of distortions of traumatic memories of children who were subjected to severe physical or sexual abuse. Third, some fantastic allegations may grow out of normal childhood fears and fantasy. Fourth, improbable allegations may be produced by misperception, confusion, and trickery. Lanning noted, "Some clever offenders may deliberately introduce elements of satanism and the occult into the sexual exploitation simply to confuse or intimidate the victims. Simple magic and other techniques may be used to trick the children. Drugs may also deliberately be used to confuse the victims and distort their perceptions." Fifth, certain allegations, for example, large satanic conspiracies that infiltrated government agencies, including the police and the FBI, may be the product of urban legend. Sixth, Lanning stated that many allegations "probably involve a *combination* of the answers previously set forth." Seventh, Lanning asserted that some overzealous professionals who were "true believers" in ritual and satanic abuse used suggestive interview practices that introduced fantastic ideas that children came to believe.[85]

In 1997, Mark Everson elaborated on Lanning's analysis of bizarre allegations. Everson explained that implausible descriptions of abuse arise from three sources. First, the event itself, that is, what actually happened to the child. Everson noted that reality is sometimes stranger than fiction. Some improbable explanations are probably true. Jean Goodwin reminds us that society has a tendency to close its eyes to child sexual abuse, a tendency that intensifies as the abuse becomes more severe. Goodwin wrote, "Human beings are always hoping for evidence that things are not as bad as we suspect. We are relieved to find anyone willing to tell us that the Holocaust was not really that bad nor Hiroshima. In the history of child abuse, this phenomenon manifests itself in the tendency for the most severe cases to be the least believed."[86]

Everson's second explanation for fantastic descriptions of abuse is the interviewing process. Of particular concern are interviewer biases and preconceptions. An interviewer who believes ritual abuse is common may consciously or inadvertently "manufacture" bizarre allegations during the interview of a young child.

Third, Everson wrote that factors apart from the investigation can distort memory. Television, videos, movies, books—all of these can influence memory. Children dream, and many children have nightmares. An occasional child may confuse reality with a scary dream. Finally, a small number of children are psychotic and suffer delusions. Everson concluded, "What is evident from this discussion of possible explanatory mechanisms for improbable and fantastic elements in children's accounts of abuse is that the presence of such material in a child's report should not lead to an automatic dismissal of the child's entire account. As we have seen, there are many reasonable explanations why such material may emerge in an otherwise credible and truthful account of abuse."[87]

In the end, nothing came of the ritual abuse "scare" of the 1990s. There was never any hard evidence of widespread ritual or satanic abuse of children. Unfortunately, the understandable skepticism aroused by the "scare" retarded efforts to prove that children can be reliable witnesses.[88]

Conclusion

During the nineteenth century and the first six decades of the twentieth, sexually abused children struggled to be believed. Beginning in the late 1970s and early 1980s, sustained efforts were made to respond to sexual abuse, and toward the end of the twentieth century, there were signs that the effort was bearing fruit. Since the mid-1990s, substantiated cases of child sexual abuse have declined nearly 40 percent.[89] Other forms of maltreatment declined as well, but not as steeply as sexual abuse. David Finkelhor and Lisa Jones analyzed possible explanations for the decline in substantiated sexual abuse and wrote in 2004, "The most optimistic explanation is that incidents of child sexual abuse are decreasing. A great deal of public awareness of the problem has developed in the past 20 years. Prevention programs that target children are widespread. A large number of offenders have been incarcerated. Many treatment programs have been directed toward offenders to prevent them from reoffending, and laws have been passed in many States to improve the monitoring of sexual offenders in the community. All of these efforts have the cumulative effect of reducing incidents of child sexual abuse."[90]

Finkelhor acknowledged less optimistic explanations for the decline in substantiated cases. Perhaps the prevalence of sexual abuse has not declined, but professionals have become less diligent in looking for it. Alternatively, it is possible that professionals have grown increasingly skeptical of the ability of child protective services to intervene effectively and are filing fewer reports. Finally, Finkelhor wrote, "It may be that fewer reports of sexual abuse are being investigated or that fewer investigations are being substantiated."

Hopefully, Finkelhor's optimistic scenario is correct—fewer children are sexually abused. One thing is certain, child sexual abuse is no longer the "hidden pediatric problem" decried by Henry Kempe in 1977. Sexual abuse is out in the open, and many resources are devoted to preventing sexual abuse, detecting and investigating cases, prosecuting and incarcerating offenders, and providing therapy for children, adult survivors, and offenders. Progress has been real and sustained.

The discussion of child sexual abuse brings part I to a close. With the history of child protection in focus, part II searches for answers to the following questions: What causes child abuse and neglect? What barriers stand in the way of substantially reducing the amount of maltreatment? Are there broad societal reforms that hold promise for reducing abuse and neglect? Even if we succeed in reducing maltreatment, we cannot stop it altogether. Therefore, what changes should be made to the existing child protection system so that it works more effectively?

Part II

THE ROAD AHEAD

Child Protection Today and Tomorrow

The rescue of Mary Ellen Wilson in 1874 led by fits and starts to the child protection system in place today. In many ways, child protection in the twenty-first century resembles nineteenth-century efforts. Reports of abuse and neglect come to agencies. Investigations are conducted. A few cases end up in court, but most are handled by social workers outside the legal system. Today as then, the child protection system fails too often but works well for thousands of children.

Although there are similarities between today's child protection system and earlier efforts, there are important differences. At one time, child protection was in the hands of private charitable organizations. Today, child protection is a function of government. Prior to 1970, many communities lacked a formal child protection system. Today, organized child protection stretches coast to coast. Modern understanding of child abuse and neglect is deeper and more nuanced than in Mary Ellen's time, but many questions remain.

We have made significant strides, yet more than a century has passed since the creation of the New York Society for the Prevention of Cruelty to Children, and maltreatment continues at discouraging levels. Every year, more than a thousand children die at the hands of adults who should cherish and protect them. Large numbers of girls and boys are sexually abused, physically assaulted, and neglected. The tide of maltreatment rolls relentlessly forward. Why is maltreatment so intractable? If there were simple answers to this question, they would have been discovered long ago. H. L. Mencken once observed, "There is an easy solution to every human problem—neat, plausible, and wrong."[1] The problem of child maltreatment is agonizingly complex. Yet, despite its complexity, it is essential to forge ahead with efforts to understand the causes of maltreatment.

Chapter 6 discusses the causes of abuse and neglect as well as some of the obstacles to preventing maltreatment. With the causes of maltreatment in focus, chapter 7 shifts gears to analysis of broad societal changes that hold promise for reducing child abuse and neglect. Even with successful efforts to reduce maltreatment, child abuse and neglect cannot be eliminated, and chapter 8 describes reforms to improve today's child protection system.

Before addressing the causes of maltreatment, it is useful to set the stage by describing the day-to-day functioning of child protection in the early twenty-first century. There are some 2,610 government child protection agencies in America.[2] Child protective services (CPS) varies slightly from state to state and county to county. The CPS agency in Los Angeles does not look much like the agency in Moab, Utah, although the work inside is similar. CPS agencies are staffed by social workers, the majority of whom hold bachelor's degrees.[3] Administrators often have a master's degree in social work from one of the 150 or so social work programs at colleges and universities. A few administrators have a doctorate. In most states, the state Department of Social Services has administrative responsibility for child protection, with implementation at the county level. In eleven states, however, counties are responsible for child protection, with the state providing policy guidance.

Every community has a child abuse hot line. Some states have a single hot line for the entire state. Other states have a hot line for each county. Hot line calls come from teachers, doctors, neighbors, family members, and others. In addition to hot lines, people may use the emergency 911 number. In 2003, an estimated 2,900,000 referrals for abuse and neglect inundated CPS hot lines. That's more than 50,000 calls a week.[4]

The U.S. Children's Bureau stated that in 2003, more than half (56 percent) of all reports to CPS came from professionals. The remaining 43 percent came from neighbors, relatives, friends, and anonymous callers. Among professionals, the most frequent reporters in 2003 were educators and law enforcement (16 percent each), social services (12 percent), medical professionals (8 percent), mental health personnel (3 percent), and child care workers (1 percent).

Child protective services does not respond in person to every call, and social workers who answer hot lines have the unenviable task of deciding which calls merit investigation and which should be screened out or "closed at intake." Some calls that are screened out do not involve abuse or neglect (e.g., "My neighbor's kids are too loud").[5] In many states, CPS responds only when maltreatment occurs in the child's home and refers abuse by strangers or neighbors to police. In some cases, the social worker refers the caller to another agency such as mental health or public assistance.

When a hot line social worker decides a call merits investigation, the call is triaged as an emergency requiring immediate response or as a case that can wait. Each state has time limits for investigating nonemergency cases. If it appears a crime has been committed, the intake worker notifies police. Child protective services and law enforcement often conduct joint investigations.

After investigation, some cases are "substantiated,"; that is, CPS concludes the child was abused or neglected. In other cases it is impossible to tell whether maltreatment occurred, and such cases are referred to as "reason to suspect," "inconclusive," or "unsubstantiated." Finally, some investigations reveal that the child was not maltreated. The labels here are "unfounded" or "unsubstantiated." As one can see, the labels are not always used consistently.

One should not equate reports that are unfounded or unsubstantiated with deliberate fabrications. In most unsubstantiated cases, callers honestly suspect abuse or neglect but are mistaken. Deliberately false reports occur but are uncommon.

Substantiation rates vary over time and from place to place. In 2002, the national substantiation rate approached 30 percent.[6] At that rate, approximately 896,000 children were neglected or abused in 2002.

When investigation discloses that a child has been abused or neglected, the CPS social worker decides whether the child is in immediate danger. If so, the worker—often with assistance from police—takes the child into emergency protective custody.[7] The child is placed in a children's receiving home, with relatives, or in a foster home. When a child is removed in an emergency, the social worker promptly initiates proceedings in juvenile court. A juvenile court hearing occurs within a day or two to decide whether the child should remain out of the home pending further investigation and court proceedings. If the child is not in immediate danger, the child remains at home while social workers decide what steps are necessary to keep the child safe.

In most communities, less than 10 percent of substantiated cases are referred to juvenile court. With cases that don't go to juvenile court, CPS helps the family deal with the problems that brought the family to official attention. In neglect cases, for example, the crux of the problem is often poverty, and the social worker endeavors to connect parents with services to improve the family's circumstances. For example, with a struggling single parent, the solution may lie in financial assistance, food stamps, low-income housing, day care for the kids, and job training. In many cases, drugs or alcohol are a roadblock to competent parenting, and the worker helps the parent locate treatment. Unfortunately, many communities lack adequate substance abuse treatment resources. Moreover, substance-abusing parents often drop out of treatment.

CPS social workers do their best to connect parents to resources. Unfortunately, in many communities, crushing caseloads combined with finite resources cause thousands of struggling parents to go without help. Yet, despite obstacles, CPS social workers routinely change lives for the better. In Sacramento, California, for example, Angela was addicted to methamphetamine and was neglecting her children. CPS removed the children and insisted Angela sober up. After Angela conquered her addiction and regained custody of her children, she remarked,

"I thank God CPS came into my life, I truly do."[8] Like Angela, maltreating parents generally want to do a better job raising their children, and assistance from CPS helps many of them turn the corner. Insoo Kim Berg spent time with CPS social workers and wrote, "By and large, what I have found are overwhelmed, over-worked, and unfortunately some unappreciated workers, supervisors, administrators, and managers all trying to do the best they can with the poor and vulnerable families in our society. . . . I came away awed that they are willing to do the society's most difficult work most of the time. I was frustrated by their lack of training and skills, but fascinated with their undiminished desire to 'make a difference' in somebody's life."[9]

When children are at risk and parents can't or won't accept voluntary help, proceedings are necessary in juvenile court. The machinery of the juvenile court varies slightly from state to state. Typically, a social worker or a government attorney files a petition in court. The petition alleges a child has been abused or neglected or is at risk of maltreatment and needs the court's protection. The petition is delivered to the parents to notify them that proceedings have been commenced. If the child was taken into emergency protective custody, the first court hearing occurs promptly and is limited to deciding whether the child should remain in out-of-home care or be returned to parents pending further proceedings.

The "parties" in juvenile court protective litigation are the CPS agency and the child's parents. In some states, the child is a party. The CPS agency is represented by a government attorney. Parents have the right to be represented by an attorney, although most cannot afford one. When parents can't afford counsel, the juvenile court judge appoints an attorney to represent the parents at county expense. Does the child need an attorney? This question is discussed in chapter 8.

The purpose of juvenile court protective proceedings is to protect children and help parents. Often, the court succeeds. Abuse and neglect stop, and children receive the therapy they need. For some parents, being hauled into juvenile court is the wake-up call that cuts through a haze of drugs, indifference, or ignorance. For maltreating parents who cannot or do not want to change, the juvenile court has authority to terminate parental rights, freeing the child for adoption. Termination of parental rights is discussed in chapter 8.

Once proceedings are underway in juvenile court, parents can admit the abuse or neglect alleged in the petition, admit to some other form of maltreatment, or deny the allegations and insist on a trial. As is true with all types of litigation—civil and criminal—only a small fraction of cases end in trial. In most cases, settlements are arranged by the attorneys. A frequent settlement in juvenile court is for parents to admit some type of maltreatment and to enter into an agreement with CPS to participate in services designed to improve parenting and reduce the likelihood of further abuse or neglect. When parents admit maltreatment as part of a settlement, or are found responsible following a trial, the juvenile court gains authority (jurisdiction) over the child. In some states, the child is called a dependent of the court. In other states, the child is a ward or a CHIP—child in need of protection.

Once the juvenile court takes jurisdiction over a child, the next step is disposition. At the dispositional phase, the judge relies heavily on advice from CPS, the court's own staff of social workers, the attorneys, the wishes of parents, and, when the child is old enough to contribute, the child's views. Typically, a social worker prepares a "disposition report" for the judge. Most of the time, the parties come to terms on a disposition and the judge approves.

The fact that the juvenile court takes jurisdiction over a child does not mean the child is removed from the parents' custody. In many cases, the child remains at home under CPS supervision. Indeed, the law requires the government to make reasonable efforts to avoid removing children from home. If a child cannot remain safely at home, the court orders the child removed from the parents' custody and placed in a foster family home, or with members of the child's extended family, or in a group home or institution. The juvenile court continues its jurisdiction over the child until maltreatment is no longer an issue, parental rights are terminated, legal guardianship is established, or the child reaches adulthood and "ages out" of the system.

America's child protection system is highly complex. Successful intervention requires professionals from different disciplines to coordinate efforts and share information and resources. Like other bureaucracies, the child protection system is not very efficient, and children fall between the cracks. Yet, despite faults, the child protection system saves children.

6

CAUSES OF CHILD ABUSE AND NEGLECT

This chapter disentangles the causes of child abuse and neglect. Among experts on maltreatment there is consensus on many of the causes. Other causes remain controversial.[1]

Child Abuse and Neglect Are Multiply Determined

There are many reasons for child abuse and neglect.[2] In a review of the literature Jay Belsky concluded,

> Child maltreatment is now widely recognized to be multiply determined by a variety of factors. . . . There not only appears to be no single cause of child maltreatment, but no necessary or sufficient causes. All too sadly, there are many pathways to child abuse and neglect. . . . Although past reviewers of the literature have identified psychiatric or psychological models of maltreatment, which focus attention on the characteristics of the perpetrator; sociological models, which focus attention on the contextual conditions that give rise to abuse and neglect; and social-interactional or effect-of-child-on-caregiver models, which underscore the dyadic nature of problematic parenting, it is clear today that no one such model is adequate.[3]

To understand maltreatment, it is necessary to examine attributes of the adult, the child, and the complex psychological interplay between them.[4] Paul Howes and Dante Cicchetti observed that physically "maltreating families are characterized by pervasive disturbances in relationships between family members in both parent-child and adult-adult relationships. Specifically, members of maltreating families exhibit a higher frequency of negative feelings and appear to have difficulty regulating negative affect."[5] In a similar vein, Belsky observed, "Repeatedly it has been found that physically abusive parents are less supportive and direct fewer positive behaviors (e.g., instructing, joining play, talking to child, praising) toward their children; are less responsive to child initiations; and express less positive affection toward the child than comparison parents."[6]

The social context in which families live plays a role in maltreatment.[7] Poverty, in particular, takes a toll on parenting and contributes to abuse and neglect. The role of poverty is discussed below and in chapter 7.

Many maltreating parents are not only poor, but they are also socially isolated. In 1973, Henry Kempe described the social isolation common among maltreating adults this way, "There is generally no lifeline or rescue operation available to the parent's life. That is, they have no close friends, relatives, or neighbors whom they can readily ask for help in moments of stress."[8] Belsky affirmed,

> There is an abundance of evidence linking social isolation and limited social ties with elevated risk of child abuse and neglect. . . . Other investigations reveal that maltreating parents have smaller peer networks, though this result is not always obtained; have less contact with, and receive less help from their family of origin and other relatives; feel lonely; are socially isolated; and are less likely to have a phone . . . Maltreating parents do not use community resources that are available; are not involved in community activities, including church-related ones; and do not discuss their problems with anyone—at least in comparison groups.[9]

In sum, child abuse and neglect result from individual, interpersonal, and societal variables that interact in myriad ways, making simple explanations counterproductive. Because there is a multiplicity of interacting causes, there is no single solution to the problem. Proposed remedies must attack maltreatment from diverse angles, each remedy making its incremental contribution to the overarching goal of reduced abuse and neglect.

Child Abuse Is in Our Genes

To some extent, mistreatment is probably inherent in the human condition, just as maltreatment is observed in other species.[10] Belsky wrote, "If one looks across the animal kingdom, it becomes apparent that the mistreatment of progeny is so widespread that it would seem to be as much a part of the 'natural' condition as is sensitive, solicitous parental behavior."[11] Lynn Fairbanks and Michael McGuire wrote that while "primate mothers form close, long-lasting affiliative bonds with their offspring, . . . early field studies provide numerous examples of primate mothers pushing away, hitting, and biting their infants."[12]

Assuming there is a genetic/evolutionary component of maltreatment, it is a safe bet that the prevalence of maltreatment far exceeds the baseline inherent in human nature. In all likelihood, abuse and neglect have more to do with culture, customs, and laws than with genetics. We have little control over the genetic/ evolutionary component of our behavior (although science may change that), but we have the ability to change the culture, customs, and laws that fuel child abuse and neglect.

Intergenerational Transmission of Child Abuse and Neglect

The tendency toward child abuse and neglect is passed from one generation to the next.[13] Professionals working to protect children have long understood intergenerational transmission of maltreatment. Charles Loring Brace, for example, was well aware of the problem in 1853. But why are adults who were abused or neglected as children at increased risk of hurting their own children?

Physical abuse causes pain and injury. In most cases, the pain subsides and the bruises, lacerations, and fractures heal. When physical abuse is inflicted by a parent, however, the trauma is fundamentally psychological. Nelson Binggeli, Stuart Hart, and Marla Brassard observed, "Psychological maltreatment can be seen as the higher-order dimension; frequently, if not always, it is the most salient aspect of the majority of both physical and sexual abuse experiences. . . . A physically abusive act may convey powerful messages of spurning, terrorizing, and exploiting/corrupting, all of which may have many immediate and long-term effects on the child, while producing no long-term physical consequences."[14]

From the child's perspective, physical abuse is an assault by the most important, most trusted, most loved person on earth. Abuse inflicted by parents is more damaging than abuse inflicted by strangers, baby-sitters, or day care providers. A child who is attacked by a stranger turns to parents for love, reassurance, and protection. A child who is attacked by a parent turns for solace to the attacker. If parental abuse persists, the child may give up on the parent as a source of unqualified love.[15] A child who is physically abused by a parent once may move forward unscathed, but a child who is beaten routinely is uniquely traumatized.

But what is it about physical abuse during childhood that pushes some victims to abuse their own children? One would think abuse would have the opposite effect. Surely, victims say, "I won't ever treat my children the way I was treated." Fortunately, most victims say and do precisely that.[16] Only a minority of adults who were abused as children abuse their own children. Katherine Pears and Deborah Capaldi note, "Intergenerational transmission of abusive behavior is by no means a certainty." Joan Kaufman and Edward Zigler add that although "being maltreated puts one at risk for becoming abusive . . . the path between these points is far from direct or inevitable." Estimates of intergenerational transmission range from less than 10 percent to an implausible 70 percent.[17]

Although most maltreated children do not repeat the pattern, some do, and part of the explanation lies in the fact that children model the behavior of their parents. The "lessons" taught by abuse and harsh discipline sink into the child's developing sense of self to reappear later. Belsky wrote

> Several mediating processes, none of which are mutually exclusive, may account for the intergenerational transmission of child maltreatment. The most obvious and thus most frequently called-on presumes that aggressive, antisocial behavior is learned in childhood and simply expressed in adulthood in the parenting role. . . . In addition to learning particular behaviors in childhood that are re-peated in adulthood, intergenerational transmission may also involve parents' philosophies of discipline. . . . In light of evidence that maltreated children have problems with emotion regulation, aggression, and empathy, it seems plausible that abusive and neglectful childhoods may promote hostile personalities that be-come a proximate cause of maltreatment.[18]

Some abused children who grow up to hurt their own children are genuinely surprised and upset when they find themselves treating their children the way they were treated. Other parents find nothing remarkable. "My old man smacked me around when I was a kid, and it didn't do me no harm. Kids need a good lickin' to learn discipline."

James Garbarino gets at the heart of intergenerational transmission in his pow-erful book about boys who commit murder, *Lost Boys: Why Our Sons Turn Violent and How We Can Save Them*:

> Child maltreatment teaches children to adapt their behavior and thinking to the harsh fact that those who are in charge of caring for them are the same people who hurt, terrify, ignore, and attack them. This very adaptation ultimately becomes the source of their problems in later years. . . . Children who are maltreated are much more likely than non-maltreated children to develop a chronic pattern of bad behavior and aggression. The key lies in the fact that the child comes to understand how the world works through the lens of his own abuse. Put another way, a child's worldview is a matter of how he draws his social map. . . .
>
> Abused children develop their social maps by adapting to an abusive environ-ment. The more they learn these lessons, the more likely it is that they will learn a code that is compatible with a pattern of bad behavior and aggression by the time they are *eight years old*.[19]

Turning from physical abuse to sexual abuse, molestation by a parent is a fun-damental betrayal of trust. Rather than protect and nurture his child, the sexually abusive father or mother places lust ahead of his child's needs. The parent exploits the child's vulnerability and dependence to quench his or her passion. At its core, sexual abuse is psychological abuse. Binggeli and his colleagues observe, "Sexual abuse always involves acts of exploiting/corrupting."[20] With chronic incest, abuse is too mild a term. Long-standing incest is psychological torture. Leonard Shengold used the term "soul murder" to describe the impact of severe abuse. Shengold writes,

> Human beings are mysteriously resourceful, and some do survive such childhoods, with their sexuality and with their souls not unscarred or unwarped but at least in some part intact. Others are crushed, predominantly or completely— body and soul, sexuality and soul. Despite vulnerability of children and the prevalence of bad parents, a completely successful soul murder is probably rare. Why this should be so *is* mysterious; part of the explanation is innate endowment. What was it that enabled one of my patients with two psychotic parents to become, from age four on, the real parent in the family—the sane caring person who was able to help her siblings and even take care of her psychotic parents?[21]

Fortunately, despite the trauma of child sexual abuse, most survivors are loving parents. Yet, the depression, low self-esteem, and substance abuse experienced by some survivors of sexual abuse interferes with effective parenting.

Chronic neglect predisposes some children to a lifetime of problems, including low educational and occupational achievement, poverty, low self-esteem, depression, mental illness, substance abuse, physical illness, and criminal behavior.[22] Many survivors of neglect lead difficult lives and are not in an optimal position to nurture the next generation.

Abusive and neglectful parents often fail to provide their children with the unconditional love and support essential for healthy development. Thus, one reason maltreatment increases the odds children will grow up to provide inadequate or abusive parenting is that maltreatment inflicts deep psychological wounds. In their book *The Irreducible Needs of Children,* T. Berry Brazelton and Stanley Greenspan describe what children need:

> To pass successfully through the stages of early childhood children require more than a lack of deprivation; they require sensitive, nurturing care to build capacities of trust, empathy, and compassion. . . . Family patterns that undermine nurturing care may lead to significant compromise in both cognitive and emotional capacities. Supportive, warm, nurturing emotional interactions with infants and young children on the other hand, help the central nervous system grow appropriately. . . . Nurturing emotional relationships are the most crucial primary foundation for both intellectual and social growth.[23]

Brazelton and Greenspan note that parents who inflict chronic physical abuse, sexual abuse, or neglect send a clear message to their children that they are not worth loving. Robbed of the essentials of healthy development, too many abused and neglected children grow up without the skills required to nurture their own offspring.

To reduce maltreatment, it is essential to break the integenerational cycle of harm. The key to breaking the cycle is to prevent abuse and neglect from occurring in the first place. When maltreatment cannot be prevented, it is essential to intervene early. Recall James Garbarino's warning that lasting damage happens early, by the time children are eight.

Poverty Is a Major Contributor to Neglect and Abuse

There is compelling evidence that poverty plays an important role in neglect and physical abuse. Sexual abuse is less closely tied to poverty.[24] Michelle DiLauro wrote, "Research has found child abuse and neglect in all socioeconomic classes, but substantial evidence shows a strong relationship between poverty and child maltreatment."[25]

Professionals working with maltreated children have always understood that physical abuse and neglect are concentrated among the poor. In a 1958 report on child protective services in New Jersey, Claire Hancock wrote, "Economic insecurity is too fancy a title to describe the financial problems of this group [of mothers who abused their children]. A great many of these mothers lived with the problem of destitution. There had not been sufficient income to depend on regularly in an amount sufficient to meet even minimal needs."[26]

In the 1960s and 1970s, some professionals, politicians, and media outlets downplayed the connection between maltreatment and poverty, arguing that maltreatment is a classless phenomenon. The argument that poverty is not responsible for maltreatment was attractive for several reasons. First, abuse and neglect occur in the suburbs, and it is important to say so. Second, during the "War on Poverty" of the 1960s, it was unfashionable to blame the poor, especially for problems shared with the middle class. Third, the media is attracted to abuse by middle-class parents. In 1962, the *Saturday Evening Post* reported, "Most battered children come from 'nice' homes. Their parents are 'average' parents—with average incomes and average educations." In 1963, *Life* stated, "Parents who beat their children come from every economic level."[27] Because it is more newsworthy when privileged parents beat or molest their children than when poor parents do, media coverage reinforced the idea that abuse is classless.

On the political front, in 1973, U.S. Senator Walter Mondale was struggling to push the first major child abuse initiative through Congress, the Child Abuse

FIGURE 6.1

A poor child in New York City in the nineteenth century. From Helen Campell, *Darkness and Daylight*. 1892. Hartford, Conn.: A.D. Worthington.

Prevention and Treatment Act (CAPTA). Mondale realized that if Congress associated child abuse with poverty, CAPTA could go down in flames as "just another welfare program." By decoupling child abuse from poverty, the Senator portrayed child abuse as a classless issue—a problem that could afflict *any* parent. During House and Senate hearings on CAPTA, witnesses were at pains to portray maltreatment as a classless phenomenon. For example, William Lunsford of the Child Welfare League of America testified that abuse "is not a problem that is confined to a particular socioeconomic group within the country, or a particular racial group within the country. It crosses all those lines, the racial and economic lines, completely." In a letter written after the enactment of CAPTA, Senator Mondale stated, "This is a problem that cuts across social and economic barriers. It occurs in all kinds of families and in all kinds of neighborhoods."[28]

In 1978, Leroy Pelton published the definitive critique of what he called the "myth of classlessness." Pelton wrote, "There is substantial evidence of a strong relationship between poverty and child abuse and neglect. . . . Poverty is not merely 'associated' with child abuse and neglect; there is good reason to believe that the problems of poverty are causative agents in parents' abusive and negligent behaviors and in the resultant harm to children."[29]

The argument that poverty does not contribute substantially to abuse and neglect waned in the 1980s and 1990s. In 1990, the U.S. Advisory Board on Child Abuse and Neglect wrote, "Although child maltreatment occurs in all socioeconomic and cultural groups in society, its reported incidence is disproportionately large within those groups that are least powerful and subjected to the most stressors. Data have shown that the higher the poverty rate is in a neighborhood, the higher the rate of maltreatment will be." In 1993, Paul Howes and Dante Cicchetti wrote, "Even though child maltreatment occurs in all socioeconomic sectors, the stressors associated with living in adverse economic circumstances increase the likelihood of maltreatment occurring in families struggling with poverty."[30] Today, there is general consensus that poverty contributes to maltreatment.

According to the U.S. Census Bureau, in 2003, thirty-six million Americans lived below the poverty line.[31] That's 12 percent of the population. The poverty rate for blacks was 24 percent, for Hispanics 22 percent, for Asians 12 percent, and for whites 8 percent. In 2003, poverty worsened.

When the Census Bureau says thirty-six million Americans are poor, they mean *poor.* In 2003, a family of two had to make less than $12,015 to qualify as poor. That's a thousand dollars a month for shelter, food, clothing, medical care, routine bills, etc. It doesn't add up. Millions of Americans, who are not "officially poor," still struggle to survive.

For children, the 2003 poverty rate was 18 percent, which means some thirteen million American children were poor. For black children, poverty worsened from 1973 through 1993 (from 40 percent to 46 percent in poverty). Beginning in 1997, the poverty rate among black children dropped and stayed below 40 percent, although the 2003 rate was a depressing 30 percent. For Hispanic children, the 2003 poverty rate was nearly 30 percent, two percentage points higher than in 1979. For white children, the 2003 poverty rate was 14 percent, 3 percent worse than in 1974.

When it comes to child poverty, America fares badly compared with other developed countries. Lee Rainwater and Timothy Smeeding wrote, "Around the end of the twentieth century there were roughly the same number of children in the United States and the twelve [European countries studied by Rainwater and Smeeding]—around seventy-two million. But we found that as many as fourteen million American children are poor compared with some seven million poor children in our comparison European countries."[32] Rainwater and Smeeding found a child poverty rate of 20 percent in the United States, followed by Italy (19 percent), United Kingdom (16 percent), Canada (14 percent), Australia (13 percent), Spain (12 percent), Germany (9 percent), France (7.2 percent), the Netherlands (7 percent), Switzerland (6 percent), Belgium (5 percent), Denmark (4 percent), Norway (4 percent), Finland (3 percent), and Sweden (2 percent).

For single-parent families headed by women in the United States, the poverty rate for blacks in 2003 was 39 percent, for Hispanics 38 percent, and for whites 26 percent. For children younger than six living with their mother alone, the poverty rate in 2003 was an astounding 53 percent.

As many middle-class readers of this book will attest, raising a family is the most challenging and rewarding experience in life. It is a challenge with adequate resources. Imagine the challenge when there isn't enough money to put food on the table or buy milk for the baby. Imagine sending kids out to play when gunfire is common in the neighborhood. Imagine you are fifteen, a child yourself, coping with the responsibilities of parenthood without financial or emotional support from the father. Little wonder so many poor parents are overwhelmed, depressed, and lost to drugs and alcohol.

Yet, it is not poverty per se that causes neglect and physical abuse. After all, most poor parents do not abuse or neglect their children. Poverty is related to maltreatment because poverty takes a toll on parents. Poor parents are under pressure to meet their family's needs for shelter, food, and clothing. Society looks down on the poor, blaming them for their plight and denigrating their efforts. Many poor families live in run down, violent neighborhoods, adding further stress. The rate of single-parent households is high among the poor. If a single parent can find work, it may not pay the bills. Moreover, a working mother must find day care for her children, and good quality day care is hard to find for middle-class parents, let alone the poor. Depression runs deep among the poor.[33] To cope with lack of resources, stress, loneliness, and depression, some turn to alcohol, drugs, or crime. It is hardly surprising that the deprivations of poverty contribute to abuse and neglect of children. What is impressive is that so many poor parents do such a good job raising their kids under such adverse conditions.

Substance Abuse Is a Key Ingredient
in Maltreatment

The relationship between alcohol and drugs and maltreatment is clear.[34] In New York City in the 1850s, Charles Loring Brace of the Children's Aid Society was acutely aware that intemperance was a major culprit. In 1881, the Massachusetts Society for the Prevention of Cruelty to Children (MSPPC) stated, "Our records show that the larger part of the cases brought to our notice have their origin in the use and abuse of intoxicating drinks." A year later, the MSPCC lamented, "So long as men and women drink to excess, parents will be brutal, children will be neglected and will suffer, and so long there will be a necessity for an organization like ours." In 1935, Jacob and Rosamond Goldberg described 1,400 New York City girls victimized by sexual abuse. The Goldbergs wrote, "The problem centers about the man who, under the influence and stimulation of alcohol, seizes upon his young daughter as a readily accessible female to give vent to his overstimulated senses."[35]

Today, approximately 80 percent of families involved with child protective services have substance abuse issues. Unfortunately, substance-abusing parents are often resistant to change.[36] Richard Famularo and his colleagues studied 136 juvenile court cases in which children were removed from parental custody due to serious maltreatment. Famularo wrote, "Cases involving parental substance abuse and/or the more severe forms of child maltreatment are most resistant to treatment interventions ordered by the courts. . . . Courts and social service agencies cannot rely upon the mere fact of court involvement to yield effective interventions or compliance with service plans."[37]

Michael Murphy and his colleagues examined 206 juvenile court cases involving serious child abuse or neglect and found a high rate of parental substance abuse. Substance-abusing parents were significantly less likely to comply with court-ordered services than maltreating parents who did not abuse drugs or alcohol. Murphy and his colleagues concluded:

> Our findings indicate that in cases of serious child mistreatment, parental substance abuse is a pervasive problem which is associated with higher risk of reinjury, recidivism, danger to the child, noncompliance with treatment, and permanent removal of children by the court. . . .
>
> The current consensus among mental health clinicians is that in cases of serious substance abuse, unless this problem is identified and treated, there is very little point in beginning other forms of treatment. Continuing substance abuse has a high probability of undoing other interventions.[38]

The relationship of alcohol to maltreatment is straightforward. Intoxication lowers the inhibitions that keep our baser drives in check. Thus, the "corking fee" for

FIGURE 6.2

A little girl stands next to her father, who has passed out due to intoxication. From Helen Campell, *Darkness and Daylight.* 1892. Hartford, Conn.: A.D. Worthington.

alcohol abuse is violence, neglect, physical abuse, sexual abuse, domestic violence, disability, disease, and death on the road and at home. Drinking to excess is like taking a stupid pill. Yet, Americans love to drink, and many drink too much. "It's Friday night, let's get wasted." Spend a little time on most college campuses and you will appreciate the social importance of alcohol.

In any society, a sign that something is important is the number of words used to describe it. Thus, Alaskan Natives have many words to describe snow. In Ireland, so the song goes, there are forty shades of green. When it comes to alcohol, there are many colloquialisms to describe getting drunk: Tie one on, blitzed, three sheets to the wind, wasted, plastered, smashed, sloshed, all fucked up, snockered, gassed, shit faced, stupefied, glassy eyed, muddled, besotted, hammered, crapulent, juiced, bashed, bombed, loaded, blind, crocked, boozed, looped, hosed, pickled, lit, zonked, drunk as a skunk, soused, high as a kite, on a bender, soaked, tanked, and liquored up. I'm sure I missed some.

Americans are ambivalent about alcohol. We love it and hate it. A "wino" is a bum, but a wine aficionado is sophisticated. We look down our noses at "the sloppy drunk," but we titter as we stand around the water cooler Monday morning describing how we "tied one on Saturday night."

Producers of alcoholic beverages spend billions encouraging young and old to drink. Although children are not allowed to imbibe, television is saturated with advertising that depicts beautiful young people drinking, partying, and having fun. The message is clear, "Grow up and join the party. If you drink, you're cool. If you don't, you're a square." In 2005, the biggest celebrity in NASCAR auto racing was Dale Earnhardt, Jr. It is ironic that Earnhardt, who is one of the world's best drivers, is sponsored by a beer company whose product regularly turns Americans into terrible drivers.

Illegal drugs are less acceptable to Americans than alcohol. Yet, intoxication has the same deleterious impact on behavior, whether the intoxicant is alcohol, drugs, or a combination of the two.

When alcohol or drug abuse sinks to the level of addiction, incompetent parenting is the norm. Children are likely to be neglected, and physical and sexual abuse are common.[39] The best hope for children when one parent is addicted is that the other parent is sober. Abuse of alcohol and drugs is a major cause of maltreatment.

Violence in American Culture

America is violent. Jay Belsky wrote, "Compared with other nations, the level of violence in America can only be characterized as extreme."[40] Jo Ann Farver and her colleagues observed, "Many school-age children and adolescents who live in inner-city neighborhoods have had direct encounters with serious acts of community violence. Consequences of these adverse experiences for children ages 6 to 15 are apparent in reports of moderate, but consistent, associations between violence exposure and symptoms of posttraumatic stress disorder (PTSD), anxiety and depression, conduct disorders, peer-related aggression, and maladaptive cognitive and socioemotional functioning."[41] James Garbarino begins his book *Raising Children in a Socially Toxic Environment* with this observation: "When I talk with American teachers who have been in the field since the 1950s, I often ask them to identify the kinds of discipline problems they used to face. Here's what they come up with: gum chewing, talking back, disorder in the halls, making a mess in the classroom, dress-code violations, and being noisy. When I talk to today's teachers and ask them the same question, their lists read like a police blotter: violence against self and others, substance abuse, robbery, and sexual victimization. Things have changed."[42]

Many aspects of modern American culture have a corrosive influence on children. Millions of kids spend many hours watching TV and playing video games. The constant drumbeat of violence and sex bombarding them is venomous. Children need injections of antitoxin to neutralize the poisonous messages that dominate popular culture. Garbarino describes the impact of growing up in the midst of social poison. "It's not that kids have changed since I was a teenager. It is the social environment in which they live that has changed. . . . It pains me greatly to recognize that boys all over America witness terrifying scenes on television or the movie screen. Although some experts dismiss this as too simplistic an explanation, I am convinced that this is one reason for the spread of lethal youth violence. . . . The evidence linking televised violence to real-life violence is about as strong as the research evidence linking smoking to cancer." Belsky adds, "Central to an ecological perspective on child maltreatment is the assumption that societal willingness to tolerate high levels of violence sets the stage for the occurrence of family violence, one form of which is physical child abuse."[43]

The most potent antitoxin for poisonous popular culture is parental love, support, and discipline. Yet, children need more than parents can provide. Outside the home, children need exposure to stimuli that teach tolerance, nonviolence, empathy, unselfishness, and the importance of children, family, and community. Unfortunately, the powers that control television, movies, and video games are unlikely to produce the antitoxin because they are busy manufacturing the poison. The antitoxin will have to be found elsewhere.

Hitting Children for Disciplinary Purposes
Contributes to Abuse

Most American parents hit their children in the name of discipline.[44] I don't use terms such as "spank" or "paddle" because these terms are euphemisms for assault. Spanking and paddling are rationalizations that allow adults to justify assaulting people who are small and defenseless.

A great deal of physical abuse is corporal punishment that goes too far because the adult is furious and gets carried away.[45] Jill Korbin wrote, "In the United States, the acceptance of physical discipline has been linked to child maltreatment." Roger Byard and Stephen Cohle wrote, "Homicide rates are greatest during infancy and the later teen years. . . . In the infantile pattern, the child is young, the assailant is a parent or carer, death is caused by blunt force, intentional burns, or neglect, and the precipitating event often involves disciplinary action." Jay Belsky added, "Abusive parents are more likely to rely on physical punishment and negative acts as control strategies."[46] David Kolko observed, "The use of harsh parenting may also relate to parental beliefs in the appropriateness of strict physical discipline and having high expectations of children's behavior. Relative to comparison parents, abusive parents have been more accepting of physical punishment and have displayed high and potentially unrealistic expectations of their children's behavior." Cindy Christian noted, "There are many physical injuries that can result when children are spanked by a frustrated parent. . . . Although physical damage is not an end result in most spankings, the danger of corporal punishment lies in its potential for physical abuse." An old children's rhyme from the Shetland Islands reads, "The child will not be quiet, the child will not be quiet. Take it by the leg and hit it against the wall. The child will not be quiet."[47]

Criminal child abuse prosecutions often involve adults who injure or kill children in the name of corporal punishment.[48] In one case an adult maliciously beat an eight-year-old to death just two weeks after the child was released from the hospital following surgery to repair a lacerated bowel that the same adult inflicted by punching the child. At his murder trial, the adult argued he was imposing "reasonable" corporal punishment. In another case, an adult hit his eight-year-old daughter multiple times on the bottom with a board that he swung like a baseball bat. In a third case, an adult immersed a young child in scalding water as punishment. In a final example, a child was punched in the face and beaten with an extension cord in the name of discipline.[49]

Most adults who hit children in the name of discipline do not cross the line into abuse. The problem with corporal punishment is that tolerating the practice at all guarantees that some adults will misuse it, maiming and killing children. Corporal punishment is a major contributor to child abuse.

Sexual Deviance

No one knows why some individuals sexually abuse children. Undoubtedly, there are many reasons. Judith Becker wrote, "In all likelihood, there is not one causative factor, but rather multiple pathways by which a person develops a sexual attraction to minors."[50]

Most sex offenders are men. The Association for the Treatment of Sexual Abusers states, "The vast majority of offenders are male. Studies indicate approximately eighty percent of sex offenses against children are committed by males and approximately twenty percent are committed by females."[51]

Although we do not know what causes sexual abuse, we know it hurts children. (See chapter 5). Fortunately, few victims of child sexual abuse grow up to repeat the cycle. Yet, some do, especially males. Thus, child sexual abuse plays a role in causing further abuse.

Domestic Violence

Slightly more than half the women who are victimized by domestic violence live in households with children under age twelve.[52] It is estimated that more than three million children are exposed to domestic violence every year in the United States.[53] Young children are more likely than older children to be exposed.[54] Many parents who are in violent relationships believe their children are unaware of the violence, but this is usually wishful thinking. Katherine Kitzmann and her colleagues wrote, "Although many parents report trying to shelter their children from marital violence, research suggests that children in violent homes commonly see, hear, and intervene in episodes of marital violence."[55]

A man who beats his wife is apt to beat his child.[56] Lundy Bancroft and Jay Silverman wrote, "Children exposed to batterers are themselves at high risk to become direct targets of physical abuse and of sexual abuse." Studies of the co-occurrence of domestic violence and child abuse indicate a co-occurrence rate of 30 percent to 60 percent. Children are sometimes injured when they try to protect their mother, and even when they do not intervene, children are injured accidentally during episodes of domestic violence.[57]

Witnessing domestic violence isn't good for anyone. Research on the psychological impact on children of exposure to domestic violence began late in the twentieth century, and by the early twenty-first century, more than one hundred studies documented associations between exposure to domestic violence and harmful consequences for children.[58] Carter and colleagues report:

> Exposure to domestic violence can have serious negative effects on children. These effects may include behavioral problems such as aggression, phobias, insomnia, low self-esteem, and depression. Children exposed to domestic violence may demonstrate poor academic performance and problem-solving skills, and low levels of empathy. Exposure to chronic or extreme domestic violence may result in symptoms consistent with posttraumatic stress disorder, such as emotional numbing, increased arousal, avoidance of any reminders of the violent event, or obsessive and repeated focus on the event.[59]

According to Baker and colleagues,

Children living with domestic violence face increased risks for direct victimization. First, they may be accidentally injured because of their close proximity to
their non-offending parent during a violent incident. Young children who are
physically near parents and older children who intervene to stop the violence
may be particularly at risk. Second, children living in a home where domestic violence is occurring are also at greater risk of experiencing neglect, emotional
abuse, sexual abuse and physical abuse. In addition, children may experience victimization if the perpetrator uses them as part of the control tactics employed
against the adult victim.[60]

Children who grow up in violent homes may come to view violence as normal.
Exposure during childhood to domestic violence is a risk factor in adults for depression, low self-esteem, and other trauma-related symptoms. In addition, "Boys
exposed to domestic violence show much higher rates of aggressiveness and bul-
lying toward peers, and both boys and girls show signs of learning to meet their
needs by manipulating, pressuring, and coercing others. . . . Exposure to domestic violence markedly increases boys' likelihood of battering their own partners
when they reach adolescence or adulthood."[61] Linda Baker and her colleagues observed, "Watching, hearing, or later learning of a parent being harmed threatens
the sense of stability and security typically provided by family." Sandra Graham-
Bermann added, "Children can be traumatized by overhearing beatings as well as
by viewing them." Robbie Rossman and her colleagues wrote, "Exposure to repetitive adult domestic violence may be just as traumatic for many young children as
personal experience of maltreatment."[62]

Children of all ages can be harmed by exposure to domestic violence. Babies
can suffer neglect because their battered mother is depressed and preoccupied
with violence.[63] Babies exposed to domestic violence may experience attachment
difficulties. Preschoolers living amid domestic violence manifest problems sleeping, nightmares, eating difficulties, acting out, withdrawal, and somatic complaints including headaches and stomachaches.[64]

School-age children suffer the harmful effects observed in preschoolers.
School-age children from violent homes are also at risk of scholastic and behavioral problems. According to Graham-Bermann, "School-age children raised in
homes with domestic violence are at risk for developing mental problems. Specifically, school-age children demonstrate high rates of internalizing and externalizing behavior problems, low self-esteem, and more difficulties in school than
children raised in nonviolent homes. Children raised in a violent home experience problems in interpersonal relationships, including heightened fear and
worry about those in the home and difficulty establishing and maintaining
friendships outside the home."[65] Some children exposed to domestic violence de-

velop aggressive and antisocial tendencies (externalizing behaviors), while others pull into a shell, expressing fearfulness and inhibition (internalizing behaviors). Some children exhibit symptoms of posttraumatic stress disorder.[66]

Adolescence has rough spots for most teens. Indeed, adolescence is difficult even with supportive, loving parents who help the teen navigate the shoals separating childhood from young adulthood. The passage is more perilous for teenagers growing up in violent homes. Witnessing domestic violence is associated with increased violence by adolescents.[67] Eating disorders such as anorexia and bulimia may set in. Feelings of fear and powerlessness may manifest in delinquency, acting out sexually, substance abuse, and even suicide. Moreover, "adolescence is when children begin establishing intimate partner relationships. They may put into practice the sex roles and communication patterns learned at home."[68]

Exposure during childhood to domestic violence can leave psychological scars that interfere with competent parenting. Thus, domestic violence contributes to child maltreatment.

Mental Illness

Mental illness is usually no impediment to competent parenting. Yet, research discloses that psychiatric illness can interfere with adequate care. Some parents are so depressed they cannot meet their children's needs. Martha Erickson and Byron Egeland wrote, "Maltreating parents have been found to have a high incidence of depression."[69]

Christine Walsh and her colleagues conducted a large study and confirmed the finding of other researchers, "A parental history of psychiatric disorder is associated with an increased risk of child physical and sexual abuse." A relationship exists between child maltreatment and parental disorders of mood, anxiety, and personality. Some abusive parents demonstrate symptoms of dissociation.[70]

Some psychotic parents, particularly those with schizophrenia, are so lost to their illness they cannot care for themselves let alone children. Small numbers of mentally deranged parents kill their children.[71]

In the legal system, cases are legion in which social workers who try to help mentally ill parents are eventually forced to remove children from home and invoke the authority of the juvenile court.[72] In *Matter of M.E.B.*, for example, the single mother of seven children suffered chronic paranoid schizophrenia.[73] The mother's four older children had been removed from her custody in an earlier juvenile court case, and the current case involved her three remaining children, aged six, five, and one. The mother refused treatment for her mental illness. The children suffered severe developmental retardation due to lack of intellectual stimulation at home. The social agencies in the community tried to help, but the mother's paranoia interfered with her capacity to accept assistance. She refused, for example, to send the school-age children to special education classes. The family's apartment was filthy, with clothes scattered everywhere and food rotting on the table. After efforts to help the mother failed, the juvenile court placed the children in foster homes, where they blossomed.

In the case of *In re Andrea G.*, Andrea's mother was diagnosed with schizotypal personality.[74] On one occasion, the mother attempted to draw blood from Andrea's arm, stating that she needed "good blood" from her daughter. Mother encouraged Andrea to eat frozen vomit covered in chocolate sauce. The mother could not maintain employment or a stable home. While Andrea was living in foster care, the mother took Andrea out to dinner, accompanied by a social worker. The mother ordered food for herself but nothing for Andrea until the social worker suggested that perhaps the child should eat. There was no question Andrea's mother loved her. Tragically, this woman's mental illness made it impossible for her to provide competent parenting.

Years ago I practiced law in Utah. My clients were children and adults with mental illness and/or developmental disability, including mental retardation. One day I was asked by a social worker to take a drive with her to visit a young couple with a six-month-old baby. The couple wanted legal advice. The two had lived nearly all their lives in an institution for the mentally retarded. As young adults they fell in love, married, and, with assistance from the county, left the institution and found an apartment. When we arrived at their modest home, father was away at work and mother was home with the baby. We knocked and mother opened the screen door for us. As we went inside, we were overwhelmed with the smell of urine. Numerous used diapers lay scattered about the apartment. Dirty clothes, bags of trash, stale food, and other refuse lay on tables and the floor.

The baby was lying awake in her crib. She was clean and appropriately dressed. What struck us was the expression on the baby's face, or, more accurately, the lack of expression. It was as though her face was made of stone—no emotion at all, no life in those little eyes staring blankly at the ceiling. The social worker picked the child up and cuddled it, but there was no response. No crying, no cooing, no smiling, nothing. I'll never forget it.

What was wrong? The baby was normal, and her parents loved her dearly. Yet, because of mental retardation, this mother and father had no idea how to care for a baby. They dressed and fed her, but they did not interact with her or nurture her. To them she was like a doll. Patricia Crittenden describes what happens when infants are denied essential human contact. "Some parents are so withdrawn that they do not respond to their children at all. Of course, the infants are fed, changed, and moved from place to place. But the contact is infrequent and rarely in response to signals from the infant. In addition, there is little affectionate play or soothing contact between parent and child. Such infants first protest their condition. If, with increasing protest, there is still no parental response, the infants usually give up and become silent, limp, dull, and depressed."[75] In the car on the way back to the office, the social worker and I agreed that to save the baby's life, we had to call child protective services.

When mental illness or retardation robs a parent of the capacity to nurture their child, the state must step in. These are sad cases because the parents are not to blame for their condition, and they love their children. Yet, when therapy or other services prove ineffective or are refused, children must be protected. Thus, mental illness and mental retardation can lead to neglect.

Deliberate Abuse—Face to Face with Evil

The large majority of adults who abuse or neglect children are not evil people. Most maltreating parents love their children and have no desire to inflict serious injury, psychological damage, or death. Yet, some adults hurt children on purpose. A few are psychopaths, and fewer still are sadists who enjoy inflicting pain. Most adults who deliberately hurt children are simply bullies.

One has only to study child abuse cases to see deliberate maltreatment—abuse and neglect that are so far beyond the pale they can only be described as evil.[76] Adults kick and hit children, breaking arms, legs, ribs, and skulls. Weapons used to assault children include fists, feet, boards, wires, and anything else handy. In one of the thousands of intentional abuse cases, Ronnie Midgett killed his eight-year-old son.[77] Midgett weighed 300 pounds. His son was severely malnourished due to Midgett's neglect and weighed 40 pounds. Midgett brutally abused his son over a substantial period of time, repeatedly punching the boy in the stomach and back. When the child died, he had bruises on his lips, head, chin, chest, back, buttocks, abdomen, and hands. His ribs were broken. He bled to death because his father hit him so hard that internal organs ruptured. It is difficult to understand this man's behavior, but it is easy to put the right label on him—murderer.

Adults find myriad ways to hurt children. In one case, a mother and her live-in partner tortured, burned, and starved the woman's five children, killing two of them. In another case, an adult encouraged a teenager to play Russian roulette with a loaded gun. The teen put the gun to his head, pulled the trigger, and blew his brains out.[78] In a third case, a father held a pellet gun next to his two-month-old baby's head and said, "Shut up or I'll shoot you." The baby did not obey, so father pulled the trigger, lodging a pellet in the infant's brain. In another case, a mother prostituted her young children for drug money.[79]

Some children are starved.[80] Others are denied liquids or forced to drink to the point that it kills them. In one case, a baby died of asphyxia when an adult stuffed a bottle in the baby's mouth and squeezed the bottle until milk came out the baby's mouth while the adult pinched the child's nose shut.[81]

Children are poisoned with barbiturates, codeine, arsenic, ipecac, detergent, pepper, sleeping pills, cooking oil, caustic chemicals, acid, and more.[82] In one case, an adult killed a baby by placing massive amounts of salt in the child's formula. In another case, a child was poisoned with caffeine and iodine. In a variant on the poisoning theme, an adult intentionally injected his baby with HIV tainted blood.[83]

To round out this chamber of horrors, one perpetrator inserted needles into the skull, abdomen, or arm of three babies. In another case, adults killed a child by repeatedly putting coins in the child's throat. Another offender repeatedly poked a child with a nail. Still another offender deliberately burned a child with a hair dryer. In one case, the abuser forced a child to stick his hand into the flame of a burning acetylene torch.[84]

Incest is deliberate, intentional abuse. Fathers who engage in incestuous relations with daughters find many ways to rationalize their behavior. All of them know it is against the law, and most feel guilt. Yet, some incest perpetrators feel no remorse at all.

Sexual predators are a frightening lot, and it is among predators that we find the highest numbers of psychopaths and sadists. Predators rape children they lure into traps. Some offenders murder their victims to avoid detection or because the kill is part of the thrill.[85]

It would be easy to list further examples of deliberate abuse, but the point is clear: Some adults do horribly cruel things to children on purpose. Thus, one cause of child abuse is deliberate cruelty—"man's inhumanity to child."

In my experience, some professionals balk at coming to terms with deliberate, intentional abuse. These professionals seem to congregate in the medical and mental health professions and in the halls of academia. Rather than forthrightly addressing the fact that some adults have a mean streak they take out on children, these professionals prefer psychological explanations for abusive behavior. In publications on maltreatment there is a dearth of analysis of deliberate, intentional, mean-spirited abuse. For example, in Jay Belsky's excellent 1993 review of the etiology of physical abuse and neglect, there is little mention of intentional abuse. David Kolko is a leading expert on physical abuse, yet in his exhaustive 2002 review of physical abuse, there is little analysis of deliberate abuse.[86] I have no doubt Belsky and Kolko understand the role of intent in maltreatment, but they and other authorities seldom forthrightly discuss deliberate abuse.

Absence of candid analysis of intentional abuse in the psychological/medical literature leaves a void in discourse about maltreatment. The void is attributable in large measure to the medical model of maltreatment, with its emphasis on illness, diagnosis, and treatment. The medical model so dominates writing and thinking about child maltreatment that it squeezes out unvarnished analysis of deliberate abuse. Moreover, the psychiatric terminology employed by the medical model obfuscates the uncomfortable reality that some abuse is deliberate and some perpetrators are dangerous, evil people.

Overreliance by professionals on the medical model and psychiatric terminology tempts perpetrators of deliberate abuse to evade responsibility by saying, "It wasn't my fault. I have a problem. I'm sick. I need therapy, not time in jail." Another drawback of conceptualizing maltreatment predominantly in medical/ psychiatric terms is that conduct that deserves moral condemnation escapes opprobrium under the guise of mental disorder. Thus, a particular act of abuse might be described two different ways: First, as "intentional, deliberate abuse," or, second, as "difficulty regulating negative affect, accompanied by poor impulse control." Characterizing the act as intentional, deliberate abuse draws the appropriate response of moral condemnation. In contrast, terms like "poor impulse control" deflect attention from individual culpability.

There is great value in seeking to understand the psychological motives of adults who hurt children. It is dangerous, however, to dilute moral responsibility with psychiatric labels that disguise individual culpability behind a psychological mask. Ron Rosenbaum wrote, "It's important to believe in 'conscientious' wickedness—if we don't, then we don't believe in free will or individual responsibility. If we don't believe in ordinary, knowing wickedness, we can't condemn Hitler for anything more than a well-meaning ideological mistake."[87] Child welfare professionals who resist seeing intentional abuse for what it is, and who insist on viewing abuse and neglect exclusively through psychological lenses, dilute the moral authority of society to condemn evil.

Thriving Despite Child Abuse

Some children survive horrible childhoods unscathed.[88] How do they do it? Research on so-called resilient children reveals that many of them have an adult in their life (grandparent, teacher, nonabusive parent) who provides a steady source of emotional nourishment, support, and love.[89] Abigail Gewitz and Jeffrey Edleson wrote, "Studies have elicited several core characteristics of resilient children and their environments—among them competent parenting and healthy attachment relationships, intellectual resources, social competence, and easy temperaments."[90]

Roadblocks to Reducing Child Abuse and Neglect

With the primary causes of child abuse and neglect in focus, it is tempting to say, "Get to work. Fix the problem." If only it were that simple. Unfortunately, there are significant roadblocks to eliminating the causes of maltreatment. Three of the most daunting roadblocks are briefly mentioned below. Other roadblocks are addressed in chapters 7 and 8.

Some Problems Are Just Too Big to Solve, So Why Try?

Some social problems are so complex, so intractable, that they seem to defy solution. Child abuse and neglect is such a problem. Maltreatment has so many intertwined and overlapping causes, especially poverty, that efforts to combat it seem futile. The shear enormity of the problem discourages efforts to solve it. What's the use?

This defeatist attitude impedes efforts to combat maltreatment. There is no gainsaying that child abuse is a tough nut to crack, but so was legalized racial segregation prior to the civil rights movement. Millions of white Americas thought segregation was "Just the way things are. The system may not be right, but there's little point trying to overturn a way of life that has existed for generations. Don't rock the boat." Fortunately, that great boat rocker Martin Luther King, Jr. would have none of it. King and his fellow soldiers of the civil rights movement eliminated all vestiges of legalized segregation. Racism remains a serious problem, but the can-do attitude that propelled the civil rights movement changed America forever.

A similar can-do attitude is required in the fight against cruelty to children. With the persistence and indomitable spirit that motivated "child savers" across time, it is possible to sustain the progress that has been achieved since the rescue of Mary Ellen in 1874. With renewed commitment, further progress is attainable against this heartbreaking personal and societal failure.

The Problem Is Distasteful, Ignore It

Child abuse is disturbing. There are the physically damaged and dead babies, the vacant eyes of unloved children, the tears of sexually abused girls and boys. These images are unsettling and distasteful. It is tempting to turn away, to ignore the problem. Again, this is defeatist thinking. Distasteful and disturbing though it is, child maltreatment is a cancer that must be faced with eyes wide open.

"I'm from the Government and I'm Here to Help"

Americans are ambivalent about government. On one hand, we expect government to solve difficult problems. On the other hand, we don't want the government poking its nose in our business. Two aspects of Americans' love/hate relationship with government have direct implications for efforts to reduce maltreatment. First, Americans are prickly about government intrusion in the family. The right of parents to the custody of their children vis-à-vis the government is considered so important that parental rights are protected by the Constitution. In a line of cases extending back to the 1920s, the U.S. Supreme Court has protected parental rights.[91] Any effort by government to help parents do a better job raising their kids is perceived by some as an attack on the family.

There is a second aspect of Americans' unease with government that impedes progress against maltreatment. Americans have mixed feelings about using tax dollars for social programs, especially for the poor. Not long after the first colonists set foot on these shores, some unfortunate soul was the first to apply for welfare or, as it was then called, "outdoor relief." It is safe to assume that the first application for outdoor relief raised eyebrows and grumbles about "taxes wasted on lazy good-for-nothings." Today, federal, state, and local governments spend billions on social programs benifiting the poor. Yet, the ambivalence of the colonists is alive and well. A sizable segment of Americans believe we spend too much on social programs. Some blame the poor for poverty. Others believe government "hand outs" exacerbate poverty by undermining initiative and breeding dependence. Whatever the motivation, ambivalence about government spending on social programs stands as a roadblock to creating the broad social safety net that would reduce child abuse and neglect.

Conclusion

Child abuse and neglect are complex social problems with multiple, intersecting, and overlapping causes. There are no simple solutions, and there are significant roadblocks to reform. We will never rid ourselves entirely of abuse and neglect. Yet, organized child protection has gained steam for more than a century. Progress has been steady, albeit slow, and today we know enough about the problem to attain higher levels of achievement. The final two chapters of this book outline steps in that direction. Chapter 7 addresses broad societal changes designed to reduce child abuse and neglect. Chapter 8 offers specific recommendations to improve the child protection system.

Implementing the reforms described in chapters 7 and 8 will not be easy. Although further progress will be difficult, child protection is a moral imperative. As Judge Gerald Knight of Washington State remarked before sentencing a father to prison for murdering his four-year-old son, "We may not be able to prevent child abuse, but we have to try. A society that tolerates child abuse is a society doomed to extinction."[92]

7

REDUCING ABUSE AND NEGLECT

The complexity of child maltreatment is addressed in chapter 6. There is no magic wand to waive over the problem, and there are no quick fixes. Ira Schwartz and Gideon Fishman caution, "The history of child welfare is littered with well-intentioned, but largely failed reform efforts."[1] Burton Cohen observed that professionals working to reform child welfare approach the topic from different and, at times, conflicting perspectives. Cohen wrote, "The child welfare situation is not a single 'problem' that can be solved or resolved through analysis or simple cause and effect approaches. It is . . . a complex system of strongly interacting problems. . . . Despite numerous efforts at reform over the past 30 years, the child welfare system continues to defy the attempts of dedicated and well-intentioned reformers."[2]

Given the complexity of the problem and how deeply embedded abuse and neglect are in society, no reform effort will eliminate maltreatment. Even if significant progress is achieved, it will take years. Moreover, progress will be expensive, controversial, and plagued by setbacks. Yet, progress is possible, and the present chapter describes broad structural changes that will reduce child abuse and neglect.

Reducing Poverty

Poverty plays a central role in neglect and physical abuse. Major progress against maltreatment will be difficult until poverty is diminished. Unfortunately, the early twenty-first century is not a propitious time to campaign against poverty. Indeed, poverty appears to be getting worse.[3]

Poverty is one of those social problems that seems to defy solution. The Bible states, "For the poor will never cease out of the land" (Deuteronomy 15:11). Jesus is purported to have said, "For you always have the poor with you" (Matthew 26:10). It is easy to become fatalistic about poverty and succumb to the belief that so little can be done that there is no point trying.

The apparent insolubility of poverty is one problem. A related problem is that most middle- and upper-income Americans don't care enough about poverty to insist on change. Most of us who are fortunate enough to live in comfort focus our energy on our busy lives, our families, and our communities. We may feel sorry for the poor, but we are insulated from them and their dilemma. As we wait in line at Starbucks for our double mocha latte, we watch poor people push shopping carts down the street, but they live in a different world.

Americans think of themselves as generous, and in many respects we are. When it comes to the poor, however, American generosity goes only so far. Many Americans have a deep-seated belief that the poor are to blame for their predicament. Common sentiments include, "This is the land of opportunity. If you're poor in America, it's because you're lazy." "I work hard for my money, and I don't intend to share it with people who won't show a little initiative." "If people are poor, they have no one to blame but themselves." Such attitudes are centuries old and show no sign of eroding. Moreover, many Americans believe welfare and other programs to help the poor make matters worse by breeding dependence.

Thus, poverty is a constant in American culture, and many Americans think there is little that can be done about it. Quite a few Americans believe the remedies of the past—welfare—made things worse. Given this state of affairs, what would it take to cause Americans to rethink their attitudes about poverty and to take meaningful steps to combat the problem? Unfortunately, the answer is a crisis. Nothing of significance is likely to reduce poverty until there is a crisis that threatens the social stability of middle- and upper-income Americans.

Two momentous crises of the twentieth century support the conclusion that it will take a crisis to bring meaningful progress against poverty. First, the Great Depression of the 1930s spurred creation in 1935 of the Social Security Act. The Depression disrupted life at all social levels, and it took this threat to the economic stability of the nation to generate support for the social programs of the Social Security Act. The second twentieth-century crisis that led to reductions in poverty was a crisis of conscience—the civil rights movement. Martin Luther King, Jr.'s moral teachings about the injustice of racism pricked the conscience of white America. When cities burned in race riots, the twin impacts of Dr. King's nonviolent message and violence in the streets forced a reluctant Congress to pass civil rights legislation and to support President Johnson's War on Poverty from 1964 through 1968. The War on Poverty contributed to reduce poverty. For a decade after 1964, poverty declined, reaching a low of 11 percent of the population in 1974. Unfortunately, the War on Poverty was interrupted by the war in Vietnam, and national attention shifted from social issues to war. As attention shifted overseas, efforts to help the poor eroded, and poverty crept up.

Today, thirty-six million Americas are poor. For children, the poverty rate in 2003 approached 18 percent. More than half of preschool age children in single parent families are poor. Surely, these figures constitute a crisis of sufficient magnitude to stir the nation to action, don't they? Commentators on the child welfare system think so. In her book on race and child welfare, Dorothy Roberts descries the "persistent gap in the economic status of Blacks and whites that shows in unemployment, poverty, and income. . . . The statistics are dismal. Black families are three times as likely as whites to be poor." Elizabeth Bartholet also writes compellingly, "The families in trouble, in which children are threatened with abuse and neglect, and from which children are removed to foster care, are disproportionately poor, and they come disproportionately from racial minority groups." Lee Rainwater and Timothy Smeeding lament, "A significant percentage of American children are still living in families so poor that normal health and growth are at risk." Duncan Lindsey writes, "If many [children] are despairing, suffering from poverty and disease, especially in the midst of plenty, not only are we as guardians called into question, but a warning is sounded for our society as well."[4]

The ugly reality of poverty stares us in the face. The effects of poverty on child development are palpable. The relationship of poverty to maltreatment is clear. Yet, America isn't listening. The impashioned writing of scholars is read primarily by other scholars, generating little interest outside the academy. (A similar fate may await the present volume, although hope springs eternal.) Apart from professionals directly involved in child welfare, there is no sense of crisis. Why not? The explanation is quite simple. At this point, poverty is not making life uncomfortable for middle- and upper-income Americans. The privileged members of society feel little pressure to do anything about poverty. Although poverty may be up, violent crime (which *is* a concern to the well-to-do) is down. The economy struggled from 2000 through 2004, but slowly picked up steam during 2005, and appears to be on the mend. The War on Terror is real and preoccupying. Poverty, on the other hand, is off the radar screen. What's more, the people directly affected by poverty have no political clout to leverage the issue onto the national stage. In 2006, and for the foreseeable future, progress against poverty is unlikely.

Given the lack of motivation to reduce poverty, there is little hope in the near term for three programs that exist in other developed nations and that would reduce maltreatment: a universal children's allowance, universal child support for one-parent families, and universal health coverage.[5]

Universal Children's Allowance

Duncan Lindsey advocates a universal children's allowance paid by the government. Lindsey writes, "For families in Europe and other industrialized countries, the children's allowance is an important part of their income and is responsible for protecting the economic viability of many poor families. Children's allowance programs, which recognize the financial burden that parents have in raising children, take the form of direct payments to every family for their children and are applied universally, from the poorest families to the wealthiest."[6]

There are at least three reasons why a universal children's allowance won't fly in America. First, the program will be perceived as too expensive. Second, although middle- and upper-income parents might be happy to accept government largess, they don't need it. Third, because middle- and upper-income parents don't need an allowance, the program will be pared down to the poor, and as soon as that happens, universal children's allowances are doomed because they will be perceived—correctly—as welfare. With the adoption in 1996 of the Temporary Assistance to Needy Families program, Americans got rid of "welfare as we know it." Americans are in no mood to resurrect welfare under a different name.

Universal Child Support

Numerous European nations guarantee child support for single-parent families when fathers cannot or will not pay. Lee Rainwater and Timothy Smeeding write that in Europe, "the well-being of the child and the mother is usually the foremost value, and the absent father's willingness and ability to pay are of secondary concern. In these countries full child support is guaranteed by governments." Along these lines, Duncan Lindsey recommends what he calls "advance maintenance payments" to provide financial support for single parents.[7] Single parents would receive child support payments from the government. To fund the program, the tax system would be altered so that noncustodial parents pay additional taxes withheld from their income.

Universal child support is a nonstarter. Critics warn against creating another large, inefficient government bureaucracy. Other critics point out that millions of noncustodial fathers have no or little income that is taxable to support the program. As a result, universal child support is simply welfare.

Universal Access to Health Care

Women who receive regular prenatal care have healthier babies. Infants and children who see the doctor and dentist on a regular basis are healthier. Good health allows children's brains and bodies to develop optimally and facilitates academic and social success. When kids are healthier, parents are happier. Poverty, however, deprives many children of access to essential health, dental, and mental health care. The Census Bureau reported that in 2003, forty-five million Americans were without health insurance. As you would expect, poor people are particularly likely to lack health coverage. About eight and a half million poor children have no medical insurance.[8]

Giving poor children access to health care is a moral imperative. Moreover, getting kids to the doctor will reduce child neglect and abuse. Families where maltreatment occurs are often socially isolated. Routine medical care, whether provided at home by visiting nurses or at a clinic, is a means to break through the isolation and connect struggling parents with essential services and support. Americans trust physicians and nurses, and medical professionals are uniquely situated to prevent maltreatment before it happens and to detect it when it is occurring.

Given the importance of medical care to child development and reduced maltreatment, isn't it time for universal health coverage? Polls indicate that a majority of Americans believe some form of help is necessary for people lacking health insurance. Timothy Jost notes, "All other developed nations of the world, including developed countries in Western Europe, Asia, North and South America, and on the Pacific Rim, provide health care for all or most of their residents. . . . No other developed country relies on private insurance as does the United States to provide primary coverage for its population. All developed nations have recognized that voluntary private insurance cannot cover everyone (as it does not in the U.S.) and have developed some form of public health insurance."[9]

Despite the need for universal health coverage, it is not presently in the cards. There may be popular support to help the uninsured, but there is no consensus on how to do it. Some advocates want a government-funded and operated system similar to England's National Health Service or Germany's social insurance model. Opponents of health care operated or funded by the government are strident and well financed. Opponents include those who believe in private insurance and free markets.[10] The free marketers have the status quo on their side. In the battle over insuring the uninsured, the opposing forces are at loggerheads, with few signs of compromise from either camp. As a result, America lags behind most of the developed world in providing health care for its citizens.

Universal health coverage is unlikely in the near term. Given this reality, what course is open for those concerned about helping poor children and reducing maltreatment? The best advice is to abandon hope of major new federal programs in the health care arena and to focus on maintaining and strengthening existing programs, particularly Medicaid. Efforts are needed to increase the reimbursement rate to professionals who treat Medicaid patients. The rates are so low that doctors, dentists, psychologists, and other health care providers find it difficult to serve Medicaid patients.[11] Additionally, initiatives are required to enroll Medicaid-eligible children who are not currently in the program. Although the twin goals of improved reimbursement rates and greater enrollment will be difficult to attain, they are realistic ones that will improve the lives of millions of children.

Significant progress against poverty—including universal health care—is unlikely in the near future. For this reason, efforts to reduce child abuse and neglect are more profitably focused elsewhere. The remainder of this chapter describes reforms that hold promise for reducing maltreatment.

Home-Health Visiting for Young Children

Home visiting is not a new idea. Use of "friendly visitors" was well established in the nineteenth century. Charles Loring Brace, Etta Wheeler, and thousands of other "charity workers" visited the poor in their own homes. In 1973, Henry Kempe testified before Congress and pleaded for home health visitors. Kempe stated, "We suggest that a health visitor call at intervals during the first months of life upon *each* young family and that she become, as it were, the guardian who would see to it that each infant is receiving his basic health rights. . . . The system must be equalitarian rather that being directed just towards the poor."[12]

Home visiting holds real potential to reduce child abuse and neglect. Regular visits from a knowledgeable outsider give new parents the skills they need to succeed. Many new parents are poorly equipped for the challenges of parenting, and a home visitor provides support, encouragement, basic information on child development, and a shoulder to lean on. Poor single parents are often socially isolated, and a home visitor has unmatched opportunities to erode the isolation and connect the parent with other parents and with outside support systems. The goal is to make parenting successful and rewarding. Jay Belsky reported:

> In two separate, prospective studies of at-risk mothers followed from the postpartum period, it was found that parents with histories of maltreatment who did not maltreat their own children (during the study period) had more extensive social supports, had experienced a nonabusive and supportive close relationship with one parent while growing up or were more openly angry and better able to give a detailed coherent account of their earlier abuse than were repeaters. . . . The common denominator in all of these inquiries seems to be emotionally supportive relationship experiences that function (apparently therapeutically) to modify, presumably, the feelings and expectations of these women.[13]

Today, hundreds of home visitation programs are at work across America.[14] Empirical research on home visiting discloses successes and failures.[15] Research suggests that home visiting by nurses is particularly effective. David Olds and his colleagues compared the impact of home visiting by paraprofessionals versus home visiting by nurses and found that nurses consistently outperformed paraprofessionals. Olds wrote,

> It is reasonable to ask whether paraprofessionals have legitimacy in the eyes of families during pregnancy and infancy. Nurses are likely to have engagement and persuasive power with pregnant women and parents of young children because

pregnant women have natural concerns about complications of pregnancy, labor and delivery, and care of newborns with which nurses are viewed as authorities. Paraprofessionals probably lack this natural legitimacy. Moreover, nurses are rated by the public as having the highest honesty and ethics standards of all professionals.[16]

Olds and his colleagues studied the impact of nurse home-visiting on a sample of low-income single white women living in a semirural area near Elmira, New York. Compared with women who were not visited by nurses, pregnant women visited by nurses reduced their use of tobacco and improved their diets. After childbirth, women visited by nurses experienced fewer pregnancies, had fewer problems with alcohol or drugs, had greater success finding employment, and relied less on welfare. The children whose mothers were visited by nurses had fewer injuries and experienced lower rates of neglect and abuse.[17]

Olds and his colleagues replicated the Elmira study in Memphis, Tennessee, with a sample of poor, urban, African-American single parents. They found enduring effects of a home visitation program on the lives of urban black women. Although the results were smaller in magnitude than those achieved in a trial with semirural white women, the direction of the effects was consistent across the two studies.[18]

Home visiting is not a panacea. Mark Chaffin, Barbara Bonner, and Robert Hill studied a broad range of home-visiting and family support programs and found mixed results. Moreover, regardless of the home-visiting model used, when a home is infected with domestic violence or substance abuse, the benefits of home visiting are reduced or eliminated.[19]

Home visiting, especially *nurse* home-visiting, is a proven method that improves the lives of low-income mothers and children. What's more, home visiting is an easy sell compared with children's allowances, universal child support, and universal health coverage, which are perceived by many as budget-busting welfare programs. There is evidence that nurse home-visiting actually saves money.[20] So long as home visiting remains a voluntary service that parents can accept or reject, home visiting need not be politically divisive and should find support across the political spectrum.

Yet, if home visiting is voluntary, won't the parents who need it most reject it? Yes. For that reason, Elizabeth Bartholet argues home visiting should be mandatory. Bartholet writes, "The most dysfunctional families are the families for whom the surveillance aspect of home visitation is most important. If home visitors had the right to be present in such families on a regular, ongoing basis, they could not only help those parents capable of being helped, but could in addition protect those children at greatest risk against harm, both by virtue of their presence in the home, and their ability to trigger more interventionist action by CPS authorities."[21]

Although I sympathize with Bartholet's concerns, home visitation will founder if it is mandatory. Home visiting is effective in part because parents view it as a helping-hand rather than as a strong-arm tactic. Most struggling parents are receptive to genuine, nonauthoritarian offers of help. But if parents view the home visitor as a spy for child protection or the police, trust will be hard to come by. If nurse home-visiting is mandatory, nurses may lose the unique entree they have into homes with babies. Finally, mandatory home visiting is likely to be so contentious that political opposition will kill it. Nearly all experts agree that home visiting should be voluntary, and they are right.

But what of children in dangerous homes where parents refuse home visitation? I'm afraid we will have to content ourselves with the existing child protection system, which responds to suspicions of maltreatment as they arise. On balance, more maltreatment will be prevented with voluntary home-visiting than will be detected with mandatory visiting.

Subsidized Day Care for Children of Working Parents

Babies and little children need constant, nurturing, interactive care from parents and from caretakers who love them. Parents know this and want to be with their children. Yet, in many two-parent families, both parents work to make ends meet. In single-parent families, work is the norm, and parents who don't work and who subsist on public assistance are not so subtly urged to find a job. The Children's Defense Fund noted, "In 2002, 64 percent of mothers with children under age six and 78 percent of mothers with children ages six to 17 were in the labor force."[22]

For working parents, day care is critical. Unfortunately, many poor parents don't have good day care for their children. Hundreds of thousands of children bide their time in inadequate day care or are left at home with little or no supervision. Advocates for children and for the poor must continue lobbying for subsidized high-quality day care.

Head Start

The War on Poverty began in 1964 and ended in defeat in 1968. Of the many programs of the War on Poverty, one of the few to survive is Head Start. Born in 1965, Head Start is a child development and school readiness program for poor children from birth to age five. Numerous studies have examined Head Start and research generally finds that the program does a good job. The Children's Defense Fund reports, "Head Start is a high quality comprehensive program that helps America's poorest children overcome the disadvantages of growing up in poverty while engaging their parents in the process."[23]

Unfortunately, Head Start is underfunded and underenrolled. In 2003, the Head Start budget was 6.5 billion dollars, a substantial number, but not enough. There are some four million poor children under age five in the United States, but Head Start serves fewer than one million. The Head Start budget should expand, and efforts should redouble to enroll eligible children.

Rebuilding a Sense of Community

Americans worry that we are losing our sense of community, our desire to get involved, and our willingness to extend a helping hand. In his book *Bowling Alone: The Collapse and Revival of American Community*, Robert Putnam makes a persuasive case that the late twentieth century witnessed a loss of community. Yet, Putnam is optimistic. He writes, "It is emphatically not my view that community bonds in America have weakened steadily throughout our history—or even throughout the last hundred years. On the contrary, American history carefully examined is a story of ups and downs in civic engagement, *not just* downs—a story of collapse *and* of renewal."[24] According to Putnam, it is possible to reverse the decline in community and to strengthen our sense of interdependence. Stronger, more connected communities help struggling parents and lower the amount of child abuse and neglect.

The Annie E. Casey Foundation is working with child welfare professionals and community leaders across the United States to implement a program called "Family to Family."[25] The program strengthens community support for struggling parents and endeavors to keep children safe at home.

In the 1990s, the U.S. Advisory Board on Child Abuse and Neglect emphasized the importance of strong communities to child safety. One member of the advisory board, Gary Melton, is leading an effort in South Carolina to prevent child maltreatment by strengthening communities. With funding from the Duke Endowment at Duke University, Melton and his colleagues at Clemson University are implementing The Strong Communities Initiative. The initiative

is built on the research premise that, to be effective, child protection must become a part of everyday life in the neighborhoods where children live, study, and play. For children to be safe and families to be strong, they must be able to count on others noticing family needs and reaching out for help. If children at greatest risk are to be protected, a standard of mutual assistance must be built for all families. . . . Strong Communities seeks to build, strengthen, and renew community norms of neighbors' helping each other and watching out for their own and their neighbors' children. . . . In effect, Strong Communities is designed to give new strength to the application of the Golden Rule in the participating communities as they care for their youngest members. The initiative reflects the developers' belief that every family and every child should be confident that someone will notice and someone will care whenever they have cause for joy, sorrow, or worry.[26]

Hopefully, this experiment, and others like it, will bear fruit.

Child protection social workers may have unwittingly contributed to the deteriorating sense of community. As child protection became a specialized field within social work, child protection agencies withdrew from the communities they served and set up shop in government buildings far removed—physically and psychologically—from clients. Social workers venture forth to investigate reports, then scurry back to the office for paperwork. Ensconced in the safety and order of government buildings, it is easy to lose touch with the people who need help. Fortunately, social workers are increasingly realizing that the isolation of the office is comfortable but ineffective. Child protection agencies across the country are placing social workers in community centers, schools, and similar locations. Child protection professionals are building relationships with citizen groups and community leaders, replacing years of distrust with a sense of shared responsibility for children. Increasingly, child protection professionals realize they cannot protect children alone and that child protection requires the coordinated efforts of government agencies, private organizations, concerned citizens, churches, and many others.[27]

Return of social workers to the communities they serve may not herald the rebirth of the settlement house movement of the late nineteenth and early twentieth centuries, but it is a step in that direction. Wouldn't it be wonderful if the leadership that emanated from the able minds of Jane Addams, Grace and Edith Abbott, Julia Lathrop, Sophonisba Breckenridge, and other settlement house pioneers blossomed anew?

Hitting Children Should Be Outlawed

Long ago under Roman law a husband had the right to beat his wife for disciplinary purposes. The husband's right to physically "chastise" his wife was carried forward to England and then to America. In several American states, early court decisions authorized chastisement of a wife with a stick no thicker than the husband's thumb, giving us "the rule of thumb."[28] By the middle of the nineteenth century, the "right" of chastisement had disappeared from American law. Today, it seems absurd that the law once allowed a man to beat a woman to "keep her in line."

If a husband's right to physically chastise a wife seems barbaric, why is a parent's right to physically chastise a child less so? One might answer, "Because women are adults." True. The law does not allow adults to assault each other. Then why is it acceptable to assault children? A child is smaller, more vulnerable to injury, and less capable of flight or fight than an adult. Yet, under American law, parents have the right to assault their children. If you hit my five-year-old, you go to jail. If I hit her, I'm a law-abiding citizen.

The traditional explanation for this remarkably unequal treatment is that parents need to assault children in the name of discipline. If you are among the majority of Americans who believe hitting children is necessary for discipline, keep in mind that not so long ago some men thought it necessary to hit women for discipline. In light of what we know today about children and about discipline, there is no greater justification for hitting children than there was for hitting women.

There is mounting evidence that hitting children for disciplinary purposes is not benign and that it has deleterious consequences for some children.[29] Clifton Flynn wrote, "Recent studies have suggested that a host of potentially harmful behavioral and psychological consequences may result from so-called 'ordinary' physical punishment. These negative outcomes include alcohol abuse, depression, suicidal thoughts, behavioral problems, low achievement, and future economic insecurity." Mary Eamon added, "Regardless of the child's age, gender, or race/ethnicity, physical punishment was related to children's socioemotional problems." Murray Straus and Glenda Kaufman Kantor studied the association between corporal punishment during adolescence and later mental health problems. Straus and Kantor wrote, "Corporal punishment in adolescence is associated with a significantly increased probability of depressive symptoms as adults." Adults who were physically punished as teenagers are more likely to think about suicide and more likely to abuse alcohol. Straus and Kantor found, "The more corporal punishment the subjects experienced when they were teenagers, the greater the risk that they will go beyond ordinary corporal punishment to acts that are severe enough to be classified as physical abuse" with their own children.[30]

Fifty years ago, many parents used belts, switches, and paddles to "wallop" children. By the last quarter of the twentieth century, societal views on hitting children were in flux, and such methods were increasingly viewed as excessive. Toward the end of the century, experts increasingly urged parents to abandon corporal punishment altogether. In the fortieth edition of his famous book *Dr. Spock's Baby & Child Care*, Benjamin Spock wrote in 1985, "In olden days, most children were spanked, on the assumption that this was necessary to make them behave. In the twentieth century, as parents and professionals have studied children here and in other countries, they have come to realize that children can be well behaved, cooperative, and polite without ever having been punished physically."[31] In 1998, the American Academy of Pediatrics concluded that the negative consequences of spanking outweigh any benefits and urged pediatricians to help parents find "methods other than spanking in response to undesirable behavior." In 2000, T. Berry Brazelton and Stanley Greenspan wrote, "Physical discipline, such as hitting or spanking a child is no longer an acceptable alternative to discipline. Discipline means teaching, *not* punishment. Physical punishment is not respectful and is bound to undermine the child's self-image. Anger may be stored up to be worked out later. In addition, we are living in a violent society and using violence to settle an issue is saying to a child 'This is the way we deal with things.

Violence is the way to handle frustration or anger.' We cannot afford such a message any longer."[32]

In 2002, Elizabeth Gershoff reviewed the literature on corporal punishment and concluded,

> At its worst corporal punishment may have negative effects on children and at its best has no effects, positive or negative. . . . The defining aspect of corporal punishment, and indeed the key to its potential for securing short-term compliance, is that it involves inflicting pain on children. Even proponents of corporal punishment argue that it should be painful. As a country, Americans need to reevaluate why we believe it is reasonable to hit young, vulnerable children when it is against the law to hit other adults, prisoners, and even animals. The difficulty of drawing the line between physical abuse and corporal punishment begs the question[:] Why should we risk harming our children when there are a range of alternative methods of punishment and discipline?[33]

In 1979, Sweden became the first nation to prohibit corporal punishment by parents. Julian Roberts reported, "Published evaluations have concluded that the Swedish law achieved its stated goal of changing public attitudes toward corporal punishment."[34] Lack of physical assault by parents has not caused Swedish children to run amuck. Since Sweden's bold move, the following nations have abolished physical chastisement: Austria, Croatia, Cyprus, Denmark, Finland, Germany, Israel, Iceland, Latvia, and Norway. Other countries are considering the issue.

Hitting children for purposes of discipline is increasingly viewed as outmoded, unnecessary, and harmful. Jay Belsky noted, "Children remain the only people in this country whom it is legal to strike." Nations that have abolished hitting have not experienced harmful effects. Millions of American parents refuse to assault their children in the name of discipline, and most research indicates their children are better off as a result. These reasons are more than sufficient to outlaw hitting for discipline. But these are not the only reasons to ban corporal punishment. There is strong evidence that physical abuse often results from corporal punishment inflicted by adults who believe they have a right to hit kids.[35] Several of the countless punishment-gone-wrong cases were described in chapter 6. Here's another. Linda Smith and her two-year-old daughter Amy lived with David Foster. One day, Amy refused to sit on the couch to eat a snack. Linda became angry, took the child to her room, spanked her, and slapped her face. Linda continued hitting Amy, knocking her to the floor. David joined in the "discipline." Eventually, Linda knocked Amy backward and she hit her head on a door. Later that night, Amy died. In the name of discipline, but in the heat of irrational anger, Amy was murdered.[36] Thousands of other children suffer bruises, lacerations, black eyes, fractures, burns, head injuries, and death due to corporal punishment.

We have to change the idea that it is acceptable to hit children. It is no more acceptable to hit your child than it is to hit your spouse, your employee, or the guy next to you at the bus stop. In the latter three scenarios you'd be arrested and hauled off to jail. Children deserve the same protection. Outlawing corporal punishment will begin the long process of helping adults understand that hitting those we love is not acceptable. Banning corporal punishment will reduce child abuse.

Alcohol

The abuse of alcohol causes so much misery that an outright ban on the stuff would do a world of good. Prohibition failed once, however, and the prospects for successful prohibition in the future are zero. Most people drink, and millions enjoy getting drunk. The problem is that while people are drunk, they often maim and kill. Alcohol is inextricably tied to neglect, physical abuse, and sexual abuse of children.

Although it is not possible to ban alcohol, it is possible to change the way people think about drinking. Fifty years ago, smoking was considered benign, cool, even healthful. In 1964, however, the Surgeon General issued his famous report on the link between smoking and cancer. Since then, smoking has come to be seen for what it is, a dangerous addiction that hurts not only the smoker but also those nearby. Although millions of Americans light up, millions more say, "No thanks. Why would I do that to myself?"

When it comes to alcohol, America is exactly where it was fifty years ago with smoking. Drinking is perceived as a harmless pastime to be enjoyed with friends. When friends or family have "one too many," most of us wink and look the other way. We need to change our perception of drinking. Consuming alcohol, like smoking, is dangerous to the imbiber and those nearby. Getting drunk—which is a goal for millions—is like standing blindfolded at the edge of a cliff. Even when getting drunk is not the goal, having one drink too often turns into "one too many," and when that happens people get hurt. The message should be that drinking, like smoking, is dangerous and can be deadly. If fewer adults drank, many fewer children would be abused, neglected, and killed.

Toward a Less Toxic Society

Child abuse and neglect are reinforced by a popular culture that inundates children with corrosive, toxic messages glorifying violence and denigrating empathy, compassion, and connection with fellow creatures. Parents are the most effective antitoxin for this poison. Yet, parents need help. The help will not come from the media moguls who produce the toxin, although pressure on the media to clean up its act is worthwhile. Nor should help for parents come from the censor. We cannot relinquish our freedom of speech in the name of a more civil society.

The factory that will produce the antitoxin for poisonous popular culture is the public school. I realize the schools are overburdened. Too often, when there's a problem with kids, people turn to the educators and say, "You fix it." But I'm not asking educators to take on a new assignment. Teachers are already working to instill the values kids need. What educators need is more resources to fulfill this vital aspect of their mission.

When the goal is preventing child abuse and neglect, I have a specific recommendation for the public schools: *bring back home economics, and make the boys attend.* I daresay many readers will brush off this suggestion as trivial, even silly. But they are wrong. It is in classes that used to be called home economics that teenagers have the opportunity to learn what it means to parent.

When I was in high school, boys went to shop class and girls went to home economics where they learned to cook, sew, and prepare for motherhood. In shop, boys learned to build a cabinet, tear down a carburetor, and lie about sex. Today, of course, things are different (sort of). Gender stereotyping is reduced, and girls-only home economics is now gender-neutral family and consumer studies. Yet, the students in family and consumer studies classes are mostly girls. It's pretty daring for a high school boy to attend, although some teachers and schools are able to attract respectable numbers of boys.

Classes in family and consumer studies provide a golden opportunity to prevent child maltreatment. These classes expose high school students to material on child development, parenting, appropriate disciplinary practices, the risks of hitting children, and the horrible damage associated with shaking babies.[37] Every high school student in America should learn this material, and family and consumer studies classes are the place to teach it.

Textbooks used in high school family and consumer studies classes discuss child abuse. Thus, Verna Hildebrand's *Parenting: Rewards & Responsibilities* tells young people, "The abuser may know little about child development and expect too much of a child. . . . If anger is a problem for you, do yourself and your child a tremendous favor and seek professional help." Holly Brisbane's *The Developing Child: Understanding Children and Parenting* has up-to-date material on child abuse. Brisbane tells students, "When you are handling a baby or young child, never-ever-shake or jiggle him or her. These actions are dangerous. Every year thousands of babies suffer serious problems due to shaken baby syndrome."[38] Verdene Ryder and Celia Decker's *Parents and Their Children* has a strong section on child abuse. Ryder and Decker caution readers, "*Never* shake [a baby]. . . . The key to preventing Shaken Baby Syndrome is to educate parents about the dangers of shaking a child. Another step is to teach parents to cope with their baby's crying."[39] Ryder and Decker offer commonsensible strategies to cope with a crying baby.

Teachers of family and consumer studies at the high school and university levels should put their heads together to devise techniques to overcome the resistance of boys and some girls to engage in learning basic information about child development and parenting. Holly Brisbane is correct when she writes in her textbook for high schoolers, "Many family problems, including child abuse, are directly related to poor parenting skills and to a lack of knowledge about child development. Classes like the one you are taking help give parents—and future parents—realistic ideas about what parenting involves."[40]

When you think of professionals focused on child abuse you think of social workers, physicians, nurses, judges, lawyers, and mental health professionals. You don't think of Ms. Jones, the family and consumer studies teacher at the local high school. Yet, Ms. Jones and thousands of teachers like her across the country are ideally situated to help teenage girls and boys—especially boys—understand the joys and tribulations of parenthood. Child abuse and neglect will be reduced when kids enroll in Ms. Jones's family and consumer studies class.

Fighting Deliberate Abuse and Neglect

Most parents who physically abuse or neglect their children want to do a better job. With support, many can be helped. Our system of child protection must extend a helping hand to parents who have stumbled. Yet, as we strive to help struggling parents, we must remember that some adults hurt children on purpose. Those who inflict deliberate abuse are not ill. They are criminals. Producers of child pornography, for example, should be hunted down and imprisoned. Scoundrels who traffic in children for purposes of commercial sexual exploitation deserve to rot in jail. The same fate should await sexual predators who target children. Prison is also a good home for adults who intentionally inflict serious injury or death on children.

Conclusion

The purpose of this chapter is to describe reforms in American culture, customs, and laws that will improve the lives of children and reduce abuse and neglect. At this point in our history it is not possible to take a significant bite out of poverty. We *can*, however, strengthen Medicaid, subsidized child care for working parents, and Head Start. In addition, the time is right to expand home visitation programs that utilize nurses. Venturing into the homes of parents with new babies is in the finest tradition of public health nursing. The nurse visitor helps parents adjust to their new role, pierces the isolation that traps so many poor families, and gives parents a much needed pat on the back and words of encouragement.

Many will strongly disagree with the recommendation to outlaw hitting children. I realize I'm swimming upstream here, but I'm right. Not because I'm an expert on corporal punishment, but because those who are—Spock, Brazelton, Greenspan, the American Academy of Pediatrics—understand that hitting children to teach a lesson does more harm than good. So much child abuse results from discipline gone awry that if we curtail hitting in the name of discipline we will markedly reduce physical abuse. The lawmakers of Sweden were prescient in 1979 when they banned hitting. Other countries are following Sweden's lead, and America should not miss this opportunity to reduce maltreatment. It is time to abandon a practice that hurts children and is as outmoded as hitting your wife to teach her a lesson.

If I'm swimming upstream when I advocate an end to hitting children, I'm drowning and going under for the third time when I urge Americans to rethink their attitude toward drinking. Yet, I'm compelled to make the argument. Drinking leads so often to drunkenness, and drunkenness leads so often to disaster for children, adults, and society that we need to see drinking for what it is: A dangerous indulgence that causes incalculable economic, emotional, and physical harm. Drinking is not benign. It is dangerous and it hurts children.

Finally, I implore educators to accept responsibility for inoculating children against the toxic popular culture. In particular, I urge teachers and leaders in the field of family and consumer studies to step up to the plate and fulfill their mission of preparing young people for parenthood. Find ways to get more high school students, especially boys, to attend and take seriously semester-long courses on child development and parenting.

If we want reduced child abuse and neglect, we are off to a good start when we support Medicaid, subsidized child care, Head Start, nurse home-visiting programs, an end to hitting in the name of discipline, a new and negative mind set about alcohol, and an expanded role for educators in family and consumer studies. Child maltreatment will not go away if these reforms are implemented, but children will be safer.

8

IMPROVING THE CHILD
PROTECTION SYSTEM

Broad structural changes designed to reduce maltreatment are addressed in the previous chapter. Even if such changes are implemented, it will not be possible to prevent all abuse and neglect. Thus, it is critical to improve the existing child protection system. The present chapter makes specific recommendations to strengthen child protection. The chapter begins with discussion of funding the child protection system. After examining the purse strings, analysis shifts to proposals by a number of experts on how to improve child protection. The remainder of the chapter discusses the lingering effects of racism, the need for more focused leadership in child welfare, creation of a less adversarial child protection system, modification of child abuse reporting laws, strengthening foster care, and improving the juvenile court.

Giving New Meaning to the Word Byzantine:
Funding Child Welfare

The full spectrum of child welfare services—hot lines, investigation, services to keep families together, courts, substance abuse and mental health treatment, efforts to return children to their parents following removal, foster care, adoption, and more—is paid for with a patchwork of federal, state, and county dollars reaching into the billions.[1] The funding structure is labyrinthine, requiring mastery of such arcane matters as Titles IV-B and IV-E of the Social Security Act, the Temporary Assistance to Needy Families Program (TANF), the Child Abuse Prevention and Treatment Act (CAPTA), Food Stamps, Supplemental Security Income, the federally financed child support program, Medicaid, the State Children's Health Insurance Program (SCHIP), the Child Care Development Fund, the federal substance abuse grant, the federal mental health grant, the federal family violence grant, the Community Services Block Grant, the Social Services Block Grant, and more. And that's just the federal programs. Every state has its own funding streams, laws, and regulations governing child welfare. Child welfare administrators know this territory well and spend much of their time traversing the money maze and patching together funding streams to keep the system afloat.

Services at the front end of child protection—hot lines, investigation, services to children and families in their own homes—are paid for largely from state and local funds, although limited federal dollars are available through the Child Abuse Prevention and Treatment Act, Medicaid, Temporary Assistance to Needy Families, Title IV-B of the Social Security Act, and other federal programs. The courts, including juvenile courts, are paid for almost entirely from state and local funds.

The federal government's largest financial contribution to the child welfare system relates to foster care. Title IV-E of the Social Security Act provides about half the cost of foster care, with states and counties picking up the rest. Unfortunately, Title IV-E dollars have not kept pace with rising costs, and foster care funds are eroding. Of equal concern, because Title IV-E provides millions of dollars for children in foster care, the title has the unintended effect of incentivizing states to keep children in foster care. The Pew Commission on Children in Foster Care reported, "Simply put, current federal funding mechanisms for child welfare encourage an over-reliance on foster care at the expense of other services to keep families safely together and to move children swiftly and safely from foster care to permanent families."[2]

Examination of federal, state, and local funding for child welfare and, more broadly, social services for the needy, reveals three noteworthy facts. First, the funding structure gives new meaning to the word "byzantine." During the seventy years since passage of the Social Security Act in 1935, social welfare programs emerged haphazardly from Congress and state legislatures as political will crystalized to support new initiatives. Although efforts are made to harmonize new programs with those already on the books, the effort is never fully successful. As a result, the system is so complex, with so many programs, so many funding sources, and so many requirements (some of which conflict or overlap), that billions are wasted on administration.

The time has arrived for a major overhaul of social welfare financing in the United States. A more streamlined, coherent system will cost less and provide more. In 2004, the Pew Commission on Children in Foster Care published recommendations to improve the funding mechanisms for child welfare.[3] Other organizations and experts are working on the issue, and the prospect of simplified funding mechanisms for child welfare may be on the horizon.

The second fact to emerge from examination of child welfare funding is that spending on child welfare is not up to the task. Of course, this is not news. Child protection has never been adequately funded. From the earliest days of organized child protection, professionals struggled to find money for the work, and the struggle continues. The truth is, the causes of child abuse and neglect are so complex, so varied, and so deeply embedded in our culture, that it is unlikely sufficient funds will ever be available. Funding for child welfare competes with national defense, the War on Terror, roads, bridges, commerce, agriculture, education, and myriad other priorities. Nevertheless, advocates for children must continue lobbying for all the money they can squeeze out of legislatures. Money will not eliminate child abuse and neglect, but it is essential for effective child protection.

The third noteworthy fact about funding for child welfare is that although funding is inadequate, it is substantial. The Urban Institute calculated that in 2002, more than twenty-two billion dollars was expended on child welfare programs.[4] The extent of these expenditures is not lost on politicians, making it awkward to ask for more. The reaction of many lawmakers and members of the public is, "Do a better job with the billions you have before you come asking for more." There is more than a kernel of truth to the critique that child welfare is inefficient and wasteful. It is incumbent on child welfare administrators to increase efficiency and accountability.

Proposals by Various Scholars to Improve Child Protection

A number of experts on child welfare, as well as the U.S. Advisory Board on Child Abuse and Neglect, have developed proposals to improve child protection. Several of these proposals are noted in the following sections.

Duncan Lindsey's Bright Line Separating
Neglect from Severe Abuse

In his 2003 book *The Welfare of Children*, Duncan Lindsey noted that the core functions of the child welfare system—foster care, adoption, child protection—are predicated on the "residual perspective," in which services are offered *after* problems arise. Lindsey argues that the residual perspective prompts social workers to devote their energy to crisis intervention and thus shortchanges prevention. According to Lindsey, child welfare was transformed from a system that offered a broad range of services into a system focused almost entirely on investigating allegations of abuse and neglect and removing children from homes. Lindsey wrote, "Over time the child welfare system became a crisis intervention service where only the most seriously harmed children received attention. The needs of families that did not require the child to be removed would have to wait."[5]

Lindsey offers a proposal to reverse what he sees as "the complete transformation of public child welfare from a system serving a broad range of disadvantaged children into one designed primarily to protect children from battering and sexual assault." Lindsey hopes to return to a system in which "child welfare social workers would be freed to return to the duties for which they are most qualified—providing effective and needful services to impoverished and disadvantaged families." To that end, Lindsey recommends drawing a bright line separating neglect from severe physical and sexual abuse. Lindsey wrote, "In the last two decades child abuse and child neglect problems have converged into a combined category of 'child abuse and neglect' or 'child maltreatment.' This approach has led to conceptual confusion. By blending these two fundamentally different problems, we have diminished our ability to deal effectively with either."[6]

Under Lindsey's proposal, severe physical abuse and sexual abuse become the responsibility of law enforcement—police investigate and prosecutors prosecute. Child welfare social workers have little to do with severe physical abuse or sexual abuse. Neglect, on the other hand, is the bailiwick of social workers. According to Lindsey, "Child neglect requires the compassionate ear and helpful hand of the social worker."[7] With their focus on neglect, Lindsey believes social workers will be able to substantially reduce the current emphasis on investigation and adversarial confrontation with parents.

Lindsey's effort to separate severe physical and sexual abuse from neglect, and to earmark one for police and the other for social work, won't work. First, it is incorrect to say that professionals confuse "child abuse" with "neglect." Indeed, one of the notable accomplishments of the twentieth century was the gradual disentanglement of neglect, physical abuse, and poverty.[8] If there is confusion, it is not because the field lacks satisfactory categories, but because the categories overlap. Often, the same child is physically abused *and* neglected, sexually abused *and* physically abused, neglected *and* psychologically maltreated. It is unrealistic to attempt to draw clear lines between categories.

Another problem with Lindsey's proposal is that it does not sufficiently acknowledge that physical abuse is on a continuum of severity from mild to severe. Lindsey does not propose prosecuting every parent who hits a child or leaves a bruise. That is why Lindsey's proposal refers only to "severe" abuse. But what are we to do with children whose physical abuse falls short of severe? Are these children—some of whom are in danger—the responsibility of the police or child welfare?

As with physical abuse, Lindsey's proposal does not sufficiently acknowledge the continuum of severity regarding neglect. Some neglect is criminal. Most isn't. Some neglect is the proper domain of police, some the territory of child welfare, and some the shared turf of law *and* social work. Neglect is not divisible into neat, water-tight compartments.

The lines separating severe from nonsevere and criminal from noncriminal maltreatment are often blurred. In many cases, it is impossible to tell the degree of severity until an investigation occurs. With this uncertainty in mind, the question becomes, What government agency should receive and investigate reports of physical abuse? If all investigations of physical abuse are the responsibility of police, with no or little involvement from child welfare, then the police will do what they are good at: look for evidence of crime, interrogate suspects and victims, and make arrests. Is this the optimal response to physical abuse? I doubt it. With intrafamilial abuse, I prefer the system in place today, in which reports of abuse are routed to police *or* social workers *or* both. When appropriate, social workers and police conduct joint investigations. In many cases it is quickly apparent that the police are not required, and they bow out and let social workers take over. I believe it is all to the good when social workers and police put their heads together to reach balanced decisions that are appropriate to the situation.

Lindsey deserves applause for his effort to make the child welfare system as effective and responsive as possible. Unfortunately, the effort to draw a clear line separating severe abuse from neglect, and assigning the former to law enforcement and the latter to social work, will not work.

Although I disagree with Lindsey on his proposal to shift severe physical abuse and sexual abuse to law enforcement, I agree wholeheartedly with him that a major roadblock to reducing maltreatment is poverty. Lindsey offers farsighted ideas for combating child poverty (see chapter 7), in which he recommends universal children's allowances, improved collection of child support, and what he calls "Child Future Savings Accounts: Social Security for Children." If the political winds shift enough to allow progress against poverty, Lindsey's ideas will have greater currency than they do today.

Leroy Pelton Cuts the Gordian Knot

In his 1989 book *For Reasons of Poverty*, Leroy Pelton argued that a child welfare agency cannot simultaneously help and investigate troubled families. Pelton asserted that the incompatibility of the investigative and helping roles is a "major reason for the failure of the child welfare system in this country." Pelton argued that *all* investigative aspects of child protection should be removed from child welfare and turned over to police. Legal definitions of child abuse and neglect should be narrowed so police investigations are limited to cases of "severe harm or endangerment resulting from clearly deliberate acts or gross abdication (deliberate or not) of parental responsibility."[9]

Pelton asserts that under appropriately narrow definitions, the vast majority of reports will be defined as child welfare problems rather than legally cognizable abuse or neglect. As a result, most reports will go to social workers who will respond nonpunitively. Investigation by police will be necessary only in a small percentage of serious cases.[10] When police do investigate, Pelton argues they should refer cases to juvenile court rather than file criminal charges.

Under Pelton's proposal cases requiring coercive intervention in families are handled by the juvenile court, not child welfare. Decisions about removing children from home, placing children in foster care, monitoring out-of-home placements, and terminating parental rights are made by the juvenile court with assistance from social workers employed *by the court*. According to Pelton, ridding child welfare of all investigative and coercive functions will allow social workers to help troubled families. Pelton wrote:

> Social workers are trained to help. That is what they go into the profession to do, and that is what they do best. The investigative role is not even taught in social work schools. We must create an agency structure in which social workers, when going into the home in child welfare cases, can say "I'm here to help," and truly mean it, with the resources to do it, and without the nagging overtones of role conflict and role ambiguity. The discovery, investigation, and judgment of individual culpability and wrongdoing is another matter entirely, and is the province of law enforcement agencies and the courts. By entangling two distinctly different roles, we have not only diminished our ability to deal firmly and effectively with true unlawful behavior, but have tied the hands of social workers in their efforts to effectively serve the child welfare policy of family preservation. . . . My primary objective here is to clear the way for the public child welfare agency to become a nonpunitive, noninvestigatory, nonplacing agency that will be a true advocate for and "friend" to families experiencing child welfare difficulties.[11]

Under Pelton's plan, child welfare will "no longer be perceived as a threat to families." Parents will feel safe approaching child welfare for help. The number of children in foster care will decline because "we would no longer be sending an army of investigators out to 'substantiate' questionable charges of child abuse and neglect and to make placements for which there is questionable need." The army of investigators will be transformed into an army of family advocates who will reduce the need for foster care.

Pelton's proposal is broader than Lindsey's. Lindsey made an effort to separate severe abuse from neglect and to assign investigation of severe abuse to police and investigation of neglect to child welfare. Pelton cuts the Gordian knot by divesting child welfare of *all* investigative functions.

Is Pelton right? Possibly. It is a bold proposal. But I question the wisdom of transferring all investigative functions to law enforcement. During the late twentieth century, efforts to protect children became too punitive. Pelton's proposal could exacerbate the punitive response by injecting the police into *all* cases requiring investigation. Pelton would likely reply that his primary objective is protecting children, not punishing parents, and that under his proposal the police will turn cases over to the nonpunitive juvenile court rather than to criminal prosecutors.

Pelton's goal is worthy, but if we entrust investigation to police, criminal prosecution is precisely what we'll get. This is not a criticism of the police; it's simply a fact. The police are in the business of detecting crime, making arrests, and laying the groundwork for punishment through the criminal justice system. That's their job. If we want nonpunitive solutions for selected cases of child abuse and neglect, the police are ill-suited for the job. What we need is social workers. We are better off with the model in which social workers and police officers work together, pooling their different but overlapping perspectives and expertise.

I agree with Pelton that the overarching goal is "protection of the child, not punishment of parents." Yet, I question his proposal to send all cases requiring investigation to juvenile court. Some maltreating parents require a criminal justice response, not referral to juvenile court. The best way to determine which parents should be arrested and which ones referred to juvenile court is for police officers and social workers to put their heads together in joint investigations.

In the final analysis, the question is: Is it wiser public policy to take a law enforcement or a social work approach to investigating suspicions of child maltreatment? When the New York Society for the Prevention of Cruelty to Children was established in 1875, Elbridge Gerry opted for the law enforcement approach. It didn't take long for others to point out the weaknesses of the law enforcement approach and to call for a blend of social work and legal action, with the emphasis on social workers conducting investigations and helping families. Eventually, supporters of the social work approach gained the upper hand. Pelton throws down the gauntlet. He argues that the century-long experiment with social workers simultaneously investigating and providing services is a failure that must be abandoned in order to save child welfare.

Elizabeth Bartholet Advocates Adoption

In 1999, Elizabeth Bartholet published *Nobody's Children: Abuse and Neglect, Foster Drift, and the Adoption Alternative*. Like Duncan Lindsey, Leroy Pelton, and others, Bartholet understands that substantial reductions in abuse and neglect require structural changes in American society that reduce poverty. Although Bartholet sees reduced poverty as the ultimate solution, she is realistic. She understands reduced poverty is not on the horizon, and she is unwilling to sacrifice children while America waits for social reform.

Bartholet challenges staunch advocates for keeping families together. She argues that too much emphasis is placed on trying to preserve families that are beyond repair. According to Bartholet, "There is no evidence that the treatment and other parent-support services which may be offered in the most serious abuse and neglect cases are helpful in reforming parents and protecting children." Bartholet believes the child welfare system needs to move aggressively to place more children in adoptive homes. She writes, "The evidence is clear that adoption works, and that it is the best of the available alternatives for children who have been subjected to abuse or neglect. . . . What matters is that the children get into homes where they can thrive."[12]

To free children for adoption, Bartholet favors early termination of parental rights when prospects for successfully rehabilitating parents are slim. As for concerns that intervention and termination of parental rights fall disproportionately on people of color, Bartholet writes, "Even if state intervention appears likely to have a disproportionate impact on poor and minority group parents, we need to act. Children, like their parents, come in black and brown skins, and suffer the ravages of poverty. We should not refuse to protect them from child maltreatment simply out of fear that this will have a discriminatory impact on their parents."[13]

Bartholet focuses particular attention on the impact of parental substance abuse on children, writing, "Seventy to eighty percent of the CPS caseload consists of cases in which a parent's substance abuse plays a role." Bartholet warns against returning children "to parents whose first love is their drug." For Bartholet, it is unconscionable that thousands of children languish in foster care while their drug-abusing parents are given repeated opportunities to kick the habit. Bartholet writes, "In cases in which the parents had a serious history of substance abuse, or a history of child abuse or neglect, and there was no good reason to believe that they were now committed to and capable of succeeding in rehabilitative efforts, CPS could move immediately to terminate parental rights, placing the child in the meantime in a pre-adoptive home." Bartholet believes parents must be held accountable and that the state should intervene more rather than less often. Bartholet wrote, "If we want to protect children from abuse and neglect, the case for intervening more aggressively both before and after such maltreatment occurs is strong."[14]

Bartholet believes there is a large pool of potential adoptive parents. According to Bartholet, this pool has not been tapped because adoption on a large scale has never been viewed as a viable option for abused and neglected children. Moreover, so much time is wasted attempting to redeem irredeemable parents that when parental rights are finally terminated, too many children are too old and too damaged to attract adoptive parents.

Bartholet has been criticized for her doubts about preserving families and for her advocacy of adoption. Dorothy Roberts, for example, wrote, "Proponents of the shift away from family preservation claim that increasing adoptions is the best way to reduce the foster care population. . . . This is a false hope. There are not enough people wishing to adopt to absorb the high volume of children already pouring into foster care." Martin Guggenheim accused Bartholet of shortchanging the rights of parents and ignoring the complexities of adoption.[15] In response, Bartholet fired back:

> The evidence indicates that adoption can and does work for children who are damaged and for children who are older. These children do have extraordinary needs. Most of them are far more likely to find the extraordinary parenting they require to overcome their history and heal their injuries in the adoptive parent population than in the families that subjected them to abuse and neglect, or in temporary foster care, or in institutional care. . . . Adoption critics point to the adoption disruption statistics [i.e., adoptions that do not work], but given the damage that so many foster care children have suffered, the fact that only roughly 10 percent of the adoptions out of the foster care system disrupt should be seen as a mark of the success achieved in these adoptive relationships. . . . But can adoptive families be found for today's population? Adoption skeptics say no. . . . The reality is that we have done more to drive prospective parents away from the foster care system than to draw them in. We could expand the existing parent pool by recruiting broadly; now we recruit on the most limited basis. We could socialize prospective parents in ways that would open their minds to the idea of parenting children born to other parents and other racial groups, and children who have physical and mental disabilities; for the most part we now do just the opposite. . . . Ours is a society that glorifies reproduction, drives the infertile to pursue treatment at all costs, socializes them to think of adoption as a second-class form of parenting to be pursued only as a last resort, and regulates adoption in a way that makes it difficult, degrading, and expensive. We could instead encourage not only the infertile but the fertile to think of adoption as a normal way to build their families. . . . Adoption skeptics say that whites are not interested in adopting the children in the foster care system. But we have done little to recruit adoptive parents among the relatively privileged white middle class. Instead we have told them that they may not be allowed to adopt children of color who make up roughly two-thirds of the foster care group, and that they are guilty of racial genocide if they try. . . . Race does matter to many adoptive parents in today's world. But our state welfare agencies have been telling adoptive parents that race *should* matter. . . . It is obvious that many whites would adopt from the foster care system if only we would eliminate the racial barriers, as the federal government's [Multiethnic Placement Act] now commands be done. If we were to affirmatively socialize whites to believe that they *should* consider adopting children of color we could expect to increase the numbers of potential adopters exponentially. . . . We know that children require nurturing environments to thrive today and to have promising prospects for tomorrow. Common sense, confirmed by research, tells us that children who are severely abused and neglected will do best if removed and placed permanently with families where they will receive the kind of nurturing likely to help them recover from their wounds. Common sense, confirmed by research, tells us they would do better yet if we moved them when abuse and neglect were first manifest. This does not mean that in all cases of severe abuse and neglect we should

immediately terminate the parents' rights and move children on to adoption. But it does mean that we should consider immediate termination of parents rights in many more cases and place a much higher priority on prompt adoptive placement.[16]

Elizabeth Bartholet has not given up on a future with less poverty and greater racial justice. Her point is that if we spend all our time gazing into the future, we turn a blind eye to children suffering right now. These children need our help today, not a decade from now. Bartholet believes it is morally wrong to sacrifice children's happiness on the altar of family preservation. Abused and neglected children deserve a future, and for many children adoption is that future.

Bartholet's proposal to significantly increase adoption of abused and neglected children holds great promise and is attainable. Indeed, the past several years witnessed substantial gains in adoption of abused and neglected children in foster care, and Bartholet's book and advocacy for adoption played a role in that accomplishment.

U.S. Advisory Board on Child Abuse and Neglect

The U.S. Advisory Board on Child Abuse and Neglect was created by Congress to evaluate and report on the child protection system. The board issued four reports between 1990 and 1993 that amounted to an indictment of the system.[17] Gary Melton, an influential member of the board, wrote, "The Board determined that the system was *fundamentally* flawed. . . . There was catastrophic failure in every part of the child protection system—a failure that resulted from errant design and that amounted in sum to a 'moral disaster.' "[18] Board members believed that the reformers who advocated for mandatory reporting in the early 1960s did not foresee the huge number of reports that overwhelmed the system. According to the board, four errors led to the failure of late twentieth century child protection:

> First, public policy has been driven by the response to the wrong question. With the focus on investigation as a prelude to court action and, ultimately, separation of maltreated children from abusive or neglectful parents, the policy debate has focused on the question, "Under what circumstances is coercive government intervention justifiable to protect children?" This question tends to elicit legalistic discussion about the definition of abuse and neglect, the standards for gathering and introducing evidence about parental behavior, and the relative strength of rights of parents and children. Remarkably little discussion occurs about the far broader question, "What can government and social and neighborhood institutions do to prevent or ameliorate harm to children?". . . .
>
> Second, the idea that "doing something" about child maltreatment means initiating an investigation has become ingrained among professionals and the pub-

lic. As a result, policymakers disturbed by the crisis in child protection commonly fail to look beyond the "solution" of hiring more CPS workers, and the professions and the public as a whole generally do not assume responsibility for action to protect children.

Third, in the same vein, at least in part because investigation has been primarily the function of CPS, child maltreatment has been identified as a social service problem, perhaps as a result, other sectors of the child protection system— elements that are necessary to address the multiple dimensions of the problem of child abuse and neglect—often have been absent from active involvement in planning the implementing of a response.

Fourth, the narrowness of the question and the responsibility assigned has contributed to the lack of comprehensive, conceptually coherent planning in the child protection system.[19]

The board concluded that the child protection system had become too focused on investigation and coercive intervention in families. The board wrote:

The most serious shortcoming of the nation's system of intervention on behalf of children is that it depends upon a reporting and response system that has punitive connotations, and requires massive resources dedicated to the investigation of allegations. State and county child welfare programs have *not* been designed to get immediate help to families based on voluntary requests for assistance. As a result, it has become far easier to pick up the telephone to report one's neighbor than it is for that neighbor to pick up the telephone to request and receive help before the abuse happens. If the nation ultimately is to reduce the dollars and personnel needed for investigating reports, more resources must be allocated to establishing voluntary, nonpunitive access to help.[20]

The board recommended a move away from what it perceived as a fixation on adversarial investigation and toward what it called a child-centered, family-focused, and neighborhood-based focus on prevention. Melton and colleagues summarized the board's five-part strategy.[21] First, neighborhoods across America must be strengthened physically and socially to create safe and healthy places for children and families.[22] Second, services to families must be relocated to the communities where they are needed. For example, prevention and treatment programs should be integrated into neighborhood institutions such as schools, where they are more visible and accessible. Third, improved government leadership is necessary in child welfare policy. Fourth, it is important to advocate for change in national values, including less tolerance for violence as a means to resolve disputes. Fifth, it is necessary to increase research into the causes of child maltreatment and into programs that are effective at preventing abuse and neglect.

I share the advisory board's belief that more must be done to establish voluntary, nonpunitive access to help for troubled parents. Unfortunately, in its zeal to condemn the child protection system, the board made mistakes of its own. First, the board exaggerated the extent to which child protection is in crisis. Child protection is not on its deathbed. Despite faults, the system rescues thousands of children from maltreatment.

The source of the board's second mistake is found in its antipathy for legal intervention in the family. The board's antagonism for legal intervention led it to undervalue the role of law in child protection. The board was too grudging in its willingness to concede that there will always be an important role for investigation, coercive intervention in families, and litigation in juvenile and criminal court.

Summary Regarding Reform Proposals

The reforms offered by Duncan Lindsey, Leroy Pelton, Elizabeth Bartholet, and the U.S. Advisory Board on Child Abuse and Neglect are valuable. One theme that ties them together is the stark reality that significant progress against physical abuse and neglect will be difficult while poverty remains high. Unfortunately, substantial progress against poverty is unlikely in the short term. Solutions that have a realistic chance of success will have to be found elsewhere.

Lingering Effects of Racism

For much of American history child welfare services were overtly racist. African-American children were excluded from many orphanages.[23] As mother's pensions became available after 1911, many localities refused pensions to African-American mothers. Today, overt racism is much reduced, but the legacy of stereotyping persists.

Children of color are overrepresented in the child welfare system, especially in foster care. Many committees, commissions, and scholars have drawn attention to the racial disparities in child welfare. Dorothy Roberts, for example, in her book *Shattered Bonds: The Color of Child Welfare*, focuses on the child welfare system's disparate treatment of African-American children and families. Roberts attributes part of the problem to the high poverty rate among African Americans. Beyond poverty, Roberts argues the child welfare system remains racist. She writes, "I have come to the conclusion that race does influence child welfare decision making. Child welfare workers and judges find it easier to break up Black families than any other families. But even without definitive proof of racial bias on the part of these individuals, it is accurate to say that the overrepresentation of Black children in the child welfare system results from racism." Roberts does not claim that large numbers of child welfare workers are intentionally racist. Rather, she asserts that negative stereotypes about African-American parents influence social workers and judges "whether they realize it or not. . . . Race must move to the center of public debate about changing the child welfare system."[24]

Like other observers, Roberts understands that significant progress against child maltreatment is unlikely without structural changes that reduce poverty and racial inequality. She writes,

> An overwhelming body of research on the negative effects of poverty on children tells us that generous public support of child welfare would drastically reduce cases of child abuse and neglect. . . . The ingredients for a strong child welfare program are clear and simple: first, reduce family poverty by increasing the minimum wage, instituting a guaranteed income, and enacting aggressive job creation policies; second, establish a system of national health insurance that covers everyone; third, provide high-quality subsidized child care, preschool education, and paid parental leaves for all families. Increasing the supply of affordable housing is also critical.[25]

Roberts is correct that these ingredients are "clear," but they are not "simple." The structural changes Roberts and others (myself included) wish for— guaranteed income, universal health coverage—are controversial in the United States and are not currently in the cards.

"Who's in Charge Here?" No One
Is at the Helm of Child Protection

In the fight against cancer, doctors are in charge, assisted by allied scientists. Politicians and industry fund research. As for the fight against crime, law enforcement takes the lead, supported by a range of disciplines dedicated to preventing crime and rehabilitating offenders. Again, politicians provide money. When it comes to child abuse and neglect, however, no one is in charge, and lack of leadership is undermining progress.

When organized child protection began in 1875, the profession of social work did not exist. Employees of societies to prevent cruelty to children were "agents," not social workers. But by the early twentieth century, social work was coming into its own and social workers were increasingly in charge of child protection. This picture remained static until 1962, with publication by pediatrician Henry Kempe of the battered child syndrome. During the 1960s and 1970s, physicians carved out leadership roles in child protection, sharing the spotlight with social work. Indeed, given the high prestige of medicine compared with social work, physicians more or less pushed social work out of the spotlight. The 1980s and 1990s witnessed significant growth in criminal prosecution of child abuse, particularly sexual abuse. Simultaneously, there was an expansion of lawyers in juvenile court. Lawyers made their own bid for leadership, and once again a high prestige profession muscled in on social work. If pediatricians pushed social workers out of the spotlight, lawyers shoved them to the edge of the stage. Finally, psychologists and psychiatrists made their way onto the now-crowded stage to treat victims and perpetrators. Mental health professionals nudged social workers across the proscenium and into the orchestra pit.

Medicine, law, psychiatry, and psychology do not claim to have all the answers. Yet, given their power and prestige, physicians, lawyers, and psychotherapists assumed increasingly dominant roles in policymaking and writing on abuse and neglect. Few professionals acknowledged this power shift away from social work. Indeed, the words on everyone's lips during the closing years of the twentieth century were "interdisciplinary cooperation," "shared responsibility," and "multidisciplinary teams." Interdisciplinary cooperation became the mantra of child protection. The reality, however, was that social workers continued to carry the laboring oar in day-to-day child protection, while physicians, lawyers, and mental health professionals dominated public discourse. Consider, for example, the U.S. Advisory Board on Child Abuse and Neglect. The chairperson was a physician. The vice-chair was an attorney.

There is nothing wrong with interdisciplinary cooperation and shared leadership. Indeed, interdisciplinary cooperation is essential for effective child protection. Unfortunately, leadership in child protection has become so fragmented that no one is in charge. Recall the old saying, "Too many chefs spoil the broth." In child protection today, there are too many chefs. Although child protection requires interdisciplinary cooperation, the field cries out for one profession to carry the overall banner of leadership. That profession is social work. Yet, social work has been relegated to the back seat.

Why should social work lead child protection? Because responding to maltreatment means responding to poverty, social dislocation, violent neighborhoods, breakdown of community, mental illness, substance abuse, criminal behavior, ignorance, and neglect. The professions of medicine, law, psychology, and psychiatry are too narrowly focused for the task. Only social workers are equipped by training, experience, and breadth of mission to respond fully. Only social work has the assessment, referral, intervention, monitoring, and prevention skills to provide the comprehensive response needed to combat child abuse and neglect. Unfortunately, at this juncture, social work is not up to the task.

To spearhead the charge against abuse and neglect, social work must once again produce leaders like Jane Addams, Julia Lathrop, Grace and Edith Abbott, Carl Carstens, Sophinisba Breckenridge, Vincent De Francis, and Florence Kelley. These pioneers ceded nothing in influence and creativity to medicine or law. Where are the leaders of social work for the twenty-first century?

There are thousands of talented social workers in child protection. Many of the most skilled are administrators in state and county departments of social services. Although these dedicated professionals move mountains to help children and families, government bureaucrats hesitate to take the kinds of courageous public stands that Jane Addams and her colleagues were famous for. Unless social workers in high-level government positions are free to speak their minds, leadership will not come from this quarter. Given the nature of bureaucracy, the necessary freedom of speech is unlikely to materialize, and innovative leadership cannot be expected from government social workers.

Nongovernmental organizations devoted to child welfare provide important leadership. In particular, the Child Welfare League of America (CWLA), the American Humane Association (AHA), and the Children's Defense Fund (CDF) make valuable contributions. Yet, with the exception of Marian Wright Edleman of the Children's Defense Fund (who happens to be a lawyer), it has been many years since nongovernmental organizations produced leaders the likes of Carl Carstens, who directed CWLA during the 1930s, and Vincent De Francis, who headed up the Children's Division of AHA from 1954 to 1977. Today, leadership in child protection is not coming from nongovernmental organizations.

If leadership in social work is not forthcoming from government bureaucrats or nongovernmental organizations, that leaves academia. A new generation of leadership in social work must come from the academy. Yet, I see little interest from social work educators in taking the bold steps necessary to improve child protection. It is true that many teachers of social work are passionate about children. Yet, too few academic social workers venture beyond the classroom and the research journals into the world of politics and public policy where the battle must be waged. Social work will not regain its position of leadership until academic social workers throw themselves into the political maelstrom as their predecessors did a century ago. Social work education must produce more professors like Richard Gelles, who combined scholarship—*The Book of David: How Preserving Families Can Cost Children's Lives*—with lobbying and testimony before Congress to change public policy on child protection.[26]

What children need from academic social workers is greater political advocacy and agitation. Only when social workers *force* other professionals, politicians, and policymakers to accord them equal status in the arena of ideas, policy, and politics will social work reclaim the mantle of leadership.

A final aspect of social work education requires mention—that is, brain drain. In most social work schools, students can select between two tracks, a clinical track and an administration/social service track. Students on the clinical track study to become psychotherapists and counselors, whereas students pursuing the administration track find their way into public and private agencies, including child protection. Should social work schools be in the business of training psychotherapists? In 1994, Harry Specht and Mark Courtney published a provocative book titled *Unfaithful Angels: How Social Work Has Abandoned Its Mission*, in which they wrote,

> We believe that social work has abandoned its mission to help the poor and oppressed and to build community. Instead, many social workers are devoting their

energies and talents to careers in psychotherapy. A significant proportion of social work professionals—about 40 percent—are in private practice, serving middle-class clients. . . . For the most part, professional associations of social workers and schools of social work are active participants in the great transformation of social work from a professional corps concerned with helping people deal with their social problems to a major platoon in the psychotherapeutic armies. . . . Social work is in a position to become little more than another mental health profession.[27]

Psychotherapists and counselors are in short supply, and clinical social workers provide much of the therapy that is vital for victims of trauma, domestic violence, abuse, and neglect. Thus, clinical training for social work students is legitimate. Yet, the attraction of clinical work is a drain on the social work profession, drawing many talented young people into the lucrative and prestigious world of psychotherapy and away from helping the poor.

How can this brain drain be stemmed? Social work educators must grapple with the issue. It is their responsibility to contribute more effectively to the production of graduates who *want* careers in child protection and related fields. Social work schools should place less emphasis on clinical training and devote more resources to classes and opportunities in public administration and service. There is a federally funded program that provides tuition assistance to social work students preparing for careers in child welfare, and Congress is considering bills to forgive student loans for graduates who enter child protection and remain in the field.[28] Social work deans should lobby for these and similar programs.

Social work educators can't do it all. Before child welfare will attract and retain more bright young social workers, the pay and working conditions of child protection workers must improve. In 2003, the U.S. General Accounting Office (GAO) published a study of working conditions in child welfare agencies.[29] The GAO confirmed that many child welfare agencies pay such low salaries that it is difficult to recruit and retain talented professionals. Add highly stressful and sometimes dangerous working conditions, responsibility for life and death decisions, crushing caseloads, insufficient training and supervision, and endless paperwork and it's a wonder anyone makes a career of child protection.[30] The General Accounting Office reported, "Turnover of child welfare staff—which affects both recruitment and retention efforts—has been estimated at between 30 percent and 40 percent annually nationwide, with the average tenure for child welfare workers being less than 2 years.[31] Brenda Smith reported, "Estimated turnover rates range as high as 23% to 85% per year, varying substantially among local agencies."[32]

Cash-strapped CPS administrators find creative ways to improve training, working conditions, and supervision for workers. What administrators don't deal with however (because they have little power to do so) is the real issue: Child protection workers are underpaid. In 2004, the average annual salary of CPS social workers was $35,553. In many communities, teachers (who are notoriously under-paid) make more than CPS social workers. It is not uncommon for social workers, who are burned out on CPS (but not their love of children), to abandon social work and enter teaching.[33] Not only do they make more money, they have fewer pressures, and, oh yes, summers off!

Social workers are not only underpaid, they have an inferiority complex. Too many social workers view themselves as members of a second-rate profession, somehow beneath medicine, psychology, and law. For their part, many physicians, psychiatrists, psychologists, lawyers, and judges share the low opinion of social work.

There is a hierarchy among professionals in child protection, and social work is at the bottom. Given the hierarchy, it is ironic that when you examine the day-to-day responsibilities of the various professions involved in child protection, social workers have far and away the most difficult job. Indeed, compared with what so-ciety demands of the average CPS social worker, being a judge, psychologist, or pediatrician is easy. Yet, CPS social workers are the least respected and lowest paid of the relevant professions. It is no wonder CPS has difficulty keeping its best and brightest.

Undercompensation and underappreciation of CPS social workers, coupled with unmanageable caseloads, seriously undermines child protection. It is no ex-aggeration to say children are hurt and killed because society refuses to pay social workers what they're worth. There is no more important issue facing child pro-tection today than better pay for social workers. We can't afford to pay CPS social workers what they're worth, of course, because the best of them are priceless, but until we substantially raise their pay and the status of their profession, there isn't a chance social work will reclaim its leadership role in child protection.

As a symbolic first step toward reclaiming leadership and shedding the inferi-ority complex that hobbles social work, the name of the state agency in charge of child welfare should be changed from the Department of Social Services to the Department of Social Work. We have state departments of justice, health, and mental health, and it is time for the *State Department of Social Work*. Naming the agency after the dedicated professionals who work there is an overdue sign of respect.

A Less Adversarial Child Protection System:
Differential Response

A key to improving child protection is to make it less adversarial. Struggling par-ents are more likely to accept help from social workers if they don't feel threat-ened. It is not possible to eliminate all elements of adversarial confrontation from child protection which, by its nature, involves uninvited and, more often than not, unwanted intervention. Yet, concrete steps can be taken to make child protection less adversarial.

Leroy Pelton comes closest to a nonadversarial child protection system with his proposal to strip child welfare of *all* authority to investigate reports, to remove children from home, and to monitor out-of-home placement and turn these functions over to police and courts. In Pelton's scheme, child welfare is a purely voluntary service agency. Although Pelton's proposal is intriguing, it is not the system in place today, nor is it likely to be implemented.

Today's system of child protection traces its roots directly to nineteenth-century societies to prevent cruelty to children, which relied heavily on investigation and criminal prosecution. Over the course of the twentieth century, the emphasis on adversarial intervention waxed and waned. The adversarial approach gained momentum toward the end of the twentieth century, as the nation adopted a "get tough on crime" mentality and as child protection staggered under a flood of cases. Yet even as child protection leaned in the direction of the adversarial/investigative end of the continuum, efforts were underway to pull it in the opposite direction. The most promising less adversarial approach is called differential or alternative response.

In her 1998 book *The Future of Child Protection*, Jane Waldfogel described two benefits of differential or alternative response. First, child protection too often takes a one-size-fits-all approach to reports of maltreatment. Many reports are screened out, meaning child protection does nothing, and families—many of which are in trouble—get no help. Cases that survive initial screening are investigated, and investigation is adversarial. Under differential response, child protection focuses less on investigation and more on assessing the needs of individual families and tailoring its response accordingly. According to Waldfogel, a second benefit of differential response relates to shared responsibility for child protection. Rather than child protective services carrying the entire responsibility for child protection, "the differential response paradigm calls for a community-based system, in which CPS continues to play the lead role but works with the criminal justice system and with other private and public agencies to provide preventive and protective services for the full range of children in need of protection. [Differential response incorporates] informal and natural helpers, drawn from families and communities to play a much more active role in child protection, in partnership with CPS and the other agencies in the community-based system."[34]

Leroy Pelton reviewed Waldfogel's book on differential response and saw little promise. Pelton wrote:

Although Waldfogel contends that her paradigm differs sharply from the current CPS approach, it merely extends it. While CPS would keep for its own caseload only "high risk" cases, it would maintain oversight over everything, and families would be "reassessed" on an ongoing basis. "Community partner agencies" and "family and community members" would be enlisted as coercive social control agents for "protective oversight" and "shared responsibility." The CPS gateway to "services" would straddle child welfare even more extensively than it does today, with the possibility of net-widening in terms of the CPS caseload itself. This will appeal to those who believe that if we don't keep a vigilant and menacing eye over the poor, who knows what horrible things they'll do.[35]

Pelton raises important questions, yet differential response holds real promise for reducing adversarial relations between social workers and parents. Particularly hopeful is differential response's emphasis on individualized assessment rather than investigation. "Investigation" smacks of law and an adversarial process for gathering evidence. Assessment, by contrast, connotes the helping processes of social work. Needless to say, differential response will fail if it is little more than semantic window dressing—a euphemistic change in terminology. It is an empty gesture to continue the investigative model under the guise of "assessment." As Waldfogel recognizes, differential response requires changed attitudes and practices, not new labels on old jars.

The states of Minnesota and Missouri are leaders in differential response.[36] In both states, reports of suspected maltreatment go to the child abuse hot line and are placed in either an investigation track or an assessment track. Cases involving immediate risk of serious harm to children are investigated. When criminal abuse is suspected, the police are involved in the investigation. The assessment track is voluntary. Parents can decline to participate, in which case an investigation may be necessary.

Both states commissioned evaluations of differential response, and the results are promising. The Missouri evaluation was conducted by Gary Siegel and Anthony Loman who wrote that the Missouri "family assessment response was meant to be non-accusatory and supportive, offering needed services as soon as possible without the trauma, stigma, or delay of the investigative process, and to involve the family in a collaborative response to problems and needs. An important element of the new approach involved establishing stronger ties to resources within the community able to assist children and families."[37]

Siegel and Loman compared differential response to the traditional investigative approach to child protection and found that differential response did not jeopardize the safety of children.[38] Indeed, children were made safer quicker. With differential response there was an increase in the percentage of cases in which social workers took action to help families. In 2002, the Missouri Department of Social Services reported that 64 percent of cases fell into assessment, whereas 34 percent required investigation.[39] With differential response, services were delivered more promptly. Use of community services increased, and recidivism decreased. The number of children removed from home did not change under differential response. Families were more cooperative and satisfied with the process. Parents felt they were respected. Differential response did not hamper investigation of cases requiring that response.

In Minnesota, Alternative Response is "a strength-based and community-oriented approach to addressing child maltreatment reports that do not meet Minnesota statutory requirements for a mandated investigative response. Eligible families may choose to participate as an alternative to the traditional investigative response. Under Alternative Response, no investigation or determination of child maltreatment is made. Instead, a family assessment is completed to determine the safety of the child, the risk of maltreatment, and to identify family needs and strengths."[40]

Minnesota commissioned an ongoing evaluation of its alternative response program, and in 2003 published an interim report describing results for two years. Compared with families that received the traditional CPS investigative response, families participating in alternative response were more likely to report "greater satisfaction with the way they were treated by child protection workers." Alternative response parents reported they were more involved in decision making. Social workers in the alternative response program were more likely to report that families were cooperative. Alternative response workers reported increased contact with parents and greater access to services for families. "[Alternative response] families reported receiving greater help meeting certain practical needs than did [traditional response] families. This included getting help to pay utilities and obtain food, clothing, appliances, furniture and home repairs, along with other financial assistance." Alternative response families tended to remain engaged with services longer than traditional response families. Alternative response did not compromise child safety. "No statistically significant differences were found in the level of new child maltreatment reports (after initial cases had closed) for alternative response compared to control families."[41]

In 2004, Minnesota issued a final report on its Alternative Response program. The authors of the evaluation, Anthony Loman and Gary Siegel, wrote, "Child safety was not compromised by the Alternative Response (AR) to child protection. No evidence was found that this approach led to a decrease in the safety of children. On the contrary, there was evidence that the safety status of children improved during cases in which AR was used and that this was related to increased service provision. Families who received the AR approach were less likely to have new child maltreatment reports than control families that received a traditional investigation. While the initial cost of AR in services provided and worker time was greater than in traditional CPS interventions, it was less costly and more cost effective in the longer term."[42]

Differential response is not a panacea. It does not "cure" poverty, and it will not eliminate child abuse and neglect. Nevertheless, differential response holds promise for creating a less adversarial environment for child protection. When the level of adversarial confrontation is reduced, parents are more likely to engage with social workers trying to help them. The task of professionals in child protection is to improve the system one brick at a time and differential response is more than a brick: It is a cornerstone.

Child Abuse Reporting Laws Require Modification

Laws requiring professionals to report suspected child abuse and neglect have been on the books since 1963. Today, some professionals argue that mandatory reporting laws should be repealed. Leading this charge is Gary Melton, who writes, "The assumptions that guided the enactment of mandated reporting laws were largely erroneous." Melton argues that the experts who lobbied for the original reporting laws seriously underestimated the scope of abuse and neglect. Mandatory reporting inundated child protection in a flood of reports, rendering it ineffective. Social workers are forced to devote almost all their time to investigating reports, with little time to help troubled families. Melton writes, "Vast human and fiscal resources that could be spent in prevention or treatment are instead expended in investigations that usually result in significant disruption of family life but little if any benefit." Melton adds, "The threat of reporting probably deters many families from seeking help."[43] Melton argues it is time to abandon mandatory reporting.

Many professionals (myself included) believe Melton exaggerates the ill effects of reporting laws and fails to give them credit for rescuing children. It would be a serious mistake to repeal the laws. Professionals who report suspicions of maltreatment are the eyes of child protection, and without their reports the system is blind. Reporting is vital to child protection.

Although Melton's call to abolish mandatory reporting goes too far, the time is ripe to rethink reporting laws. One insightful reform proposal is from David Finkelhor and Gail Zellman who describe a system they call "flexible reporting options for skilled child abuse professionals." Finkelhor and Zellman note that many competent and well-intentioned professionals occasionally decline to report. Professionals fail to report for several reasons. First, in some cases the abusive parent or the child is already in therapy and the professional concludes that reporting will destroy the trust that is essential for therapy. Second, child protective services often provides few or no services to families that are reported, and the professional may conclude that reporting will simply disrupt a family that is trying to improve. Third, doctors worry that if they report a parent, the parent will not bring the child back to the clinic for necessary medical care. Finally, many professionals believe that in some cases they can do a better job than child protective services. Research discloses that up to 40 percent of professionals periodically decline to report.[44]

Finkelhor and Zellman propose a system in which certain highly trained and experienced professionals will have the option to defer reporting in appropriate cases. These professionals will have the option to file a "report in confidence, defer-ring an investigation until later, or indefinitely." Finkelhor and Zellman describe one of the benefits of their system: "The tremendously overloaded child abuse reporting system could be spared from having to immediately investigate certain kinds of cases that are already under the supervision of skilled child abuse professionals."[45]

Finkelhor and Zellman's proposal would harmonize the reporting law with what professionals do in practice and would increase professional support for the reporting law and for child protective services. Finkelhor and Zellman argue, "A more flexible system might well result in better protective practices. The overbur-dened CPS bureaucracies increasingly can do little more than conduct investiga-tions with insufficient resources and intervene in a small number of extremely severe cases. If a flexible reporting system allowed and encouraged other commu-nity professionals and agencies to take more responsibility for the investigation, monitoring, and treatment of abusive families who might not otherwise get much attention from CPS, then more CPS resources might be available for children who are wholly dependent on CPS."[46]

In line with Finkelhor and Zellman, I do not believe the reporting law should be modified in cases of sexual abuse or serious physical abuse. Professionals should be required to report these matters—which are crimes—to law enforce-ment or child protection. On the other hand, so long as hitting children for disci-plinary purposes remains legal, minor bruises associated with such discipline should not be reported if a professional believes reporting is not the best way to handle the situation.

Neglect requires a nuanced approach. Neglect that poses an immediate risk of serious injury or death must be reported. Absent immediate threat, however, re-porting neglect to child protective services should be optional. In states where differential response is in place, a professional concerned about neglect can con-tact a social worker in the "assessment" branch of differential response to discuss options.

In the previous chapter, I argued for expanded home-visitation programs staffed by nurses. Under a modified reporting law, nurse home-visitors should be given reporting options along the lines described by Finkelhor and Zellman. Af-fording nurse visitors a measure of discretion about reporting will help them con-nect to parents. In addition to nurse home-visitors, physicians and mental health professionals should have discretion regarding whether to report relatively minor maltreatment.

Giving professionals a measure of discretion over reporting runs the risk that professionals will occasionally fail to report maltreatment that requires immedi-ate intervention. Indeed, this result is certain to occur. Children who could be protected won't be. Balanced against this stark reality are two facts. First, current reporting laws require professionals to report every suspicion of abuse or neglect, with the result that child protection is overwhelmed. An overwhelmed child protection system probably misses more cases of serious maltreatment than will be missed under a modified reporting system. Second, reporting to child protective services is not always the most appropriate option. Giving professionals a measure of discretion over reporting in nonsevere cases allows professionals to help families in ways that are impossible under current law. The net result will be positive for children and parents.

Strengthening Foster Care

Children who cannot remain safely at home are placed in out-of-home care. During the nineteenth century, children frequently wound up in orphanages or almshouses. Charles Loring Brace and other reformers struggled to remove children from institutions and place them in foster homes. Debate over the merits of foster care versus institutional care continued from the 1850s into the twentieth century. Eventually, supporters of foster care prevailed and almshouses, followed by orphanages, disappeared.[47]

Foster care is not ideal for children. No one doubts that children are better off with loving biological parents than with substitute caretakers. Many children living in foster care have problems. But are the problems caused by foster care or by the conditions the children experienced at home that led to placement in foster care? Davidson-Arad wrote:

> The problem with these studies is that it is not at all clear that the multitudinous difficulties to which they point stem from the children's placement in out of home care. Several researchers have pointed out that the prevalence of these problems among persons who have been removed from home is not significantly different from that among persons who grew up in poor socioeconomic circumstances, suggesting that the problems may stem from their socioeconomic deprivations before coming into care.
>
> Furthermore, clinical and empirical findings show that children who grow up in neglectful or abusive homes suffer from similar problems, including impairments in their basic trust, self-esteem, and ability to form and maintain relationships. . . . The problems of children removed from home may have preceded their removal and been anchored in the neglect and abuse on account of which they were removed.[48]

There are biological parents who parent in name only: Parents who are so incompetent, stoned, drunk, perverted, mentally ill, or violent that they cannot or will not provide what children need. Children in such "families" are better off with foster parents.

Some people view foster care as a problem rather than a solution. They lament that half a million children live in foster care. This is a legitimate concern, yet we must not lose sight of the fact that for many abused and neglected children, foster care is better than whence they came. Joseph Reid observed, "For thousands of children foster care is preferable to their being in their own homes, for there simply is no own home and no possibility for one. . . . The need for foster care programs cannot be eliminated and communities should not blame themselves for this necessity."[49] Foster care works well for thousands of children. The goal is not elimination of foster care, but reducing the number of children who need such care.

Research on Foster Care

The earliest in-depth study of foster care was Henry Maas and Richard Engler's 1959 classic *Children in Need of Parents*. Maas and Engler studied hundreds of foster children in nine urban and rural communities and documented that many children live for years in foster care. Maas and Engler wrote, "Of all the children we studied, better than half of them gave promise of living a major part of their childhood years in foster families and institutions. Among them were children likely to leave care only when they came of age, often after having had many homes—and none of their own—for ten or so years. Children who move through a series of families or are reared without close and continuing ties to a responsible adult have more than the usual problems in discovering who they are. They are the children who learn to develop shallow roots in relationships with others, who try to please but cannot trust, or who strike out before they can be let down." Maas and Engler found low rates of adoption from foster care. When adoption did occur, the child was usually a baby. Older children, children with mental or physical handicaps, and children of color were seldom adopted.[50]

Why did so many children languish so long in foster care? Maas and Engler attributed foster care drift to several factors. First, in the 1950s, the law made it difficult to terminate parental rights so children could be freed for adoption. Second, social agencies did not push adoption. Third, agencies received money for children in out-of-home care, creating incentives to keep children in care. Fourth, in many communities little effort was made to reunify children with parents. Fifth, many agencies didn't know how many children were in care. Sixth, for children of color, discrimination was a roadblock to adoption.

The second classic study of foster care was David Fanshel and Eugene Shinn's 1978 *Children in Foster Care: A Longitudinal Investigation*. In Fanshel and Shinn's study of 624 foster children, 36 percent were in care more than five years. Of children in long-term care, more than half were not visited by their parents. How did the children in long-term care fare? Contrary to expectations, Fanshel and Shinn did not find that long-term foster care was inevitably harmful. Indeed, when Fanshel and Shinn compared outcomes for children who remained in foster care with outcomes for children who returned to parents, they found, "Continued tenure in

foster care is not demonstrably deleterious with respect to IQ change, school performance, or the measures of emotional adjustment we employed. We do not say
that the children are in a condition that is always reassuring—but staying in care
as opposed to returning home does not seem to compound the difficulties of the
children."[51]

Fanshel and Shinn certainly did not advocate long-term foster care for children.
Between 25 and 33 percent of Fanshel and Shinn's foster children showed signs of
emotional impairment. Along with other child welfare experts, Fanshel and Shinn
urged greater resources to prevent the problems that lead to out-of-home care. Yet,
Fanshel and Shinn remind us that for many abused and neglected children, a
good foster home is better than a dysfunctional, drug infested, and abusive biological family.

The number of children in foster care has fluctuated over time. Unfortunately,
until recently there were few national statistics on foster care, making it difficult
to tell how many children were in care at any given time. Moreover, getting a fix
on foster care is complicated by the fact that during the twentieth century, the
federal government's definition of "foster care" included *all* types of out-of-home
care: foster family care, orphanages, group homes, even preadoptive homes.[51] Examining various sources, it appears that across the twentieth century about 1 percent of American children were in foster care at any given time.[52] The percentage
of poor children in foster care always exceeded 1 percent. Leroy Pelton estimated
that in 2001, nearly 5 percent of poor children were in out-of-home care.[53] Today,
the foster care population hovers around 500,000. Although half a million children is unacceptably high, it is well to remember that foster children make up a
tiny fraction of the total child population. Most children are not abused or neglected, and most who are are not in foster care.

Children of all ages live in foster care.[54] Approximately 4 percent of foster children are infants. In 2001, almost 39,000 infants entered foster care, often because
their mother was on drugs. Preschoolers make up nearly a quarter of children in
foster care, with elementary school-age kids comprising another quarter. Teens
from eleven to fifteen make up 30 percent of foster children, and older teens represent approximately 16 percent.

Every year, approximately 20,000 foster children reach eighteen and "age out"
of the child welfare system.[55] Unfortunately, many of these young people do not
fare well. "Youth in foster care are twice as likely as the rest of the school-age population to dropout before completing high school."[56] Children who age out of foster care have increased rates of homelessness and incarceration. Some sell drugs
to earn money.[57] In 2005, Mark Courtney and his colleagues described a longitudinal study of former foster youth in Illinois, Iowa, and Wisconsin:

> In Summary, youth making the transition from foster care are faring worse than
> their same-age peers, in many cases much worse, across a number of domains of
> functioning. They approach the age of majority with significant educational

deficits and relatively few of them appear to be on a path that will provide them with the skills necessary to thrive in today's economy. They are less likely to be employed than their peers, and earnings from employment provide few of them with the means to make ends meet. This is reflected in the economic hardships many of them face and the need that many of them have for government assistance. A large number continue to struggle with health and mental health problems. Too many of them have children for whom they cannot provide a home. They are much more likely than their peers to find themselves involved with the criminal justice system.[58]

To help foster youth prepare for adulthood, Congress in 1986 amended the Social Security Act to create the Independent Living Program.[59] The program provided federal funds to states to help foster youth achieve independence. In 1999, Congress strengthened the program with the Foster Care Independence Act, including the John H. Chafee Foster Care Independence Program. Under the Chafee program, federal funds allow states to pay educational expenses for foster youth aging out. Additional funds are available to extend Medicaid eligibility to age twenty-one. Money is also available to assist former foster youth with housing.

African-American children are overrepresented in the child welfare system. Today, African Americans make up 15 percent of the U.S. population and 41 percent of the foster care population. Native Americans represent 1 percent of the U.S. population, with 2 percent of children in foster care. By contrast, whites are 61 percent of the population and only 40 percent of the foster care population.

It is sad that some children cannot live safely with their parents. Earlier in our history such children were indentured or apprenticed. Thousands of hapless children were consigned to almshouses and orphanages, and thousands lived on the street. Gradually, reformers like Charles Loring Brace won the argument that such children deserve something better; they deserve a substitute family, a foster family. The foster care system has faults: Too many children are in care too long, and too many children are shifted from home to home.[60] Despite the problems, however, we are fortunate that hundreds of thousands of adults open their homes and hearts to abused and neglected children. The great majority of foster parents provide competent, stable homes. Although researchers, policymakers, and legislators must continue efforts to improve foster care, they should devote just as much effort to supporting the existing system. The foster parents, foster children, and professionals in the child welfare system deserve praise and support. My colleague Melissa Knight provides therapy for disabled infants and young children, many of whom are rescued from abuse and are living in foster homes. Knight describes the foster parents whose homes she visits and marvels at their commitment and their abiding love of children. "They're angels," she says, and she's right.

It is doubly tragic when a child who has been abused at home is abused again in foster care. Although abuse occurs in some foster homes, it is uncommon. In 2000, the rate of abuse in foster care varied from less than 1 percent in one state to a little over 3 percent in another, with the median across the country of less than 1 percent. If we assume a rate of abuse in foster care of 0.5 percent, then some 2,500 children were abused in foster care in the year 2000. Although 2,500 is unacceptably high, the fact that the national rate of abuse in foster care is less than 1 percent is a testament to success, not failure, and to the hard work of foster parents and the professionals who license and supervise foster homes.

Finding a permanent home for children in foster care means working toward reuniting children with parents or, when reunification is unwise, moving toward adoption, guardianship, or long-term foster care. Efforts to improve permanency planning got seriously underway in the 1970s, spurred by Maas, Engler, Fanshel, Shinn, and others. For most abused or neglected children in out-of-home care, the plan is to work toward reunifying the family. Services are offered to help parents overcome the problems that led to removal. Some states are better than others at reunifying foster children with parents. The U.S. Children's Bureau reported that in 2000, the percentage of children reunified with parents within twelve months of entry into foster care ranged from a high of 87 percent reunified in one state to a low of 35 percent reunified in another.[61] Unfortunately, following reunification, some children are abused again and returned to foster care. Here, too, states vary. In one state in 2000, the reentry rate was 1 percent, whereas in another state 28 percent of reunified children returned to foster care. States that are quicker to reunify foster children with parents tend to have higher rates of reabuse and reentry into foster care. One explanation is that some children are reunified too quickly, before maltreating parents have reformed.

When efforts to reunify a family fail, social workers seek another stable arrangement for the child, with formal adoption the ideal for most children. The federal Adoption Assistance and Child Welfare Act of 1980 established the goal of reducing the time it takes to move foster children to adoption. In 1997, the Adoption and Safe Families Act (ASFA) reinforced this goal. ASFA requires states to seek termination of parental rights for foster children who have been abandoned and for children in foster care for 15 of the most recent 22 months. ASFA promotes adoption by expanding adoption subsidies.

Since the passage of ASFA in 1997, states have worked hard to speed adoption.[62] Cornelia Ashby of the U.S. General Accounting Office reported, "The annual number of adoptions have increased by 57 percent from the time ASFA was enacted through fiscal year 2000."[63] The Pew Charitable Trusts reported, "From 1998 to 2002, states placed over 230,000 children in adoptive homes. More children were adopted during this five-year period than the previous 10 years combined."[64] Mark Testa and his colleagues wrote, "The past decade has seen unparalleled success in finding adoptive homes for children in foster care. This achievement—including states' answering the federal challenge to double adoptions out of foster care in five years—was the result of coordinated efforts across multiple fronts."[65]

Guardianship is an increasingly popular option for foster children who cannot return to parents and for whom adoption is unlikely. Often, the guardian is a member of the child's extended family such as a grandparent, aunt, or uncle. Guardianship is a legal relationship established by a judge. A child's guardian receives legal custody of the child, including the decision-making authority normally exercised by parents. Once formal guardianship is established the child leaves the child welfare system. Guardianship lasts until the child turns eighteen. The principal advantage of guardianship is that the child has a permanent family. An additional advantage in many cases is that the biological parents can remain part of the child's life because guardianship does not terminate parental rights.

Many adults, especially family members who are willing to become guardians to foster children, can't afford the expense of raising a child. Subsidized guardianship provides an answer. Massachusetts established the first subsidized guardianship program in 1983, and today some thirty-five states have subsidized guardianship programs.[66] Child welfare administrators cobble together state, local, and federal dollars to subsidize guardianship. Efforts are underway to increase federal money for subsidized guardianship.

TEPAC — Temporary Permanent Attachment Care: Reducing Uncertainty in Out-of-Home Care

Under current practice, when a child is removed from home and placed in foster care, the emphasis in most cases is working toward reunification. To that end, social workers create reunification plans, judges approve the plans, and parents work on the problems that led to removal. Meanwhile, children reside with foster parents or relatives.

From the moment a child enters foster care, everyone anticipates the "big day" when the child returns home. Reunification with parents is the primary measure of success. Reunification is the brass ring on the foster care merry-go-round. The merry-go-round spins in cycles of periodic review, and with each revolution the child reaches for the ring that signifies, "I'm going home." Every review that ends in "not yet" is viewed as a shortfall, a failure to reunify. Indeed, every day in foster care is a "could have been" day, a day when many foster children think, "I could have gone home today, but there's still something wrong with me."

Not only are there nagging questions about going home, but there is also the very real possibility of moving from one foster home to another, undermining a sense of security. At least 20 percent of foster children live in three or more homes. Some foster children are moved seven or more times.[67] The foster child wonders, "If I can't go home, will they move me somewhere else? Will they move me today? Tomorrow? Next week? I'd better not get too comfy here cause I might leave soon. I better not get attached to these people cause I might never see them again. All the grownups say they care about me, but it's hard to feel loved."

For parents, the uncertainty of foster care is agonizing. Every day the child is away is a failure, another day when the sign around the parent's neck reads "Unfit." Parents wonder, "Will I ever get my baby back? Can I defeat the addiction this time or will I fall off the wagon like I've done in the past? Will my child forget me? Will I ever make the social worker and the judge happy? Do I have the strength to keep fighting? Am I really a horrible parent?"

Foster parents have struggles of their own. A foster parent must balance their commitment to the child against the "danger" of getting too attached. Foster care, after all, is a holding pattern while parents get their act together. Yet, foster care is a holding pattern that discourages too much holding. The "job description" for foster parents is a contradiction: Care for the child, but not too much. Provide for the child, but withhold the full measure of commitment that is so important for healthy development. Keep this child in a state of suspended animation while we fix mom and dad.

Social workers, like foster parents, are devoted to children. Yet, social workers are cogs in a bureaucracy, and bureaucracy by nature is inflexible, rule-bound, and insensitive to individual needs. The best child welfare bureaucracy on earth is not very efficient, and inefficiency is magnified by overwhelming caseloads and inadequate financial and human resources. Social workers are buried in so many rules, regulations, and reports that there is little time for children.

The uncertainty that exemplifies today's foster care system is hardly optimal for child development. Sigrid James wrote, "Children with a higher number of placement changes are known to experience a decreased likelihood of reunification, greater severity of behavior problems, and more time in residential care."[68] Foster children lack the certainty of knowing who will take care of them over time. At a fundamental level, foster children are deprived of the unqualified love and security that constitutes the essence of the child–parent relationship and that is critical for the development of a healthy sense of self. Given these concerns, it is a testament to the dedication of foster parents and social workers, and to the resilience of children's spirits, that so many foster children turn out so well.

Foster care will always be an important component of child protection. Because of the uncertainty of traditional foster care, however, it is worth considering a new type of out-of-home placement for selected children. Currently, a foster child is like a boat cast upon the ocean without a port to call home. Each foster placement is a temporary anchorage, with no guarantee the anchor will hold. The child must always be on watch, and it is never safe to relax because the anchor could slip at any moment, casting the child adrift. Children need a safe harbor, a homeport. When the goal is reunifying the child with biological parents or close kin, it may take months or years to achieve this objective. In the meantime, the child needs certainty. The child needs a safe harbor that won't change with every tide. The child needs "temporary permanence."

Temporary permanence not a contradiction in terms. Temporary permanence describes out-of-home care in which a child is assured a stable placement for an extended period, typically a year. Temporary permanence removes the uncertainty that plagues foster care and that prevents kids from putting down roots. Temporary permanence encourages bonding with competent, caring adults. Adults providing temporary permanent care operate with a longer frame of reference that allows them to help children achieve a sense of stability, a safe harbor.

This new, more stable form of out-of-home care may be called Temporary Permanent Attachment Care (TEPAC). Implementation of TEPAC will require changes in attitude, aptitude, practice, and law. Under current practice, foster children can be moved from one placement to another with relative ease.[69] A foster parent may request a change if "the child isn't a good fit," if the child's behavior is too much for the provider, and for other major or minor reasons. With TEPAC, providers will assume enhanced responsibilities. Unlike the present system, in which foster parents can bail out at the first sign of trouble, TEPAC requires providers (no longer called foster parents) to "stick it out through thick and thin." The role of a TEPAC provider is similar to the role of a biological parent. Biological parents don't have the option of requesting a "new placement" when things get rocky. Biological parents are committed to their child, and as a result, biological parents find ways to help the child negotiate developmental hurdles and difficulties. The same commitment is needed of TEPAC providers.

With competent biological parents, the child knows at a primal level that the parent's love is unconditional. The child understands that the parent's attachment is secure and the parent won't reject the child even when the child goes astray. TEPAC strives to approximate this sense of security. The TEPAC child knows the adult is committed and won't toss them out on a whim. The TEPAC child— unlike the child in traditional foster care—can put down roots. I am not suggesting TEPAC affords all the benefits of a loving biological or adoptive child–parent relationship. Temporary permanence, after all, is not permanent permanence. I believe, however, TEPAC is a substantial improvement over the uncertainty of today's foster care system.

For TEPAC to be effective, providers must have a larger measure of control than today's foster parents. In the current system, nearly all decision-making authority rests with social workers. Foster parents have little authority to make decisions on behalf of children. With TEPAC, the provider has legal custody of the child and the right to make minor and most major decisions for the child, including where the child goes to school, whether the child plays basketball or soccer, where to go on vacation, how to discipline the child (without hitting), who the child's playmates are, and so on. In other words, the TEPAC provider acts as a parent. The major responsibility of TEPAC providers is ladling up copious servings of stability, support, and love.

TEPAC providers do not have the full measure of parental rights enjoyed by biological or adoptive parents. The TEPAC provider shares responsibility with the social worker. What changes under TEPAC is the nature of the provider–social worker relationship. In today's foster care system, social workers call the shots and foster parents obey. With TEPAC, the provider and the social worker are equals— colleagues working in tandem for the child's future. The TEPAC provider has legal custody of the child but consults the social worker on a regular basis, especially about important decisions. The social worker supports the provider's authority, employing the skills unique to social work to coordinate the services needed by the child, the provider, and the child's biological parents. The social worker does most of the paperwork so the provider can concentrate on parenting.

Most of today's foster parents are intelligent, caring people who could transition easily into TEPAC providers. Yet, more is demanded of a TEPAC provider than is required of a traditional foster parent. A TEPAC provider is a professional with expertise in child development. Before social workers will be willing to relinquish a large measure of control to TEPAC providers, social workers will have to be convinced that TEPCA providers deserve that trust. The same level of confidence will be required by juvenile court judges who will bestow legal custody on TEPAC providers.

For TEPAC to be successful, four requirements must be fulfilled. First, TEPAC providers must be licensed by appropriate authorities. TEPAC providers should pass a licensing examination similar to the examination required of teachers, social workers, nurses, lawyers, and other professionals. Second, a college degree or equivalent life experience should be required to be a TEPAC provider. Colleges and universities will create training programs to prepare students for careers as TEPAC providers. Young people entering college should be able to major in TEPAC. Although it is important to recruit young people to the profession, it is equally if not more important to recruit older students, especially adults who are successful parents. Many adults, including thousands of retired people, will return to university to become certified TEPAC providers.

Third, a TEPAC provider must be a professional in fact as well as in name. A TEPAC provider is much more than a 24-hour-a-day childcare provider. A TEPAC provider is part therapist, part parent, and part child advocate. Intelligent individuals will not be drawn to this work unless TEPAC providers have status equal to teachers, nurses, and social workers. If TEPAC is looked down on as a third-class profession—as little more than glorified baby-sitting—it will fail. Finally, TEPAC providers must make a good living. TEPAC providers must be paid as much as professionals in comparable professions.

Temporary permanent attachment care should be added to the existing foster care system. TEPAC providers will provide stability for thousands of children.

Care must be taken to ensure placing children in TEPAC does not relieve the pressure to move children toward reunification with parents or permanence through adoption. Delicate case-by-case assessment is required.

Temporary permanent attachment care fills a gap between traditional foster care and legal guardianship. Traditional foster care does not give children the certainty they need to prosper. Guardianship is generally reserved for older children who are not likely to be adopted. TEPAC gives infants, young children, and, as appropriate, older children a secure, lengthy placement in which to thrive. Looking at TEPAC with a child's sense of time, a year of stability is a long time. Moreover, TEPAC placements can be extended. TEPAC gives children a safe harbor in which to drop anchor.

Foster Children Speak for Themselves

In the literature on foster care and child protection we seldom hear from children themselves. An early exception is the 1885 *Annual Report* of the Massachusetts Society for the Prevention of Cruelty to Children (MSPCC). A motherless girl was rescued by the Society from a brutal and drunken father. Following her placement in a rural foster home, she wrote the Society, "I had a lovely time last winter, sliding down hill. I went to private school last winter. I have been may-flowering and got some lovely ones. I sent you a box of them, which I hope you received all right. I think I am a happy girl, and would not exchange for anything of my own accord."[70]

Another little girl was removed from an "intemperate mother" who forced the child to sing in saloons. From her foster home in the country the child wrote, "I like my place very much. I love Mr. and Mrs. C. and call them papa and mamma. I have been going to school. The teacher is Miss C. and she is very nice. We spelt for headmarks and I got the second prize. I can play 'Sweet By and By' and 'Yankee Doodle' on the organ, and mamma is learning me the notes. I had a splendid Christmas and New Years. I have four pets; two pigs, a chicken and a calf."[71]

In a report on the early work of the MSPCC, Ray Hubbard described "The Happy Solution of Ruth's Problem":

> Since she was eight months old, Ruth had lived with a woman and her son whom she had known as her mother and brother. Constant friction and quarreling, with frequent punishment of Ruth by the woman and nagging by the son, finally caused the fourteen-year-old girl to flee to a neighbor's house.
>
> The "mother" brought Ruth into court as a stubborn child. At the request of the court, S.P.C.C. investigated the whole affair. Then came the discovery that the woman was not Ruth's mother. She told conflicting tales concerning Ruth's origin, claiming that the girl had been born to her, and even giving date of birth. Since none of her statements could be verified, and because Ruth herself declared that

she would rather "be put away" than return to her home, the Society took her in custody and placed her in the Children's Home.

She was given medical attention for eyes and teeth, and revealed an intelligence quotient of 118 on tests at the Psychopathic Hospital. There it was discovered that because of her turbulent home life she was threatened with St. Vitus's dance [involuntary nervous twitching] and a different environment was recommended.

Further identification of Ruth was not possible, so she became a State ward. While in State care she kept up frequent correspondence with the Society's visitor. In her foster home she was very happy and became an honor pupil at school. Victor in a district spelling bee, she became a contestant in the State finals, and received fourth place and a silver loving cup.

In one letter she tells her former agent, "I will think of you (because I do) and that will help me, because whenever I think of you I am inspired. I guess that is partly because you believe in me and I've got to make good, and partly because I admire you so."

Ruth became an honor high school graduate, and though considered college material, preferred to go into training as a nurse. She won a scholarship and was accepted for training at a hospital.[72]

We would hardly expect the Massachusetts Society to publish children's letters longing for parents or complaining about foster care. Some children weren't happy, and unfortunate placements occurred. Child welfare isn't perfect. Yet, these touching letters attest success.

How about today? What do today's foster children say about their circumstances? A report on California's foster care system compiled in 2000 provides insights.[73] Foster children were asked a series of questions, including "In what ways has your social worker been helpful to you?" Among children's answers we find a twelve-year-old saying, "Every Monday she takes me to the library, she takes me shopping, and she came to my graduation." A seven-year-old said, "She helped me because she came to my school and talked to my teacher." A ten-year-old remarked, "She takes me places. She makes sure I get to see my mom, I have what I need, that I'm happy." An eight-year-old stated, "She helps my mommy learn to take care of us better." A ten-year-old said, "She takes care of things when I have a problem. She plays with me and always answers my questions."

Obviously, being away from parents is difficult for most children. Foster youth were asked, "Is there anything else that you think I should know about what it's like for children who live separate from their birth mother?" An eleven-year-old spoke for many when she said, "It's sad. It's not fun. You cry sometimes. You miss them a lot. You want to be with them every day." A ten-year-old remarked, "It's scary, and you don't know what's gonna happen." One child simply said, "I miss my mom."

When asked what they liked about foster care, a twelve-year-old said, "They are taking care of me. They treat us right. They do not beat us." An eight-year-old replied, "I have friends. I love my sisters." A nine-year-old's answer was, "It has lots of toys and food, and my mom cooks good too." A thirteen-year-old said, "I like it good. We eat chicken every day. Good house. Clothes on my back." An eight-year-old stated, "My foster mom is the best. She treats me well. When she puts me in the corner I know why. And I like it here a lot." A thirteen-year-old said, "I feel how it is to have a family that loves you."

Every foster child has a story. Some are happy, some sad. I am fully aware of research showing that for many foster children, the passage into adulthood is stormy. Yet, as I read the quotes from these and other foster children, I see young people who are better off in foster homes than in their own homes. I see children who are cared for and in many cases loved by substitute moms and dads. I see children with a future thanks to foster care.

Despite its flaws, the child protection system (or, more accurately, the professionals and foster parents who are the system) rescues children every day from abuse, neglect, and death. Our long-term priority must be to reduce the amount of abuse and neglect. Our short-term priority must be to strengthen and support the existing system.

Juvenile Court

From the time of its creation in 1899, the juvenile court played a key role in child protection. The focus of the present section is on three issues facing today's juvenile court. First, should children in juvenile court have attorneys? Second, when is it proper to terminate the child-parent relationship? Third, does today's juvenile court need revitalization?

Attorneys for Children in Juvenile Court

In juvenile court, does the child need a lawyer? This question must be answered from two perspectives: first, juvenile delinquency cases and, second, child abuse and neglect cases. In the early days of the juvenile court, lawyers seldom appeared in either type of case. The order of the day was informality and the judge, assisted by a probation officer, listened to witnesses and decided what to do. In 1967, however, the U.S. Supreme Court ruled in the famous case of *In re Gault* that children accused of delinquency have a constitutional right to an attorney.[74] As attorneys made their way to juvenile court for delinquency cases, the question arose: What about child protection cases? Shouldn't children in protective proceedings have an attorney?

Critics of attorneys for children in protective proceedings point out that the adversaries in such cases are the CPS agency and the parents. Both have lawyers to protect their interests. The child does not need an attorney because the judge keeps a watchful eye over the child's interests. Adding another lawyer simply complicates an already complicated situation, detracting from the informality that is desirable in juvenile court. In addition, although the point is seldom discussed candidly, critics of counsel for children worry about the cost of adding a third lawyer. Critics note that on a national scale taxpayers spend millions of dollars on lawyers for parents and protective services agencies. Is it wise to spend additional millions on more lawyers? Wouldn't it be wiser to spend the money on services to help families and children? We could buy a lot of homemaker services, therapy, parenting classes, and job training with the money we spend on attorneys for children.

Supporters of attorneys for children in protective proceedings argue that the child needs someone whose sole responsibility is advocating for the child. The lawyer for the parents can't guard the child's interests because the parents' lawyer is advocating for the parents. If the child's interests are at odds with the wishes of the parents, the parents' lawyer is duty-bound to advocate the parents' wishes. The lawyer for CPS is not in a position to represent the child. Although child protection usually seeks the outcome that is best for the child, this is not always the case. Suppose, for example, that a psychologically traumatized child needs expensive therapy in a hospital. The cash-strapped CPS agency may instruct its attorney to ask the judge for less expensive outpatient therapy, and the attorney is obligated to go along. In some cases, then, the interests of CPS and the child diverge, and the lawyer cannot serve two masters.

How about the judge? Can't the judge sort through the arguments of the attorneys for the parents and CPS and decide what is best for the child? Although the judge has the child's interests in mind, the judge is supposed to be impartial, not an advocate for the child. Moreover, the judge is unlikely to gain a full appreciation of the child's needs, unless the child has independent representation to articulate the child's side of the story. The only way to ensure that the child does not fall through the cracks is to give the child a voice in court.

Supporters of representation for children have the stronger argument. Yet, conceding that children need a voice in juvenile court is not to say that the voice must be a lawyer. A trained volunteer with a caseload of one or two children might do a better job than an attorney responsible for 100 kids. Indeed, an attorney with 100 cases can be one of the cracks kids fall through.

Many communities assign volunteer advocates to children. The volunteers are typically known as court-appointed special advocates or CASAs. Increasingly, states have laws authorizing CASA programs, and there is a national CASA organization. CASA volunteers include retirees, college students, and others. Responsible for only one or two children at a time, CASAs make sure kids' needs are met and that busy attorneys, social workers, and judges don't drop the ball. CASA volunteers often know the child better than the professionals and offer insights that would otherwise be missed.

Supporters of attorney representation for children don't dispute the value of CASAs. Proponents of attorneys, however, ask the following question: If the parents and CPS need attorneys to properly represent their views in court, why does the child whose entire future is at stake need something less? Only lawyers are equipped by training and experience to fully understand the complexities of litigation. Although CASA volunteers do a wonderful job and should be used along with attorneys, CASAs are not attorneys. Children deserve the same level of representation as parents and agencies—*legal* representation.

The debate over attorney versus nonattorney representation for children is resolving in favor of attorneys. Once this debate is put to rest, however, another issue arises: What is the proper role of the child's attorney in protective proceedings? In juvenile delinquency proceedings, the role of the youth's attorney is relatively well defined. The youth's attorney acts for the most part like a defense attorney representing an adult who is charged with a crime. The youth's attorney counsels the youth on the nature of the charges, possible defenses, the likelihood of success if the case goes to trial, whether it would be wise for the youth to testify if there is a trial, whether to admit the charges, whether to accept a negotiated plea, and the range of possible punishments. As with criminal litigation against adults, the youth in delinquency proceedings is entitled to make the critical decisions, and the attorney's job is to advocate the youth's wishes. Thus, after counseling from the attorney, the youth decides whether to admit responsibility or plead not guilty and insist on a trial. If there is a trial, the youth decides whether to take the witness stand and testify in his own behalf. The difference between adult and youth clients is that children are immature and need more guidance from their attorneys. In the final analysis, however, in delinquency litigation, the attorney's job is to be a zealous advocate for the youth's wishes.

Although clients in criminal and delinquency litigation are entitled to make the critical decisions, candor requires three admissions. First, there are plenty of adult defendants who are adult in name only and who require as much guidance as youth. Second, in most cases the client, whether young or old, goes along with the attorney's advice. Third, when criminal defense attorneys are candid, they admit they occasionally overrule their clients' wishes. Defense attorneys don't say to clients, "No, you can't do that. I won't permit it." Rather, attorneys lean on clients until they come around. Such "leaning on" occurs with adults, and it certainly occurs with youth. In delinquency cases, youthful indiscretion requires a degree of reigning in to protect the client's interests. Conceding that defense counsel in delinquency cases exert influence over critical decisions, the role of the defense attorney remains clear: The attorney's responsibility is to zealously defend the youth and to carry out the youth's wishes on key issues such as admitting or denying the charges, going to trial, and testifying.

Unlike delinquency, where the role of the youth's attorney is relatively clear, the proper role for a child's attorney in juvenile court protective proceedings is anything but clear. Indeed, there is considerable debate among attorneys about the proper role of the child's attorney in protective proceedings. Although there are several strands to the debate, two predominate: Some attorneys favor a paternalistic, guardian ad litem approach to representation. Other attorneys favor an autonomy-based, child's wishes approach.

Supporters of the guardian ad litem approach argue that the child's lawyer should advocate in court for what the lawyer determines is in the child's best interest, even if the lawyer's determination differs from the child's wishes. The guardian ad litem approach is paternalistic because it rests on the belief that children are not sufficiently mature to determine their best interests. The guardian ad litem approach is the tradition in protective proceedings and is the law in most states.

On the other side of the debate are attorneys who argue the child's attorney should advocate for what the child wants, regardless of the attorney's views. The "child's wishes" approach is the norm in delinquency litigation but is a relative newcomer in protective proceedings. The child's wishes approach is based on two principles. First, respect for children's autonomy. Many children are capable of rational decision making, and attorneys should respect and advocate their client's wishes. Second, supporters of the child's wishes approach lack confidence in the ability of attorneys to decide what is best for children.

Few participants in the debate take an absolutist position on the role of the attorney. I know no supporters of the child's wishes approach who believe attorneys should be bound by the wishes of three-year-olds. By the same token, supporters of the guardian ad litem approach agree that by age fourteen or so, teenagers should have a controlling voice in their representation. Moreover, devotees of the guardian ad litem approach agree that when the attorney's views differ from the child's, the attorney is duty bound to inform the judge of the child's wishes.

At its core, the debate centers on the age at which children should be deemed competent to direct the attorney. Proponents of the child's wishes approach tend to draw the line at an early age. Sarah Ramsey, for example, proposed that lawyers assume seven-year-olds are capable of directing their attorney.[75] Those who favor the guardian ad litem approach tend to draw the line at a later age, sometime during adolescence. Supporters of both approaches justify their position by drawing on the child development literature. Supporters of the child's wishes approach point to literature indicating that children can think rationally by age seven. On the other hand, guardian ad litem supporters argue that the ability to reason should not be confused with the ability to reason responsibly. Children lack experience and tend to overvalue short-term interests. Moreover, some abused and neglected children lag behind developmentally.

There is no psychological research that directly addresses the age at which children are capable of directing attorneys in juvenile court protective cases. However, there is research on children's decision-making capacity in delinquency cases. Commenting on the delinquency research, Thomas Grisso wrote, "Current evidence suggests that compared with adults, youth under age fifteen are at greater risk of having poor knowledge of matters related to their participation in trials. . . . For youths under fourteen years old, the balance of evidence . . . suggests that as a group they are at greater risk than most adults for deficits in abilities associated with adjudicative competence."[76] I asked Dr. Grisso his thoughts on the age at which children would be able to direct their attorneys in protective cases. He opined that most children below fourteen or fifteen lack the capacity to meaningfully direct attorneys. Rona Abramovitch, Michele Peterson-Badali, and M. Rohan reinforce Grisso's judgment that it is not until adolescence that children begin acquiring the knowledge and maturity needed to meaningfully participate in legal decision making.[77] Melinda Schmidt, N. Dickon Reppucci, and Jennifer Woolard wrote, "In general, children under the age of 15 have significantly poorer understanding of legal matters relevant to their participation in trials than do adults."[78]

Thus, research on children's decision-making capacity in delinquency cases suggests that in protection cases there are problems with the child's wishes model for children under age fourteen. Nevertheless, many academics, along with the American Bar Association and the National Association of Counsel for Children, favor broad application of the child's wishes approach in protective cases.

The preference for the child's wishes model can be traced to a conference held at Fordham University Law School in 1995. More than seventy lawyers, judges, and mental health professionals attended. The conferees concluded, "Lawyers serve children best when they serve in the role as an attorney, not as guardian ad litem. . . . If the child can direct the representation, the lawyer has the same ethical obligations as the lawyer would have when representing an adult." To test the courage of their convictions, the conferees considered the case of a child who wants to leave foster care to return to a sexually abusive father. The conferees suggested that the attorney should counsel the child and urge her not to go home. If the child is adamant, however, the conferees concluded, "The attorney must either advocate the child's wishes or withdraw."[79]

It is clear from the proceedings of the Fordham conference that the conferees doubted the ability of attorneys to competently determine what is best for children. The conferees wrote, "Nothing about legal training or traditional legal roles qualifies lawyers to make decisions on behalf of their clients." Martin Guggenheim, one of the conferees, wrote, "Liberating lawyers for children to advocate results they believe are best for their clients will ensure the randomness and chaos that a rational legal system would avoid whenever possible."[80] Another conferee, Peter Margulies, wrote, "The potential for arrogance and ignorance is greatest when a lawyer appointed to represent a child" advocates for what the lawyer thinks is best for the child.[81] Thus, distrust in the ability of lawyers to perform the guardian ad litem role is at the core of the child's wishes approach.

As mentioned above, the American Bar Association (ABA) favors the child's wishes model. The ABA Standards of Practice for Lawyers Who Represent Children in Abuse and Neglect Cases provide, "The child's attorney should represent the child's expressed preferences and follow the child's direction throughout the course of litigation." The Standards also state, "If the child's attorney determines that the child's expressed preference would be seriously injurious to the child, the lawyer may request appointment of a separate guardian ad litem and continue to represent the child's expressed preference, unless the child's position is prohibited by law or without any factual foundation. The child's attorney shall not reveal [to the judge] the basis of the request for appointment of a guardian ad litem which would compromise the child's position."[82] The *Standards* acknowledge that in rare cases a lawyer may need to reveal confidential information to protect a child from serious injury or death—a rather grudging concession to the reality of child abuse. The ABA *Standards* are only a model and are not binding on states or on attorneys.

The National Association of Counsel for Children (NACC) adopted the ABA *Standards*, but with judicious amendments. The NACC is the nation's only organization devoted entirely to improving the quality of legal representation for children. Founded in 1977, the NACC has some 2,000 members. Most members are attorneys, but some are social workers, judges, pediatricians, or mental health professionals. The NACC version of the ABA *Standards* recognizes "there will be occasions when the client directed model cannot serve the client and exceptions must be made."[83] On such occasions, the NACC authorizes an attorney to serve as a guardian ad litem.

The ABA and NACC standards recognize that some children are too immature to direct the attorney. Unfortunately, neither set of standards offers much help determining when a child is, in the words of the ABA *Standards*, "impaired." Thus, once again we are left to wonder, how old is old enough? The primary failing of the ABA *Standards*, the NACC *Standards*, and the literature on this subject is that no one offers particularly good advice on how to make the most important decision in the entire process: Is this child able to direct the attorney?

Dodging for a moment the ticklish issue of how old is old enough, and assuming we are dealing with a child who is *not* able to direct the attorney, what is the attorney's role? If the attorney is a guardian ad litem, the answer is clear: The attorney conducts an investigation, including consultation with the child if the child is old enough to be interviewed, and the attorney advocates in court for what the attorney thinks is best for the child. The answer is not so clear for those who believe attorneys are incompetent to determine what is best for children, and who reject the attorney guardian ad litem role. Critics of the guardian ad litem model suggest several options, four of which are: (1) the Martin Guggenheim "legal interests" position, (2) the Jean Peters "rely on the child development literature" position, (3) the Emily Buss "take no position" position, and (4) the "appoint another adult" position.

The "legal interests" position is developed most thoroughly by Martin Guggenheim and is incorporated into the ABA *Standards*. Guggenheim wrote, "The proper role of young children's lawyers should simply be to enforce their clients' rights. Those rights derive from substantive law. For this reason, we should be encouraging lawyers to study the substantive law that defines the rights of children and instructing lawyers to enforce those rights assiduously."[84] Guggenheim is skeptical of the ability of lawyers to determine what is best for children. He argues that by requiring lawyers to focus exclusively on enforcing children's legal rights, it is possible to cabin lawyer discretion within acceptable limits.

But what are children's legal rights in protective litigation? Guggenheim concedes this can be difficult to determine. According to Guggenheim, the child's primary legal right is to live with her parents unless the parents have maltreated the child. If the child is removed from maltreating parents, Guggenheim argues the child has a legal right to visitation with the parents. Guggenheim asserts the child's attorney should not form an opinion about what the *attorney* thinks is best for the client. Rather, the lawyer should confine herself to enforcing the child's legal rights.

Although Guggenheim has years of experience representing children, I don't think his "legal interests" approach works. Try as he might to divest attorneys of discretion, he can't do it, and here's why. According to Guggenheim, the child has a legal right to remain with parents unless removal is essential to protect the child. If removal is needed, however, the child has a legal right to removal. No matter how you cut it, the lawyer has to decide: Should the child stay at home or not? To make that decision, the lawyer has to look beyond the law to the facts of the case, and once the lawyer delves into the facts, the lawyer must decide what is best for the child. There's no escaping it. Guggenheim's "legal rights" model fails because it ignores the fact that before an attorney can enforce a child's legal rights, the attorney must decide between alternative legal rights, thereby exercising precisely the kind of professional judgment Guggenheim deplores.

Like Martin Guggenheim, Jean Peters is a leading authority on attorney representation for children in protective proceedings.[85] With children too young to direct counsel, Peters recommends that the attorney consult the child development literature and pursue the course of action that the literature suggests is best for the child. Although I have great respect for Peters' expertise, her model won't work. A look at the child development literature reveals competing theories and unanswered questions. How is the attorney to decide on the proper theory? How does the attorney deal with the unanswered questions? Peters lacks confidence in the ability of lawyers to decide what is best for children. Given her lack of confidence in lawyers, why does Peters believe lawyers will be successful at finding, synthesizing, understanding, and selecting appropriately from the various theories of child development and behavior? In all likelihood, the child's attorney will pick the developmental theory that supports what the attorney thinks is best for the child, and once again we are back to lawyers exercising judgment about what is in the child's best interests. Peters is no more successful at stripping discretion from attorneys than Guggenheim.

Donald Duquette is an experienced attorney for children. Duquette analyzed the child's wishes model and wrote, "The so-called client-directed models have not eliminated unreviewed, ad hoc, and potentially idiosyncratic lawyer discretion. The ABA/NACC Standards and Fordham Recommendations merely move that unfettered discretion to other parts of the process—parts not as easily open to review as the ultimate best interests determination. The ABA/NACC and the Fordham approaches aspire to be pure attorney models, but pull their punches in various ways. They create so many points of discretion and so many loopholes that they provide little guidance to the practicing lawyer."[86]

Emily Buss may be the only contributor to the literature who gets close to eliminating attorney discretion. Buss argues that when a child cannot direct the attorney, the attorney should take no position in court.[87] Under Buss's "no-position" position, the child's attorney essentially serves as a watchdog to ensure that other lawyers are doing their jobs.

For those who don't trust attorneys to decide what's good for kids, Buss's no-position position has the best shot at restricting attorney discretion. By depriving the attorney of the opportunity to take *any* position, the attorney cannot make the kinds of mistakes that the anti-guardian ad litem forces worry about. However, I would argue that if the child's attorney can't take a position, why waste money on the attorney? Let's spend the money on somebody who can help the judge figure out what to do. The do-nothing position does not further the interests of children.

The fourth option when a child is too young to direct the attorney is to appoint a guardian ad litem to decide what is best for the child. The child's attorney then advocates in court for the guardian's decisions. This is another well-intended bad idea. There is no reason to believe that a guardian ad litem will be any better than an attorney at deciding what is best for a child. Moreover, who will pay for the thousands of guardian ad litems required by this approach? Taxpayers are already paying for attorneys for parents, CPS agencies, and children. If that isn't enough, are we going to inject another adult into the equation and pay them too? Remember, none of the money that pays for attorneys and guardians ad litem is available to pay for services for children and families. All the money disappears into the legal system.

In response to the cost argument, supporters of the additional guardian ad litem approach assert that volunteer guardians can be recruited and trained to make decisions in children's best interests. Wouldn't it be smarter to skip the volunteers and train the attorneys? There's no reason to think volunteers will make better post-training decisions than attorneys. The extra guardian ad litem idea is impractical and unwise.

Where does all this lead? Children who are mature enough to direct their counsel have the right to do so, and for these children, the child's wishes model is proper. For mature children, the ABA and NACC standards are appropriate. Where I part company with most of those who address this issue is the age at which children should be allowed to direct counsel. I'm an unabashed paternalist. The clear message from the psychological literature is that fourteen is the minimum age. Below fourteen, children are too young to be responsible decision makers.

For children too immature to decide for themselves what to advocate in court—and that is nearly all children under age fourteen—the proper role for the child's attorney is guardian ad litem. The attorney conducts a thorough investigation and makes a judgment about what is best for the child. I'm not saying this is easy, and I'm not suggesting that the training lawyers get in law school equips them for the task. I *am* saying that experience doing this difficult work, combined with ongoing training and consultation with professionals in other disciplines, gives children's attorneys the tools they need to make wise decisions most of the time. The guardian ad litem role for attorneys is more likely than the child's wishes approach to serve children better. Children deserve representation from an adult with their best interests at heart, and that is precisely what they get with an attorney guardian ad litem.

When Should the Child–Parent Relationship Be Terminated?

The legal relationship between parent and child ends three ways: death of parent or child, voluntary relinquishment of parental rights, or involuntary termination of parental rights by a judge. By any measure, a judge's order ending the legal relationship between parent and child is a serious matter. Yet, there are times when the only way to secure a child's future is to sever ties to their parents. Indeed, we need to be more aggressive in ending the rights of parents who cannot or will not live up to their responsibilities.

Parenting is biological, psychological, cultural, and legal. The biological bond to children is instinctive. We are born to parent.[88] At the psychological level, the attachment between parent and child is unparalleled. The drive to protect and nurture one's child is innate and powerful, often more powerful than the will to live. Incorrigible villains are often doting parents. Consider Aaron in Shakespeare's *Titus Andronicus*. Shakespeare portrays Aaron as the embodiment of evil. As Aaron contemplates his imminent demise, his primary regret is that he will no longer be able to wreak havoc, murder, rape, betrayal, and misery on others. Yet, he will stop at nothing to protect his infant child. Aaron is an exceedingly bad man but a good daddy.

Culture mirrors the interwoven biological and psychological dimensions of parenting. In turn, culture influences the biopsychological sphere. Two recent cultural developments demonstrate this symbiotic relationship: changing attitudes toward corporal punishment, and the role of fathers in day-to-day care of babies. Hitting children in the name of discipline has long been normative in American culture. Not long ago, it was common to use paddles, belts, and other instruments to discipline children. By the late twentieth century, however, such methods of punishment were increasingly viewed as unacceptable. Although many parents still hit their children in the name of discipline, the cultural trend is away from such punishment. Hopefully, twenty-second-century parents will view corporal punishment as a barbaric relic of an unenlightened past.

In the typical American family of the 1950s, father went to work and mother stayed home with the children. When dad returned at the end of the day, he dandled Junior on his knee but called in the expert when diapers needed changing. Fathers played an important role in child rearing, but moms carried most day-to-day parenting responsibilities. In the latter part of the twentieth century, cultural attitudes toward fathering changed, fueled by greater egalitarianism and a flood of women into the workforce. Increasing numbers of fathers are actively, albeit generally not equally, involved in caring for babies and little children. In this way, culture influences and reinforces the psychology of parenting.

Law is an expression of cultural norms. The U.S. Constitution protects the right of parents to custody of children. The Constitution creates a "private realm of family life which the state cannot enter."[89] In sum, parenting is embedded in our law, in our culture, and in who we are.

In addition to rights, parents have responsibilities. Fortunately, parents are biologically, psychologically, culturally, and legally driven to fulfill these responsibilities. At the level of biology, instinct propels us to protect and nurture offspring, and psychology reinforces this instinct. Our culture values competent parenting and stigmatizes parents who neglect their children. Finally, the law insists that parents meet their child's needs for food, clothing, shelter, medical care, and support. When parents fail in their responsibilities toward their children, as when they inflict abuse or neglect, criminal law punishes the parent and juvenile court protects the child. In drastic cases, the juvenile court terminates the legal child–parent relationship.

Legal Grounds to Terminate Parental Rights. Only a judge has authority to sever the legal child–parent relationship against the parents' wishes. Every state has laws establishing grounds for termination. Typically, the grounds consist of parental misconduct that harms the child and demonstrates persistent parental incompetence. In juvenile court, proceedings to terminate parental rights are instituted by the government, and the government has the burden of proving one or more grounds for termination.

In litigation, there are three levels of proof. From lowest to highest, the levels are preponderance of the evidence, clear and convincing evidence, and proof beyond a reasonable doubt. The higher the level of proof required in a particular type of litigation, the more difficult it is for the party with the burden of proof to prove its case. The higher the level of proof required, the more confident we are that the result is correct. Thus, in criminal litigation, where the liberty, reputation, and, in capital cases, the life of the defendant are at stake, the highest and most difficult level of proof—beyond a reasonable doubt—is imposed on the prosecution. The prosecution's evidence must satisfy the jury of the defendant's guilt beyond a reasonable doubt. If there is a reasonable doubt, the jury *must* acquit the defendant.

The easiest level of proof to satisfy is the preponderance of evidence standard, which is employed in most civil litigation. The preponderance standard requires the party with the burden of proof to bring forth evidence that convinces the jury or judge that it is more likely than not that the party should win. In a typical auto accident case, for example, the plaintiff driver has the burden of proving that it is more likely than not that the defendant driver was negligent.

Clear and convincing evidence lies somewhere between preponderance of evidence and proof beyond a reasonable doubt, precisely how far between is unclear. Although percentages do not convey the full meaning of levels of proof, they provide a rough sense of the certainty required. Thus, the preponderance standard is sometimes described as 51 percent certainty, proof beyond a reasonable doubt is in the neighborhood of 95 percent certainty. Clear and convincing evidence is roughly 75 percent certainty.

Clear and convincing evidence is required in several types of civil cases where the interests at stake are so important that a level of certainty higher than a preponderance of evidence is necessary. The U.S. Supreme Court ruled, for example, that the Constitution requires clear and convincing evidence to involuntarily civilly commit a mentally ill person to a psychiatric hospital. California's juvenile courts use the preponderance standard to determine whether a child is abused or neglected. If the state seeks to remove the child from the home, however, the state must justify removal with clear and convincing evidence. The U.S. Supreme Court ruled in *Santosky v. Kramer* that because of the importance of the parent–child relationship, the Constitution requires clear and convincing evidence to terminate parental rights.[90]

The legal grounds to terminate parental rights have not changed significantly since the early twentieth century. For example, California in 1917 authorized courts to terminate parental rights in seven situations: (1) when parents left their child in the care of another without provision for the child's support and with the intent to abandon the child; (2) when a child was "cruelly treated or neglected by his parent or parents"; (3) when the parent was "habitually intemperate"; (4) when the parent was incurably insane; (5) when the parent was mentally retarded; (6) when the parent was divorced because of the parent's adultery or cruelty to the other spouse; and (7) when the parent was convicted of a serious crime that resulted in loss of civil rights (i.e., loss of the right to vote and hold public office).

Focusing on the last two grounds to terminate parental rights, in the early twentieth century, adultery was a crime and was equated by the legislature with parental incompetence. Today, adultery is frowned on but is not a basis to terminate parental rights. Conviction of a crime is no longer automatic justification to terminate parental rights.

The other grounds to terminate parental rights set forth in California's early law—abandonment, maltreatment, substance abuse, mental illness, and mental retardation—are as viable today as they were in 1917. Other states have similar grounds for termination. Each state sets a time limit for abandonment. Maltreatment must be serious or repeated. Substance abuse has to be chronic. Mental illness alone is not sufficient to terminate parental rights. The parent's mental illness must seriously compromise the capacity to parent and must be chronic. Finally, mental retardation itself is not grounds to terminate parental rights. A parent's low intelligence must seriously compromise their capacity to parent.

Impact of Federal Law on Termination of Parental Rights.   The federal government plays an important role in shaping policy on termination of parental rights. In 1980, Congress passed the Adoption Assistance and Child Welfare Act (AACW). AACW provides funds to support child welfare services. One goal of AACW was to reduce the number of children in foster care by requiring states to make "reasonable efforts" to prevent removal of children from their homes, and, when removal was necessary, to make "reasonable efforts" to reunify families. Unfortunately, AACW did not reduce the foster care population, and in 1997, Congress responded with the Adoption and Safe Families Act (ASFA). Although ASFA continues the "reasonable efforts" requirement, ASFA increases the circumstances in which states terminate parental rights.

Under ASFA, every abused or neglected child in foster care must have a case plan that is reviewed by a judge or an administrative body at least every six months. Within twelve months of entering foster care, the state must hold a permanency hearing to determine the child's future. ASFA encourages states to begin proceedings to terminate parental rights when a child has been in foster care for fifteen of the most recent twenty-two months.

In the following aggravated circumstances, ASFA urges states to forego any effort to reunify the family and move directly to termination of parental rights: the child has been abandoned; the parent assaulted the child and caused serious injury; the parent subjected the child to sexual abuse, chronic abuse, or torture; the parent murdered another child; or the parent's rights to another child have been terminated.

A More Aggressive Approach to Termination of Parental Rights.   Many social workers struggle to come to terms with termination of parental rights. Social work is about helping people improve their circumstances. Social workers want to help struggling parents do a better job so children can remain safely at home. The desire to help families stay together runs deep in social work. In 1909, the social workers attending the influential White House Conference on the Care of Dependent Children stated, "Home life is the highest and finest product of civilization. It is the great molding force of mind and of character. Children should not be deprived of it except for urgent and compelling reasons."[91]

The importance of keeping children with their parents was reiterated by the attendees at the 1930 White House Conference on Child Health and Protection in these words:

> The family is the richest medium for the nurture and development of the child. Where the essentials of family life exist, even incompletely, every effort should be made to keep the child with his own mother and father. Their home is his rightful place. The sense of belonging meets one of his fundamental needs. He feels himself secure as part of a stable and resourceful family group, in a world of strangers and of dangers. Almost certainly in later life he will be a member of some other family; what is more important than to secure for him as a child a normal preparatory experience in his own home? Here he learns to meaning of loyalty, that fundamental factor in character. The child's own family sees him intimately, sees him under all circumstances and conditions, has a more continuous opportunity to understand him, is more certain to cherish a continuing confidence in him, and to respect his aims and accomplishments than any other group. Parents add to these considerations an enduring loyalty and confidence, for nature gives to parents rose tinted glasses in viewing their offspring.[92]

Social workers are so imbued with the desire to help that some of them view termination of parental rights as a personal and professional failure. With this in mind, we need to expand the definition of success in child welfare. When parents can be helped, that's great. In appropriate cases, however, promptly terminating the rights of incompetent parents *is* the measure of success. Some parents don't parent, and no amount of services, counseling, or parenting classes will help. In such cases, our eyes need to be on the child and on finding a nurturing and permanent home for the child. Terminating the child–parent relationship as quickly as possible can be the key to the child's future. The longer we wait to sever parental ties, the longer the child languishes in foster care, and the less likely the child is to be adopted. When we drag our heels trying to help hopeless parents, we fail children. Success in child welfare means taking families apart as well as keeping them together.

Terminating the child–parent relationship due to parental substance abuse raises complex issues. Substance abuse plays an enormous role in child abuse and neglect. Parents with serious substance abuse problems, particularly addiction, seldom provide competent parenting. Yet, most substance-abusing parents who hurt or neglect their children deserve a chance to kick the habit before parental rights are terminated. When a juvenile court determines that substance abuse contributes to child abuse or neglect, the parent should be ordered into treatment unless the parent's addiction is chronic and previous treatments have failed. In the face of previous failures, the judge should move decisively toward termination of parental rights.

When maltreating parents with serious substance abuse problems are court ordered into treatment, they should be clearly informed that they are being afforded a limited opportunity to get clean and sober to regain custody of their children. The parent deserves prompt admission to a quality treatment program tailored to their needs, not prompt addition to a waiting list. Every time a substance-abusing parent with a child in foster care is put on a waiting list, society fails the child.

Once in treatment, the parent should have six months to get clean and sober. No more than six months, and few second chances. But what of the fact that many people who ultimately succeed at substance abuse treatment relapse, fall off the wagon? For many addicts it takes years to kick the habit. There are four reasons it is wrong to give substance-abusing parents multiple chances at treatment. First, when substance-abusing parents fall off the wagon, they pull their kids off with them. The parent falls to the pavement in a stupor. The child falls further into the uncertainty of long-term foster care. Giving substance-abusing parents multiple opportunities at treatment is unfair to children. Second, substance abuse treatment is expensive and in short supply. It is a waste of resources to provide treatment to people who can't or won't put in the effort required to help themselves. Third, giving substance-abusing parents multiple bites at the treatment apple sends the message that we are not serious when we insist on reform. Fourth, parents have responsibilities: Parents have a moral and a legal duty to take care of their children, and when they allow addictions to interfere with that responsibility, they are making a choice—a choice to abdicate responsibility.

An increasing number of communities have a "drug court," which is a specialized court for selected individuals whose legal difficulties are tied to alcohol or substance abuse. When a substance-abusing parent is a good candidate for drug court, the juvenile court judge may approve this option.

Judges are loath to terminate the child–parent relationship, a reticence that is understandable in view of the enormity of the decision. Moreover, every time a judge considers termination, she comes face-to-face with a long line of U.S. Supreme Court and state supreme court decisions placing parental rights on a pedestal.[93] The U.S. Supreme Court has stated, "It is cardinal with us that the custody, care and nurture of the child reside first in the parents, whose primary function and freedom include preparation for obligations the state can neither supply nor hinder."[94] Elsewhere the court wrote, "The family has a privacy interest in the upbringing and education of children . . . which is protected by the Constitution against undue state interference."[95]

No one gainsays the importance of parental rights. I believe, however, that constant pronouncements by appellate judges about the importance of parental rights make some trial judges so timid that they hesitate to "pull the trigger" when termination is appropriate. The justices of the U.S. Supreme Court and state appellate courts could help their colleagues on the trial bench by finding opportunities to discuss the importance of ending the child–parent relationship. Recognizing that some child–parent relations are not worth saving does nothing to undermine respect for families.

In some ways, a family is like a human body. Severing the parent–child relationship is like cutting off an arm or leg. Yet, there are times when an arm or leg is so infected, so riddled with gangrene that the only way to save the body is to sever the limb. Similarly, with the parent–child relationship, some parents are so incompetent, cruel, or addicted that they infect their children and the only remedy is a legal scalpel. Termination is painful but necessary for the child's future. Just as the surgeon does not hesitate to amputate the gangrenous limb, so the judge must sever the parent–child relation that is poisoned beyond repair. The child welfare system must move more rapidly to help parents who can be helped. At the same time, the system must move more decisively to terminate parental rights when help is unavailing or rejected.

Rejuvenating the Juvenile Court

When the juvenile court was born in 1899, its creators eschewed formal legal procedures and rules of evidence in favor of informality. In delinquency as well as abuse and neglect cases, lawyers seldom played a role. The judge listened to the evidence and decided what was best for the child. It was believed that legal technicalities, including lawyers, were unnecessary and interfered with the judge's ability to dispense individualized justice. In delinquency cases, however, critics of the juvenile court argued that children accused of crime should have rights similar to the rights of adults accused of crime. Adults have the right to remain silent, the right to notice of the charges against them, the right to appeal if they are convicted, and the right to an attorney. In 1967, the U.S. Supreme Court addressed children's rights in delinquency proceedings in *In re Gault*.[96] The Supreme Court ruled that children accused in juvenile court of delinquency are entitled to most of the rights afforded adults, including the right to counsel. The effect of *In re Gault* was to formalize delinquency proceedings. Before long, delinquency trials in juvenile court looked a lot like criminal trials in adult court.

Although *Gault* was a delinquency case, the decision had spillover effects on juvenile court proceedings to protect abused and neglected children. Prior to this case, lawyers were uncommon in abuse and neglect cases. The child protection agency was typically represented by a social worker, who presented the agency's position to the judge. Parents, most of whom were poor, seldom had legal representation. Rules of evidence and procedure were downplayed or ignored, and informality was the order of the day. Following *Gault*, however, lawyers became increasingly common in abuse and neglect cases. Today, the child protection agency is represented by a district attorney or another government lawyer. Parents who can't afford an attorney are represented by appointed counsel. As discussed earlier, judges increasingly appoint attorneys for children. One by-product of attorneys is greater formality and a more adversarial approach to cases. Although informality has not been sacrificed entirely, *Gault* transformed the juvenile court's handling of abuse and neglect.

Does a more legalistic and adversarial juvenile court produce a net benefit for maltreated children and their parents? Reasonable minds differ on this question. No one disputes that parents have important interests at stake in juvenile court. To offset the power differential between parents and the state, one can make a strong argument that parents need attorneys to defend their interests. On the other hand, it can be argued that the juvenile court's ability to protect children and help parents is undermined by the loss of flexibility that comes with multiple attorneys and rules of procedure and evidence. Even when courts function at their best, they are not very good at solving complex human problems. I believe transforming the juvenile court from an informal sociolegal institution into an adversary forum crippled the court's ability to respond to families in crisis. To my mind, *Gault* has done more harm than good to the juvenile court's ability to deal effectively with abuse and neglect. Parents certainly deserve fair treatment. Moreover, attorneys have an important role to play. However, the juvenile court of the early twenty-first century has lost the flexibility and informality required to respond effectively to abuse and neglect. The juvenile court needs an overhaul, a return to the informality of an earlier day.

Part of the solution to what ails the juvenile court lies in alternative dispute resolution (ADR). ADR is a well-established field of expertise that seeks to resolve disputes without litigation. Two ADR techniques that hold promise for recapturing a measure of the informality of the early juvenile court are family group conferencing and mediation.

Family group conferencing (FGC) originated in New Zealand in the 1980s.[97] The idea is to remove cases from the adversary system and to involve the child's extended family in finding amicable solutions to family problems. The FGC process typically involves four steps. First, a referral is made for a conference. Referrals come from social workers, judges, parents, and other interested persons. Second, a professional with special training, often called a coordinator, prepares the meeting. The coordinator invites the parents, extended family members, and relevant professionals to attend. A key aspect of preparing for a family group conference is taking the time—often quite a bit of time—to equip parents with the information and self-confidence they need to participate as equals in the conference. The parents are encouraged to invite persons they think can contribute. The coordinator gathers records and other information that will be needed at the conference.

Third, the conference is held at a time and place convenient for the family. Typically, a number of professionals attend the conference (e.g., social worker, family doctor, minister). In some places, attorneys attend family group conferences. In other communities, attorneys are not invited. When the child is old enough to participate meaningfully, the child attends. Following initial discussion, the family meets privately to formulate a plan to protect the child. When the family is satisfied, the professionals rejoin the conference and the family's plan is discussed. In most cases, the family and the professionals agree. Communities vary on which professional or professionals can veto a family's plan. Assuming there is agreement, the coordinator documents it, and, in some communities, the agreement is submitted to the juvenile court judge for approval. Fourth, the agreement emerging from a family group conference contains provisions for post-conference services and monitoring by child welfare. If all goes well, the agreement expires and the family goes on with life.

A small number of states have statutes authorizing family group conferencing (e.g., Kansas, Montana, Oregon, South Carolina, and Washington).[98] Other states are experimenting with FGC sans statutory authorization (e.g., California).

To date there is little empirical research on the effectiveness of FGC. The research that does exist is not very encouraging. The first published study comparing FGC with traditional child protection is from Sweden. Knut Sundell and Bo Vinnerljung compared 67 families who went through FGC with 106 families who received traditional child protective services.[99] Sundell and Vinnerljung found that although the family group conferences themselves went well, the long-term outcome for FGC families was not superior to traditional protective services. Indeed, during a three-year follow-up period, more FGC families were re-referred to child protection for physical abuse than families that received traditional services. The jury is still out on the effectiveness of family group conferencing.

An alternative to family group conferencing is mediation, which is a time-tested method of resolving disputes without litigation. An impartial mediator, who may or may not be an attorney, brings the sides together in an effort to find common ground and reach agreement. Mediation has been used successfully for years in a wide range of legal arenas, including custody disputes in family court. Mediation is a relative newcomer in juvenile court protective proceedings but is finding increasing acceptance. An evaluation of juvenile court mediation in Essex County, New Jersey, found that most participants—parents and professionals— were satisfied with the process. When parents are properly prepared, mediation gives them a sense that they are listened to and respected.[100]

Alternatives to litigation are important in the effort to rejuvenate the juvenile court. Yet, with mediation and family group conferencing, something is missing. What key ingredient do these techniques omit? The judge. It seems that the more we embrace nonadversarial solutions in juvenile court, the less we see of the judge. Of course, the judge is still there to preside over trials of cases that don't settle and over proceedings to terminate parental rights. Perhaps we will have to content ourselves with a juvenile court judge whose role is limited to presiding over trials, much like judges in criminal court. Yet, don't we lose something when juvenile court judges are limited to the residue of cases that can't be resolved without a fight? Yes. We lose the tradition of the wise juvenile court judge meeting informally with troubled parents and helping them solve their problems. The judge is the ultimate authority in the legal system. The judge carries an aura of authority that is unique to the judicial role. Given the prestige and power of the office, judges have unparalleled problem-solving capacity—capacity that is squandered when judges are limited to presiding over trials.

Today, we risk losing the century-old tradition of the juvenile court judge as informal, hands-on problem solver. The loss, if it occurs, will be a direct result of *In re Gault*. The *Gault* decision led to the introduction of lawyers in protective proceedings. As lawyers entered the front door, informality left by the rear exit, crowded out by the winner-take-all mentality at the heart of the adversary system of justice.

The attorneys who devote themselves to the juvenile court don't do it for the money. They do it to help children and families, and they often succeed. Yet, attorneys are ingrained in the traditions of adversarial litigation. Many attorneys in juvenile court realize the drawbacks of an adversarial approach and work hard to reach amicable solutions. In the end, however, attorneys behave like attorneys because they're attorneys. If the tradition of the judge as informal problem solver is worth saving, we'll need a little less lawyering in juvenile court.

I recommend a return to the original model in which the judge meets in an office (not a courtroom) with the parents, social worker, and, as appropriate, others. Lawyers do not attend. Rules of evidence and formal testimony are replaced with informal discussion. Everyone has an opportunity to talk to the judge and each other. Everything that is said is confidential so parents can feel comfortable being candid. The judge decides what is needed to help the family and keep the child safe. The judge discusses her ideas with the others and comes to a resolution.

Does this proposal differ from mediation? Yes. The difference is that with this proposal the judge is once again at the heart of the process. The judge brings to the table the entire legal and moral authority of the judicial office. The judge is not separated physically and psychologically from the parties by a bench and a robe. Sitting at the same table, the judge is first among equals. The skillful judge brings a chemistry to the meeting that lowers barriers and inspires the participants toward compromise and consensus. This model of judging is the genius of the juvenile court, and we can't afford to lose it. To fulfill its potential as a vital component of society's response to abuse and neglect, the juvenile court must return to its roots in the early twentieth century, prior to the unintended but corrupting influence of *In re Gault*.

Under the proposal described above, parents would not be forced to forego a trial where they are represented by counsel. Parents desiring the type of informal meeting described here are volunteers. Moreover, parents who are dissatisfied with the judge's decision at an informal meeting can request a trial before a different judge.

Prior to becoming a judge, relatively few attorneys have experience with child abuse, neglect, poverty, substance abuse, and the host of social issues that take center stage in juvenile court. In many states, judges rotate judicial assignments, and a stint in juvenile court may last only a year or two. Experienced judges know it takes a year to begin learning the ropes in juvenile court. To fulfill the Solomon-like judicial role described here, we need judges who are committed to the juvenile court for extended periods, preferably as a career. Juvenile court judges should be encouraged to earn masters or doctoral degrees in social work, sociology, or psychology.

Utah is at the head of the class when it comes to selecting judges who are committed to the juvenile court. In Utah, the juvenile court is separate from the rest of the judiciary. When a Utah attorney applies to become a juvenile court judge, she knows from the outset she will always serve that court. Thus, the attorneys who apply are committed to helping children and families. Utah's approach is worthy of emulation.

Conclusion

In 1938, that great advocate for children, Grace Abbott, penned the words that begin this book, "The progress of a state may be measured by the extent to which it safeguards the rights of its children." As we look back across American history, we ask: What progress has America made in its effort to safeguard children from abuse and neglect? Can we feel pride in what has been accomplished? Or should we lower our eyes in shame at how little has been achieved?

The first colonists reached these shores in 1607, and, from the earliest days, people of good will rescued children from abuse and neglect. Yet, more than two-and-a-half centuries elapsed before organized child protection began in 1875 with the creation of the New York Society for the Prevention of Cruelty to Children (NYSPCC). From the time the NYSPCC opened its doors, it took another century for America to patch together a nationwide system of child protective services. Although early progress was slow, the pace of child protection quickened significantly in the last quarter of the twentieth century and shows no signs of waning. Progress has been made.

What is the state of child protection today? Newspaper and television reports often portray a child protection system in trouble—failing to protect children in obvious danger, randomly tearing families apart, and haphazardly dumping children into dangerous and poorly supervised foster homes. Many well-informed experts believe child protection is in crisis.[101] Leroy Pelton wrote, "Public child welfare is in chaos. Nationally, more than two million reports of alleged child abuse and neglect overwhelm public child welfare agencies each year."[102] Alvin Schorr wrote that a "series of blows" left child welfare in "shambles."[103] Schorr attributes the mounting crisis to worsening poverty, substance abuse, increasing numbers of single-parent families, and the flood of reports to child protective services. In 1990, the U.S. Advisory Board on Child Abuse and Neglect warned that fundamental change is needed to keep the child protection system from collapsing.

There is no gainsaying that child protection has too much to do. Child protection is burdened with so many cases that it cannot function optimally. Yes, child protection is in trouble, but is it in danger of collapse? Before we push the panic button, remember: There has never been a time when the child protection system wasn't overburdened. There has never been a time when the system was adequately funded and staffed. Consider six quotes spanning the twentieth century:[104]

1933: "Large areas, especially in rural sections where it is frequently most needed, are without child protective services of any kind." (Theodore Lothrop)

1939: "The lack of systematic children's protective work is still a serious gap in the children's work of many cities and states." (Carl Carstens)

1958: "The number of families and children being served by the agency has increased steadily year by year. The allocation of staff has never been able to match the increased demands." (Claire Hancock)

1967: "No state and no community has developed a Child Protective Service program adequate in size to meet the service needs of all reported cases of child neglect, abuse and exploitation." (Vincent De Francis)

1993: "Whether the focus is prevention, investigation, adjudication, or treatment, resources have failed to grow at a rate anything close to the explosive rise in the number of reports of child maltreatment and the parallel increase in the complexity of reported cases." (U.S. Advisory Board on Child Abuse and Neglect)

Child protection has always been stretched thin. I see no evidence, however, that the system is collapsing. For well over a century, child protection has been running at breakneck speed just to keep pace. Today's underpaid and undervalued social workers have to run a little faster than their nineteenth-century counterparts, but they keep up most of the time. Pay a visit to a child protection agency and you will find dedicated professionals working to help children and families. You will find stress and frustration, but you won't find a sense that child protection is futile or that the system is bankrupt. You'll find persistence, not panic.

When it comes to holding the child protection system accountable, keep in mind the enormity of the responsibilities entrusted to child protection. We are asking a lot when we ask the social workers, judges, lawyers, nurses, and doctors of the child protection system to fulfill the responsibilities that are clearly theirs. We must not hold them accountable for things over which they have no control. In particular, the child protection system is not responsible for the social ills that cause maltreatment, including poverty, racism, substance abuse, crime, and violence. Responsibility for the precursors of child abuse and neglect lies with society at large and with our political institutions and our lack of will to do something about these problems, *not* with the child protection system. The child protection system is overworked because society has failed to fulfill its responsibilities, not because the system is inherently flawed.

If you want evidence that the child protection system works, look no further than the personal stories of children whose lives are safer and happier because someone stepped in to stop abuse. Recall Mary Ellen Wilson, whose rescue in 1874 led to the creation of the New York Society for the Prevention of Cruelty to Children. Mary Ellen was rescued from cruelty, enjoyed a happy childhood, married, had children, and devoted herself to helping others by serving on the Board of Directors of the American Humane Association. The movement that grew out of Mary Ellen's rescue has saved millions of children. Given the enormity of its responsibilities, it is a wonder the child protection system works as well as it does. The mission is to improve the system, not start from scratch.

With an eye toward improving the child protection system, chapter 6 outlined the major causes of abuse and neglect, along with roadblocks to reform. Chapter 7 discussed broad steps that will reduce maltreatment. These steps include home visiting by nurses, subsidized day care for working parents, expanding the Head Start program to give poor children an academic jump start, creating a less toxic society, teaching parenting skills through the implementation of family and consumer studies, strengthening communities, outlawing hitting children in the name of discipline, and rethinking attitudes toward drinking.

Chapter 8 shifted the focus from broad reforms to specific steps designed to improve today's child protection system, including redoubled efforts to weed out the lingering effects of racism, challenging social work to reclaim its leadership position in child protection, creating a less adversarial child protection system, modifying child abuse reporting laws to give professionals discretion on what and when to report, strengthening foster care and adding Temporary Permanent Attachment Care, and rejuvenating the juvenile court by recapturing the informality that was a major component of the genius of the court.

Even if *none* of these improvements are made, Americans should be proud of their child protection system. We do not have to lower our eyes in shame at how little has been done. A great deal has been accomplished. If Grace Abbott were here today, we could look her in the eye and say, "We have made the progress you demanded. America has a system in place to safeguard the rights of its children from maltreatment." Abbott would be happy but not satisfied. She would note with satisfaction that almshouses and orphanages have disappeared. Today, most children who cannot stay at home live with relatives or foster parents. Abbott would be pleased with the growth of child welfare as a specialty within her beloved profession of social work. She would nod approvingly when she learned that America's child protection system now reaches coast to coast, and that federal, state, and local governments spend generously on child welfare programs.

Organized child protection was invented in America and shared with the world. The sustained drive to protect children from maltreatment is a major accomplishment toward human progress and common decency. Yet, the work of child protection is far from complete, and redoubled efforts must begin today so children are guaranteed the future they deserve.

NOTES

Part I

1. See U.S. Children's Bureau, *Child Maltreatment 2003* (2005; U.S. Department of Health and Human Resources). The Children's Bureau report states, "For 2003, an estimated 1,500 children died due to abuse or neglect" (p. xvii).

2. David Davis, *The Unquiet Death of Eli Creekmore*. Documentary film produced in 1987 by Public Television station KCTS, Seattle, Washington.

3. Barbara Feaster, personal communication, 2004.

4. Jamal's story is based on a case from California. See People v. Ruby Pointer, 199 Cal. Rpt. 357 (Ct. App. 1984). I am grateful to Dr. Loretta Rao for taking the time to describe to me her vital role in this case. Dr. Rao saved Jamal's life.

5. Olivia Waggoner, personal communication, 2004.

Chapter 1

1. The word "outdoor" relief was used because the relief was granted to poor people living outside the doors of an almshouse. Relief in the almshouse was "indoor" relief.

2. Robert H. Bremner (Ed.), *Children and Youth in America: A Documentary History*, vol. 1, p. 104 (1970; Cambridge, MA: Harvard University Press).

3. See Michael Wald, State Intervention on Behalf of "Neglected" Children: A Search for Realistic Standards, 27 *Stanford Law Review* 985 (1975). In this important article, Wald was among the first to call for clear distinctions between poverty and neglect.

4. Bremner, *Children and Youth*, pp. 262, 265, 272. Bremner quoted from the "Rules for the Government of the Almshouse," October 6, 1800, as found in the New York City Council Minutes, 1784–1831, II, p. 671.

5. See Homer Folks, *The Care of Destitute, Neglected, and Delinquent Children* (1902; New York: MacMillan Co.). Folks wrote (pp. 167–168) that Massachusetts poor law authorized local authorities to bind out neglected children.

6. Bremner, *Children and Youth*, p. 123.

7. See Clyde E. Buckingham, Early American Orphanages: Ebenezer and Bethesda, 26 *Social Forces* 311–321, p. 314 (1948).

8. A description of this case was sold to the public as a pamphlet titled, "The Trial of Amos Broad and His Wife on Three Several Indictments for Assaulting and Beating Betty,

A Slave, and Her Little Child Sarah, Aged Three Years." The pamphlet is reproduced in Paul Finkelman (Ed.), *Slavery, Race, and the American Legal System: 1700–1872. A Sixteen Volume Facsimile Series Reproducing Over One Hundred and Seventy Rare and Important Pamphlets* (1988). Series VI, vol. 1, pp. 179–209. *Free Blacks, Slaves, and Slave Owners in Civil and Criminal Courts* (New York: Garland).

9. Report of the Trial of Susanna. Pamphlet reproduced in Paul Finkelman (Ed.), *Slavery, Race*, pp. 211–260.

10. Folks, *Care of Destitute*, pp. 168–169; Murray Levine & Adeline Levine. *Helping Children: A Social History*, p. 207 (1992; New York: Oxford University Press).

11. See Maurice O. Hunt, Child Welfare. In Russell H. Kurtz (Ed.), *Social Work Yearbook 1960*, vol. 14 (1960; New York: Russell Sage Foundation); June Axinn & Mark J. Stern, *Social Welfare: A History of the American Response to Need*, 5th ed. (2000; Boston: Allyn & Bacon).

12. Folks, *Care of Destitute*, p. 13 (1902; New York: MacMillan).

13. In a report in 1821, Josiah Quincy of Massachusetts condemned outdoor relief and praised the almshouse. Josiah Quincy, *Report of the Massachusetts Committee on the Pauper Laws in 1821*. In Sophonisba P. Breckenridge, *Public Welfare Administration in the United States: Selected Documents* (1927; Chicago: University of Chicago Press). In another report, John Yates, the Secretary of State of New York State, recommended the creation of workhouses. John V.N. Yates, *Report of the Secretary of State on the Relief and Settlement of the Poor* (1824). Yates' report is reprinted in *Poverty, U.S.A., The Almshouse Experience* (1971; New York: Arno Press and New York Times).

14. Grace Abbott, *The Child and the State*, vol. 1, p. 5 (1938; Chicago: University of Chicago Press).

15. Breckenridge, *Public Welfare Administration*, pp. 146, 169; Henry Smith Williams, What Shall Be Done with Dependent Children? 164(485) *North American Review* 404–415, pp. 404–405 (April, 1897).

16. Homer Folks, The Removal of Children from Almshouses. In *Proceedings of the National Conference of Charities and Corrections*, p. 1 (1894; Boston).

17. See Sister Jane Frances Heaney, *A Century of Pioneering: A History of the Ursuline Nuns in New Orleans—1727 to 1827* (1993; New Orleans: Ursuline Sisters of New Orleans). See also Henry Churchill (Ed.), *The Ursulines in New Orleans and Our Lady of Prompt Succor: A Record of Two Centuries. 1727–1925* (1925; New York: P.J. Kennedy and Sons).

18. Historians differ slightly on the number of orphanages in existence before 1800. See Bremner, *Children and Youth*, p. 275. Bremner noted, "Prior to 1800 orphan homes or asylums for unfortunate children were rare" (p. 282).

19. Folks, *Care of Destitute*. Folks created a table (p. 55) describing the founding of orphanages:

Founded prior to 1801: 6
Founded 1800 to 1811: 2
Founded 1811 to 1821: 7
Founded 1821 to 1831: 6
Founded 1831 to 1841: 26

Founded 1841 to 1851: 30
Total   : 77

See also LeRoy Ashby, *Endangered Children: Dependency, Neglect, and Abuse in American History* (1997; New York: Twayne). Ashby wrote, "Between 1820 and 1860, 150 private orphanages were founded across the country" (p. 28).

20. See Hastings H. Hart, *Preventive Treatment of Neglected Children*, p. 1 (1910; New York: Russell Sage Foundation).

21. For biographical information on Charles Loring Brace, See Emma Brace, *The Life of Charles Loring Brace: Chiefly Told in His Own Letters* (1894; New York: Charles Scribner's Sons). Emma Brace was Charles Loring Brace's daughter.

22. Five Points was razed to the ground in the 1880s.

23. Charles Dickens, *American Notes*, pp. 100–102 (1900 printing; New York: Oxford University Press).

24. See Edwin G. Burrows & Mike Wallace, *A History of New York City to 1898* (1999; New York: Oxford University Press).

25. Letter reproduced in Emma Brace, *The Life of Charles Loring Brace*, pp. 154–155.

26. See Stephen O'Connor, *Orphan Trains: The Story of Charles Loring Brace and the Children He Saved and Failed*, p. 38 (2001; Boston: Houghton Mifflin);

Richard A. Meckel, Protecting the Innocents: Age Segregation and the Early Child Welfare Movement, 59 *Social Service Review* 455–475, at 462 (1985).

27. Manhattan was the most populous of New York City's boroughs. Manhattan's population rose dramatically from 1790, when the island was home to 33,000. By 1880, Manhattan's population exceeded 1,160,000. At relevant times, Manhattan's population was:

1790—33,000
1810—96,000
1820—123,000
1840—312,000
1850—515,000
1860—813,000
1880—1,160,000

(Source: *Comprehensive Census of the United States*, p. 192 [1850]). Looking at the percentage of New York City's population that was native born versus foreign born, we find that in 1845, residents of foreign birth comprised 36 percent of the city's population of 371,223. In 1850, foreign-born residents comprised 45 percent of the population of 515,547. In 1855, foreign born residents comprised 51 percent of the population of 629,904. In 1860, foreign-born residents comprised 47 percent of the population of 813,669.

28. The country suffered a depression from 1857 to 1859. See Meckel, Protecting the Innocents. Meckel wrote, "Mid-century immigration was accompanied by a series of economic disruptions, culminating in the depression of 1857, which, along with the housing and job shortages produced by the massive influx of immigrants, served to increase significantly the ranks of the homeless, destitute, and criminal in America's cities" (p. 472).

29. Bremner, *Children and Youth*. Bremner wrote, "From the 1840's on, most immigrants arrived virtually penniless. Unable to continue their journey inland, many remained in the coastal cities to swell the roles of unskilled labor and the dependent poor" (p. 398).

30. Burrows & Wallace, *A History of New York City*, p. 790.

31. See Thomas E. Cone, Jr., *History of American Pediatrics* (1979; Boston: Little, Brown and Co.). Cone described in detail the problems associated with impure milk:

> Milk and other perishable foods, in the absence of reliable refrigeration, were subject to the whims of the weather. Milk was commonly adulterated, as well as contaminated with pathogenic bacteria. The milk might come from diseased cows, improperly fed, often with swill from neighboring distilleries, and they were housed in filthy dairies.
>
> It was not until 1896 that the New York City Board of Health adopted a section of the sanitary code prohibiting the sale of milk except under a permit. . . . (p. 106)
>
> Even in the early twentieth century, dirty milk was usually found in most large American cities. . . . (p. 142)

32. Burrows & Wallace, *A History of New York City*, p. 788.

33. In *Children and Youth*, Bremner wrote, "Industrial child labor began in America at the end of the eighteenth century. The novelty of this development should not obscure the fact that during the eighteenth and nineteenth centuries most children continued to work in their homes, on the farm, and in their parents' workshops. . . . The cotton industry in New England brought the industrial revolution to America, and with it the introduction of children as an industrial labor force" (p. 145). Ibid., p. 103.

34. Ashby, *Endangered Children*, p. 41 (1997; New York: Twayne).

35. Emma Brace, *The Life of Charles Loring Brace*, p. 156 (1894; New York: Charles Scribner's Sons).

36. Charles Loring Brace, *The Dangerous Classes of New York, and Twenty Years' Work Among Them*, third edition, p. 223 (1872; New York: Wynkoop & Hallenbeck); emphasis in original. As Brace discussed the ill-effects of alcohol, he hinted at child sexual abuse, writing that in the home of a man who drinks, "Here the hearts of young women are truly broken, and they seek their only consolation in the same magic cup; here children are beaten, or maimed, or half-starved, until they run away" (p. 65). Brace's daughter and biographer, Emma Brace, found among Brace's papers notes hastily written in pencil, probably for a sermon, in which Brace wrote of "The girl old in crime and suffering." Emma Brace, *The Life of Charles Loring Brace*, p. 193.

37. New York Children's Aid Society, *First Annual Report*, p. 6 (1854).

38. Charles Loring Brace, *Dangerous Classes*. In chapter 10, Brace discussed street girls. His primary concern was sexual abuse, although he did not describe it directly in his writing. In this book, Brace wrote, "Among a million people, such as compose the population of this city and its suburbs, there will always be a great number of misfortues; fathers die, and leave their children unprovided for; parents drink, and abuse their little ones, and they float away on the currents of the street; step-mothers or step-fathers drive out, by neglect and ill-treatment, their sons from home" (p. 28).

39. Circular of the New York Children's Aid Society (March, 1853).

40. In *The Life of Charles Loring Brace*, Emma Brace, wrote:

No sooner was the office of the Children's Aid Society opened at 683 Broadway, than there was an immediate response of the children to this effort for them. Crowds of wandering little ones found their way there. Ragged young girls who had nowhere to lay their heads, children driven from drunkards' homes, pickpockets and child beggars and flower-sellers, all came. Mr. Brace says in "The Dangerous Classes of New York": —"All this motley throng of infantile misery and childish guilt passed through our doors, telling their simple stories of suffering and loneliness and temptation, until our hearts became sick; and the present writer, certainly, if he had not been able to stir up the fortunate classes to aid in assuaging these fearful miseries, would have abandoned the post in discouragement and disgust." (pp. 158–159)

41. Charles Loring Brace, The Little Laborers of New York City, 47(279) *Harper's New Monthly Magazine* 322–332, p. 327 (August, 1873). Among the industrial schools operated by CAS, one taught girls to use sewing machines. See Emma Brace, *The Life of Charles Loring Brace*, p. 305.

42. Charles Loring Brace, Little Laborers, pp. 327–328.

43. Brace wrote: "Besides this lodging-house are four other lodging-houses, for newsboys, boot-blacks, and other street lads. The best known of these is the Newsboys' Lodging-House, No. 49 Park Place, the first ever opened in any country, founded in 1854. During nineteen years it has sheltered 91,426 different boys, restored 7196 lost and missing ones to friends, provided 7108 with homes, furnished 576,493 lodgings, and 426,580 meals" (ibid., p. 329). The remarkable precision of Brace's recordkeeping attests to his administrative skill and that of his staff. Brace's daughter and biographer, Emma Brace, in *The Life of Charles Loring Brace*, provided interesting detail on the opening of the first lodging-house:

> The early spring of 1854 saw the opening of the first "Newsboys-Lodging-House." After many efforts, the society finally obtained money enough to pay for a loft in the old Sun Building, and an excellent superintendent, Mr. C.C. Tracy, was procured. A well-ventilated dormitory was fitted up for ninety boys, with comfortable, single beds; there was a large schoolroom (serving also for chapel and playroom), with library, melodeon, and saving bank, besides bath and washrooms, and private lock-closets for clothes for each boy. . . . The boys, nothing loth to obtain the good things, were much puzzled as to what it all meant. It did not occur to them that discipline was to be the order of the place, and they prepared for a grand frolic. But when it was suddenly discovered that the first boots flying about were a signal for the lively ones to be lifted quietly from bed, and left to shiver over their folly, they concluded that the part of discretion was to nestle in their warm beds. Little sleeping, however, was there among them that night. But ejaculations sounded out, such as, "I say, Jim, this is rayther better 'an bumming". "My eyes! What soft beds these is!" "Tom, it's 'most as good as a steam-gratin'', and "There ain't no M.P.'s to poke neither. I'm glad I ain't a bummer to-night." (pp. 187–188).

44. See Emma Brace, *The Life of Charles Loring Brace*: "It seemed to Mr. Brace that if these boys could have a place to which they felt at liberty to go when they chose, with no restrictions beyond a small charge and the necessity for decent behavior, if, in short, he could institute a sort of 'hotel for boys,' this convenience might become an agency for immense good" (p. 168). She went on to describe a shelter for girls opened by Brace and his associates, "The Girls' Lodging-House," where "any drifting, friendless girl could go for

a night's lodging. . . . Agents were sent out on the docks and into the slums, the police were informed of the refuge, notices were posted in station-houses, and near ferries and railroad-stations, and everything was done to reach out the hand of welcome to the homeless girl" (p. 252).

45. Emma Brace, *The Life of Charles Loring Brace*, p. 191.

46. See Janet Liebl, *Ties That Bind: The Orphan Train Story in Minnesota* (1994); Jeanne F. Cook, A History of Placing-Out: The Orphan Trains, 74 *Child Welfare* 181–197 (January–February, 1995). See also The American Experience, *The Orphan Trains*. Public Broadcasting Service. Program number AMEX-904. This extraordinary sixty-minute video is available from public television. The program was produced in 1995 by Janet Graham and Edward Gary. Graham and Gary interviewed elderly women and men who rode Brace's orphan trains as youngsters. The interviewees tell their stories in their own words. Graham and Gary even managed to find one elderly gentleman who had adopted an orphan train rider. The film is informative and touching and provides further evidence that although Brace and his employees made mistakes, their hearts were in the right place. Many of the orphan train riders were better off and happier for Brace's efforts.

47. See Abbott, *The Child and the State*. Abbott wrote:

Agencies that arranged for free foster-home care also developed during the years immediately before and following the Civil War. The New York Children's Aid Society founded by Charles Loring Brace in 1853 specialized in the placement of children on the farms of the Middle West and in upstate New York and did much to popularize this method of care. Other early child-placing societies were the Henry Watson Children's Aid Society, Baltimore, 1860; Boston Children's Aid Society, 1864; Brooklyn Children's Aid Society, 1866; New York State Charities Aid Association, 1872; Children's Aid Society of Pennsylvania, 1882; Connecticut Children's Aid Society, 1892. The state "Children Home Societies" movement which began in Illinois in 1883 spread rapidly. These state-wide child-placing agencies, originally fostered by the Protestant churches, were established in thirty-six states. For many years all these agencies, as Hastings Hart had pointed out, received children with little investigation and placed them with little knowledge of the foster-parents. (p. 8)

48. During many summers, Brace and his family vacationed at Lake Placid.

49. See Emma Brace, *The Life of Charles Loring Brace*. Emma Brace described her father's belief in the benefits of life on a western farm. She quoted her father, "In pleading for the superiority of a home life in the West for the child, he says that it is often plain that no human power can save these street children if left in their own surroundings, and pictures the change to pure country air, instead of the gases of sewers, trees and fields and harvests in place of narrow alleys" (p. 201–202); Charles Loring Brace, *Dangerous Classes of New York*, p. 45.

50. In *The Life of Charles Loring Brace*, Emma Brace wrote:

[Charles Loring Brace's] friend, Miss Schuler, in speaking after his death, of the distinctive character of his work, wrote: "His genius solved the problem which had baffled the philanthropists of preceding centuries. He saw that home life, and not institution life, was needed for children, and so he set himself to finding homes for homeless children. It seems so simple to us now, now that we know all about it; but it required his penetration, his genius, to reveal to us what is self-evident when once our eyes are opened. (p. 171–172)

In *Dangerous Classes of New York,* Charles Loring Brace wrote, "The Asylum has its great dangers, and is very expensive. The Emigration-plan must be conducted with careful judgment, and applied, so far as is practicable, to children under, say, the age of fourteen years. Both plans have defects, but, of the two, the latter seems to us still to do the most good at the least cost" (p. 244). In *Children and Youth in America,* Bremner wrote, "In the 1850's and for forty years thereafter, the most outspoken critic of both almshouse and asylum care for children was Charles Loring Brace, secretary of the New York Children's Aid Society. . . . [Brace opposed] institutional life of any kind, and his insistence that the best place for dependent or needy children was in foster homes, preferably on western farms" (p. 632).

51. Charles Loring Brace, What is the Best Method for the Care of Poor and Vicious Children? 2 *Journal of Social Science* 93–98, p. 95 (1880). Brace's paper sparked a vigorous response. A letter to the journal regarding Brace's paper was penned by Mr. L. P. Alden, principal of the State Public School for Poor Children, Coldwater, Michigan. In the letter, Alden wrote:

> I think that Mr. Brace has done a great thing for the city of New York in relieving it of so many incipient criminals, for which that city could well afford to erect him a monument. From all the testimony, however, that has reached me, it seems quite improbable that the West, where these children are sent, feel so grateful that it will contribute much towards its erection. 2. Without doubt, many children have been saved to good citizenship, through Mr. Brace's system, who would have grown up in vice and been lost, had they remained in the streets of New York, and certainly none have been made worse by diffusing them through the West. 3. But, nevertheless, I am very certain that a very much larger *percentage* of these children would have been saved had they been placed in well regulated industrial institutions, where, for a term of months or years, they would have been placed under a course of instruction, training and discipline, such as the average country home cannot possibly secure. . . . My experience in placing out children with all the care we can exercise in securing for them good homes, and with the help that the excellent county agent system, which Michigan has established, has led me to a very different conclusion from that which has generally been arrived at, viz.: that "a poor home is better than the best institution." I *know* that this is not so.

52. Charles Loring Brace, *Dangerous Classes of New York,* p. 228.

53. See Kristine E. Nelson, Child Placing in the Nineteenth Century: New York and Iowa, 56 *Social Service Review* 107–120 (1985): "In response to charges of lack of care in placement and supervision of children in the west, Charles Loring Brace . . . outlined its procedures to the public in lectures and annual reports. Visitors of the society located deserted or homeless children or those in 'such a state of poverty as to be improved by being taken to good homes in the country,' and told the children and their parents of the great advantages of going West; however, they were not to induce children or to take them without the written or witnessed verbal consent of their parents" (p. 108).

54. O'Connor, *Orphan Trains.* O'Connor wrote, "The first orphan train company left New York by river boat on the evening of September 28, 1854. There were thirty-seven boys and girls in the group. Nine others who had been scheduled for the trip apparently arrived at the [Children's Aid Society] offices too late to make the boat and were sent by train to join the company in Albany the following morning" (p. 106).

55. The children were not indentured, that is, they were not legally obligated to stay with their foster parents. Many of the older teenagers moved. In *Dangerous Classes of New York*, Charles Loring Brace wrote, "The children are not indentured; but are free to leave, if ill-treated or dissatisfied; and the farmers can dismiss them, if they find them useless or otherwise unsuitable. This apparently loose arrangement has worked well, and put both sides on their good behavior. We have seldom had any cases brought to our attention of ill-treatment. The main complaint is that the older lads change places often" (p. 243).

56. See O'Connor, *Orphan Trains;* Donald Dale Jackson, It Took Trains to Put Street Kids on the Right Track Out of the Slums, 17 *Smithsonian* 94–102 (August, 1986). Jackson interviewed surviving orphan train riders, and wrote: "By today's standards the orphan trains and the traumatic auction like lineups at journey's end seem callous and even barbaric. But in fairness they should be judged in the context of a time when the law treated ten-year-olds as adults and boys sweated beside their fathers in coal mines. In its own day the placing-out program, though controversial, was generally accepted and applauded as a reasonable solution to a painful dilemma" (p. 95).

57. In *The Life of Charles Loring Brace*, Emma Brace wrote, "Mr. Brace believed fully that the system of not requiring indentures was a wise one" (p. 202). See also Homer Folks, Family Life for Dependent and Wayward Children. In Anna G. Spencer & Charles W. Birtwell (Eds.), *The Care of Dependent, Neglected and Wayward Children: Being a Report of the Second Section of the International Congress of Charities, Correction and Philanthropy, Chicago, June, 1893*, pp. 69–80 (1894; Baltimore: Johns Hopkins Press). Folks wrote:

> While among progressive institutions the terms of indenture have been much modified in the interest of the child, there is a growing feeling that any legal contract compelling a child to serve a master for a certain term of years, mortgaging his future to pay for his present, affects unfavorably the standing of the child in the community and in the mind of the foster-parent, degenerating in its worst phases into something little better than slavery. Nor is it apparent that any inflexible contract can meet varying conditions. If the agreement is to be based, as it should be, on equity, it must take into account the age of the child when placed, his physical strength, his previous training, the amount of attendance at school, and many other factors. The Children's Aid Societies of New York, Boston, Pennsylvania, and perhaps others, use no written agreement whatever, but adjust the terms from year to year as the developments of each individual case seem to require, excepting, of course, in cases of legal adoption. This method gives perfect flexibility and is undoubtedly the best plan, provided it is guarded by an ever-vigilant supervision, but is possibly the worst plan of all if not so guarded. (p. 76)

58. See Emma Brace, *The Life of Charles Loring Brace*: "The assistant secretary in the office in New York was in constant communication with the children sent out by the society, and tried to keep himself informed of every change in the boys' careers, both through letters and through visits of the Western agents" (p. 202).

59. In *Orphan Trains*, O'Connor wrote:

> The Emigration Plan had many grievous faults, in particular its failure to provide adequate screening of and assistance to foster parents and employers, adequate monitoring and supervision of placements, and adequate help to birth families so that they could remain intact. But the program also provided children with many real and important

benefits. At a time when it was necessary for poor children to work, the Emigration plan got children jobs, and at a time when even very young children would travel great distances to find work, the CAS not only provided them with free transportation but, if things did not work out with one employer, sent them a ticket to another or back to New York. (p. 155)

60. In *Dangerous Classes of New York*, Brace wrote, "A great obstacle . . . was . . . the superstitious opposition of the poor. This was undoubtedly cultivated by the priests, who seem seldom gifted with the broad spirit of humanity of their brethren in Europe. They apparently desire to keep the miserable masses here under their personal influence. Our action, however, in regard to these waifs, has always been fair and open. We know no sect or race. Both Catholic and Protestant homes were offered freely to the children. No child's creed was interfered with. Our committees themselves in the Western villages have frequently had Roman Catholics" (p. 244). See also Ralph E. Pumphrey & Muriel W. Pumphrey, *The Heritage of American Social Work* (1961; New York: Columbia University Press). The Pumphreys wrote, "Rightly or wrongly, Catholics felt that the Children's Aid Society was a device for Protestant proselytizing among the children of Catholic immigrants. Their response was to set up an agency in which the faith of such children might be protected and strengthened rather than lost." (p. 147). The agency was the Catholic Protectory.

See also Stephen O'Connor, *Orphan Trains: The Story of Charles Loring Brace and the Children He Saved and Failed* (2001; Boston: Houghton Mifflin). O'Connor wrote, "Although it is perfectly true that Brace and many of his coworkers were deeply prejudiced against Catholics, and that most Catholic children who were sent west did in fact end up being raised Protestant, their conversion was never an overt aim of the charity" (p. 172). See also Tim Hacsi, From Indenture to Family Foster Care: A Brief History of Child Placing, 74 *Child Welfare* 162–180 (January–February, 1995). In this article on the development of foster care, Hacsi states that Brace was anti-urban, anti-immigrant, and anti-Catholic. In my opinion, Hacsi's statement is inaccurate. It is true that Brace loved the countryside, and built his house away from the city, but he worked virtually his entire adult life in New York City. If he was "anti-urban," why did he labor in the tenements of New York City? As for being anti-immigrant, I find nothing in Brace's writing or career to support this statement. Indeed, Brace devoted his life to *helping* immigrant children. Brace had difficulty with certain members of the Catholic Church. I believe, however, that it is wrong to call Brace anti-Catholic.

61. Richard Wexler, Take the Child and Run: Tales from the Age of AFSA, 36 *New England Law Review* 129 (2001).

62. The best review of the various evaluations of the Children's Aid Society's placing out efforts in the Midwest is contained in Nelson, Child Placing in the Nineteenth Century. Nelson described studies conducted by employees of CAS, which suffered, of course, from concerns about bias.

63. Hastings H. Hart, *Placing Out Children in the West*, Proceedings of the Eleventh Annual National Conference of Charities and Correction, pp. 143–150 (1884). Over the years, the New York Children's Aid Society took steps to supervise the children it placed via orphan trains. See Comments of Charles Loring Brace, Jr. on the paper of Francis H. White,

cited below. Brace, Jr. said, "At this time, as the Professor said, we have a great many inspectors. We have four inspectors traveling all the time, and four inspectors who are residents of western states, who visit the homes and see that the children are sent to school and well taken care of" (p. 90).

64. Hart, *Placing Out Children in the West*, p. 150.

65. Francis H. White, The Placing-Out System in the Light of Its Results. In Spencer & Birtwell, *Care of Dependent*, pp. 81–89. White was a professor of history and political science at Kansas State Agricultural College. Prior to moving to Kansas, White was superintendent of the Brooklyn Children's Aid Society. With the cooperation of the New York Children's Aid Society, White followed up on two groups of children sent by the Society to Kansas.

66. For discussion of this study, see Nelson, Child Placing in the Nineteenth Century, pp. 110–111 (1985).

67. Ibid., p. 117.

68. Charles Loring Brace, *Dangerous Classes of New York*, pp. 234–242.

69. Nelson, Child Placing in the Nineteenth Century: "By the turn of the century, out-of-state placement was discredited in the eyes of child welfare professionals, and the practice discouraged by several Midwestern states that required a bond of up to $10,000 to be filed for each out-of-state child placed" (p. 107). Nelson reviewed the evaluations of the effectiveness of the New York Children's Aid Society's placement programs.

70. O'Connor, *Orphan Trains*, p. 256. See also Address of Amos W. Butler of Indianapolis, Indiana, Secretary, State Board of Charities, presented at the 1909 White House Conference on the Care of Dependent Children. *Proceedings of the Conference on the Care of Dependent Children: Held at Washington, D.C., January 25, 26, 1909*, pp. 56–58. 60th Congress, 2nd Session, vol. 13, S.D. 721 (1909). Butler wrote, "In years past great numbers of dependent children were brought into some of the Western States. While some were placed with care and given supervision, others were not well placed and many became poor citizens or public charges. In consequence, some States have passed laws regulating the bringing of dependent children within their borders" (p. 57).

71. In *Orphan Trains*, O'Connor wrote that following the 1909 White House Conference, " 'Orphan trains' continued to go west for more than twenty years, but they were vastly different affairs than they had been during the program's heyday in the nineteenth century. These parties were considerably smaller. No longer ranging between thirty and one hundred, they were rarely larger than fifteen, and sometimes they contained only two or three children. . . . the average age of the orphan train riders dropped significantly during the final years, and many of the riders were infants" (p. 308).

72. Jackson, It Took Trains. Jackson wrote:

> But if imitation connoted success, the program was a smash. New York Catholics, who had attacked Brace for sending Catholic children to Protestant homes and even charged they were enslaved, began transporting kids from the New York Foundling Hospital to new homes in the country about 1875. The hospital's system differed from the Children's Aid Society's in that children were assigned to specific families before they boarded a westbound train. Institutions in Boston, Chicago and other cities launched their own versions. A Chicago agency advertised children "free on 90 days trial," and provided winsome descriptions: "One boy baby, has fine head and face, black eyes and hair, fat and pretty: three months old." (p. 98)

Chapter 2

1. For historical documentation and greater detail about the rescue of Mary Ellen, see John E. B. Myers, *A History of Child Protection in America*. This lengthy document is available from the author at jmyers@pacific.edu.

2. Etta Angell Wheeler, *The Story of Mary Ellen: Which Started the Child Saving Crusade Throughout the World*, p. 1 (no date; Denver, CO: American Humane Association).

3. Etta Wheeler, *Report to the 37th Annual Meeting of the American Humane Association*. October 13–16, 1913. Rochester, NY. Reprinted under the title Child Protection Begins, 50 *The National Humane Review* 16–17 (January–February, 1962). Wheeler provided another version of the case, different in a few details, in a publication titled "The Story of Mary Ellen: Which Started the Child Saving Crusade Throughout the World," available from the American Humane Association in Denver, Colorado.

The "cowhide" was described by the neighbor who informed Etta Wheeler of Mary Ellen's plight. See *New York Herald*, April 12, 1874. The paper reported,

> During the first week after the Connollys came there a witness saw the cowhide lying on the table; it is like what a man uses when on horseback; it is about two and a half feet long; it has lashes (she don't know how many) about the size of a finger, something like a cat-o'-nine-tails; she used to hear Mrs. Connolly licking the child every morning "up and down" the room, the child crying "Oh, mamma! mama!" all the time; in conversation with Mrs. Connolly the latter said she never knew such a child; she said it was a little devil, that she knew more than a girl of ten or eleven, and that she couldn't have a bit or a sup unknown to her husband, as the child told him everything; she had seen the child lying in a corner of the room under the window, and believes that was where she slept; and passed all her time.

4. Wheeler, *Story of Mary Ellen*, pp. 2–3.

5. See *New York Times*, April 10, 1874, p. 8, "Upon this petition, Judge Lawrence issued, not an ordinary writ of habeas corpus, but a special warrant, provided for by section 65 of the Habeas Corpus act, whereby the child was at once taken possession of and brought within the control of the court."

6. Wheeler, *Story of Mary Ellen*, p. 3.

7. We do not know precisely what Mary Ellen said to the judge. The quote in the text is drawn from newspaper coverage of the case. *New York Sun*, Friday, April 10, 1874.

8. See Sidney H. Coleman, *Humane Society Leaders in America*, p. 74 (1924; Albany, NY: American Humane Association).

9. See Lela B. Costin, Unraveling the Mary Ellen Legend: Origins of the "Cruelty" Movement, 65 *Social Service Review* 203–223 (1991). See also *New York Times*, April, 10, 1874, which stated:

> Mr. Bergh, who, though the case was not within the scope of the special act to prevent cruelty to animals, recognized it as being clearly within the general laws of humanity, and promptly gave it his attention. . . .
>
> Before adjournment the child was removed into the Judge's private room, apart from all parties to the proceedings, she corroborated before Judge Lawrence her statement as herein given. Counsel on behalf of Mr. Bergh, in his statement to the court, desired it to be

clearly understood that the latter's action in the case has been prompted by his feelings and duty as a humane citizen; that in no sense has he acted in his official capacity as President of the Society for Prevention of Cruelty to Animals, but is none the less determined to avail himself of such means as the law place within his power to prevent the too frequent cruelties practiced on children. (p. 8)

10. See Stephen Lazoritz, Whatever Happened to Mary Ellen? 14 *Child Abuse & Neglect* 143–149 (1990).

11. Elbridge Gerry was born Christmas day 1837 into a distinguished family. His grandfather, also Elbridge Gerry, signed the Declaration of Independence and was vice president of the United States under James Madison. In 1858, the twenty-one-year old Elbridge Gerry graduated from Columbia University and began studying law. In short order he had a thriving law practice and was active in civic affairs. Early in the history of the American Society for the Prevention of Cruelty to Animals, Gerry became Henry Bergh's chief advisor and legal counsel. Gerry wrote most of the animal protection legislation that Bergh lobbied through the New York legislature.

12. Elbridge Gerry's close ties to the courts, and his emphasis on prosecution, have been criticized. See Lela B. Costin, Howard J. Karger, & David Stoesz, *The Politics of Child Abuse in America* (1996; New York: Oxford University Press). The authors wrote, "In the end, Gerry's coercive domination of the placement of children away from their parents, and his refusal to collaborate with the existing children's agencies; forestalled well into the twentieth century the development of a rational system of children protection within a larger system of social services" (p. 75).

13. SPCCs around the country used prosecution as a tool to force parents to take better care of their children. See Eugene Morgan, The Why and How of Societies for the Prevention of Cruelty to Children, 6 *The National Humane Review* 186–187 (October 1918). Morgan was secretary of the Humane Society of Columbus, Ohio. He wrote,

> It is part of the business of the Humane Societies to rehabilitate deficient homes and to make them fit places for the proper rearing of children. . . . As a rule our Society compels delinquent parents who are under suspended sentences to report for two years, during which time we endeavor to keep in close touch with family conditions. . . . it is my firm conviction that the greatest service a Humane Society can render to the community is to see that every child gets a square deal to the extent of not only proper and necessary home, food, care and clothing, but as to what is really of greater importance, proper environment. (p. 186)

14. Quoted in Roswell C. McCrea, *The Humane Movement: A Descriptive Survey*, pp. 139–140 (1910; New York: Columbia University Press).

15. Ibid., p. 135.

16. Theodore A. Lothrop, Correction and Prevention of Neglect of Children. In *White House Conference on Child Health and Protection*. Section IV—The Handicapped: Prevention, Maintenance, Protection. Carl C. Carstens, Chair. Committee on Socially Handicapped—Dependency and Neglect. Homer Folks, Chair. J. Prentice Murphy, Vice-Chair, pp. 353–389, at 386 (1933; New York: Appleton-Century).

17. Charles H. Warner, Handling Cases of Improper Guardianship, 5 *The National Humane Review* 173–174, p. 173 (September 1917).

18. Quoted in Alfred J. Kahn, *Planning Community Services for Children in Trouble*, p. 314 (1963; New York: Columbia University Press). Kahn quotes from the Brooklyn Society for the Prevention of Cruelty to Children, *Fiftieth Annual Report* (1930):

> The Society looked back on its accomplishments both with pride and sorrow. . . . Its sorrow stemmed not from anything it has wilfully done wrong, but rather from the things it has left undone or done inadequately . . . In its early days too much emphasis had been placed on prosecution and not enough on rehabilitation and prevention and only the most casual inquiry had been made into the causes of individual family breakdown—children were too quickly removed from homes that were labeled unfit. They were then placed in institutions or sent to foster homes about which little or nothing was known. (p. 340).

Kahn continued, "The Manhattan society long stressed 'law enforcement' and 'rescue' work, narrowly defined, but was described in the 1930s as beginning to place more stress on the adjustment of children in their own homes and on the use of court as a last resort." (p. 342).

19. Massachusetts Society for the Prevention of Cruelty to Children, *First Annual Report, 1881*, p. 22 (1882; Boston: Wright & Potter). See also Robert H. Bremner (Ed.), *Children and Youth in America: A Documentary History*, vol. 2 (1970; Cambridge, MA: Harvard University Press). Bremner wrote that after 1912, the most important advances in casework came about as a result of the growth of public agencies charged with child protection and with improvement in the administration of child welfare services (p. 118). See also Ray S. Hubbard, Child Protection. In Fred S. Hall (Ed.), *Social Work Yearbook*, vol. 1, 65–67 (1929; New York: Russell Sage Foundation). Hubbard wrote that most early SPCCs followed the law enforcement approach, noting that "Massachusetts was the first to advance beyond this position. In 1907 the police badge was discarded for the most part and case work methods were first applied. . . . Although the rank and file of societies for the prevention of cruelty to children have persisted in the traditional manner, a few have followed the example of Massachusetts" (p. 66). See also Emma O. Lundberg, Child Welfare Services. In Russell H. Kurtz (Ed.), *Social Work Yearbook*, vol. 5, pp. 63–76 (1939; New York: Russell Sage Foundation). Lundberg wrote, "The Massachusetts Society for the Prevention of Cruelty to Children differed from the New York Society in that its agents did not have police power, but for almost thirty years it confined itself mainly to the legal aspects of protecting children from active cruelty" (p. 68).

20. Annual Meeting of MSPCC, 1906, Boston, MA. p. 2. Carl C. Carstens was an important leader in American child welfare. He lived from 1865 to 1939. See Paul G. Anderson, *The Good to be Done: A History of Juvenile Protective Association of Chicago, 1898–1976* (1988; Ph.D. dissertation, Department of History, University of Chicago), provided a useful biographical sketch:

> Carl Carstens's credentials were impressive. After having attended New York School of Philanthropy in 1899 he had enrolled at University of Pennsylvania's Wharton School of Finance and Commerce to study social economy under Simon Patten. While a graduate student Carstens had apprenticed under Mary Richmond at Philadelphia Society for Organizing Charity. After earning his doctorate in 1903 he had apprenticed under Edward Devine at New York Charity Organization Society. Carstens had had no training or experience in anti-cruelty work, conceded President Grafton Cushing of Massachusetts Society

for the Prevention of Cruelty to Children at the December 1906 Annual Meeting, "but he is a notable organizer, and will bring us a large experience in charitable work, a broad knowledge of the social problems of the day, a keen intelligence, and a modern point of view."

Carl Carstens's task was to reorient Massachusetts Society for the Prevention of Cruelty to Children from law enforcement to social work by cooperating with other social agencies and by developing a casework service. (pp. 377–378)

21. Vincent De Francis, Help or Punishment: Which Shall it Be? 44 *The National Humane Review*, 19–21, p. 20 (emphasis in original) (March–April 1956). See also Vincent De Francis, *Child Protective Services in the United States: Reporting a Nationwide Survey* (1956; Denver, CO: American Humane Association). In this report, De Francis wrote:

Many of the Societies for the Prevention of Cruelty to Children added other services to children or merged with other child service agencies so that today [1956] we find many of them carrying out the child protective function and in addition they are providing services in the area of foster home placement, adoptions, aid to unmarried mothers, and homemaking. Others, having merged with family and children's agencies, provide those services in addition to the carrying out of the original functions. Still others have continued to concentrate on the primary function of child protection and carry that as their sole responsibility.

A few Societies for the Prevention of Cruelty to Children and Humane Societies, after such mergers, completely lost their identities and in many instances this resulted in an abandonment of the child protective function.

The transition from law enforcement to casework was a slow one. (p. 5)

See also William A. Ekwall, Better Child Protection; Fewer Juvenile Delinquents, 35 *The National Humane Review* 20–22 (June 1947). Judge Ekwall wrote: "Actually there are few prosecutions against adults compared to the number of cases handled but in extreme cases such prosecutions and the authority to make them are vital to the efficiency of preventive work" (p. 22).

22. See Eugene Morgan, The Why and the How. Morgan was secretary of the Humane Society for Columbus, Ohio. He emphasized that prevention is as important as prosecution, and that once intervention occurs, the Society should provide services to help the family.

23. See American Humane Association, *Standards for Child Protective Agencies* (no date; Albany, NY: American Humane Association). The standards were accepted by AHA's Board of Directors in 1950. During his tenure as director of the Children's Division of American Humane, from 1954 to 1977, Vincent De Francis strongly advocated the social work approach to child protection. See De Francis, Help or Punishment. De Francis recognized that prosecution is warranted in cases of "gross physical abuse, extreme cruelty, or barbarous treatment," and "extreme gross neglect, willfully committed" (p. 20). In other cases, however, De Francis believed prosecution was futile.

24. See E. Marguerite Gane, Child and Youth Protection. In Russell H. Kurtz (Ed.), *Social Work Yearbook*, vol. 4, pp. 57–61 (1937). Gane wrote in 1937, "The transition from a program of rescue to one of prevention is widespread" (p. 60). See also Ralph P. Truitt, All Casework is One, Child Welfare League of America, 5(7) *Bulletin* 2-3 (September, 15, 1926). Truitt was

director of the Division on Prevention of Delinquency of the National Committee for Mental Hygiene. He wrote:

> Caseworkers have a habit of speaking of family casework, child-placing, institutional work, protective work, probation work and child guidance as if they were fundamentally different in methods and aims and this habit of speaking has been confirmed into a habit of thinking and acting. As a matter of fact, in our sober moments all of us recognize that though we are organized according to the special facilities our agencies provide, we are or should be united by the fundamental purpose of casework which is to understand our clients and their situations well enough to adjust them to the best social advantage. (p. 2)

See also Vincent De Francis, *The Fundamentals of Child Protection: A Statement of Basic Concepts and Principles in Child Protective Services* (1955; Denver, CO: American Humane Association). Referring to the original SPCCs, De Francis wrote:

> This pioneering group began operations in an era before the science and practice of social work was born. Nurtured as they were under what were tantamount to police powers, their orientation was legalistic. Their early adherence to a law enforcement approach met the needs of the times and produced the kind of relief which was contemplated by the enabling legislation which authorized their creation. With the turn of the [twentieth] Century and with the growing public consciousness that prevention is a better cure than punishment, we began to see leaders in the field of child protection turning the emphasis away from prosecution and toward the application of remedial measures. (p. 5)

25. Frank B. Fay, The Protection of Neglected and Abused Children. In Anna G. Spencer & Charles W. Birtwell (Eds.), *The Care of Dependent, Neglected and Wayward Children: Being a Report of the Second Section of the International Congress of Charities, Correction and Philanthropy, Chicago, June, 1893*, pp. 130–134, at 133–134 (1894; Baltimore: Johns Hopkins Press).

26. Sonya Michel, *Children's Interests/Mothers' Rights: The Shaping of America's Child Care Policy*, p. 14 (1999; New Haven, CT: Yale University Press).

27. Ibid., p. 43. Half-orphans continued to populate orphanages in the twentieth century. See Child Welfare League of America, Why Continue to Call Children's Institutions Orphanages? 4(1) *Bulletin* 3 (January 15, 1925). The brief anonymous article stated:

> "Better Times" reports that a recent study of so-called orphan asylums in New York state shows that of 29,277 children in these institutions in a single year, 45 percent had both parents living, while an additional 44 percent had one parent living. Of the 14,671 children discharged from these institutions 72 percent were returned to parents or relatives. Twenty-five percent of the children remained in the institutions less than one year and 42 per cent were discharged within two years.
>
> These figures are additional evidence that orphans are scarce. It would be a blessing to many children in these institutions if the terms orphan and orphanage, which have come to have a technical meaning even to the child, and have given it the impression of being different from other children, were eliminated. How many "orphanages" will note to change their names in 1935? (p. 3)

28. *Cowley v. People*, 21 Hun. 415 (New York Supreme Court, 1880).

29. Massachusetts Society for the Prevention of Cruelty to Children, *Ninth Annual Report*, p. 13 (1889).

30. Linda Gordon, *Heroes of Their Own Lives: The Politics and History of Family Violence*, p. 44 (1988; New York: Penguin Books).

31. California Society for the Prevention of Cruelty to Children, President's Address in the *Third Annual Report for the Year Ending December 31, 1879*, p. 2 (San Francisco: Society for the Prevention of Cruelty to Children).

32. Oscar L. Dudley, Saving the Children: Sixteen Years' Work among the Dependent Youth of Chicago. Committee on the History of Child-Saving Work. Twentieth Conference of the National Conference of Charities and Correction, *History of Child Saving in the United States.* pp. 99–115, at 106 (1893, reprinted in 1971).

33. Laws of New York, chapter 428 (1877).

34. California Society for the Prevention of Cruelty to Children, *Third Annual Report,* 1880, p. 6.

35. 96 Pa. 112 (1880).

36. The father asserted that he did not believe in traditional medicine. He employed a device by which he pricked the skin of his spouse and children with needles and then rubbed the area with ointment.

37. Alfred M. Kerchley, The Enforcement of Medical Care for Children, 8 *The National Humane Review* 205 (November 1920).

38. See Massachusetts Society for the Prevention of Cruelty to Children, *Crusading for Children: 1878–1943* (no date, probably 1943; Boston: MSPCC). The monograph stated, "Serious intemperance stood out as a factor in 47.7 per cent of the cases in 1916. During the first year after National Prohibition (1921), the percentage as 16.8; in 1940, 26.6; and in 1943, 27.6" (p. 37). See also Frank Fay, The Protection of Neglected and Abused Children. Fay, who was the general agent of the Massachusetts Society for the Prevention of Cruelty to Children, wrote, "It is apparent that two-thirds of our work comes from the use and abuse of intoxicating drink." (p. 132). See also Travis Gibb, Indecent Assault Upon Children. In Allan McLane Hamilton & Lawrence Godkin (Eds.), *A System of Legal Medicine*, vol. 1. pp. 649–657 (1894; New York: E.B. Treat). Gibb was the examining physician for the New York Society for the Prevention of Cruelty to Children. He wrote of child sexual abuse, "In my experience, criminal assaults upon children are usually perpetrated by men who are insane, old men beyond the age of virility, men under the influence of liquor, and those suffering from some form of perversion of the sexual instinct which may be akin to insanity" (p. 652).

39. Massachusetts Society for the Prevention of Cruelty to Children, *First Annual Report, 1881* (1882; Boston: Wright & Potter). The report stated, "It will be a cause of surprise to many to know how often the intemperance is on the part of the mothers" (p. 3).

40. Massachusetts Society for the Prevention of Cruelty to Children, *Annual Report for 1882* (1883; Boston: Wright & Potter). Frank Fay, the Society's general agent, wrote, "We feel safe in saying that nearly three-fourths of our work is directly or indirectly from the excessive use of intoxicating drink" (p. 21). In his 1885 Annual Report, Fay wrote, "Intemperance continues to be an active agent in producing neglect and abuse of children. Reference to our statistics shows this, although we feel assured more cases ought to be noted, but we record only those positively ascertained. . . . The prevalent effort to check this evil, we trust, will shed its benign influence upon those who need it most." Massachusetts Society for the Prevention of Cruelty to Children, *Fifth Annual Report for 1885*, pp. 20–21 (1886; Boston: Wright & Potter).

41. Jacob A. Goldberg & Rosamond W. Goldberg, *Girls on City Streets: A Study of 1400 Cases of Rape* (1935; New York: American Social Hygiene Association). Reprinted as part of Leon Stein & Annette K. Baxter (Advisory Editors), *Women in America from Colonial Times to the 20th Century*, p. 187 (1974; New York: Arno Press).

42. McCrea, *The Humane Movement.*

43. To conduct research on the Sacramento Society for the Prevention of Cruelty to Children, I examined microfilm copies of the *Sacramento Union* maintained by the Sacramento County Archives. Years ago, someone compiled an index of stories in the early editions of the *Union*. By looking under the subject heading "children," I located stories describing the work of the Society. The *Union* routinely sent a reporter to the meetings of the board of directors of the society.

44. The Children's Society: Many Cases are Treated—Society Commended in the East—Manual Training and Domestic Science in Schools, *Sacramento Union*, p. 2, August 6, 1907. On July 2, 1907, the *Union* discussed Healy's annual report, in which he indicated 320 "offenders cautioned" (p. 5).

45. Friends of the Children: Interesting Meeting of the Society Held Last Evening for the Purpose of Considering Complaints, *Sacramento Union*, p. 5, April 3, 1906.

46. In Interest of Children, *Sacramento Union*, p. 3, May 7, 1907.

47. Keep Children at Home: Society for Prevention of Cruelty to Children Wins in Case of Mere Lads on Streets at Night Selling Papers, *Sacramento Union*, p. 7, April 9, 1907. Healy informed the SPCC board of the case.

48. Work Among the Children: What the Society and Its Officer Has Done During the Past Month Regarding Wayward Youngsters, *Sacramento Union*, p. 5, January 8, 1907.

49. Friends of the Children: Interesting Meeting of the Society Held Last Evening for the Purpose of Considering Complaints, *Sacramento Union*, p. 5, April 3, 1906.

50. Children's Society Says These Two Boys Can and Must be Saved: Lads of Nine and Eleven, Who Have Commenced to Prey on Property Are Landed in Jail, *Sacramento Union*, p. 12, August 16, 1907. "Meum" and "tuum" is Latin, which translates roughly to mine and yours.

51. Breaks Up Den of Vice: Officer Dan Healy and Police Raid Room Into Which Boys and Girls Were Enticed and Taught to Steal, *Sacramento Union*, p. 10, June 15, 1907.

52. Ibid.

Chapter 3

1. See Nathan E. Cohen, *Social Work in the American Tradition*, pp. 68–69 (1958; New York: Dryden Press). Cohen wrote, "By the end of the century the charity organization societies began to employ paid workers, to engage in social reform, and to recognize the need for trained staff. Many of these societies established training courses for their workers." (pp. 68–69). There is some debate regarding where the first school of social work was established. See Carol Coohey, Letter to the Editor: Notes on the Origins of Social Work Education, 73 *Social Service Review* 418–422 (1999).

2. Ralph E. Pumphrey & Muriel W. Pumphrey, *The Heritage of American Social Work*, pp. 202, 255 (1961; New York: Columbia University Press).

3. Grace Abbott lived from 1878 to 1939. She was born in Grand Island, Nebraska, two years after her equally famous sister, Edith Abbott. Grace Abbott graduated from Grand Island College in 1898, and became a teacher. From 1908 to 1917, Abbott was director of the Immigrants Protective League of Chicago. She lived at Hull House. Julia Lathrop sparked Abbott's interest in child labor, and, in 1917, Abbott moved to the Children's Bureau in Washington, D.C., to administer the child labor law. Abbott succeeded Lathrop as head of the Children's Bureau in 1921. In 1934, Abbott became a professor of public welfare in the School of Social Service Administration of the University of Chicago. For a wonderful biography of Grace and Edith Abbott, see Lela B. Costin, *Two Sisters for Social Justice: A Biography of Grace and Edith Abbott* (1983; Chicago: University of Illinois Press).

4. Florence Kelley lived from 1859 to 1932. Born in Philadelphia, Kelley's undergraduate degree was from Cornell. She also received a law degree from Northwestern University. Kelley investigated sweatshops as an agent of the Bureau of Labor Statistics. In 1892, she was appointed director of the Factory Inspection Department. Eventually, she became the Director of the National Consumers' League. Florence Kelley was a strong advocate for child labor laws.

5. Robert C. Reinders, Toynbee Hall and the American Settlement Movement, 56 *Social Service Review* 39–54, pp. 45–46, 49 (March, 1982).

6. William Healy was born on his family's farm some twenty-five miles from London, England in 1869. His father managed the farm, which was small but stable. Part of the farm contained clay suitable for brick making, and the family operated a small tile and brick making operation. William's father lost the farm in a family squabble, and William's family moved to southern England, where William's father got a loan to start a brick making operation. Unfortunately, just as the business was getting started, a storm destroyed the facility, and the family fell on hard times. William's uncle lived in Buffalo, New York, and he urged the family to move to America, which they did when William was nine. The family stayed in Buffalo a short time then moved to Chicago, where William's father got a low-level job with the city.

When he was thirteen, William left school to work in a bank to help support his family. William worked at the bank ten years, rising to head bookkeeper. As he worked, he saved for college. In 1893, at age twenty-three, Healy was accepted by Harvard, a rather remarkable feat considering he never completed grammar school. He studied his way into the medical school at Harvard, although he completed his medical education in 1900 at Chicago's Rush Medical College. Initially, Healy had a general medical practice in North Chicago, but before long he became interested in neurology, and, eventually, psychiatry.

7. Kathleen W. Jones, *Taming the Troublesome Child: American Families, Child Guidance, and the Limits of Psychiatric Authority*, p. 9 (1999; Cambridge, MA: Harvard University Press).

8. Margo Horn, *Before It's Too Late: The Child Guidance Movement in the United States, 1922–1945*, p. 2 (1989; Philadelphia: Temple University Press).

9. Enactment of child labor laws had a relationship to the development of mothers' pensions, beginning in 1911. When children did not work, family income declined, increasing the need for mothers' pensions.

10. Lawrence T. Royster, The Care of the Dependent Child, 8 *The National Humane Review* 113 (June, 1920). Royster was president of the Norfolk Society for the Prevention of Cruelty to Children in Norfolk, Virginia.

11. Susan Whitelaw Downs & Michael W. Herraden, The Orphan Asylum in the Nineteenth Century, 57 *Social Service Review* 272–290, p. 273 (1983).

12. Homer Folks, The Removal of Children from Almshouses. In *Proceedings of the National Conference of Charities and Corrections*, p. 130 (1894). See also Homer Folks, Child-Saving Work in Pennsylvania. In Committee on the History of Child-Saving Work, Twentieth Conference of the National Conference of Charities and Correction, *History of Child Saving in the United States*, pp. 138–153 (1893, reprinted in 1971).

Homer Folks was born in Hanover, Michigan, on February 18, 1867, to Esther Woodliffe and James Folks, who were farmers. Folks obtained bachelors degrees from Albion College and Harvard. Folks considered the ministry, but opted for a career in social work. While at Harvard, Folks was influenced by professors Francis G. Peabody and George Herbert Palmer, who emphasized ethics and social responsibility. In 1890, Folks became general superintendent of the Children's Aid Society of Pennsylvania. While at the Children's Aid Society, Folks pioneered in placing out. In 1893, Folks became executive secretary of the New York State Charities Aid Association in New York City. Folks remained with the association until his retirement in 1946. Folks was at the forefront of Progressive Era reforms. He understood that poverty lay at the root of child dependency and neglect. His 1902 book *The Care of Destitute, Neglected and Delinquent Children* is a classic. Folks helped establish the juvenile court in New York. In 1907, he helped establish the New York State Probation Commission, which he chaired for ten years. Folks was involved in the creation of the National Child Labor Committee and chaired the committee. In 1909, Folks presided over the White House Conference on the Care of Dependent Children. In addition to his work for children and families, Folks played a leading role in combating tuberculosis, diphtheria, and venereal disease. In all, Folks's career of public service spanned nearly sixty years. He passed away February 13, 1963. [This biographical information is drawn largely from Walter I. Trattner, Folks, Homer. In John A. Garraty & Mark C. Carnes (Eds.). *American National Biography*, vol. 8, pp. 172–174 (1999; New York: Oxford University Press).

13. Folks, Removal of Children, p. 131 (1894). For a detailed description of the Massachusetts approach to dependent, neglected, and delinquent children, see Anne B. Richardson, The Massachusetts System of Caring for State Minor Wards. Committee on the History of Child-Saving Work. Twentieth Conference of the National Conference of Charities and Correction, *History of Child Saving in the United States*, pp. 54–67 (1893, reprinted in 1971).

14. Hastings H. Hart, *Preventive Treatment of Neglected Children*, pp. 67–68 (1910; New York: Charities Publication Committee). Reprinted as part of David J. Rothman (Advisory Ed.), *Poverty, U.S.A.: The Historical Record* (1971; New York: Arno Press and the New York Times).

15. Address of Charles W. Birtwell at the 1909 White House Conference on the Care of Dependent Children. *Proceedings of the Conference on the Care of Dependent Children: Held at Washington, D.C. January 25, 26, 1909*, pp. 133–134, at 134. 60th Congress, 2nd Session, vol. 13, S.D. 721. Birtwell was hired by the Boston Children's Aid Society in 1885. He graduated with honors from Harvard, where he met Homer Folks. Birtwell was an extremely hard worker. Under his leadership, the Boston Children's Aid Society became a model for placing children in foster homes.

16. *Proceedings of the Conference on the Care of Dependent Children*, p. 10.

17. Hart, *Preventive Treatment.* Hart wrote, "We no longer build orphan asylums; we build 'children's homes.' We no longer house children in great buildings like summer hotels, nor do we build institutions with dormitories where 200 girls sleep in a single room; but we build cottages, with 'house fathers' and 'house mothers,' and gather the children in smaller groups" (p. 63). See also *1930 White House Conference on Child Health and Protection, pp.* 319–340 (1931; New York: Century). Homer Folks chaired the committee "Socially Handicapped—Dependency and Neglect." The committee wrote, "Encouraging progress has been made. Many old-time congregate institutions have been rebuilt into cottage groups, and have moved from crowded city streets into the suburbs. Others have altered their large buildings so as to provide for care of their children in small groups, each group having its own facilities" (pp. 328–329).

18. *Proceedings of the Conference on the Care of Dependent Children,* p. 11.

19. *White House Conference on Child Health and Protection.* Section IV—The Handicapped: Prevention, Maintenance, Protection. Carl C. Carstens, Chair. Committee on Socially Handicapped—Dependency and Neglect. Homer Folks, Chair, J. Prentice Murphy, Vice-Chair (1933; New York: Appleton-Century).

20. Address of Lillian D. Wald at the 1909 White House Conference on the Care of Dependent Children. *Proceedings of the Conference on the Care of Dependent Children,* p. 171.

21. See Rochelle Beck, The White House Conferences on Children: An Historical Perspective, 43 *Harvard Educational Review* 653–668 (1973).

22. See Letter to President Roosevelt dated December 22, 1909, urging the president to convene a White House conference to address issues related to dependent and neglected children. The letter was signed by Homer Folks, Secretary, New York State Charities Aid Association, Hastings Hart, superintendent, Illinois Children's Home and Aid Society, John Glenn, secretary and director of the Russell Sage Foundation, Thomas Mulry, president, St. Vincent de Paul Society of the United States, Edward Devine, editor, *Charities and the Commons,* Julian Mack, juvenile court judge, Cook County, Illinois, Charles Birtwell, general secretary of the Boston Children's Aid Society, Theodore Dreiser, editor of the *Delineator,* and James West, secretary of the National Child Rescue League. The letter is reproduced in *Proceedings of the Conference on the Care of Dependent Children,* pp. 17–18 (1909).

23. Ibid., p. 5. Child welfare professionals had reached consensus on the benefits of family life long before the 1909 White House Conference. See, e.g., Charles Richmond Henderson, The Relief and Care of Dependent Children. In *Study of the Dependent, Defective, and Delinquent Classes* (1901). Henderson wrote, "It is a first principle of charity to avoid breaking up the natural relations of the family so long as the interests of the children are not in jeopardy. Parental responsibility must not be weakened, and the affections which cling to offspring and parents must not be lightly destroyed" (p. 98).

The importance of keeping children with their parents was reiterated by the attendees at the 1930 White House Conference on Child Health and Protection:

The family is the richest medium for the nurture and development of the child. Where the essentials of family life exist, even incompletely, every effort should be made to keep the child with his own mother and father. . . . Almost certainly in later life he will be a member of some other family; what is more important than to secure for him as a child a normal preparatory experience in his own home? Here he learns the meaning of loyalty, that fundamental factor in character. The child's own family sees him intimately, sees him under all circumstances and conditions, has a more continuous opportunity to understand him, is more certain to cherish a continuing confidence in him, and to respect his aims and accomplishments than any other group. Parents add to these considerations an enduring loyalty and confidence, for nature gives to parents rose tinted glasses in viewing their offspring. (p. 8).

24. *Proceedings of the Conference on the Care of Dependent Children*, p. 9.

25. *White House Conference on Child Health and Protection*, p. 4. The committee wrote, "It is estimated that in the 44 states administering mothers' aid laws there was expended a total of thirty million dollars to keep an average of some two hundred and twenty thousand children with their mothers" (p. 11). In 1931, the U.S. Children Bureau estimated that 253,298 children in 93,620 families received financial support from mothers' pensions. U.S. Children's Bureau, *Mothers' Aid, 1931*. Publication No. 220 (1933).

26. Barbara Machtinger, The U.S. Children's Bureau and Mothers' Pensions Administration, 1912–1930, 73 *Social Service Review* 105–118, p. 115 (1999).

27. Lillian Wald lived from 1867 to 1940. Born in Cincinnati, Ohio, she received training as a nurse at New York Hospital, graduating in 1891. In addition to many accomplishments in the field of public health, Wald was a tireless advocate for children, and was among the founders of the New York Child Labor Committee.

28. Dorothy Zietz, *Child Welfare: Services and Perspectives*, p. 255 (2nd ed., 1968; New York: John Wiley & Sons).

29. Florence Kelley, *Some Ethical Gains Through Legislation*, pp. 100–101 (1905; New York: MacMillan).

30. Costin, *Two Sisters*, p. 125.

31. *United States Statutes at Large*, vol. 37, p. 79.

32. Grace Abbott, acceptance speech at awarding of medal by the national Institute of Social Sciences, 1931. quoted in Kristie Lindemeyer, "*A Right to Childhood*": The U.S. Children's Bureau and Child Welfare, 1912–1946, pp. 175–176 (1997; Urbana: University of Illinois Press).

33. See Barbara Finkelstein, Uncle Sam and the Children: A History of Government Involvement in Child Rearing. In N. Ray Hiner & Joseph M. Hawes, *Growing Up in America: Children in Historical Perspective*, pp. 255–266 (1985; Chicago: University of Illinois Press). Finkelstein stated that the first federal involvement in matters of child welfare occurred in 1819, when Congress passed the Civilizing Act, appropriating funds to hire teachers for Native American Children. "Between 1819 and 1865, American Indians were the sole recipients of congressional social largess" (p. 258). After the Civil War, Congress established pensions for families of Union soldiers. Additionally, the Freedmen's Bureau provided educational and other support for children of former slaves.

34. President Franklin D. Roosevelt, Executive Order Number 6757. June 29, 1934.

35. See Edwin E. Witte, *The Development of the Social Security Act* (1962; Madison: University of Wisconsin Press). Mr. Witte prepared the manuscript of his book as he worked on the Social Security Act. The book is a fascinating first-hand account of the making of the Social Security Act.

36. Wilbur J. Cohen & Robert J. Lampman, Introduction. In ibid., pp. xi-xvi, at xii.

37. See the Social Security Act, *U.S. Statutes at Large*, vol. 49, part 1, title V, part 1, section 501, 74th Congress, 1st Session, chapter 531 (August 14, 1935). The statute provided: "For the purpose of enabling each State to extend and improve as far as practicable under the conditions in such State, services for promoting the health of mothers and children, especially in rural areas and in areas suffering from severe economic distress, there is hereby authorized to be appropriated for each fiscal year, beginning with the fiscal year ending June 30, 1936, the sum of $3,800,000."

For a concise discussion of the child welfare aspects of the Social Security Act, see Katharine F. Lenroot, Maternal and Child Welfare Provisions of the Social Security Act, *Law and Contemporary Problems*, pp. 253–262 (1936).

38. See the Social Security Act, *U.S. Statutes at Large*, vol. 49, part 1, title V, part 3, section 521, 74th Congress, 1st Session, chapter 531. (August 14, 1935). Section 521(a) provided in part:

> For the purpose of enabling the United States, through the Children's Bureau, to cooperate with State public-welfare agencies in establishing, extending, and strengthening, especially in predominantly rural areas, public-welfare services (hereinafter in this section referred to as "child-welfare services") for the protection and care of homeless, dependent, and neglected children, and children in danger of becoming delinquent, there is hereby authorized to be appropriated for each fiscal year, beginning with the fiscal year ending June 30, 1936, the sum of $1,500,000.

Initially, there was no definition of the term "child welfare services." Edwin Witte, wrote, "I suggested the definition which occurs in the final act." Witte, *The Development of the Social Security Act*, p. 170.

39. Ernest K. Coulter, *The Children in the Shadow*, p. 39 (1913; New York: McBride, Nast & Co.).

40. Herbert H. Lou, *Juvenile Courts in the United States*, p. 16 (1972; New York: Arno Press and the New York Times). Lou was referring to Laws of Massachusetts, 1877, chapter 210.

41. Coulter, *Children in the Shadow*, p. 33.

42. Julian W. Mack, The Juvenile Court, 23 *Harvard Law Review* 104–122, at 107 (1909). Judge Mack became a federal judge on the United States Court of Appeals for the Seventh Circuit. See also Julian W. Mack, The Chancery Procedure in the Juvenile Court. In Jane Addams (Ed.), *The Child, the Clinic, and the Court*, pp. 310–319 (1925; New York: New Republic).

Mack graduated from Harvard Law School in 1887 and then did graduate work in Germany. He was a professor of law first at Northwestern University and then at the University of Chicago. In 1903 Mack was appointed to the Chicago Civil Service Commission and, also in that year, he was elected as a Democrat to Cook County Circuit Court, from which his peers selected him to serve on the juvenile court bench. Mack was a leader of Chicago's Associated Jewish Charities. He presided at the 1906 National Conference of Jewish Charities and at the 1912 National Conference of Charities and Correction (Paul G. Anderson, *The Good to be Done: A History of Juvenile Protective Association of Chicago, 1898–1976* [1988; Ph.D. dissertation, Department of History, University of Chicago]).

43. Illinois Juvenile Court Law, section 1.

44. Anderson, *Good to be Done*, p. 90 (emphases in original).

45. Ben B. Lindsey, Colorado's Contribution to the Juvenile Court. In *The Child, the Clinic and the Court* (Eds.), pp. 274–289, at 277 (1925; New York: New Republic).

46. Address of Benjamin B. Lindsey at the 1909 White House Conference on the Care of Dependent Children. *Proceedings of the Conference on the Care of Dependent Children*, p. 217.

47. *The Real Mother Goose* (1916; New York: Rand McNally).

48. See Eugene Morgan, The Why and How of Societies for the Prevention of Cruelty to Children, 6 *The National Humane Review* 186–187, p. 187 (October 1918). Morgan was secretary of the Humane Society of Columbus, Ohio.

49. Douglas P. Falconer, Child and Youth Protection. In Fred S. Hall, *Social Work Yearbook*, vol. 3, pp. 63–66, at 64 (1935; New York: Russell Sage Foundation).

50. Alan Sussman, Sex-Based Discrimination and PINS Jurisdiction. In Lee E. Teitelbaum & Aidan R. Gough (Eds.), *Beyond Control: Status Offenders in the Juvenile Court, pp.* 179–199 (1977; Cambridge, MA: Ballinger). See also Sophonisba P. Breckendridge & Edith Abbott, *The Delinquent Child and the Home* (1912; New York: Russell Sage Foundation).

51. See Hart, *Preventive Treatment*; Benjamin Karpman, *The Sexual Offender and His Offenses*, p. 67 (1962; New York: Julian Press). Karpman wrote, "The most common form of delinquency in girls is antisocial sex behavior. Even where the prominent features of misconduct are something else—stealing, truancy, blackmail, they are nearly always found to be associated with the instinctive urge. The reason for this frequency is in our social standards. Boys who indulge in sex relations are seldom apprehended for that reason alone, but the girl comes under the social ban" (p. 58). See also Anne T. Bingham, Determinants of Sex Delinquency in Adolescent Girls Based on Intensive Studies of 500 Cases, 13 *Journal of the American Institute of Criminal Law and Criminology* 528 (1923); June Purcell-Guild, Study of One Hundred and Thirty-One Delinquent Girls Held at the Juvenile Detention Home in Chicago, 1917, 10 *Journal of the American Institute of Criminal Law and Criminology* 443–476 (1920).

52. See U.S. Children's Bureau, *Children's Bureau Statistical Series: Juvenile Court Statistics: 1946–1949*. No. 8 (1951). This publication documented the different treatment of teenage girls and boys. Cases

> dismissed, adjusted or held open without further action were proportionately higher for boys than girls. . . . Differences . . . are attributable in part to the different reasons for which boys and girls are brought to courts. Boys are most frequently referred to court for such reasons as stealing, destroying property, and other types of malicious mischief. Such offenses can frequently be understood or excused as the expression of mischievousness or an adventuresome spirit where continuing court care is not considered necessary. Their cases are often dismissed. Girls, on the other hand, usually come before the court because of sexual misconduct or offenses of a related nature. As indicated previously, this type of misconduct is viewed more seriously than that of boys. Consequently, the probation and commitment rate for girls is much higher than for boys. (p. 6)

53. Hart, *Preventive Treatment*, p. 72.

54. Following his tenure at the MSPCC, Carstens went on to become the director of the Child Welfare League of America. He was an influential leader in early twentieth-century

child welfare. See Carl Carstens, Annual Report of Executive Director: Boston, June 12, 1930. Child Welfare League of America, 9(6) *Bulletin* 1-3 (June, 1930). In his report, Carstens stated, "One of the striking developments in child welfare work during the last ten years has been in the field of public service. Although there are still States where no definitely organized public service to children is being rendered it is reasonable to look forward to the establishment at an early day of public children's bureaus, preferably as parts of state departments of public welfare in all of the separate States" (p. 2).

55. Ray S. Hubbard, Child Protection. In Fred S. Hall (Ed.), *Social Work Yearbook*, vol. 1, pp. 65–67, at 67 (1929; New York: Russell Sage Foundation).

56. Douglas P. Falconer, Child and Youth Protection. In Fred S. Hall (Ed.), *Social Work Yearbook*, vol. 3, pp. 63–66, at 65 (1935; New York: Russell Sage Foundation).

57. U.S. Children's Bureau, *Public Social Services to Children: A Decade of Progress*, p. 4 (April 1946). In 1946, the U.S. Children's Bureau wrote:

When the Social Security Act was under consideration in Congress, only one-fourth of the States had made provision for local public services for children through public county organization for child welfare work under State leadership. In only one State was the program in effect in practically all counties. Now, in approximately half of the States, county welfare agencies have fairly broad responsibility for services to children who are dependent, neglected, or handicapped. Every State, Territory, and the District of Columbia has a plan which includes public child welfare services provided by local child welfare workers in at least some of the counties or other local subdivisions. (p. 6)

58. Falconer, Child and Youth Protection, p. 65.

59. U.S. Children's Bureau, *Child Welfare Statistics, 1959*, p. 2 (1960).

60. Herschel Alt, A Critical Appraisal of the Functions of Private Agencies in Meeting the Needs of Children. Paper presented at the Child Welfare League section of the National Conference of Social Work, Grand Rapids, Michigan (May 1940; New York: Child Welfare League of America).

61. Carl C. Carstens, Children's Protective Work in a Community's Programs, Child Welfare League of America, 18(2) *Bulletin* 4 (February 1939).

62. Vincent De Francis, *Child Protective Services in the United States: Reporting a Nationwide Survey* (1956; Denver: American Humane Association). There was an earlier attempt at a nationwide survey. See Theodore A. Lothrop, Correction and Prevention of Neglect of Children. In *White House Conference on Child Health and Protection*, pp. 353–389. Lothrop sent questionnaires to fifty-three SPCCs, 334 humane societies, and fifty-six other agencies doing protective work. "From a total of 443 questionnaires sent out, 201 replies were received" (p. 385). Lothrop wrote, "The returns do not permit an accurate appraisal of the present status of child protection service throughout the country" (p. 368).

63. De Francis published throughout his career at American Humane. His practice, however, was to publish his book-length works and his articles as "in house" publications of the American Humane Association rather than to publish through commercial book publishers or in the professional literature. Because his articles did not appear in journals, they did not find their way into the various indexes to the literature, nor did they end up in very many libraries. The same was true for De Francis's book-length publications. Much of Vincent De Francis's work was years ahead of its time—especially his research on child

sexual abuse—yet his contributions to the field and to the literature are little known today. I am convinced that De Francis's decision to publish "in house" is a major reason why he is not more well known. His name should be familiar to every student of child protection. Additional publications included Vincent De Francis, *No Substitute for Child Protection* (1957; Denver, CO: American Humane Association); Vincent De Francis, *Interpreting Child Protective Services to Your Community* (1957; Denver, CO: American Humane Association); Vincent De Francis, *Protective Services and Community Expectations* (1961; Denver, CO: American Humane Association); Vincent De Francis, To Protect the Battered Child, 51 *The National Humane Review* 26–27 (March–April 1963); Vincent De Francis, Who Said There's No More Cruelty to Children? 50 *The National Humane Review* 18–19 (March-April 1962).

64. Vincent De Francis, *The Court and Protective Services: Their Respective Roles*, p. 6 (1960; Denver, CO: American Humane Association).

65. Vincent De Francis, *Let's Get Technical: The "Why and What" of Child Protective Services*, p. 9 (1959; Denver, CO: American Humane Association). See also Vincent De Francis, Anytown, U.S.A., 28 *The National Humane Review* pp. 22-24 (November–December, 1955). De Francis wrote, "Most damaging is the failure to give a child the love and affection, the sense of belonging and the security which is so important to a proper personality development" (p. 24). De Francis was not alone in understanding the harm of psychological maltreatment. See, e.g., Thomas D. Gill, The Legal Nature of Neglect, 6(1) *NPPA National Probation and Parole Association Journal* 1–16 (January 1960). Gill was a juvenile court judge in Hartford, Connecticut.

66. Testimony before the House Subcommittee on Juvenile Delinquency, U.S. House of Representatives, May 29, 1957. See also Vincent De Francis, *The Court and Protective Services*. De Francis wrote, "Child neglect is a first step in the development of a delinquent" (p. 3).

67. De Francis, *Child Protective Services*, p. 15.

68. Ibid., p. 18.

69. De Francis, *Child Protective Services*, pp. 7, 146, 169.

70. Ibid., pp. 80, 83, 87.

71. Child Welfare League of America, *Standards for Child Protective Organizations* (1937; New York: Russell Sage Foundation). The standards provided, "The forms of the work of child protection and its auspices are so various that child protection should be regarded as a service rendered by many different units in different communities and often in the same community rather than the function of one kind of agency" (p. 6). See also Fred DelliQuadri, Child Welfare. In Russell H. Kurtz (Ed.), *Social Work Yearbook*, vol. 13, pp. 146–157 (1957; New York: National Association of Social Workers). DelliQuadri wrote, "The most successful results being obtained today are in agencies where the functions have been clearly identified and where workers are assigned exclusively to the difficult task" (p. 150).

See also Emma O. Lundberg, Child Welfare. In Russell H. Kurtz (Ed.), *Social Work Yearbook*, 93–103 (1947; New York: Russell Sage Foundation). Lundberg wrote, "All states now have departments of social welfare, of health, and of education. The majority of departments of social welfare and health include special bureaus or divisions relating to children" (p. 100).

See also Barbara Smith, Helping Neglectful Parents to Become Responsible, 14(3) *The Child* 36–47 (September, 1949). Smith, a case supervisor in protective services for the Baltimore Department of Public Welfare, wrote: "The trend is toward making the protective service of a community distinct and specialized in order to emphasize to the parents who are referred to it as one of its main differences from other casework services. This difference is that in protective services the relations of parents to the agency are not entirely voluntary" (p. 36).

72. See De Francis, *Child Protective Services*. Responding to De Francis's survey, an Arkansas official wrote, "Services are given through a county office. In cases where there is a local child welfare worker the service is given by this person. In counties where it is done through the county welfare office, it is part of the general work load and not specifically assigned" (p. 59). De Francis wrote that in Colorado, "Twenty-one of the 54 counties which reported child protective services carry them as a segregated service" (p. 69). A Georgia official wrote, "Protective services are a part of an unsegregated caseload in the county departments, although at one time Fulton county had a separate unit" (p. 84). A respondent from Illinois wrote, "Direct services in protective cases are provided by child welfare staff operating from regional offices of the Department as part of an unsegregated caseload, only upon referral from a County Court. Most of the child welfare workers have some graduate training in a school of social work. We do not have a plan of in-service training in the special area of protective services" (p. 90).

See also Report on the Child Abuse Prevention and Treatment Act, 93rd Congress, 1st Session, H.R. 93-685. The reported stated, "Although effective programs exist in some communities, for many years the problem of child abuse has lacked a focus within broader social service programs. Moreover, the very social service agencies with the responsibility to deal with this problem have often lacked the necessary resources" (p. 3). See also Alfred J. Kahn, *Planning Community Services for Children in Trouble* (1963; New York: Columbia University Press). Kahn wrote, "A community needs, but many do not have, a widely known agency or unit with sufficient staff to explore such situations on referral" (p. 344). "Occasionally, some specialized staff handles the work, but it is usually part of the child welfare task" (p. 345). "Protective casework is now generally defined either as a specialty within the scope of child welfare services or as part of the general child welfare job" (p. 337).

73. U.S. Children's Bureau, *Trends and Developments in Public Child Welfare Services*. Child Welfare Reports, no. 4, p. 14 (May 1949).

74. De Francis, *Child Protective Services*. Responding to De Francis's request for information, a Delaware official wrote, "Protective services are provided as a segregated part of the child welfare program and staff is selected on the basis of special qualifications. . . . Delaware is a small state and our protective load is such that only one worker is needed in each county" (p. 76). A Minnesota official wrote, "In the urban counties these services are usually given in a separate unit or division with especially skilled workers. However, in the counties which have no specialized child welfare workers protective service becomes the responsibility of the regular worker" (p. 124). See also Louise Foresman, Nelle Martin, Ruth Safier, & Lorena Scherere, The Team Approach in Protective Service, 42 *Child Welfare* 135–138 (March 1963). This article described the role on homemaker services in child protection. Discussing St. Louis County, the authors wrote, "We have developed a well-defined protective service program composed of a single-function unit of nine child welfare workers and one full-time and one half-time child welfare supervisor" (p. 136).

75. Vincent De Francis, *Child Protective Services: A National Survey*, p. 11 (1967; Denver, CO: American Humane Association).

76. Ibid., p. vii. De Francis wrote, "Data supports the finding that there is a legal base in the welfare laws of each of the 50 States to authorize responsibility for Child Protective Services under public child welfare auspices" (p. vii). De Francis went on to comment that "Great variation was found in the language of the welfare laws of the 50 states. In many of the statutes there is direct mention of Child Protective Services as an identifiable area of responsibility. In most, this responsibility may be implied from broad language which frequently speaks of services to "neglected and dependent children, or children in danger of becoming delinquent." This phrase is borrowed from the original language of the Social Security Act passed by Congress in the early thirties" (p. 15).

77. E. Elizabeth Glover & Joseph H. Reid, Unmet and Future Needs. In Alan Keith-Lucas (Special Editor), Thorsten Sellin (Ed.). Marvin E. Wolfgang (Acting Associate Editor), 355 *The Annals of the American Academy of Political and Social Science* 9–19, p. 14 (September 1964; Philadelphia: The American Academy of Political and Social Science).

78. See National Study Service, *Planning for the Care and Protection of Neglected Children in California* (August 1965). The National Study Service was a joint project of the Child Welfare League of America, the Family Service Association of America, and the National Council on Crime and Delinquency. In the transmittal letter regarding the report, Maurice O. Hunt, Director of the National Study Service wrote, "There are major gaps in California's effort to protect children who are in jeopardy. This study shows that many children who are in serious danger are not receiving the help they need from the community until too late and then that the aid is often inadequate." The report stated, "The county welfare departments are not regarded by their communities as child protective agencies, and have little specialized protective service except as demonstration projects or limited units covering a part of the county" (p. 32). The report commented, "One of the common subjects of comment by the public health nurses interviewed was their concern about the unavailability of protective services which are divorced from law enforcement" (p. 100). The report stated that in 1957 counties "were authorized to establish protective services on a permissive basis. This provision is little used to date" (p. 111).

79. De Francis, *Child Protective Services*, p. 21. De Francis wrote, "Caseload differentiation, with Child Protective cases in specialized protective units, is not a common practice. Three states use specialized protective service units exclusively, 2 more have specialized units for handling and treating reports of child abuse. Eighteen additional states have one or more specialized protective service units serving a single district, county or city" (p. viii).

80. In his 1956 nationwide survey of child protection, De Francis found seventy-four communities that claimed to have no protective service agency, public or private. De Francis, *Child Protective Services in the United States*, p. 28. See also Glover & Reid, Unmet and Future Needs. Glover and Reid wrote: "In hundreds of counties in the United States, there is no protective service for children, other than police services, and, in many of the nation's largest cities, the only protective service is provided by voluntary agencies that are not sufficiently financed to give total community coverage. . . . In the writers' opinion, every county and city should have a publicly financed and administered child protective service, operated on a twenty-four-hour, seven-days-a-week basis under the direction of professional social workers" (p. 14).

See also Inez M. Baker, Upholding Rights of Parents and Child, 13 *The Child* 27-30 (August, 1948). Baker was Parish Supervisor of the Children's Division of the Orleans Parish Department of Public Welfare. Baker wrote, "Space does not permit full discussion of the so-called 'protective' function sometimes assumed by children's agencies. In brief, we might say that families affected by this rather undefined function are those in which the right of the parents to retain full responsibility for their children is questioned, at least by some part of the community" (p. 28). See also William A. Ekwall, Better Child Protection; Fewer Juvenile Delinquents, 35 *The National Humane Review* 20-22 (June, 1947). Judge Ekwall wrote, "Can anyone argue that there are sufficient organizations now existing to take care of such cases and to alleviate such conditions? The answer is no!" (p. 21).

81. See Anonymous, Authentic Stories from the Case Files of a Child Protective Agency, 51 *The National Humane Review* 20-21 (January–February, 1963). This short article described a series of cases in which protective services assisted children and families. See also Anonymous, "I Don't Want to Go Home": Excerpts from the Notebook of a Social Worker with the Children's Society, 51 *The National Humane Review* 26-27 (1963). This article described a case where the juvenile court was not needed to help a child.

82. Claire R. Hancock, *A Study of Protective Services and the Problem of Neglect of Children in New Jersey*, p. 36. (1958; State of New Jersey, Department of Institutions and Agencies, State Board of Child Welfare).

83. African-American mothers and children were often excluded from mothers' pensions. See Ira DeA. Reid, Child Dependency as Affected by Race, Nationality, and Mass Migration. In *White House Conference on Child Health and Protection*, pp. 279–350. Reid wrote: "In North Carolina, the only southern state having state supervision, mothers' aid is granted in 75 of its 100 counties. In the biennial report of the State Department of Charities and Public Welfare for 1924 to 1926 there were only 4 Negro families in the 246 (less than 2 per cent) that had been aided. . . . In the practical working out of mothers' aid in North Carolina, the impression still prevails among many county officials that all white mothers should be cared for before aid can be given Negro mothers . . . Only two grants are known to have been made to Negro mothers in Florida. . . . In Richmond, Virginia, the Negro Survey Committee found that "in not a single instance is a mothers' pension or allowance being paid to a Negro mother" (p. 302).

See also Marian J. Morton, Cleveland's Child Welfare System and the "American Dilemma," 1941–1964, 71 *Social Service Review* (March 1998); General Report, Dependent and Neglected Children. In *White House Conference on Child Health and Protection*. The report stated, "Large numbers of needy children, additionally handicapped by color, national origin, or mass migration do not share in the provision made by public and private agencies for dependent children." (p. 7). Later, the report stated, "The unfortunate situation of four ethnic groups has aroused deep concern. The children of Negroes, Mexicans, Puerto Ricans, and Indians present special problems of great importance. Public and private agencies for dependent and neglected children have not concerned themselves as a rule with children of these races and nationalities" (p. 17).

See also Olive David Streater, Some Aspects of Illegitimacy Among Negroes. Child Welfare League of America, 10(5) *Bulletin* 7-8 (May 1931); Herschel Alt, *A Critical Appraisal of the Functions of Private Agencies in Meeting the Needs of Children*. Paper presented at the Child Welfare League section of the National Conference of Social Work, Grand Rapids, Michigan

(May 1940; New York: Child Welfare League of America). In 1939, Alt sent a questionnaire to child welfare professionals in thirty-five cities with populations over 250,000. He noted the increase in care for special groups of children (e.g., those with health and behavioral problems, and Negro children). Today, it seems odd to put African-American children in the same category as pre-psychotic children. Alt, however, wrote well before the civil rights movement, and saw nothing unusual in the juxtaposition. See also Linda Gordon, *The Great Arizona Orphan Abduction* (1999; Cambridge, MA: Harvard University Press).

84. Examples of racial insensitivity abound. In the Child Welfare League of America *Bulletin* for June 15, 1928, there is a story of funding for Ellis College, a private "institution for white, fatherless girls under the age of thirteen" [vol. 7(6), p. 1]. In 1934, Carol Hayes, the principal of a "school for Negroes" in Birmingham, Alabama gave a moving speech at the Southern Regional Conference of the Child Welfare League of America. Carol Hayes, The Negro Child in Our Social Pattern, Child Welfare League of America, 8(9) *Bulletin* 1, 4-6 (November 1934). The *Bulletin* published excerpts of Hayes' speech. The *Bulletin* editor introduced the speech with the following: "Speech, in part, made at Southern Regional Conference of the Child Welfare League of America, Birmingham, Alabama, October 13. The speaker, himself a Negro, is principal of one of the public schools for Negroes in Birmingham. The Conference was held in a leading hotel, the Tutwiler, which permitted attendance of Negroes."

The system of boarding schools for Native American children, originally designed to undermine Native American culture, had a long history. See Margaret Connell Szasz, Federal Boarding Schools and the Indian Child: 1920–60. In N. Ray Hiner & Joseph M. Hawes, *Growing Up in America: Children in Historical Perspective*, pp. 210–218 (1985; Chicago: University of Illinois Press). Szasz wrote that Congress funded the first off-reservation schools in 1882. Szasz observed that by 1928, "There were seventy-seven boarding schools with an enrollment of 21,000. By 1941 only forty-nine boarding schools remained with an enrollment of 14,000" (p. 213).

85. See California Society for the Prevention of Cruelty to Children, *Twenty-Seventh Annual Report* (1902). In the director's address to the members of the society, he reported on the founding of a "Colored Children's home." See also Hayes, The Negro Child. In an eloquent speech that was careful not to offend the largely white audience, but which powerfully described the racial injustice of the South, Hayes praised the Birmingham Children's Aid Society for helping African-American as well as white children.

See also Priscilla Ferguson Clement, Families and Foster Care: Philadelphia in the Late Nineteenth Century. In N. Ray Hiner & Joseph M. Hawes, *Growing Up in America: Children in Historical Perspective*, pp. 135–146 (1985; Chicago: University of Illinois Press). Clement described the practices of the Philadelphia Children's Aid Society and the Home Missionary Society of Philadelphia, both of which placed children in foster homes: "The majority of children in the care of both agencies were native-born Protestants, and, in addition, about 90 percent were Caucasian. Still, there is no evidence that either society deliberately discriminated against nonwhites. Actually the opposite may have been true since both agencies cared for a higher percentage of blacks than their proportion of the city's population would warrant" (p. 140).

See also Crystal M. Potter, The Institutional Care of Negro Children in New York City, Child Welfare League of America, 25(6) *Bulletin* 1-5 (June 1946). Potter was second deputy commissioner in the New York City Department of Welfare. Her article described how institutions in New York City worked to comply with a 1942 rule called the Race Discrimination Amendment which prohibited distribution of government funds to institutions that discriminated on the basis of color. See also Richard Paul, Negro Children at the Leake and Watts School, Child Welfare League of America, 25(6) *Bulletin* 5-7, 12 (June 1946); Patricia M. Collmeyer, From "Operation Brown Baby" To "Opportunity": The Placement of Children of Color at the Boys and Girls Aid Society of Oregon, 74 *Child Welfare* 242–263 (January-February 1995); Paul H. Stuart, The Kinsley House Extension Program: Racial Segregation in the 1940s Settlement Program, 66(1) *Social Service Review* 112–120 (March 1992). The Kinsley House conducted a biracial recreation program in a southern city from 1945 to 1949.

86. Emma Brace, *The Life of Charles Loring Brace: Chiefly Told in His Own Letters*, p. 57 (1894; New York: Charles Scribner's Sons); Child Welfare League of America, The Crusade for Children, 7(6) *Bulletin* 6-7 (June 15, 1928). The *Bulletin* described a recent publication from the New York Children's Aid Society: "During its 75 years, the Children's Aid Society has cared for white children, for colored children, for sick and crippled children, and for 'bad' boys and girls" (p. 6).

87. See Reid, Child Dependency as Affected by Race, Nationality, and Mass Migration. In *White House Conference on Child Health and Protection*, pp. 279–350:

> Next, although exact comparison is difficult, the proportion of young Negro children left daily in homes without the care of a mother or of any other unoccupied female adult is apparently much greater than that of white children, 15 per cent of all Negro children under sixteen were thus left without care. This is in no sense due to neglect, but because so large a number of Negro mothers are bearing the double burden of homemaking and child care, plus the necessity for gainful employment outside the home. . . . (p. 288)
> . . . In addition to discussing problems affecting African American children, Reid discussed "The Mexican in California," writing, "Among a majority of Americans racial prejudices exist against the Mexican which manifests itself in the common classification of the Mexican as *not white*, and the Mexican, sensitive to this social ostracism, does not force himself where he feels the pressure against him." (p. 312, emphasis in original)

88. Marshall B. Jones, Decline of the American Orphanage, 1941–1980, 67(3) *Social Service Review* 459-480 (1993).

89. Matthew A. Crenson, *Building the Invisible Orphanage: A Prehistory of the American Welfare System*, p. 314 (1998; Cambridge, MA: Harvard University Press).

90. Alfred Kadushin, Child Welfare: Adoption and Foster Care. In John B. Turner (Ed.). *Encyclopedia of Social Work*, vol. 1, p. 115 (1977; Washington, D.C.: National Association of Social Workers).

91. Dorothy Berkowitz, Protective Case Work and the Family Agency, 24(7) *The Family* 261–266, p. 261 (November 1943).

92. Vincent De Francis, *The Fundamentals of Child Protection: A Statement of Basic Concepts and Principles in Child Protective Services*, p. 25 (1955; Denver, CO: American Humane Association).

93. See Vincent J. Fontana, *The Maltreated Child: The Maltreatment Syndrome in Children* (2nd ed., 1971; Springfield, IL: Charles C. Thomas). Dr. Fontana, a pediatrician, wrote concerning physical abuse:

In discussing this problem with other physicians, it became apparent that a blind spot existed concerning the importance or frequency of this pediatric entity. I also realize that society, social workers, public health officials, and law enforcement agencies have failed to recognize the maltreatment syndrome in children, partly because of their disbelief. . . . (p. xii)

. . . This disease has been hidden medically and socially for many years, and in view of our obvious ignorance of the subject, it has also been hidden statistically. The maltreatment of children has not been considered important enough to be included in the curricula of medical schools; it has not been given notice in any of the major pediatric textbooks, and it has been ignored by both society and physicians for many years. This seems to be a result of society's disbelief that such inhumane cruelties could wilfully be inflicted upon children. (p. 5)

Chapter 4

1. In 1860, French physician Ambroise Tardieu, professor of legal medicine at the University of Paris, described a condition remarkably similar to battered child syndrome. See Frederic N. Silverman, Rigler Lecture: Unrecognized Trauma in Infants, the Battered Child Syndrome, and the Syndrome of Ambroise Tardieu, 104 *Radiology* 337–353 (1972). Tardieu was also far ahead of his time regarding sexual abuse of children.

2. See Vincent J. Fontana, *The Maltreated Child: The Maltreatment Syndrome in Children*, 2nd ed., 2nd printing (1972; Springfield, IL: Charles C. Thomas). Fontana wrote: "This disease has been hidden medically and socially for many years, and in view of our obvious ignorance of the subject, it has also been hidden statistically" (p. 5). He went on to say, "Presently, stimulated by the recent reports on this pediatric problem of serious import, the education process of bringing this syndrome to the attention of the medical student, the hospital trainee and the practicing physician has begun" (p. 22).

3. John Caffey, Multiple Fractures in the Long Bones of Infants Suffering from Chronic Subdural Hematoma, 56 *American Journal of Roentgenology* 163–173 (August 1946). For biographical information on Caffey, see Frederic N. Silverman, Presentation of the John Howland Medal and Award of the American Pediatric Society to Dr. John Caffey, 67(5) *Journal of Pediatrics* 1000–1007 (November 1965). This article contains fascinating personal information about Caffey, including the fact that as a young man he was an avid poker player, loved sports, and, during his years in New York City, spent many an afternoon at Yankee Stadium. As a teacher, Caffey was very demanding and often gruff with students, although many former students remembered him fondly as a brilliant instructor. See also Frederic N. Silverman, Profiles in Pediatrics II: John P. Caffey, 124 *Journal of Pediatrics* 825–827 (May 1994); N. Thorne Griscom, John Caffey and His Contributions to Radiology, 194 *Radiology* 513–518 (February 1995).

4. My rendition of this event is borrowed from Silverman, Profiles in Pediatrics, p. 826. Silverman wrote of Caffey, "He recounted this story to several of his close associates, usually punctuating it will chuckles." See John Caffey, *Pediatric X-ray Diagnosis* (1945; St. Louis: Mosby). Caffey labored five years on the book, which went through numerous editions. See also Frederic N. Silverman (Ed.), *Caffey's Pediatric X-ray Diagnosis* (1985; Chicago: Year Book Medical Publishers).

5. John Caffey, On the Theory and Practice of Shaking Infants, Its Potential Residual Effects of Permanent Brain Damage and Mental Retardation, 124(2) *American Journal of Diseases of Children* 161–169 (August 1972); John Caffey, The Whiplash Shaken Infant Syndrome: Manual Shaking by the Extremities with Whiplash-Induced Intracranial and Intraocular Bleedings, Linked with Residual Permanent Brain Damage and Mental Retardation, 54(4) *Pediatrics* 396–403 (October 1974). Caffey was not the first to describe injuries caused by shaking. See A.N. Guthkelch, Infantile Subdural Haematoma and its Relationship to Whiplash Injuries, 2 *British Medical Journal* 430–431 (May 22, 1971). Guthkelch wrote, "It seems clear that the relatively large head and puny neck muscles of the infant must render it particularly vulnerable to whiplash injury. . . . One cannot say how commonly assault in the form of violent shaking rather than of direct blows on the head is the cause of subdural haematoma in infants who are maltreated by their parents" (p. 430).

6. See Griscom, John Caffey. Griscom wrote:

> He also knew that for most injuries in infants, a good history of the injury was immediately and freely available to the questioner but that this was not the case with these subdural hematomas and the associated long-bone abnormalities. Nevertheless, Dr Caffey declined to draw sweeping conclusions, for reasons of scientific caution and concern about legal repercussions, and because the culture of the time found it so unthinkable that parents and other caregivers could injure the infants in their trust maliciously or unthinkingly. The most he would say was that the injurious episodes "were either not observed or were denied when observed. The motive for denial has not been established. It is unlikely that trivial unrecognizable trauma caused the . . . fractures. . . ." Despite his caution, however, Dr Caffey's articles were crucial to the slow acknowledgment of the existence of the battered child syndrome, which was not fully accepted until the early 1960s. (p. 516)

7. John Caffey, Multiple Fractures, pp. 163, 172. See also John Caffey, Some Traumatic Lesions in Growing Bones Other Than Fractures and Dislocations: Clinical and Radiological Features, 33(353) *The British Journal of Radiology* 225–238 (May 1957). See also Harry Bakwin, Multiple Skeletal Lesions in Young Children Due to Trauma, 49 *Journal of Pediatrics* 7–15 (1956). Bakwin wrote of Caffey, "Since then [1946] he has called attention repeatedly, in conferences and teaching sessions, to the frequency with which trauma produces skeletal changes in infants and young children" (p. 7).

8. Frederic N. Silverman, The Roentgen Manifestations of Unrecognized Skeletal Trauma in Infants, 69(3) *American Journal of Roentgenolgy* 413–427, p. 413 (March 1953).

9. Paul V. Woolley, Jr. & William A. Evans, Jr., Significance of Skeletal Lesions in Infants Resembling Those of Traumatic Origin, 158 *Journal of the American Medical Association* 539–543, p. 540 (June 18, 1955).

10. Samuel H. Fisher, Skeletal Manifestations of Parent-Induced Trauma in Infants and Children, 51 *Southern Medical Journal* 956–960, p. 956 (August 1958). Fisher described three children, two of whom died from abuse.

11. Donald H. Altman & Richard L. Smith, Unrecognized Trauma in Infants and Children, 42-A(3) *The Journal of Bone and Joint Surgery* 407–413, p. 409 (April 1960).

12. John L. Gwinn, Kenneth W. Lewin, & Herbert G, peterson, Roentgenographic Manifestations of Unsuspected Trauma in Infancy, 176(11) *Journal of the American Medical Association* 926–929, pp. 926, 929, 926, 927 (emphasis in original) (June 17, 1961).

13. Lester Adelson, Slaughter of the Innocents: A Study of Forty-Six Homicides in Which the Victims Were Children, 264(26) *New England Journal of Medicine* 1345–1349, pp. 1348–1349 (June 29, 1961). Dr. Adelson's study covered Cuyahoga County, which includes Cleveland.

14. Elizabeth Elmer, Abused Young Children Seen in Hospitals, 5(4) *Social Work* 98–102, p. 99 (October 1960). Elmer wrote:

> It will be helpful first to inspect another phenomenon that beclouds the issue at every turn: the repugnance felt by most of our society for the entire subject of abused children. . . . First, we are led in many subtle ways to believe that our society is an enlightened one which offers to every child at least the bare minimum of care and protection. . . . Second, so strong is our current cultural emphasis on the rights of children and the responsibilities of parents that many parents will not even admit to the occasional spanking they administer. . . . These two factors do not fully explain the strength of the universal repugnance that is so easily observed. . . . Whatever the conscious or concealed components, the emotion of repugnance is common enough to warrant the label of cultural norm, at least in middle-class American society. In the opinion of the author, this repugnance is the chief reason so little systematic study has been devoted to abused children and their families. (p. 98)

15. Helen E. Boardman, A Project to Rescue Children from Inflicted Injuries, 7(1) *Social Work* 43–51, at 44 (January 1962).

16. C. Henry Kempe, Frederic N. Silverman, Brandt F. Steele, William Droegemueller, & Henry K. Silver, The Battered-Child Syndrome, 181(1) *Journal of the American Medical Association* 17–24, pp. 17–18 (July 7, 1962). In 1959, Kempe and Henry K. Silver made a presentation about child abuse at the Sixty-Ninth Annual Meeting of the American Pediatric Society in Buckhill Falls, Pennsylvania. Their presentation was titled "The Problem of Parental Criminal Neglect and Severe Physical Abuse of Children." A brief description of the presentation appeared at 98 *American Journal of Diseases of Children* 134/528 (October 1959), as follows:

> The recognition of criminal neglect and physical abuse of children requires a certain degree of realistic open-mindedness on the part of the pediatrician, who may, on emotional grounds, tend to reject the concept that parents can and do severely neglect or physically harm their children. A number of recent instances of criminal neglect and severe physical assault in more than one sibling in a family will be briefly reviewed. These cases illustrate that the pediatrician must have an awareness of the problem when the first instance of abuse in a family occurs so that he may be prepared to make a specific diagnosis and recommendations that will lead to the institution of protective measures for the remaining children. The frequent failures of physicians, social services, and the law, in coping with felonious neglect and physical abuse of a degree that leads to severe injury or death, require a frank reappraisal of this difficult problem. (p. 134)

In 1961, Kempe, Steele, and others made a presentation about Battered Child Syndrome in Chicago at the Thirtieth Annual meeting of the American Academy of Pediatrics.

17. Breslau is now Wroclaw, Poland. Biographical information about Dr. Kempe was drawn in part from Pierre E. Ferrier, C. Henry Kempe Remembered, 9 *Child Abuse & Neglect* 133–136 (1985); Henry K. Silver, C. Henry Kempe, MD—A Biographical Sketch, 138 *American Journal of Diseases of Children* 224–227 (March 1984); and Henry K. Silver,

Presentation of the Howland Award: Some Observations Introducing C. Henry Kempe, M.D., 14 *Pediatric Research* 1151–1154 (1980).

18. Vincent J. Fontana, Denis Donovan, & Raymond J. Wong, The "Maltreatment Syndrome" in Children, 269(26) *New England Journal of Medicine* 1389–1394, p. 1389 (December 26, 1963). Fontana and his colleagues preferred the term "maltreatment syndrome in children" to "battered child syndrome." Fontana viewed abuse as on a continuum of seriousness, with battering toward the life-threatening end of the continuum. Fontana believed the term "maltreatment syndrome" would help physicians be on the lookout for milder forms of abuse. Fontana and his colleagues explained:

> Kempe et al. have described this repeated physical abuse of children and called it the "battered child syndrome." Other reports in the medical literature have referred to this disease of maltreatment as "unrecognized trauma." Unfortunately, both these terms do not fully describe the true picture of this often life-threatening condition. A more precise and descriptive term that could be applied to this clinical entity is that of the "maltreatment syndrome in children." A maltreated child often presents no obvious signs of being "battered" but has multiple minor physical evidences of emotional and at times nutritional deprivation, neglect and abuse. (p. 1389)

Kempe was aware that battered child syndrome represented one end of the continuum. He wrote, "The battered child syndrome must be thought of as only the extreme form of a whole spectrum of non-accidental injury and deprivation of children." C. Henry Kempe, Pediatric Implications of the Battered Child Syndrome, 46 *Archives of Disease in Childhood* 28–37, p. 28 (1971). See also Vincent J. Fontana & Esther Robinson, A Multidisciplinary Approach to the Treatment of Child Abuse, 57(5) *Pediatrics* 760–764 (May 1976). Fontana and his colleagues pioneered a program in which abusive mothers lived with their children in a supportive, therapeutic environment, where they received intensive intervention; Vincent J. Fontana & Valerie Moolman, *Save the Family, Save the Child: What We Can Do to Help Children at Risk* (1991; New York: Dutton).

19. See U.S. Congress, Report of the Advisory Council on Child Welfare Services, 86th Congress, 2nd Session, S.D. 92 (1960).

20. Public Welfare Amendments of 1962, Public Law 87-543, Section 528. *U.S. Statutes at Large*, vol. 76, p. 172.

21. Vincent De Francis, *Child Protective Services: A National Survey*, p. 4 (1967; Denver, CO: American Humane Association). Vincent De Francis, Statement Submitted at the Hearing of the Senate Subcommittee on Children and Youth. Held at Denver, Colorado, March 31, 1973. Hearings Before the Subcommittee on Children and Youth of the Committee on Labor and Public Welfare, United States Senate, 93rd Congress, 1st Session, March 26, 27, 31, and April 24, pp. 301–314, at 303 (1973; Washington, DC: U.S. Government Printing Office).

22. States seeking child welfare services under the Social Security Act must submit a proposed state plan to the federal government. The requirement for universal child welfare services by July 1, 1975 was imposed as a requirement for approval of state plans. See Public Welfare Amendments of 1962, *U.S. Statues at Large*, p. 172. See also Wilbur J. Cohen & Robert M. Ball, Public Welfare Amendments of 1962 and Proposals for Health Insurance for the Aged. *Social Security Bulletin* (October 1962). Cohen was assistant secretary for legislation in the Department of Health, Education, and Welfare, now Health and Human

Services. Ball was the commissioner of Social Security. Cohen and Ball wrote, "Beginning July 1, 1963, State child welfare plans must provide for coordinating their services with the services provided for dependent children under title IV, and they must also show by that date that they are working toward making child welfare services available by July 1, 1975, to all children in the State who need them" (p. 3).

23. A brief perusal of the *Readers' Guide to Periodical Literature* revealed the following. Under the subject heading "cruelty to children," there were two entries for the period March 1959 to February 1961; three entries for the period March 1961 to February 1963; nine entries for the period March 1963 to February 1965; and two entries for the period March 1965 to February 1966. Thus, it appears there was brief peak of interest shortly following publication of the "Battered Child Syndrome." See Barbara J. Nelson, *Making an Issue of Child Abuse: Political Agenda Setting for Social Problems* (1984; Chicago: University of Chicago Press). Nelson wrote that while she was doing research on child abuse for her book, "I was confronted by a startling finding. An examination of the *Reader's Guide to Periodical Literature* and the *Social Science and Humanities Index* showed that absolutely no articles on child abuse (regardless of what term one used) had been published before 1962. Later research in other indexes proved me slightly wrong, but at that moment I was surprised and intrigued by the finding" (p. ix). See also American Humane Association, Children's Division, Legislative Review, part II. A Study of Laws Enacted in 1963 for the Protection of the Battered Child, 52 *The National Humane Review* 24–25 (May–June 1964).

24. Their "Prison" Was Home. *Newsweek*, p. 43 (August 8, 1960). *Life* described the same three children in its August 29, 1960 issue, vol. 49, pp. 29–30.

25. "When They're Angry . . ." *Newsweek*, p. 74 (April 16, 1962).

26. Battered-Child Syndrome. *Time*, p. 60 (July 20, 1962).

27. Cry Rises from Beaten Babies. *Life*, pp. 38–39 (June 14, 1963).

28. *Good Housekeeping*, pp. 87–89, 195, at 87–88 (March, 1964). This article was impressive for its thoroughness and objectivity. Chris's mother got psychiatric help for her anger.

29. Statutes: Saving Battered Children. *Time*, p. 43 (January 8, 1965).

30. See Charles Flato, Parents Who Beat Children 235 *Saturday Evening Post* 30–35 (October 6, 1962). This was an in-depth article that included compelling photographs of abused children. See also Katherine Brownell Oettinger, Protecting Children from Abuse, 39 *Parents Magazine* p. 12 (November 1964). As chief of the U.S. Children's Bureau, Oettinger wrote:

Horrifying as it may be, the ugly truth is that every day children in this country are being physically abused, neglected, beaten and battered by their own parents, suffering injuries that have led to crippling—and death! And the problem is increasing.

A battered child needs immediate help—protection, perhaps even removal from the home. But we must remember, too, that the parent who hurts his child does so because of deep-seated emotional conflicts. He, too, urgently needs help and attention if his inadequacies and hostility are to be properly dealt with. (p. 12)

31. Elizabeth Elmer, Identification of Abused Children, 10(5) *Children* 180–184 (September–October 1963). Elmer wrote:

Abundant material is available about individual mistreated children and particular abusive families but data are lacking on comparable groups of children or families selected for study according to carefully defined criteria. This means that few objective guidelines for child protection have been formally established; for example, little is known about the long-term effects of abuse on the child or about the nature of the factors which determine the outcome of rehabilitative efforts with the families.

Perhaps the chief reason for this state of affairs is the taboo in contemporary society regarding abuse and gross neglect. The acute discomfort aroused by the topic leads to extremes of emotion and unquestionably accounts in part for the disregard of the subject by research workers. (p. 180)

32. Fontana, *The Maltreated Child*, pp. xii, 5. See also Vincent J. Fontana, Letter to the Editor, *New England Journal of Medicine*, p. 1044 (November 8, 1973). Fontana wrote:

Child maltreatment is an ugly symptom of the times, but it is more than that: it is inextricably linked with unbearable stress, with impossible living conditions, with material or spiritual poverty, alcoholism, assaults, robberies, murders and the other ills in the midst of which we live and for which we must find massive healing. It is born of this illness and violence and it will breed more of it. If we cannot, as physicians, feel for the children who are even now being neglected and abused, at least we must feel for ourselves and the kind of future we are shaping for ourselves and our children. (p. 1044)

33. U.S. Children's Bureau, *Bibliography on the Battered Child* (July 1969; Children's Bureau: Washington, DC). See also National Institute of Mental Health, *Selected References on the Abused and Battered Child* (1972; Rockville, MD; NIMH).

34. In the journal *Children* [9(3), 123 (May–June 1962)], published by the U.S. Children's Bureau, brief news reported: "Prompted by reports of apparent increases of the numbers of infants and young children who have been subjected to physical harm, the Children's Bureau held an all-day conference in Washington in mid-January to discuss ways the Bureau might help States and communities combat the problem. At the conference, which was attended by 25 pediatricians, judges, lawyers, social workers, and other specialists from various parts of the country, numerous incidents were cited of evidence of past injuries being discovered in children brought to hospitals for treatment of an 'accidental' injury" (p. 123) See also Dorothy E. Bradbury, *Five Decades of Action for Children: A History of the Children's Bureau*, p. 119 (1962; U.S. Department of Health, Education, and Welfare).

35. Vincent De Francis, Who Said There's No More Cruelty to Children? 50 *The National Humane Review* 18–19 (March–April 1962).

36. U.S. Children's Bureau, U.S. Department of Health, Education, and Welfare, *The Abused Child—Principles and Suggested Language for Legislation on Reporting of the Physically Abused Child* (1963). See also Monrad G. Paulsen, Child Abuse Reporting Laws: The Shape of the Legislation, 67 *Columbia Law Review* 1–49 (January 1967); Monrad G. Paulsen, Legal Protections Against Child Abuse, 13 *Children* 43–48 (March-April 1966); American Humane Association, Children's Division, *Guidelines for Legislation to Protect the Battered Child.* (Denver, CO: American Humane Association); American Medical Association, *Physical Abuse of Children—Suggested Legislation* (1965; Washington, DC: AMA); Council of State Governments, Committee of State Officials on Suggested State Legislation, *Suggested State Legislation* (1965; Washington, DC: Council of State Governments).

37. American Medical Association, Office of the General Counsel, Battered Child Legislation, 188 *Journal of the American Medical Association* 386 (April 27, 1964). On June 24,

1964, the AMA House of Delegates approved the position stated by the Office of the General Counsel.

38. Ibid.; Vincent De Francis, *Child Abuse Legislation: Analysis and Study of Mandatory Reporting Laws in the United States*, p. 18 (1966; Denver, CO: American Humane Association).

39. American Humane Association, AHA Children's Division Survey on Abuse, 51 *The National Humane Review* 24–27, pp. 24–25 (July–August 1963). De Francis was fully aware of the methodological weaknesses of his study, writing, "We saw this as only *one* index of the incidence of child abuse. We also saw that at best this could give us information only about the battered child whose case came to the attention of public authorities and whose abuse was severe enough and sensational enough to make a 'newsworthy' story" (p. 24). See also Vincent De Francis, *Child Abuse—Preview of a Nationwide Survey* (1963; Denver, CO: American Humane Association).

40. David G. Gil, *Violence Against Children: Physical Child Abuse in the United States* (1970; Cambridge, MA: Harvard University Press).

41. James Garbarino & Cyleste C. Collins, Child Neglect: The Family with a Hole in the Middle. In Howard Dubowitz (Ed.), *Neglected Children: Research, Practice, and Policy* pp. 1–23, at 3 (1999; Thousand Oaks, CA: Sage). See also Margaret G. Smith & Rowena Fong, *The Children of Neglect: When No One Cares* (2004; New York: Brunner-Routledge). Smith and Fong wrote, "What all definitional proposals regarding child neglect seem to have in common is the concept that one or more of a child's basic needs (e.g., food, shelter, and clothing; safety; love, and affection; health care; education; and/or socialization) are not being met and as a result the child suffers harm or is at risk of harm" (p. 12). See also *In re K.S.*, 737 P.2d 170, 173 (Utah 1987).

42. Isabel Wolock & Bernard Horowitz, Child Maltreatment as a Social Problem: The Neglect of Neglect, 54 *American Journal of Orthopsychiatry* 530–543, pp. 531, 535 (1984).

43. See Martha Farrell Erickson & Byron Egeland, Child Neglect. In John E. B. Myers, Lucy Berliner, John Briere, C. Terry Hendrix, Carole Jenny, & Theresa A. Reid (Eds.), *The APSAC Handbook on Child Maltreatment*, 2nd ed., pp. 3–20 (2002; Thousand Oaks, CA: Sage): "Although abuse still garners more public attention, neglect is the most common type of reported maltreatment" (p. 7); see also Dubowitz (Ed.), *Neglected Children*, p. 19; Smith & Fong, *Children of Neglect*: "In terms of overall reports of child maltreatment, not just fatalities, neglect is the most prevalent type of child maltreatment. . . . Studies have shown that the ratio of neglect to abuse reports ranges from 3:1 to 10:1" (p. 3).

44. U.S. Children's Bureau, *Child Maltreatment 2003* (2005; Washington, DC: U.S. Department of Health and Human Resources); Smith & Fong, *Children of Neglect*, p. 3; Erickson & Egeland, Child Neglect, p. 7.

45. See Jay Belsky, Etiology of Child Maltreatment: A Developmental-Ecological Analysis, 114 *Psychological Bulletin* 413–434, p. 413 (1993); R. McGee, D. Wolfe, S. Yuen, S. Wilson, & J. Carnochan, The Measurement of Maltreatment: Which Method is Best? Paper presented at the biennial meetings of the Society for Research in Child Development, March 1993, New Orleans, LA. Cited in Belsky, Etiology of Child Maltreatment.

46. Smith & Fong, *Children of Neglect*, p. 2; U.S. Children's Bureau, *Child Maltreatment 2002*, p. 25 (2004; U.S. Department of Health and Human Resources). See also Erickson & Egeland, Child Neglect: "Neglect is often fatal, due to inadequate physical protection, nutrition, or health care" (p. 3).

47. Smith & Fong, *Children of Neglect*, pp. 4, 64.

48. Garbarino & Collins, Child Neglect, p. 19; Erickson & Egeland, Child Neglect, p. 3; James Garbarino & John Eckenrode, *Understanding Abusive Families: An Ecological Approach to Theory and Practice*, p. 17 (1997; San Francisco: Jossey-Bass).

49. See Nelson J. Binggeli, Stuart N. Hart, & Marla R. Brassard, *Psychological Maltreatment of Children*, pp. 6–7 at 6 (2001; Thousand Oaks, CA: Sage).

50. Stuart N. Hart, Marla R. Brassard, Nelson J. Binggeli, & Howard A. Davidson, Psychological Maltreatment. In J. Myers et al. (Eds.), *APSAC Handbook on Child Maltreatment*, pp. 79–103, at 79; Binggeli, Hart, & Brassard, *Psychological Maltreatment*, p. xi (emphasis in original). See also James Garbarino, *The Psychologically Battered Child* (1986; San Francisco: Jossey Bass).

51. Robin A. McGee, David A. Wolfe, Sandra A. Yuen, Susan K. Wilson, & Jean Carnochan, The Measurement of Maltreatment: A Comparison of Appoaches, 19 *Child Abuse & Neglect* 233–249, p. 243 (1995).

52. Vincent J. Felitti et al., Relationship of Childhood Abuse and Household Dysfunction to Many of the Leading Causes of Death in Adults: The Adverse Childhood Experiences (ACE) Study, 14 *American Journal of Preventive Medicine* 245–258 (1998).

53. See Shanta R. Dube, Robert F. Anda, Vincent J. Felitti, Daniel P. Chapman, David F. Williamson, & Wayne H. Giles, Child Abuse, Household Dysfunction, and the Risk of Attempted Suicide Throughout the Life Span, 286 *Journal of the American Medical Association* 3089–3096 (2001). Every year, more than 30,000 people commit suicide in the U.S. "An ACE score of at least 7 increased the likelihood of childhood/adolescent suicide attempts 51-fold and adult suicide attempts 40-fold" (p. 3093). "The current analysis suggests that approximately two thirds (67%) of suicide attempts are attributable to the types of abusive or traumatic childhood experiences that we studied. Although preventing, treating, and understanding the effects of adverse childhood experiences is difficult, progress in this area may substantially reduce the burden of suicide. . . . In conclusion, we found that adverse childhood experiences dramatically increase the risk of attempting suicide" (p. 3095).

54. Patricia M. Dietz et al., Unintended Pregnancy among Adult Women Exposed to Abuse or Household Dysfunction During Their Childhood, 282 *Journal of the American Medical Association* 1359–1364 (1999).

55. Felitti et al., Relationship of Childhood Abuse, p. 254 (1998); Robert F. Anda et al., Adverse Childhood Experiences and Smoking During Adolescence and Adulthood, 282 *Journal of the American Medical Association* 1652–1658 (2000).

56. See Social Security Act, *U.S. Statutes at Large*, vol. 49, part 1, title V, part 3, section 521, 74th Congress, 1st Session, chapter 531 (August 14, 1935).

57. Letter of Transmittal from Walter F. Mondale to Harrison A. Williams dated March 15, 1974. Located at Child Abuse Prevention and Treatment Act, 1974, Public Law 93-247 (S. 1191). Questions and Answers, Analysis, and Text of the Act, prepared for the Subcommittee on Children and Youth of the Committee on Labor and Public Welfare, U.S. Senate. 93rd Congress, 2nd Session, p. VII (April, 1974).

58. See report to accompany S. 1191, Child Abuse Prevention and Treatment Act. Senate Report 93-308, 93rd Congress, 1st Session (July 10, 1973). In this report it is stated, "On March 18, 1973, Senator Mondale introduced, with the cosponsorship of 13 other Senators, S. 1191, the Child Abuse Prevention and Treatment Act. A similar bill, H.R. 6380, was

introduced in the House of Representatives" (p. 2). See also Hearings Before the Subcommittee on Children and Youth of the Committee on Labor and Public Welfare, United States Senate, 93rd Congress, 1st Session (March 26, 27, 31, and April 24, 1973); Hearings Before the Select Subcommittee on Education of the Committee on Education and Labor, House of Representatives, 93rd Congress, 1st Session, on H.R. 6379, H.R. 10552, and H.R. 10968 (October 1, 5, and November 2, 1973).

59. Senator Mondale chaired the Subcommittee on Children and Youth of the Senate Committee on Labor and Public Welfare. In 1978, in a short introduction to a symposium on child maltreatment in the *Chicago-Kent Law Review*, then Vice-President Mondale described how he became interested in child abuse. In the summer of 1972, Senator Mondale received a news clipping describing an abused little boy. The picture accompanying the story showed the child's scarred and bruised back. Although Mondale had served on numerous Senate committees, "nothing I witnessed during that period was as disturbing or horrifying, or as compelling, as the stories and photos of children, many of them infants, who had been whipped and beaten with razor straps; burned and mutilated by cigarettes and lighters; scalded by boiling water; bruised and battered by physical assaults; and starved and neglected and malnourished." Walter F. Mondale, Introductory Comments, 54 *Chicago-Kent Law Review* 635–639, p. 636 (1978). Also instrumental were Congressmen Mario Biaggi, John Brademas, and Peter Peyser.

60. Other medical witnesses employed photographs of abused children.

61. C. Henry Kempe, Position Paper for Hearing of the Subcommittee on Children and Youth of the Committee on Labor and Public Welfare, United States Senate, March 31, 1973, Denver, Colorado. Hearings Before the Subcommittee on Children and Youth of the Committee on Labor and Public Welfare, pp. 179–208 at 184, 193 (1973; Washington, DC: U.S. Government Printing Office).

62. Ibid. (emphases in original).

63. Testimony of Vincent De Francis. Hearings Before the Subcommittee on Children and Youth of the Committee on Labor and Public Welfare, U.S. Senate, pp. 293–314 at 293.

64. See Report to accompany S. 1191, Child Abuse Prevention and Treatment Act. In this report, Senator Mondale wrote, "In the majority of cases, witnesses testified, parents, who abuse their children were themselves abused when they were young. This suggests the vital importance of trying to treat child abuse so that a cycle is not repeated from generation to generation" (p. 3). See also Testimony of Brandt Steele, Hearings Before the Subcommittee on Children and Youth of the Committee on Labor and Public Welfare, U.S. Senate, pp. 227–229. Steele, a psychiatrist, testified, "One of the things that we find in the parents who have this pattern of extreme abuse of their children, the background that they themselves were treated very much the same way" (p. 227).

Regarding intergenerational abuse, see Marian G. Morris, Robert W. Gould & Patricia J. Matthews, Toward Prevention of Child Abuse 11(2) *Children* 55–60 (March-April 1964).

65. Testimony of Vincent Fontana. Hearings Before the Select Subcommittee on Education of the Committee on Education and Labor, House of Representatives. Bills to provide for the establishment within the Department of Health, Education, and Welfare of a National Center on Child Development and Abuse Prevention, to provide financial assistance for a demonstration program, and for other purposes (October 1, 5 and November 2, 12, 1973).

66. See Report to accompany S. 1191, Child Abuse Prevention and Treatment Act. In this report, Senator Mondale wrote, "Members of the committee were encouraged to learn that in recent years a number of promising new approaches to child abuse have been developed and put into effect on a limited basis." (p. 3). The senator referred specifically to interdisciplinary child abuse teams in Washington, DC, New York City, and Denver. Senator Mondale also mentioned the value of "lay therapists" and Parents Anonymous. The report stated, "Dr. John Allen, a representative of the American Academy of Pediatrics testified: 'We believe strongly that about 80 percent of these families (of abused children), and maybe even 90 percent, with proper multidisciplinary coordination, could be rehabilitated' " (p. 3).

See also Irene B. Shapaker, Intake in Children's Protective and Court Work. Child Welfare League of America, 26(10) *Bulletin* 4–7 (December 1947). Shapaker was a supervisor with the Children's Aid Society and the SPCC in Buffalo, New York. She wrote, "The worker's role is to take to the parents the community's concern when children are neglected and at the same time to know that the children will be helped most when their parents are seen as people who are in trouble rather than as people who do not care about the welfare of their children" (p. 7). See also American Academy of Pediatrics, Committee on Infant and Pre-School Child, Maltreatment of Children: The Physically Abused Child, 37(2) *Pediatrics* 377–382 (February 1966). The committee stated that mandatory reporting of suspected cases of child abuse is justified and that legislation should be primarily protective rather than punitive. See also Sidney Wasserman, Understanding Comes First in Helping the Abused Parent of the Abused Child, 14(5) *Children* 175–179 (September-October 1967).

67. Testimony of Vincent Fontana before the Select Subcommittee on Education of the Committee on Education and Labor, House of Representatives, 93rd Congress, 1st Session, H.R. 6379, H.R. 19522, H.R. 10968.

68. Kempe, Pediatric Implications of the Battered Child Syndrome, p. 30 (emphases in original). The speech was the Windermere Lecture for 1970. The article was included along with Dr. Kempe's testimony in the proceedings of the Congressional hearings on CAPTA.

69. See Statement of Stephen Kurzman, Assistant Secretary for Legislation, Department of Health, Education, and Welfare, Before the Subcommittee on Children and Youth, Committee on Labor and Public Welfare, United States Senate, March 27, 1973. Mr. Kurzman wrote, "The actual provision of needed services to children and families, suffering from this problem is a role which we believe is appropriately performed by States and localities" (p. 1). "The Department, through the administration of Titles IV-A and IV-B of the Social Security Act, provides funds for child protective services in each State" (p. 13). "[Mr. Kurzman pointed out additional ways federal agencies, e.g., National Institute of Mental Health, assisted states] . . . The Department believes that additional legislation is unnecessary to carry out the Federal role of assisting States and local communities in coping with child abuse" (p. 20). See also Letter from Secretary of Health, Education, and Welfare Casper W. Weinberger to Senator Harrison A. Williams, Jr., Chairman of the Committee on Labor and Public Welfare. Found at Report to accompany S. 1191, Child Abuse Prevention and Treatment Act, pp. 8–10.

70. See *Code of Federal Regulations*, Title 45, § 1340.1-1 et seq., § 1340.3-3 (1975).

71. Douglas J. Besharov, The Need to Narrow the Grounds for State Intervention. In Douglas J. Besharov (Ed.), *Protecting Children from Abuse and Neglect: Policy and Practice* 47-90 (1988; Springfield, IL: Charles C. Thomas). Besharov wrote: "The new Child Abuse Act required the Secretary of Health, Education and Welfare (now Health and Human Services) to establish a National Center on Child Abuse and Neglect (National Center). The National Center was to serve as a clearinghouse for the development and dissemination of information about child protective research and programs" (p. 51).

72. Public Law 95-608. *United States Code Annotated*, title 21, § 1901 et seq. See House Report No. 95-1386. July 24, 1978, pp. 8–9.

73. Public Law 96-272.

74. Howard Altstein & Ruth McRoy, *Does Family Preservation Serve a Child's Best Interests?* (2000; Washington, DC: Georgetown University Press). The authors debated the efficacy of family preservation.

75. Richard J. Gelles, *The Book of David: How Preserving Families Can Cost Children's Lives* (1996; New York: Basic Books).

76. Ibid., p. 148 (emphasis in original).

77. See Transracial Adoption—Congress Forbids Use of Race as a Factor in Adoptive Placement Decisions, 110 *Harvard Law Review* 1352–1358 (1997).

78. The position paper was developed at a conference of the National Association of Black Social Workers in Nashville, Tennessee, April 4–9, 1972.

79. Elizabeth Bartholet, *Nobody's Children: Abuse and Neglect, Foster Drift, and the Adoption Alternative* pp. 124–125 (1999; Boston: Beacon Press); Cynthia G. Hawkins-Leon & Carla Bradley, Race and Transracial Adoption: The Answer is Neither Simply Black or White Nor Right or Wrong, 51 *Catholic University Law Review* 1227 (2002).

80. MEPA is found at Title 42 *United States Code* Sections 671(18) and 1996b. Section 671 provides: "Neither the State nor any other entity in the State that receives funds from the Federal Government and is involved in adoption or foster care placements may—(A) deny to any person the opportunity to become an adoptive or foster parent, on the basis of the race, color, or national origin of the person, or of the child involved; or (B) delay or deny the placement of a child for adoption or into foster care, on the basis of the race, color, or national origin of the adoptive or foster parent, or the child, involved." Section 1996b(3) provides that nothing in MEPA "shall be construed to affect the application of the Indian Child Welfare Act of 1978."

81. National Association of Black Social Workers position paper, 1972. Available at http://www.nabsw.org.

82. Public Law 105-89.

Chapter 5

1. See Lucy Berliner & Diana M. Elliott, Sexual Abuse of Children. In John E. B. Myers, Lucy Berliner, John Briere, C. Terry Hendrix, Carole Jenny, & Theresa A. Reid (Eds.), *The APSAC Handbook on Child Maltreatment*, 2nd ed., pp. 55–78 (2002; Thousand Oaks, CA: Sage): "The precise incidence and prevalence of sexual abuse in the general population are

not known. It is difficult to establish incidence rates because most sexual abuse is not reported at the time it occurs" (p. 56); Kamala London, Maggie Bruck, Stephen J. Ceci, & Daniel W. Shuman, Disclosure of Child Sexual Abuse: What Does the Research Tell Us About the Ways that Children Tell? 11 *Psychology, Public Policy, and Law* 194–226 (2005):

> it is not known how many children are victims of sexual abuse in the United States. There are two major reasons for this lack of data. First, present estimates of the incidence of child sexual abuse (CSA) are primarily based on reports received and validated by child protection agencies. These figures, however, do not reflect the number of unreported cases or the number of cases reported to other types of agencies (e.g., sheriff's offices) and professionals (e.g., mental health diversion programs). Second, the accuracy of diagnosis of CSA is often difficult because definitive medical evidence is lacking or inconclusive in the vast majority of cases, and because there are no gold standard psychological symptoms specific to sexual abuse. (p. 194)

2. David Finkelhor, Current Information on the Scope and Nature of Child Sexual Abuse, 4 *The Future of Children* 31–53, pp. 32, 34 (1994; available online at www.future ofchildren.org).

3. Ibid., p. 31; Berliner & Elliott, Sexual Abuse of Children, p. 56; Sonja N. Brilleslijper-Kater, William N. Friedrich, & David L. Corwin, Sexual Knowledge and Emotional Reaction as Indicators of Sexual Abuse in Young Children: Theory and Research Challenges, 28 *Child Abuse & Neglect* 1007–1017 (2004): "Research indicates that between 25% and 35% of all sexual abuse victims involve children under the age of 7" (p. 1007).

4. See Martin A. Finkel & Allan R. DeJong, Medical Findings in Child Sexual Abuse. In Robert M. Reece & Stephen Ludwig (Eds.), *Child Abuse: Medical Diagnosis and Management* 207–286 (2001; Philadelphia: Lippincott, Williams & Wilkins): "Most children are sexually abused by individuals who have ready access to them and are known, loved, and trusted by the child" (p. 219).

5. Finkelhor, Current Information, p. 45.

6. See Esther Deblinger, Julie Lippmann, & Robert Steer, Sexually Abused Children Suffering Post Traumatic Stress Symptoms: Initial Treatment Outcome Findings, 1 *Child Maltreatment* 310-321 (1996): "Approximately one third of sexually abused children demonstrate no apparent symptomatology, and no single symptom or syndrome is characteristic of the majority of sexually abused children" (p. 310).

7. Kathleen A. Kendall-Tackett, Linda Meyer Williams, & David Finkelhor, Impact of Sexual Abuse on Children: A Review and Synthesis of Recent Empirical Findings, 113 *Psychological Bulletin* 164–180, p. 171 (1993).

8. John N. Briere & Diana M. Elliott, Immediate and Long-Term Impacts of Child Sexual Abuse, 4 *The Future of Children* 54–69, p. 57 (1994) (available online at www.future ofchildren.org).

9. Kendall-Tackett, Williams, & Finkelhor, Impact on Sexual Abuse, p. 171, 165.

10. See Arlene McCormack, Mark-David Janus, & Ann Wolbert Burgess, Runaway Youths and Sexual Victimization: Gender Differences in an Adolescent Runaway Population, 10 *Child Abuse & Neglect* 387–395 (1986); Briere & Elliott, Immediate and Long-Term

Impacts, p. 60; Berliner & Elliott, Sexual Abuse of Children, p. 56; Cathy S. Widom & M. Ashley Ames, Criminal Consequences of Childhood Sexual Victimization, 18 *Child Abuse & Neglect* 303–318 (1994); Cathy S. Widom & Joseph B. Kuhns, Childhood Victimization and Subsequent Risk for Promiscuity, Prostitution, and Teenage Pregnancy: A Prospective Study, 86 *American Journal of Public Health* 1607–1612 (1996).

11. Kendall-Tackett, Williams, & Finkelhor, Impact of Sexual Abuse, p. 165.

12. Berliner & Elliott, Sexual Abuse of Children: "As a group, sexually abused children do not always self-report clinically significant levels of emotional distress. Most studies find, however; that they have more depressive symptoms and more anxiety or lower self-esteem than nonabused comparison children" (p. 59); Kendall-Tackett, Williams, & Finkelhor, Impact of Sexual Abuse, p. 165; Briere & Elliott, Immediate and Long-Term Impacts, p. 57.

13. See Berliner & Elliott, Sexual Abuse of Children: "Sexual abuse appears to constitute a major risk factors for a variety of problems in adult life. The effects of abuse on adult living are not uniform, however. Some survivors report no or very few symptoms, whereas others experience life as overwhelming in many domains" (p. 61); Anna C. Salter, *Transforming Trauma: A Guide to Understanding and Treating Adult Survivors of Child Sexual Abuse* (1995; Thousand Oaks, CA: Sage). But see Bruce Rind, Phillip Tromovitch, & Robert Bauserman, A Meta-Analytic Examination of Assumed Properties of Child Abuse Using College Samples, 124 *Psychological Bulletin* 22–53 (1998). Rind and colleagues argued that factors other than sexual abuse (e.g., family dysfunction) may account for problems experienced by college-age adults. This article generated a great deal of controversy. See U.S. House of Representatives Resolution 107, rejecting the notion that sex between adults and children could be positive. *Congressional Record*, p. H5341 (July 12, 1999).

14. See John Briere & Lisa Zaidi, Sexual Abuse Histories and Sequelae in Female Psychiatric Emergency Room Patients, 146 *American Journal of Psychiatry* 1602–1606 (1989); Widom & Ames, Criminal Consequences.

15. Salter, *Transforming Trauma;* Patricia Coffey, Harold Leitenberg, Kris Henning, Tonia Turner, & Robert T. Bennett, Mediators of the Long-Term Impact of Child Sexual Abuse: Perceived Stigma, Betrayal, Powerlessness, and Self-Blame, 20 *Child Abuse & Neglect* 447-455, p. 447 (1996); Joseph M. Chandy, Robert Wm. Blum, & Michael D. Resnick, Female Adolescents with a History of Sexual Abuse: Risk Outcomes and Protective Factors, 11 *Journal of Interpersonal Violence* 503–518, p. 503 (1996).

16. See Esther Deblinger, Lori B. Stauffer, & Robert A. Steer, Comparative Efficacies of Supportive and Cognitive Behavioral Group Therapies for Young Children Who Have Been Sexually Abused and the Nonoffending Mothers, 6 *Child Maltreatment* 332–343 (2001; cognitive behavioral therapy helped children and their nonoffending parents); William B. Friedrich, *Psychotherapy with Sexually Abused Boys* (1995; Thousand Oaks, CA: Sage); Karen J. Saywitz, Anthony P. Mannarino, Lucy Berliner, & Judith A. Cohen, Treatment for Sexually Abused Children and Adolescents, 55 *American Psychologist* 1040–1047 (2000): "The available research suggests that abuse-specific [cognitive behavioral therapies] are probably efficacious for alleviating many of the chief symptoms displayed by sexually abused children" (p. 1047).

17. David Finkelhor & Lucy Berliner, Research on the Treatment of Sexually Abused Children: A Review and Recommendations, 34 *Journal of the American Academy of Child and Adolescent Psychiatry* 1408–1423, at 1414 (1995).

18. C. Henry Kempe, Sexual Abuse, Another Hidden Pediatric Problem: The 1977 C. Anderson Aldrich Lecture, 62(3) *Pediatrics* 382–389, p. 382 (September 1978). Kempe stated, "Often, pediatricians will simply not even consider the diagnosis of incest in making an assessment of an emotionally disturbed child or adolescent of either sex" (p. 383); Erna Olafson, David L. Corwin, & Roland C. Summit, Modern History of Child Sexual Abuse Awareness: Cycles of Discovery and Suppression, 17 *Child Abuse & Neglect* 7–24, p. 8 (1993); Judith L. Herman & Lisa Hirschman, *Father-Daughter Incest*, p. 7 (1981, 2000; Cambridge, MA: Harvard University Press).

19. Linda Gordon, *Heroes of Their Own Lives: The Politics and History of Family Violence*, p. 215 (1988; New York: Penguin Books); Massachusetts Society for the Prevention of Cruelty to Children, *Tenth Annual Report for 1890* (1891; Boston: Wright & Potter). The report continued, "The penalty is very severe, and no one will ask for merciful treatment of such criminals" (p. 14). *Sacramento Union*, vol. XI, June 20, 1856.

20. Ambrose A. Tardieu, *Etude Medicale-Legale Sure Les Attentats Aux Moeurs*, 6th ed. (1873; Paris); Roland C. Summit, Hidden Victims, Hidden Pain: Societal Avoidance of Child Sexual Abuse. In Gail Elizabeth Wyatt & Gloria Johnson Powell (Eds.), *The Lasting Effects of Child Sexual Abuse*, pp. 39–60, at 46 (1988; Newbury Park, CA: Sage).

21. Summit, Hidden Victims; Brouardel quoted in Jeffrey M. Mason *The Assault on Truth: Freud's Suppression of the Seduction Theory*, p. 44 (1984; New York: Farrar, Strauss & Giroux).

22. Tardieu, however, was not entirely forgotten. In 1894, Travis Gibb, the examining physician for the New York Society for the Prevention of Cruelty to Children, published one of the earliest American reports on sexual abuse of children. Travis Gibb, Indecent Assault Upon Children. In Allan McLane Hamilton & Lawrence Godkin (Eds.), *A System of Legal Medicine*, vol. 1, pp. 649–657, at 650 (1894; New-York: E.B. Treat). Gibb referred briefly to Tardieu.

23. Masson, *Assault on Truth*, p. 192. In the Introduction to the 1985 edition of his book, Masson wrote:

> In the end, it is the reality and the extent of the abuse that matters, and, equally important, the fact that both are routinely denied or in some other fashion neglected by psychoanalysts and psychiatrists. It is irrelevant where this neglect originates. I believe that Freud is largely responsible for this neglect by having given intellectual sophistication to a wrong view (that women invent rape) for the perpetuation of a view that is comforting to male society; but I do not believe that this is the reason we persist in ignoring the reality of this abuse. To understand this, one must take into account the wider issues raised by Florence Rush and Judith Herman and other feminist authors. There is no doubt in my mind that it was the feminist literature of the 1970s that finally broke the silence about the incidence and prevalence of incest. (p. xvii)

24. Sigmund Freud quoted in Jeffrey Masson, *The Assault on Truth: Freud and Child Sexual Abuse*, p. 10 (1984, 1992; New York: HarperCollins).

25. Herman & Hirshman, *Father-Daughter Incest*, pp. 9, 11. See also Diana E. H. Russell, *The Secret Trauma: Incest in the Lives of Girls and Women* (1986; New York: Basic Books). Russell wrote that "all the blame for the mistreatment of incest victims in this century cannot rightly be heaped on Freud. Responsibility should also be placed on those clinicians

who, following in his footsteps, have refused to take seriously the experiences of incestuous abuse reported by their clients" (p. 6).

26. See Leroy G. Schultz, Interviewing the Sex Offender's Victim, 50 *Journal of Criminal Law, Criminology, and Political Science* 448–452 (1959–1960). Schultz wrote,

> Many studies have pointed out that the victim may offer little or no resistance, that some are cooperative to an unusual degree and that in certain instances the so-called victim may be the seducer or aggressor. . . . In cases of incest one can almost always assume a close relationship between victim and offender. So great can the role of the victim be in sex offenses that many should be considered offenders themselves, and it has been recommended that the victims be mentally examined along with the offender. (pp. 448–449)

See also Estelle Rogers & Joseph Weiss, Study of Sex Crimes Against Children. In Karl M. Bowman, *California Sexual Deviation Research*, pp. 47–53 (January 1953; Sacramento: California Department of Mental Hygiene, printed by the Assembly of the State of California). Rogers and Weiss studied 59 girls and 15 boys victimized by sexual abuse. Rogers and Weiss wrote: "it was clearly shown that a certain number of children did participate in the sexual act or acts with the offender; that is, they encouraged in some way the initiation or continuation of the sexual relationship with him. The degree of their participation ranged from simple compliance with the offender's wishes to actual solicitation of his sexual advances" (p. 48). Rogers and Weiss described what they called "participant victims" as young as six. See also Benjamin Karpman, *The Sexual Offender and His Offenses*, p. 67 (1962; New York: Julian Press). Karpman summarized Lauretta Bender & Abram Blau, The Reaction of Children to Sexual Relations with Adults, 7(4) *American Journal of Orthopsychiatry* 500–518 (1937), as follows: "Usually, the child victims had unusually attractive and charming personalities. They made every effort to attract attention from adults. . . . Children may not resist; they often are active, or initiate the role. Even where physical force is involved it does not account for the frequent repetition of the act; apparently it was fundamentally satisfactory" (p. 67).

See also Marjorie Van De Water, Sex Criminal Not a "Fiend," 72(2) *Science News Letter* 26–27, p. 27 (July, 13, 1957).

27. Bender & Blau, Reactions of Children, p. 513. Bender lived from 1897 to 1987 and had a long and distinguished career in psychiatry.

28. Karl Abraham, The Experiencing of Sexual Traumas as a form of Sexual Activity. In Karl Abraham (Ed.), *Selected Papers*, pp. 47–62, at 48 (1927; London: Hograth).

29. Alfred Kinsey, Wardell B. Pomeroy, Clyde E. Martin, & Paul H. Gebhard, *Sexual Behavior in the Human Female*, p. 118 (1953; Philadelphia: W.B. Saunders). See David Finkelhor, *Sexually Victimized Children* (1979; New York: Free Press). Referring to Kinsey, Finkelhor wrote:

> Kinsey was another central figure in the history of research on child sexuality, and he too had a rather ambivalent impact on the study of sexual victimization. On the one hand, Kinsey's studies broke new ground, establishing that child sexual experiences were virtually universal and thus giving assurance to many people that their previously imagined deviance was in fact shared by many others. However, in spite of evidence from his survey that child molesting, sexual abuse, and incest were far more widespread than anyone had previously been able to show, he gave these findings very little attention. He made

pronouncements that he thought incest was more in the imaginations of psychotherapists than it was in the experience of their patients, and he wondered why any child should be so distraught at having its genitals fondled by a stranger. (p. 9)

30. D. James Henderson, Incest. In A. M. Freedman, H. I. Kaplan, & B. J. Sadock (Eds.), *Comprehensive Textbook of Psychiatry,* 2nd ed., pp. 1530–1543, at 1536 (1975; Baltimore: Williams and Wilkins); Finkelhor, *Sexually Victimized Children,* p. 24.

31. Jacob A. Goldberg & Rosamond W. Goldberg, *Girls on City Streets: A Study of* 1400 *Cases of Rape* (1935; New York: American Social Hygiene Association). Reprinted in 1974 as part of Leon Stein & Annette K. Baxter (Advisory Editors), *Women in America from Colonial Times to the 20th Century* (New York: Arno Press). The Goldbergs, aware of the blame the victim mentality, wrote: "One matter insisted upon was that the consent of a female person should be no defense and should be immaterial. This is generally accepted as sound procedure in this country, and serves to counteract the contentions of some, usually the guilty persons, that there are sexually precocious girls who lead on men and youths and that the females should share in the responsibilities involved" (p. 215).

32. See J. Weiss, E. Rogers, M. R. Darwin, & C. E. Dutton, A Study of Girl Sex Victims, 29 *Psychiatric Quarterly* 1–28 (1955); Anna C. Salter, *Treating Child Sex Offenders and Victims,* p. 25 (1988; Newbury Park, CA: Sage); Theresa Reid, Father-Daughter Incest in Contemporary Fiction. Unpublished manuscript, p. 13 (1995).

33. Herman & Hirschman, *Father-Daughter Incest,* pp. 36, 42 (1981, 2000; Cambridge, MA: Harvard University Press) (p. 42).

34. Herbert Blummer, Social Movements. In Barry McLaughlin (Compiler), *Studies in Social Movements: A Social Psychological Perspective,* pp. 8–9 at 9 (1969; New York: Free Press); Ferracuti, Incest Between Father and Daughter, p. 170. Ferracuti wrote, "Weiner reports international incidences ranging between one and five per million per year, worldwide. In the United States, Weinberg reports incidences ranging from 1.2 cases per million in 1910 to 1.1 per million in 1930, with the highest rates 7 per million in the State of Washington, and 9 per million in New Zealand" (p. 169). Ferracuti was referring to K. S. Weinberg, *Incest Behavior* (1955; New York: Citadel); and I. B. Weiner, On Incest: A Survey, 4 *Excerpta Criminologica* 607 (1962).

35. Ferracuti, Incest Between Father and Daughter, p. 179. In *The Sexual Offender,* Karpman wrote, "Regarding offenses against children, there are two mistaken beliefs: (1) that children have no sexual interests (2) that sexual experiences are harmful to them. There is slight evidence for either of these. Blau and Bender conclude that emotional reactions of children are remarkably devoid of guilt, fear or anxiety. Sexual experiences with adults, however, tended to complicate or impede development. The child's sexuality is best permitted to lie dormant" (p. 68). See also Charles H. McCaghy, Child Molesting, 1 *Sexual Behavior* 16-24 (August 1971). McCaghy provided a thorough review of the literature available in 1971.

In Paul Sloan & Eva Karpinski, Effects of Incest on the Participants, 12 *American Journal of Orthopsychiatry* 666–673 (1942), the authors wrote: "The 'traumatic' aspect furthermore loses some of its significance when it is realized that the child itself often unconsciously desires the sexual activity and becomes a more or less willing partner in the act" (p. 666). Sloan and Karpinski concluded that incest with young children was not inherently harmful, but that incest later in life was. They wrote, "Indulgence in incest in the post-adolescent period leads to serious repercussions in the girl, even in an environment in which the moral standards are relaxed" (p. 673). See also Joseph Wortis, Sex Taboos, Sex Offenders and the Law, 9(3) *American Journal of Orthopsychiatry* 554–564 (July 1939).

36. Anna C. Salter, *Transforming Trauma: A Guide to Understanding and Treating Adult Survivors of Child Sexual Abuse*, p. 161 (1995; Thousand Oaks, CA: Sage).

37. Lauretta Bender & Alvin E. Grugett, A Follow-Up Report on Children Who Had Atypical Sexual Experience, 2 *American Journal of Orthopsychiatry* 825–837, p. 827 (1952); Heinz Brunhold, Observations after Sexual Trauma Suffered in Childhood, 11 *Excerpta Criminological* 5–8, p. 7 (1964); Herman & Hirschman, *Father-Daughter Incest*, pp. 22–23.

38. Kinsey et al., *Sexual Behavior*, pp. 121–122.

39. Goldberg & Goldberg, *Girls on City Streets*. See also William I. Thomas, *The Unadjusted Girl: With Cases and Standpoint for Behavior Analysis* (1923; Boston: Little, Brown). Thomas wrote:

> The worst cases of all are those of the delinquent girls who come from depraved homes where the mother is a delinquent woman, or from homes still more tragic where the father has himself abused the person of the child. As a result of the interviews with the girls in the State Training School at Geneva, it appeared that in 47 cases the girl alleged that she had been so violated by some member of her family. In 19 cases the father, in 5 the uncle, in 8 the brother or older cousin had wronged the child for whom the community demanded their special protection. In addition to these cases discovered at Geneva, the court records show that in at least 78 other cases the girl who was brought in as delinquent had been wronged in this way in 43 of these cases by her own father. (p. 101)

See also Benjamin Apfelberg, Carl Sugar, & Arnold Z, pfeffer, A Psychiatric Study of 250 Sex Offenders, 100 *American Journal of Psychiatry* 762–770 (1944): "Of all the sex offenses those involving small children, particularly those under ten, should be regarded as the most dangerous to the community, especially in view of the strong compulsion to repeat such offenses" (p. 768).

40. Articles were located through the *Index to Legal Periodicals and Books*. In 2006, the *Index to Legal Periodicals and Books* has a subject heading for "child sexual abuse." This was not always so, however. Indeed, "child sexual abuse" did not become a separate subject until 1991, prior to 1991, "child sexual abuse" was listed under "child abuse." The subject heading "child abuse" first appeared in 1970, prior to 1970, physical child abuse was listed under the crime of "assault and battery," and articles on child sexual abuse were listed under "rape." Thus, to locate law review articles on child sexual abuse prior to 1970, it was necessary to look under "rape." As it turned out, it was useful to read law reviews on rape of adult women as well as articles on sexual abuse of children. The pre-1970 attitude of law review authors was similar toward adult and child victims.

Employing the *Index to Legal Periodicals and Books*, I read every law review article I could find on rape from 1888 to 1975. At first blush, this sounds like quite a chore. Actually, it was easy because so little was written about rape and sexual abuse during this lengthy period. On average, three to five articles a year addressed rape of adult women. Fewer discussed child sexual abuse. Of the small number on child sexual abuse, most dealt with statutory rape. Very little was written about incest. It is revealing that in the voluminous law review literature before 1970, so little was written about sexual assault. Silence speaks volumes.

41. But see Ira S. Wile, Sex Offenders Against Young Children: What Shall Be Done About Them? 25 *Journal of Social Hygiene* 33–44 (1939). Wile wrote, "Sexual aggression upon young boys and young girls is common, as the records of Juvenile Courts attest" (p. 36).

42. Matthew Hale, *The History of the Pleas of the Crown,* vol. 1, p. 635 (1736; London). Judge Hale lived from 1609 to 1676. His book was published posthumously. From 1671 until his death, Hale served as chief justice of the Court of King's Bench, England's most important trial court. During the feminist critique of rape law in the 1970s, Judge Hale was subjected to considerable criticism. See, e.g., Susan Brownmiller, *Against Our Will: Men, Women and Rape* (1975; New York: Simon & Shuster). In fairness to Judge Hale, he was no apologist for sex offenders. Indeed, Hale viewed rape as a despicable crime that "ought severely and impartially to be punished with death" (p. 635) As far as I can tell, Hale's famous statement did not spring from exaggerated skepticism about women. Rather, Hale's concern arose from his experience as a judge. Hale described several cases involving apparently false allegations of rape; one involving an old man who, according to the evidence, was physically incapable of the crime. Referring to these cases from his judicial experience, Hale wrote, "I only mention these instances, that we may be the more cautious upon trials of offenses of this nature, wherein the court and jury may with so much ease be imposed upon without great care and vigilance; the heinousness of the offense many times transporting the judge and jury with so much indignation, that they are over hastily carried to the conviction of the person accused thereof by the confident testimony, sometimes of malicious and false witnesses" (p. 636).

43. *State v. Chamley,* 568 N.W.2d 607, at 615 (S.D. 1997).

44. Ernst W. Puttkammer, Consent in Rape, 19 *Illinois Law Review* 410–428, p. 421 (1925); Morris Ploscowe, Sex Offenses, The American Legal Context, 25 *Law and Contemporary Problems* 217–224, p. 223 (1960); Anonymous, Statutory Rape Desirability of Evidence that Female was Previously Unchaste or Married in Mitigation of Punishment, 24 *Virginia Law Review* 335–341, p. 338 (1938). (Prior to the 1970s, law review articles written by law students were often anonymous.)

45. Anonymous, The Corroboration Rule and Crimes Accompanying a Rape, 118 *University of Pennsylvania Law Review* 458–472, p. 460 (1970); Anonymous, Forcible and Statutory Rape: An Exploration of the Operation and Objective of the Consent Standard, 62 *Yale Law Journal* 55–83, p. 56 (1952).

46. Ploscowe, Sex Offenses, pp. 222–223 (1960).

47. Anonymous, Forcible and Statutory Rape, p. 69; Anonymous, The Resistance Standard in Rape Legislation, 18 *Stanford Law Review* 680–689, at 682 (1966).

48. John H. Wigmore, *Evidence in Trials at Common Law,* vol. 3A, § 924a, pp. 736–737 (1904 [James H. Chadbourn editor of the 1978 edition]; Boston: Little, Brown & Co.).

49. Quoted in ibid., p. 757.

50. Anonymous, Resistance Standard p. 682. Quoting from R. Slovenko, A Panoramic Overview: Sexual Behavior and the Law. In R. Slovenko (Ed.), *Sexual Behavior and the Law,* pp. 5–51, at 51 (1965).

51. Anonymous, Forcible and Statutory Rape, pp. 66–67, 69 (1952).

52. Anonymous, Rape and Battery Between Husband and Wife, 6 *Stanford Law Review* 719–728, at 728 (1954).

53. See, e.g., *State v. Eli*, 62 N.W.2d 469 (N.D. 1954; in statutory rape cases, cross-examiner may ask about intercourse with others to attack the victim's general credibility); *People v. Collins*, 186 N.E.2d 30 (Ill. 1962); *State v. Wood*, 122 P.2d 416, 418 (Ariz. 1942); *Lee v. State*, 179 S.W. 145, 145 (Tenn. 1915); Anonymous, Statutory Rape, p. 336.

54. Ploscowe, Sex Offenses, p. 222.

55. See, e.g., Wile, Sex Offenders. In September 1950, the entire issue of *Federal Probation* was devoted to articles on sex offenders. In January 1936, *Mental Hygiene* contained several articles on sex offenders.

56. Gibb, Indecent Assault; Gordon, *Heroes of Their Own Lives*, pp. 7, 207.

57. New York Citizens Committee, 1939. Quoted in Karpman, *The Sexual Offender*, p. 66. See also Anonymous, Forcible and Statutory Rape.

58. Bowman, *California Sexual Deviation Research*, p. 11. Bowman wrote, "Sex offenders convicted by superior courts represented an annual conviction rate of about 11 per 100,000 population as compared to an over-all conviction rate on all charges of 121 per 100,000 population in the same counties" (p. 12).

59. See John E. B. Myers, Susan Diedrich, Devon Lee, Kelly McClanahan Fincher, & Rachel Stern, Professional Writing on Child Sexual Abuse from 1900 to 1975: Dominant Themes and Impact on Prosecution, 4(3) *Child Maltreatment* 201–216 (August 1999).

60. William Blackstone, *Commentaries on the Law of England*, p. 214 (1769; Oxford: Clarendon).

61. Victor P. Arnold, What Constitutes Sufficient Grounds for the Removal of a Child from his Home. In U.S. Children's Bureau. *Standards of Child Welfare: A Report of the Children's Bureau Conferences: May and June 1919*. U.S. Children's Bureau Publication No. 60, p. 345 (1919). Arnold was a judge of the Chicago Juvenile Court.

62. See Philip Jenkins, *Moral Panic: Changing Concepts of the Child Molester in Modern America* (1998; New Haven, CT: Yale University Press); Apfelberg, Sugar, & Pfeffer, A Psychiatric Study of 250 Sex Offenders: "Because children have often been the sexual objects of perverts, the community has demanded swift and severe punishment for such offenders" (p. 765); Crime: Horror Week, *Newsweek*, (November 28, 1949): "Either there was an unusual spate of ghastly sex crimes against children last week or some quirk in the week's news reporting made it seem so. In Los Angeles, headlines told of the discovery of the body of 6-year-old Linda Joyce Glucoft, stabbed with an ice pick and strangled with a necktie about the neck. The body was found in a rubbish heap in the yard of Fred Stroble, 67-year-old baker already wanted on a child-molestation charge" (p. 19). The story contained pictures of Stroble in his jail cell, his victim while she was alive, and her distraught parents. Ralph Brancale & F. Lovell Bixby, How to Treat Sex Offenders, 184 *The Nation* 293–295 (April 6, 1957): "spectacular and brutal sex crimes have a special power to inflame public resentment which quickly embraces all sex offenders, the harmless as well as the dangerous" (p. 293). See also Crime: The Sex Rampage, *Newsweek*, p. 22 (February 13, 1950). The article begins, "A sex crime against a child is so horrible that it arouses the wrath of the community in which it occurs like no other event. Several of them arouse the whole nation and, if spread over the front pages of newspapers, become a 'sex crime wave.' "

63. Edwin H. Sutherland, The Diffusion of Sexual Psychopath Laws, 56 *American Journal of Sociology* 142–148 (1950); J. Edgar Hoover, War on the Sex Criminal, *New York Herald Tribune* (September 26, 1937).

64. See Medicine: Sex Psychopaths, *Newsweek*, p. 50 (March 9, 1953), stressing the importance of protecting the innocent while catching the guilty; Edith M. Stern, The Facts on Sex Offenders, 29 *Parents Magazine* 42–43, 137–138, 140 (1954): "When such a sexual offense against a child is reported, our habitual feeling of safety is blown to bits. Sickened, frightened, appalled, we feel that something, anything must be done to protect our children from such experiences. . . . The very best protection you can give your children against sex offenders is plenty of wholesome parental love, for then there is little danger of their seeking unwholesome affection and approval" (p. 140).

65. Charles Harris, Sex Crimes: Their Cause and Cure, 20(4) *Coronet* 3–9, p. 4 (August 1946).

66. Robert A. Esser, Commitments Under the Criminal Sexual Psychopath Law in Criminal Court of Cook County, Illinois, 105 *American Journal of Psychiatry* 420–425 (1948), describes examples of child sexual abuse and efforts to stop it.

67. Bowman, *California Sexual Deviation Research*, p. 34. Bowman wrote, "More than 1,000 persons have been committed for indeterminate periods of care and treatment under the Sex Psychopath Law" (p. 35).

68. Sutherland, The Diffusion of Sexual Psychopath Laws. Sutherland wrote, "The states which have enacted such laws make little or no use of them" (p. 142). See also Philip Jenkins, *Moral Panic*.

69. *Doe v. Poritz*, 662 A.2d 367, at 422 (N.J. 1995).

70. *Kansas v. Henricks*, 521 U.S. 346 (1997).

71. Vincent De Francis, *Protecting the Child Victim of Sex Crimes Committed by Adults*, p. vii (1969; Denver, CO: American Humane Association).

72. David Finkelhor, *Sexually Victimized Children*, p. 1.

73. Ibid., p. 53.

74. Diana E. H. Russell, The Incidence and Prevalence of Intrafamilial and Extrafamilial Sexual Abuse of Female Children, 7 *Child Abuse & Neglect* 133–146, p. 137 (1983). Russell's research was supported by the National Institute of Mental Health and the National Center on Child Abuse and Neglect. Russell's interviews were conducted in 1978. See also Diana E.H. Russell, *The Secret Trauma: Incest in the Lives of Girls and Women* (1986; New York: Basic Books); Diana E.H. Russell & Rebecca M. Bolen, *The Epidemic of Rape and Child Sexual Abuse in the United States* (2000; Thousand Oaks, CA: Sage). Russell began publishing on rape in 1971. See Diana E.H. Russell, *The Politics of Rape: The Victim's Perspective* (1971; New York: Stein & Day).

75. My description of the McMartin case is culled from many sources, including conversations with Kee MacFarlane and others. I also drew from Mary A. Fischer, In Search of Justice, 11 *Life* 164–166 (May 1988); Jill Waterman, Robert J. Kelly, Mary Kay Oliveri, & Jane McCord, *Behind the Playground Walls: Sexual Abuse in Preschools* (1993; New York: Guilford); Mary A. Fischer, Ray Buckey: An Exclusive Interview—McMartin's Controversial Defendant Tells All, 35(4) *Los Angeles Magazine* 90–100 (April 1990); Susan Schindehette, Jack Kelley, Doris Bacon, Lee Wohlfert, Robin Micheli, & Civia Tamarkin, After the Verdict, Solace for None: California's Notorious McMartin Case Ends in Acquittals, Leaving a Legacy of Anger and Anguish, *People*, 70–80 (February 5, 1990).

76. Waterman et al., *Behind Playground Walls*.

77. In 2000, I was retained as an expert witness by a California county that was being sued by individuals who claimed they were improperly prosecuted for child sexual abuse during the early 1980s. At the request of the county, I reviewed training materials that were in use in the late 1970s and early 1980s (prior to McMartin) to train police officers and social workers on how to investigate child sexual abuse. Although there was a lot of material available for training, the materials I examined contained almost no mention of the dangers of suggestive questions and children's suggestibility. It was only after McMartin and cases like it that investigators were trained in suggestibility and proper interviewing practices.

78. Baginsky quoted in Guy M. Whipple, The Psychology of Testimony, 8 *Psychological Bulletin* 307-309, at 308 (1911); Varendonck quoted in Gail S. Goodman, Children's Testimony in Historical Perspective, 40 *Journal of Social Issues* 9–31, p. 9 (1984).

79. See John E. B. Myers, *Evidence in Child, Domestic, and Elder Abuse Cases* (2005; New York: Aspen Law and Business).

80. This case is described in David P. H. Jones & Richard D. Krugman, Can a Three-Year-Old Child Bear Witness to Her Sexual Assault and Attempted Murder? 10 *Child Abuse & Neglect* 253–258 (1986). See also Russell Watson, Gerald C. Lubenow, Nikkifinke Greenberg, Patricia King, & Darby Junkin, A Hidden Epidemic: Sexual Abuse of Children is Much More Common that Most Americans Suspect, 103 *Newsweek* 30–34 (May 14, 1984).

81. Jones & Krugman, Can a Three-Year-Old Child.

82. See Gail S. Goodman, Jodi A. Quas, Bette L. Bottoms, Jianjian Qin, Phillip R. Shaver, Holly Orcutt, & Cheryl Shapiro, Children's Religious Knowledge: Implications for Understanding Satanic Ritual Abuse Allegations, 21 *Child Abuse & Neglect* 1111–1130 (1997). The authors wrote:

> In the 1980s, child welfare advocates were shocked by allegations of a new and startling form of child maltreatment, satanic ritual abuse. Ritual abuse was said to occur in the context of bizarre satanic activities involving murder, torture, and sacrifice of humans and animals, cannibalism, and other horrendous atrocities. Reports came from "adult survivors," that is, adults who claimed to have experienced ritual abuse during their childhood, as well as from children who also described ritual abuse, often in day care settings (p. 1112).

See also Bette L. Bottoms, Gail S. Goodman, & Philip R. Shaver, An Analysis of Ritualistic and Religion-Related Child Abuse Allegations, 20 *Law and Human Behavior* 1–20 (1996); Bette L. Bottoms & Suzanne L. Davis, The Creation of Satanic Ritual Abuse, 16 *Journal of Social and Clinical Psychology* 112–132 (1997).

83. Jan Graham, Attorney General, Utah Attorney General's Office, *Ritual Crime in the State of Utah*, p. 47 (1995).

See also Goodman et al., Children's Religious Knowledge. The authors noted that as more and more investigations came up empty handed, "The reality of ritual abuse was questioned. Indeed, converging sources of evidence now suggest that the threat of highly organized, secret satanic cults was almost surely exaggerated. Large-scale survey research has failed to find corroborative evidence of the satanic elements of ritual abuse cases, alleged victims have recanted their claims, or been discredited, and neither police nor FBI agents have found physical evidence that organized satanic cults are actively engaged in the abuse of children" (p. 1112).

84. Constance J. Dalenberg, Karen Z. Hyland, & Carlos A. Cuevas, Sources of Fantastic Elements in Allegations of Abuse by Adults and Children. In Mitchell L. Eisen, Jodi A. Quas, & Gail S. Goodman (Eds.), *Memory and Suggestibility in the Forensic Interview*, pp. 185–204, at 186 (2002; Mahwah, NJ: Lawrence Erlbaum).

85. Kenneth V. Lanning, *Child Sex Rings: A Behavioral Analysis*, p. 22 (1992; Washington, DC: National Center for Missing and Exploited Children).

86. Mark D. Everson, Understanding Bizarre, Improbable, and Fantastic Elements in Children's Accounts of Abuse, 2 *Child Maltreatment* 134–149 (1997); Jean M. Goodwin, Credibility Problems in Sadistic Abuse, 21 *Journal of Psychohistory* 479–496, p. 480 (1994).

87. Everson, Understanding Bizarre, p. 147.

88. See Goodman et al., Children's Religious Knowledge. Goodman and her colleagues offer insight into how ritual abuse allegations might arise. They write,

From a psychological perspective, vulnerable individuals (perhaps due to histories of real abuse or inherent suggestibility) might be inadvertently led to believe they were abused after exposure to suggestive media, leading forensic interviews, or therapy involving suggestive memory recovery techniques. Media coverage and special seminars dealing with satanism and satanic abuse have provided adults and children with considerable knowledge about the prototypical features of ritual abuse claims, professionals (e.g., social workers, clinicians, legal investigators) and nonprofessionals (e.g., parents, friends) may transfer such information to children through questions asked in the context of formal or informal interviews. (pp. 1112–1113)

89. See Lisa M. Jones & David Finkelhor, Putting Together Evidence on Declining Trends in Sexual Abuse: A Complex Puzzle, 27 *Child Abuse & Neglect* 133–135(2003).

90. David Finkelhor & Lisa M. Jones, Explanations for the Decline in Child Sexual Abuse Cases. *Juvenile Justice Bulletin*, p. 4 (January 2004; Washington, DC: U.S. Department of Justice).

Part II

1. Henry Louis Mencken, *"The Divine Afflatus,"* A Mencken Chrestomathy, p. 443 (1949; New York: Knopf).

2. U.S. Children's Bureau, *National Study of Child Protective Services Systems and Reform Efforts*, p. 3 (May 2003). Available on at http://aspe.hhs.gov/hsp/CPS-status03/summary/.

3. See Sue D. Steib & Wendy Whiting Blome, Fatal Error: The Missing Ingredient in Child Welfare Reform: Part 1, 82(6) *Child Welfare* 747–750 (2003): "Agencies today typically require only that caseworkers have a bachelor's degree in any field. At one point in the mid-1980s, almost half of the states required no degree at all. As of 2000, only four states required a bachelor's in social work (BSW) for caseworkers, and two specified a master's in social work (MSW) for supervisory positions. Although social work has long been associated with child welfare, only about one-fourth of child welfare services today are delivered by staff with BSWs or MSWs" (p. 748).

4. See U.S. Department of Health & Human Services, Administration for Children and Families, Children's Bureau, *Child Maltreatment 2003* (2005; Washington, DC: DHHS);

U.S. Department of Health and Human Services, Administration for Children and Families, Children's Bureau, 12 *Years of Reporting: Child Maltreatment* 2001 (2003; Washington, DC: DHHS).

5. In 2002, 67.1 percent of referrals to CPS were screened in, and 32.9 percent were screened out. U.S. Department of Health & Human Services, *Child Maltreatment 2002*, p. 5 (2004).

6. See U.S. Department of Health & Human Services, *Child Maltreatment 2003* (reporting that 0 percent of reports in 2003 were thought to be intentionally false). In 2003, 57.4 percent of reports were unsubstantiated. The percentage of reports substantiated was 26.4 percent.

7. See U.S. Children's Bureau, *National Study of Child Protective Services Systems and Reform Efforts*, p. 3. The National Study reported, "It is estimated that during 2001, 21 percent of victims were removed during or as an immediate result of an investigation, with State-level percentages ranging from 6 percent to 49 percent" (p. 9). See also U.S. Department of Health & Human Services, *Child Maltreatment 2002*: "Almost one-fifth of victims (18.9%) were placed in foster care as a result of an investigation or assessment" (pp. 68–69).

8. Cameron Jahn, Hard Journey from Addiction to Inspiration, *Sacramento Bee* (March 12, 2005).

9. Insoo Kim Berg & Susan Kelly, *Building Solutions in Child Protective Services*, p.13 (2000; New York: W.W. Norton).

Chapter 6

1. For reviews of the theoretical literature see Martha Farrell Erickson & Byron Egeland, Child Neglect; David J. Kolko, Child Physical Abuse; and Lucy Berliner & Diana M. Elliott, Sexual Abuse of Children, all in John E. B. Myers, Lucy Berliner, John Briere, C. Terry Hendrix, Carole Jenny, & Theresa A. Reid (Eds.), *The APSAC Handbook on Child Maltreatment*, 2nd ed. (2002; Thousand Oaks, CA: Sage).

2. See Paul W. Howes & Dante Cicchetti, A Family/Relational Perspective on Maltreating Families: Parallel Processes Across Systems and Social Policy Implications. In Dante Cicchetti & Sheree L. Toth (Eds.), *Child Abuse, Child Development, and Social Policy*, pp. 249–299 (1993; Norwood, NJ: Ablex Pub).

3. Jay Belsky, Etiology of Child Maltreatment: A Developmental-Ecological Analysis, 114 *Psychological Bulletin* 413–434, p. 413 (1993).

4. See Jay Belsky & Peter Stratton, An Ecological Analysis of the Etiology of Child Maltreatment. In Kevin Browne, Helga Hanks, Peter Stratton, & Catherine Hamilton, *Early Prediction and Prevention of Child Abuse: A Handbook*, pp. 95–110 (2002; New York: John Wiley & Sons); James Garbarino & John Eckenrode, *Understanding Abusive Families: An Ecological Approach to Theory and Practice* (1997; San Francisco: Jossey-Bass). See also Michelle D. DiLauro, Psychosocial Factors Associated with Types of Child Maltreatment, 83 *Child Welfare* 69–96 (2004). DiLauro wrote: "Research has shown that abusive parents display less ability to solve problems, a lack of awareness of age-appropriate behavior, and harsher discipline than nonabusive parents. They also have fewer interactions with their children but are more intrusive, are less attentive and affectionate, communicate less

frequently, and provide fewer consistent and positive parenting behaviors than parents who are not abusive" (p. 73).

5. See Howes & Cicchetti, A Family/Relational Perspective, pp. 251–252.

6. Belsky, Etiology of Child Maltreatment, p. at 421.

7. Ibid.

8. C. Henry Kempe, Position Paper for Hearing of the Subcommittee on Children and Youth of the Committee on Labor and Public Welfare, U.S. Senate, March 31, 1973, Denver, CO. 93rd Congress, 1st Session, March 26, 27, 31, and April 24, 1973, pp. 179–208, at 184 (1973).

9. Belsky, Etiology of Child Maltreatment, p. 422.

10. See Kelly A. Carroll & Dario Maestripieri, Infant Abuse and Neglect in Monkeys: A Discussion of Definitions, Epidemiology, Etiology, and Implications for Child Maltreatment: Reply to Cicchetti (1998) and Mason (1998), 123 *Psychological Bulletin* 234–237 (1998).

11. Belsky, Etiology of Child Maltreatment, p. 424 (1993).

12. Lynn A. Fairbanks & Michael T. McGuire, Parent–Offspring Conflict and Corporal Punishment in Primates. In Michael Donnelly & Murray A. Strauss (Eds.), Corporal Punishment of Children in Theoretical Perspective, pp. 21–40 at 21 (2005; New Haven, CT: Yale University Press). Fairbanks and McGuire do not refer to the use of physical force as abuse. Rather, they construe the behavior as corporal punishment.

13. See John Eckenrode, Jane Levine Powers, & James Garbarino, Youth in Trouble Are Youth Who Have Been Hurt. In Garbarino & Eckenrode, *Understanding Abusive Families*, pp. 166–193. Eckenrode and his colleagues wrote,

> Children come into the world without any frame of reference. They have no inherent scale upon which to judge their worth; they must ascertain their value from the messages they receive, parents largely determine the ratings that children give themselves, at least until they enter school and begin to reevaluate themselves based upon the feedback they receive there. It is no wonder that youth whose parents show signs of emotional pathology have trouble making value judgments, especially when it comes to assessing their own personal worth. Considering the impact that parents have upon the lives of their children, it is also not surprising that maltreatment can have devastating consequences that may show up years later in the form of self-destructive and antisocial behavior; when a vulnerable youth suffers maltreatment, the result can be physical damage, low self-esteem, anxiety, lack of empathy, poor social relationships, drug or alcohol abuse, suicide, delinquency, or homicide. (pp. 166–167)

See also Belsky, Etiology of Child Maltreatment; Byron Egeland, Michelle Bosquet, & Alissa Levy Chung, Continuities and Discontinuities in the Intergenerational Transmission of Child Maltreatment: Implications for Breaking the Cycle of Abuse. In Kenvin Browne, Helga Hanks, Peter Stratton, & Catherine Hamilton, *Early Prediction and Prevention of Child Abuse: A Handbook*, pp. 217–232 (2002; New York: John Wiley & Sons); Howes & Cicchetti, Family/Relational Perspective.

14. Nelson J. Binggeli, Stuart N. Hart, & Marla R. Brassard, *Psychological Maltreatment of Children*, p. 16 (2001; Thousand Oaks, CA: Sage).

15. See James Garbarino, *The Psychologically Battered Child* (1986; San Francisco: Jossey-Bass).

16. See Jay Belsky, Sara R. Jaffee, Judith Sligo, Lianne Woodward, & Phil A. Silva, Intergenerational Transmission of Warm-Sensitive-Stimulating Parenting: A Prospective Study of Mothers and Fathers of 3-Year-Olds, 76 *Child Development* 384–396 (2005): "Whether considering research on harsh-insensitive parenting or documented child maltreatment, it is by no means the case that every parent with a problematic childrearing history proceeds to mistreat their own offspring" (p. 385).

17. Katherine C. Pears & Deborah M. Capaldi, Intergenerational Transmission of Abuse: A Two-Generational Prospective Study of an At-Risk Sample, 25 *Child Abuse & Neglect* 1439–1461, p. 1440 (2001); Joan Kaufman & Edward Zigler, Do Abused Children Become Abusive Parents? 57 *American Journal of Orthopsychiatry* 186–192, p. 190 (1987). See also Belsky, Etiology of Child Maltreatment, pp. 415, 424.

18. See Belsky, Etiology of Child Maltreatment, pp. 415–416.

19. James Garbarino, *Lost Boys: Why Our Sons Turn Violent and How We Can Save Them,* pp. 80–81 (1999; Free Press: New York; emphasis added).

20. Binggeli, Hart, & Brassard, *Psychological Maltreatment,* p. 16. See also Berliner & Elliott, Sexual Abuse of Children; Kathleen Coulborn Faller, *Understanding Child Sexual Maltreatment* (1990; Thousand Oaks, CA: Sage); Anna C. Salter, *Transforming Trauma: A Guide to Understanding and Treating Adult Survivors of Child Sexual Abuse* (1995; Thousand Oaks, CA: Sage); Marla R. Brassard & Linda E. McNeill, Child Sexual Abuse. In Marla R. Brassard, Robert Germain, & Stuart N. Hart (Eds.), *Psychological Maltreatment of Children and Youth,* pp. 69–88 (1987; New York: Pergamon Press).

21. Leonard L. Shengold, Child Abuse and Deprivation: Soul Murder, 27 *Journal of the American Psychoanalytic Association* 533–559, p. 549 (1979). In his classic paper, Shengold wrote, "Treating soul murder means first of all discovering it. The psychotherapist must be aware of the possibility of the kind of parental pathology that can contribute to crushing the child's sense of identity and capacity for feeling. The therapist must be able to suspend belief in the patient's stories of cruelty and incest—in order to help him with the most difficult task of differentiating fantasies from actual events" (p. 554).

22. See DiLauro, Psychosocial Factors. Research has shown "depressed mothers as more distant, irritable, and punitive, and less tolerant of perceived behavior problems in their children. . . . Neglectful and abusive mothers had a significantly greater incidence of depressive disorders" (p. 72).

23. T. Berry Brazelton & Stanley I. Greenspan, *The Irreducible Needs of Children: What Every Child Must Have to Grow, Learn, and Flourish,* pp. 1–2 (2000; Cambridge, MA: Perseus).

24. See Howes & Cicchetti, A Family/Relational Perspective; Margaret G. Smith & Rowena Fong, *The Children of Neglect: When No One Cares* (2004; New York: Brunner-Routledge); Brassard & McNeill, Child Sexual Abuse: "Child sexual abuse does not appear to be related to social class, although reliable data are lacking" (p. 72).

25. DiLauro, Psychosocial Factors, p. 74.

26. Claire R. Hancock, *A Study of Protective Services and the Problem of Neglect of Children in New Jersey,* p. 4 (1958; Trenton, NJ: Department of Institutions and Agencies, State Board of Child Welfare).

27. Charles Flato, Parents Who Beat Children, 235 *Saturday Evening Post* 30–35 at 32 (October 6, 1962); Cry Rises from Beaten Babies, 63 *Life* 38 (June 14, 1963).

28. Hearings to Establish a National Center on Child Abuse and Neglect. Before the Select Subcommittee on Education of the Committee on Education and Labor, House of Representatives. 93rd Congress, 1st Session on H.R. 6379. H.R. 10552, and H.R. 10968, p. 153. October 1, 5, 1973; November 12, 1973; letter of Transmittal from Walter F. Mondale to Harrison A. Williams. March 15, 1974. Located at Child Abuse Prevention and Treatment Act, 1974, public Law 93-247. Senate Bill 1191. Questions and Answers, Analysis, and Text of the Act, prepared for the Subcommittee on Children and Youth of the Committee on Labor and Public Welfare, U.S. Senate. 93rd Congress, 2nd Session, p. vii. April 1974.

29. Leroy H. Pelton, Child Abuse and Neglect: The Myth of Classlessness, 48 *American Journal of Orthopsychiatry* 608–617, pp. 609, 614 (1978).

30. U.S. Advisory Board on Child Abuse and Neglect, U.S. Department of Health and Human Services, *Child Abuse and Neglect: Critical First Steps in Response to an National Emergency* 17 (1990; Washington, DC: U.S. Government Printing Office); Howes & Cicchetti, A Family/Relational Perspective, p. 250. See also David K. Shipler, *The Working Poor: Invisible in America* (2005; New York: Vintage): "The federal poverty line cuts far below the amount needed for a decent living. . . . The result burnishes reality by underestimating the numbers whose lives can reasonably be considered impoverished" (p. 9).

31. The information on poverty is drawn from Carmen DeNavas-Walt, Bernadette D. Proctor, & Robert J. Mills, *Income, Poverty, and Health Insurance Coverage in the United States: 2003* (2004; Washington, DC: U.S. Census Bureau).

32. Lee Rainwater & Timothy M. Smeeding, *Poor Kids in a Rich Country: America's Children in Comparative Perspective*, p. 17 (2003; New York: Russell Sage Foundation).

33. See Belsky, Etiology of Child Maltreatment.

34. See Mark Chaffin, Kelly Kelleher, & Jan Hollenberg, Onset of Physical Abuse and Neglect: Psychiatric, Substance Abuse, and Social Risk Factors from Prospective Community Data, 20 *Child Abuse & Neglect* 191–203 (1996): "Studies examining mental health characteristics of abusive and neglectful parents have noted the prevalence of two main disorders: depression and substance abuse" (p. 192); DiLauro, Psychosocial Factors: "According to the National Center on Addiction and Substance Abuse, children were three times more likely to be abused and four times more likely to be neglected if they had parents who were substance abusers" (p. 72).

35. Massachusetts Society for the Prevention of Cruelty to Children, *First Annual Report, 1881*, p. 2 (*1882*; Boston: Wright & Potter); Massachusetts Society for the Prevention of Cruelty to Children, *Annual Report for* 1882, pp. 12–13 (1883; Boston: Wright & Potter); Jacob A. Goldberg & Rosamond W. Goldberg, *Girls on City Streets: A Study of 1400 Cases of Rape*, p. 187 (1935; New York: American Social Hygiene Association). Reprinted in 1974 as part of Leon Stein & Annette K. Baxter (Advisory Eds.), *Women in America from Colonial Times to the 20th Century* (New York: Arno Press).

36. See Smith & Fong, *The Children of Neglect*, p. 212. See Stephen M. Butler, Nick Radia, & Michael Magnatta, Maternal Compliance to Court-Ordered Assessment in Cases of Child Maltreatment, 18 *Child Abuse & Neglect* 203–211 (1994). Maltreating mothers with substance abuse problems were less likely than non–substance-abusing mothers to comply with court orders. "This study suggests that alcohol and drug abuse, previous history of criminal charges, transiency, and spousal violence are factors that increase the probability of noncompliance with mental health interventions mandated by the court" (p. 209);

Richard Famularo, Robert Kinscherff, Doris Bunshaft, Gayl Spivak, & Terrence Fenton, Parental Compliance to Court-Ordered Treatment Interventions in Cases of Child Maltreatment, 13 *Child Abuse & Neglect* 507–514 (1989).

37. Famularo et al., Parental Compliance, p. 512.

38. J. Michael Murphy, Michael Jellinek, Dorothy Quinn, Gene Smith, Francis G. Poitrast, & Marilyn Goshko, Substance Abuse and Serious Child Mistreatment: Prevalence, Risk, and Outcome in a Court Sample, 15 *Child Abuse & Neglect* 197–211, pp. 208–209 (1991).

39. See Jan Bays, Substance Abuse and Child Abuse: The Impact of Addiction on the Child, 37 *Pediatric Clinics of North America* 81 (1990); DiLauro, Psychosocial Factors.

40. Belsky, Etiology of Child Maltreatment, p. 422.

41. Jo Ann M. Farver, Yiyuan Xu, Stefanie Eppe, Alicia Fernandez, & David Schwartz, Community Violence, Family Conflict, and Preschoolers' Socioemotional Functioning, 41 *Developmental Psychology* 160–170, p. 160 (2005).

42. James Garbarino, *Raising Children in a Socially Toxic Environment*, p. 1 (1995; San Francisco: Jossey-Bass).

43. James Garbarino, *Lost Boys*, pp. 100, 108.

44. See Clifton P. Flynn, Regional Differences in Spanking Experiences and Attitudes: A Comparison of Northeastern and Southern College Students, 11 *Journal of Family Violence* 59–80 (1996); Anthony M. Graziano, Corinne M. Lindquist, Linda J. Kunce, & Kavita Munjal, Physical Punishment in Childhood and Current Attitudes: An Exploratory Comparison of College Students in the United States and India, 7 *Journal of Interpersonal Violence* 147–155 (1992).

45. One has only to study legal cases addressing physical abuse to understand that a great deal of physical abuse is discipline gone too far.

46. Jill E. Korbin, Culture and Child Maltreatment. In Mary Edna Helfer, Ruth S. Kempe, & Richard D. Krugman (Eds.), *The Battered Child*, 5th ed., pp. 29–48, at 38 (1997; Chicago: University of Chicago Press); Roger W. Byard & Stephen D. Cohle, Homicide and Suicide. In Roger W. Byard (Ed.), *Sudden Death in Infancy, Childhood, and Adolescence*, 2nd ed., pp. 77–163, at 77 (2004; Cambridge: Cambridge University Press); Belsky, Etiology of Child Maltreatment, p. 421 (1993).

47. Kolko, Child Physical Abuse, p. 27; Cindy W. Christian, Etiology and Prevention of Abuse: Societal Factors. In Stephen Ludwig & Allen E. Kornberg (Eds.), *Child Abuse: A Medical Reference*, 2nd ed., pp. 25–37 at 29 (1992; New York: Churchill Livingstone); rhyme quoted in B. Knight, The History of Child Abuse, 30 *Forensic Science International* 135–141 (1986).

48. See John E. B. Myers, *Myers on Evidence in Child, Domestic, and Elder Abuse Cases* (2005; New York: Aspen Law and Business).

49. *Branstetter v. State*, 57 S.W.3d 105 (Ark. 2001); *State v. Williams*, 571 S.E.2d 619 (N.C. Ct. App. 2002); *United States v. Ray*, 44 M.J. 835 (A.C.M.R. 1996); *In re C. Children*, 564 N.Y.S.2d 354 (A.D. 1991).

50. Judith V. Becker, personal communication, May 17, 2005; Judith V. Becker, Offenders: Characteristics and Treatment, 4 *The Future of Children* 176–197, p. 181 (1994).

51. See Association for the Treatment of Sexual Abusers, *Reducing Sexual Abuse Through Treatment and Intervention with Abusers*, position paper available on the association's website: www.atsa.com (accessed May 14, 2005).

52. See J. Chaiken, Violence by Intimates: Analysis of Data on Crimes by Current or For- mer Spouses, Boyfriends, and Girlfriends, publication no. NJC167237 (March 1998; Wash- ington, DC: U.S. Department of Justice, Bureau of Justice Statistics). Available online: http://www.ojp.usdoj.gov/bjs); Joy D. Osofsky, Prevalence of Children's Exposure to Do- mestic Violence and Child Maltreatment: Implications for Prevention and Intervention, 6 *Clinical Child and Family Psychology Review* 161–170 (2003); one study "indicated that chil- dren under the age of 12 resided in more than 50% of these households" (p. 162).

53. See B. E. Carlson, Children's Observations of Interparental Violence. In A. R. Roberts (Ed.), *Battered Women and Their Families,* pp. 147–167 (1984; New York: Springer); Lundy Bancroft & Jay G. Silverman, *The Batterer as Parent: Addressing the Impact of Domestic Vio- lence on Family Dynamics,* p. 1 (2002; Thousand Oaks, CA: Sage). See also Jeffrey L. Edle- son, Should Childhood Exposure to Adult Domestic Violence Be Defined as Child Maltreatment Under the Law? In Peter G. Jaffe, Linda L. Baker, & Alison J. Cunningham, *Protecting Children from Domestic Violence: Strategies for Community Intervention,* pp. 8–29 at 9 (2004; New York: Guilford); Osofsky, Prevalence of Children's Exposure, p. 162; Lucy Salcido Carter, Lois A. Weithorn, & Richard E. Behrman, Domestic Violence and Children: Analysis and Recommendations, 9 *The Future of Children* 4–20 (1999): "The often-cited fig- ures of 3.3 million and 10 million are estimates derived from methodologically limited studies" (p. 5); Sandra A. Graham-Bermann, Child Abuse in the Context of Domestic Vio- lence. In John E. B. Myers, Lucy Berliner, John Briere, C. Terry Hendrix, Carole Jenny, & Theresa A. Reid (Eds.), *The APSAC Handbook on Child Maltreatment,* 2nd ed., pp. 119–129 at 122 (2002; Thousand Oaks, CA: Sage). There has been no national prevalence study of children's exposure to domestic violence.

54. See Linda L. Baker, Peter G. Jaffe, Steven J. Berkowitz, & Miriam Berkman, *Children Exposed to Violence: A Handbook for Police Trainers to Increase Understanding and Improve Community Response* p. 1 (2002; London, Ontario, Canada: Centre for Children and Fami- lies in the Justice System; the handbook can be accessed from www.lfcc.on.ca/pubs.html or www.nccev.org); J. Fantuzzo, R. Boruxh, A. Berianna, M. Atkins, & S. Maracus, Domestic Violence and Children: Prevalence and Risk in Five Major U.S. Cities, 36 *Journal of the American Academy of Child and Adolescent Psychiatry* 116–122 (1997); Katherine M. Kitz- mann, Noni K. Gaylord, Aimee R. Holt, & Erin D. Kenny, Child Witnesses to Domestic Vi- olence: A Meta-Analytic Review, 71 *Journal of Consulting and Clinical Psychology* 339–352, (2003): "research suggests that physical violence is highest early in the marital relationship, when children are likely to be young" (p. 339); Osofsky, Prevalence of Children's Exposure, p. 163.

55. See Stephen E. Doyne, Janet M. Bowermaster, & J. Reid Meloy, Custody Disputes In- volving Domestic Violence: Making Children's Needs a Priority, 50 *Juvenile and Family Court Journal* 1 (1999); P. Jaffe, D. Wolfe, & S. Kaye Wilson, *Children of Battered Women* (1990; Thousand Oaks, CA: Sage); Osofsky, Prevalence of Children's Exposure: "In general, parents tend to underestimate the extent to which their children may be exposed to both community and domestic violence" (p. 164); Kitzmann et al., Child Witnesses, p. 339.

56. See Edleson, Should Childhood Exposure, p. 17; Jeffrey L. Edleson, Studying the Co- Occurrence of Child Maltreatment and Domestic Violence in Families. In Sandra A. Graham- Bermann & Jeffrey L. Edleson (Eds.), *Domestic Violence in the Lives of Children: The Future of Research, Intervention, and Social Policy,* pp. 91–110 (2001; Washington, DC: American

Psychological Association); Carolyn C. Hartley, Severe Domestic Violence and Child Maltreatment: Considering Child Physical Abuse, Neglect, and Failure to Protect, 26 *Children and Youth Services Review* 373–392 (2004) (discusses the complexity of the relationship between domestic violence and child abuse and neglect); Jeffrey L. Edleson, Lyungai F. Mbilinyi, Sandra K. Beeman, & Annelies K. Hagemeister, How Children Are Involved in Adult Domestic Violence: Results from a Four City Anonymous Telephone Survey, 18(1) *Journal of Interpersonal Violence* 18–32 (2003); Carter, Weithorn, & Behrman, Domestic Violence and Children, p. 9.

57. Bancroft & Silverman, *Batterer as Parent*, p. 1; Edleson et al., How Children Are Involved, p. 19; Osofsky, Prevalence of Children's Exposure: "A striking report in 1990 revealed that in homes where domestic violence occurs, children are physically abused at a rate 15 times higher than the national average. Several studies have found that in 60–75% of families where a woman is battered, children are also battered" (p. 166); Graham-Bermann, Child Abuse in the Context, p. 120.

58. See John W. Fantuzzo & Wanda K. Mohr, Prevalence and Effects of Child Exposure to Domestic Violence, 9 *The Future of Children* 21–32 (1999): "Research to date indicates that children who live in households with domestic violence are at greater risk for maladjudgment than are children who do not live with such violence" (p. 22); Abigail Gewitz & Jeffrey L. Edleson, Young Children's Exposure to Adult Domestic Violence: The Case for Early Childhood Research and Support. Series paper no. 6, pp. 113–139; George W. Holden, Introduction: The Development of Research Into Another Consequence of Family Violence. In George W. Holden, Robert Geffner, & Ernest N. Jouriles, *Children Exposed to Marital Violence: Theory, Research, and Applied Issues*, pp. 1–18, (1998; Washington, DC: American Psychological Association); Kitzmann et al., Child Witnesses to Domestic Violence: (Judges are aware of the damage caused children by exposure to domestic violence. See *People v. Johnson*, 95 N.Y.2d 368, 740 N.E.2d 1075, 718 N.Y.S.2d 1 [2000].) See also Edleson, Should Childhood Exposure: "children exposed to domestic violence may experience a variety of negative developmental outcomes and may also be at risk for direct physical abuse" (p. 8); Gewitz & Edleson, Young Children's Exposure, p. 121.

59. Carter, Weithorn, & Behrman, Domestic Violence and Children, p. 6.

60. Baker et al., *Children Exposed to Violence*, p. 17.

61. Bancroft & Silverman, *The Batterer as Parent*, pp. 47–48. See also Edleson et al., How Children Are Involved; L. Silvern, J. Karyl, L. Waelde, W. F. Hodges, J. Starek, E. Heidt, & K. Min, Retrospective Reports of Parental Partner Abuse: Relationships to Depression, Trauma Symptoms and Self-Esteem among College Students, 10 *Journal of Family Violence* 177–202 (1995).

62. Baker et al., *Children Exposed to Violence*, p. 16; Graham-Bermann, Child Abuse in the Context, p. 124; B. B. Robbie Rossman, Jacqueline G. Rea, Sandra A. Graham-Bermann, & Perry M. Butterfield, Young Children Exposed to Adult Domestic Violence. In Peter G. Jaffe, Linda L. Baker, & Alison J. Cunningham (Eds.), *Protecting Children from Domestic Violence: Strategies for Community Intervention*, pp. 30–48 at 30 (2004; New York: Guilford).

63. See National Resource Center on Domestic Violence, *Children Exposed to Intimate Partner Violence* (2002; Harrisburg, PA: NRCDV):

Many people still believe that infants and very young children are not aware of the violence in their homes. In reality, infants exposed to domestic violence frequently present with any number of issues related to the violence. Many babies appear detached and are unresponsive to adult attention. Battered women may be unable to nurture and care for their babies the way they would wish. In response, the babies may become passive, not expecting needs to be met, or conversely seem inconsolable—crying and fussing incessantly for attention or in reaction to the stress in the home. Sleep disturbances and eating disorders are common with infants. (p. 6)

64. Gewitz & Edleson, Young Children's Exposure: "initial research has suggested that domestic violence might jeopardize the development or maintenance of such attachment" (p. 116); National Resource Center on Domestic Violence, *Children Exposed:* "Expected to be 'little adults', they are often denied the exploration and experimentation necessary for development. Speech, motor skill and cognitive delays may result. Many preschoolers show signs of depression and anxiety and may find it difficult to express any emotion but anger" (p. 6).

65. See Graham-Bermann, Child Abuse in the Context, p. 124. See also National Resource Center on Domestic Violence, *Children Exposed*, p. 6.

66. See Edleson, Should Childhood Exposure; Osofsky, Prevalence of Children's Exposure, p. 164; Graham-Bermann, Child Abuse in the Context, p. 124.

67. Baker et al., *Children Exposed to Violence*, p. 2.

68. National Resource Center on Domestic Violence, *Children Exposed*, p. 7.

69. Martha Farrell Erickson & Byron Egeland, Child Neglect. In John E.B. Myers, Lucy Berliner, John Briere, C. Terry Handrix, Carole Jenny, & Theresa A. Reid (Eds.), *The APSAC Handbook on Child Maltreatment*, 2nd ed., pp. 3–20, at 13 (2002; Thousand Oaks, CA: Sage). See also Christine Walsh, Harriet MacMillan, & Ellen Jamieson, The Relationship Between Parental Psychiatric Disorder and Child Physical and Sexual Abuse: Findings from the Ontario Health Supplement, 26 *Child Abuse & Neglect* 11–22 (2002); Patricia McKinsey Crittenden, Child Neglect: Causes and Contributions. In Howard Dubowitz (Ed.), *Neglected Children* 47–68 (1999; Thousand Oaks, CA: Sage). Crittenden wrote, "These parents experience chronic depression in which there is little feeling or thought. The failure to use either affect or cognition to organize information about reality closes the doors to both relationships and learning. Under these conditions, it will be very difficult to intervene to create change" (p. 64).

70. Walsh, MacMillan, & Jamieson, Relationship Between Parental Psychiatric Disorder, pp. 19, 12.

71. Ibid. But see Chaffin, Kelleher, & Hollenberg, Onset of Physical Abuse: "No association was found between schizophrenia and either type [physical abuse or sexual abuse] of maltreatment" (p. 200); Josephine Stanton, Alexander Simpson, & Trecia Wouldes, A Qualitative Study of Filicide by Mentally Ill Mothers, 24 *Child Abuse & Neglect* 1451–1460 (2000).

72. See, e.g., *In re S.G.*, 611 S.E.2d 86 (Ga. Ct. App. 2005). The mother's parental rights were terminated; the mother had chronic schizophrenia. "The psychologist testified that, as a result of appellant's chronic mental problems, it was her opinion that, even with medication and therapy, appellant was struggling to take care of herself and was not capable of caring for a child."

73. 436 A.2d 1158 (N.J. Juv. Ct. 1981).

74. 279 Cal. Rprt. 534 (Ct. App. 1990).

75. Crittenden, Child Neglect, p. 63 (1999; Thousand Oaks, CA: Sage).

76. See Myers, *Myers on Evidence.*

77. *Midgett v. State,* 729 S.W.2d 410 (Ark. 1987).

78. *Forrester v. Bass,* 397 F.3d 1047 (8th Cir. 2005); *People v. Hanson,* 59 Cal. App. 4th 473, 68 Cal. Rptr. 2d 897 (1997).

79. G.L. Campbell-Hewson, A. D'Amore, & A. Busuttil, Non-Accidental Injury Inflicted on a Child with an Air Gun, 38 *Medical Science and the Law* 173–176 (1998); *In re S. B.,* 348 Ill. App. 3d 61, 808 N.E.2d 1094 (2004).

80. See *Hill v. State,* 64 Ark. App. 6, 977 S.W.2d 234 (1998; starvation); *Cardona v. State,* 641 So. 2d 361 (Fla. 1994; child died of multiple injuries inflicted over time, including malnutrition); *G.Q.A. v. Harrison County Department of Human Services,* 771 A.2d 331, 334 (Miss. 2000; "Dr. Davidson's expert opinion was that A.N.A. was intentionally malnourished."); *State v. Fritsch,* 351 N.C. 373, 526 S.E.2d 451 (2000; starvation); *Hill v. State,* 913 S.W.2d 581 (Tex. Crim. App. 1996; child starved to death); *In re* Danielle T., 195 W. Va. 530, 466 S.E.2d 189 (1995; termination of parental rights case; child was, among other things, severely malnourished).

81. See *State v. Stewart,* 663 A.2d 912 (R.I. 1995; dehydration). See also Allen I. Arieff & Barbara A. Kronlund, Fatal Child Abuse by Forced Water Intoxication, 103 *Pediatrics* 1292–1295 (1999; describing three cases of fatal child abuse due to forced drinking of large quantity of water as punishment); *State v. Gray,* 230 Wis.2d 746, 604 N.W.2d 33 (1999; unpublished disposition).

82. See Jan Bays & Kenneth W. Feldman, Child Abuse by Poisoning. In Robert M. Reece & Stephen Ludwig (Eds.), *Child Abuse: Medical Diagnosis and Management,* 2nd ed., pp. 405–441, at 406–408 (2001; Philadelphia: Lippincott Williams & Wilkins). See also J. Goebel, D. A. Gremse, & M. Artman, Cardiomyopathy from Ipecac Administration in Munchausen Syndrome by Proxy, 92 *Pediatrics* 601 (1993; intentional poisoning with ipecac); Roy Meadow, Non-Accidental Salt Poisonings, 68 *Archives of Diseases of Childhood* 448–452 (1993); Joseph A. Zenel, Child Abuse by Intentional Iron Poisoning Presenting as Shock and Persistent Acidosis, 111 *Pediatrics* 197–199 (2003); *State v. DePiano,* 926 P.2d 494 (Ariz. 1996; mother prosecuted for endangering children; mother attempted to kill herself and her two children with exhaust fumes from car); Shipley v. State, 620 N.E.2d 710 (Ind. Ct. App. 1993; pepper poisoning); Commonwealth v. Robinson, 30 Mass. App. Ct. 62, 565 N.E.2d 1229 (1991); State v. West, 103 N.C. App. 1, 404 S.E.2d 191 (1991; parent forced child to consume large quantities of water, leading to hyponatremia or low sodium level; child died; parent's conviction for involuntary manslaughter and nonfeloneous child abuse upheld).

83. *Commonwealth v. Robinson,* 30 Mass App. Ct. 62, 565 N.E.2d 1229 (1991); *State v. Davis,* 205 W. Va. 569, 519 S.E.2d 1999 (1999); *State v. Stewart,* 18 S.W.3d 75 (Mo. Ct. App. 2000).

84. C. Fearne, J. Kelly, J. Habel, & D. P. Drake, Needle Injuries as a Cause of Non-Accidental Injury, 77 *Archives of Diseases of Childhood* 187 (1997); K. B. Nolte, Potential Fatal Mechanisms: Esophageal Foreign Bodies as Child Abuse, 14 *American Journal of Forensic Medical Pathology* 323 (1993; report on an infant who died when caretakers repeatedly put coins in child's esophagus); *State v. Prince,* 131 Md. App. 296, 748 A.2d 1078 (2000); Mario Darok & Sebastian Reischle, Burn Injuries Caused by a Hair-Dryer—An Unusual Case of Child Abuse, 115 *Forensic Science International* 143–146 (2000); *Beaugureau v. State,* 56 P.3d 626 (Wyo. 2002; the child suffered a severe burn requiring a skin graft).

85. See, e.g., *State v. Timmendequas,* 737 A.2d 55 (N.J. 1999). The defendant, a convicted sex offender, lived close to the victim's home; he lured Megan Kanka into his home, raped her, strangled her with a belt, and dumped her body nearby.

86. See, e.g., Mary Edna Helfer, Ruth S. Kempe, & Richard D. Krugman (Eds.), *The Battered Child*, 5th ed. (1997; Chicago: University of Chicago Press); Belsky, Etiology of Child Maltreatment; Kolko, Child Physical Abuse.

87. Ron Rosenbaum, Degrees of Evil, *The Atlantic Monthly* 63, 68 (February 2002).

88. See Baker et al., *Children Exposed*, p. 18; Gewitz & Edleson, Young Children's Exposure; Kitzmann et al., Child Witnesses: "An effect size of this magnitude indicates that about 63% of child witnesses were faring more poorly than the average child who had not been exposed to interparental violence. Notably, however, this result also means that about 37% of the child witnesses showed outcomes that were similar to, or better than, those of nonwitnesses." (p. 345).

89. See Bancroft & Silverman, *Batterer as Parent:* "The quality of children's relationship with a nurturing parent has been established to be among the best predictors of their thriving and of their ability to recover from marital conflict or parental psychopathology" (p. 104); Baker et al., *Children Exposed*, p. 19; Suniya S. Luthar, Dante Cicchetti, & Bronwyn Becker, The Construct of Resilience: A Critical Evaluation and Guidelines for Future Work, 71 *Child Development* 543–562 (2000); Carter, Weithorn, & Behrman, Domestic Violence and Children, p. 6; Edleson, Should Childhood Exposure, p. 15.

90. Jeffrey L. Edleson, Young Children's Exposure to Adult Domestic Violence: "At present, we have little systematic data on what risk and protective factors are most important for the healthy development of children exposed to domestic violence" (p. 127).

91. See *Prince v. Massachusetts*, 321 U.S. 158 (1944); *Pierce v. Society of Sisters*, 268 U.S. 510 (1925).

92. The judge is quoted in *The Unquiet Death of Eli Creekmore*. Documentary film produced by David Davis in 1987 by Public Television station KCTS, Seattle, WA.

Chapter 7

1. Ira M. Schwartz & Gideon Fishman, *Kids Raised by the Government*, p. 117 (1999; Westport, CT: Praeger).

2. Burton J. Cohen, Reforming the Child Welfare System: Competing Paradigms of Change, 27 *Children and Youth Services Review* 653–666, p. 654 (2005).

3. See Margaret G. Smith & Rowena Fong, *The Children of Neglect: When No One Cares*, p. 98 (2004; New York: Brunner-Routledge); Carmen DeNavas-Walt, Bernadette D. Proctor, & Robert J. Mills, *Poverty, and Health Insurance Coverage in the United States: 2003* (2004; U.S. Census Bureau). The report states, "Both the number of people in poverty and the poverty rate increased between 2002 and 2003" (p. 1). See also David K. Shipler, *The Working Poor: Invisible America*, p. 6 (2005; New York: Vintage Books. Forty years after the War on Poverty, the gap between rich and poor has widened.

4. Dorothy Roberts, *Shattered Bonds: The Color of Child Welfare*, p. 45 (2002; New York: Civitas Books); Elizabeth Bartholet, *Nobody's Children: Abuse and Neglect, Foster Drift, and the Adoption Alternative*, p. 4 (1999; Boston: Beacon Press); Lee Rainwater & Timothy M. Smeeding, *Poor Kids in a Rich Country: America's Children in Comparative Perspective*, p. 132 (2003; New York: Russell Sage Foundation); Duncan Lindsey, *The Welfare of Children*, 2nd ed., p. 319 (2003; New York: Oxford University Press).

5. See Swedish Ministry of Health and Social Affairs, *Swedish Family Policy: Fact Sheet* (2003).

6. Lindsey, *Welfare of Children*, p. 319.

7. Rainwater & M. Smeeding, *Poor Kids* p. 137; Lindsey, *Welfare of Children*.

8. DeNavas-Walt, Proctor, & Mills, *Poverty and Health Insurance.*

9. See Timothy Stoltzfus Jost, Why Can't We Do What They Do? National Health Reform Abroad, 32 *Journal of Law, Medicine, and Ethics* 433 (2004).

10. Ibid.

11. See Peter J. Cunningham, Mounting Pressure: Physicians Serving Medicaid Patients and the Uninsured, 1997–2001. Available at the website for Center for Studying Health System Change, www.hschange.com. (accessed February 7, 2005).

12. C. Henry Kempe, Position Paper for Hearing of the Subcommittee on Children and Youth of the Committee on Labor and Public Welfare, United States Senate, March 31, 1973, Denver, Colorado. Hearings Before the Subcommittee on Children and Youth of the Committee on Labor and Public Welfare, United States Senate, 93rd Congress, 1st Session, March 26, 27, 31, and April 24, pp. 197–198 (emphasis in original) (1973).

13. See Jay Belsky, Etiology of Child Maltreatment: A Developmental-Ecological Analysis, 114 *Psychological Bulletin* 413–434, p. 416 (1993).

14. See John M. Leventhal, Getting Prevention Right: Maintaining the Status Quo Is Not an Option, 29 *Child Abuse & Neglect* 209–213, at 209 (2005). Leventhal reported on two models of home visiting focused on high-risk, first-time mothers: the paraprofessional model and the nurse home visitation model.

15. See Mark Chaffin, Invited Commentary. Is It Time to Rethink Healthy Start/Healthy Families? 28 *Child Abuse &* Neglect 589–595 (2004); Anne Duggan, Elizabeth McFarlane, Loretta Fuddy, Lori Burell, Susan M. Higman, Amy Windham, & Calvin Sia, Randomized Trial of a Statewide Home Visiting Program: Impact in Preventing Child Abuse and Neglect, 28 *Child Abuse & Neglect* 597–622, at 614 (2002). This experimental study of the Hawai'i Healthy Start Program found that the program did little to prevent child abuse. See also Mark Chaffin & Bill Friedrich, Evidence-Based Treatments in Child Abuse and Neglect, 26 *Children and Youth Services Review*, 1097–1113 (2004). Chaffin and Friedrich wrote:

> Although perinatal home-visiting has been widely lauded as effective for preventing future abuse and neglect among new parents, the randomized trial evidence is largely disappointing. . . . The Nurse Family Partnership model has amassed considerable randomized trial evidence for a range of benefits, and is probably the best-supported model currently being practiced. However, evidence of reduced child maltreatment outcomes has been only indirectly measured in some trials, appeared only as a long-delayed effect where it was directly measured, and appeared weak for cases where there was substance abuse or domestic violence. (pp. 1106–1107)

16. David L. Olds et al., Home Visiting by Paraprofessionals and by Nurses: A Randomized, Controlled Trial, 110 *Pediatrics* 486–496, p. 494 (2002). See also David Olds, Charles Henderson, & John Eckenrode, Preventing Child Abuse and Neglect with Prenatal and Infancy Home Visiting by Nurses. In Kevin Browne, Helga Hanks, Peter Stratton, & Catherine Hamilton, *Early Prediction and Prevention of Child Abuse: A Handbook*, pp. 166–182 (2002; New York: John Wiley & Sons).

17. See David L. Olds et al., Improving the Life-Course Development of Socially Disadvantaged Mothers: A Randomized Trial of Nurse Home Visitation, 78 *American Journal of Public Health* 1436–1445 (1988); David L. Olds et al., Long-Term Effects of Home Visitation on Maternal Life Course and Child Abuse and Neglect: 15-Year Follow-Up of a Randomized Trial, 278 *Journal of the American Medical Association* 637–643 (1997).

18. Harriet Kitzman, David L. Olds, et al., Enduring Effects of Nurse Home Visitation on Maternal Life Course, 283 *Journal of the American Medical Association* 1983–1989 (2000).

19. Mark Chaffin, Barbara L. Bonner, & Robert F. Hill, Family Preservation and Family Support Programs: Child Maltreatment Outcomes Across Client Risk Levels and Program Types, 25 *Child Abuse & Neglect* 1269–1289 (2001); John Eckenrode et al., Preventing Child Abuse and Neglect with a Program of Nurse Home Visitation, 284 *Journal of the American Medical Association* 1385–1391 (2000).

20. See Washington State Institute for Public Policy, *Benefits and Costs of Prevention and Early Intervention Programs for Youth* (2004; available online at www.wsipp.wa.gov).

21. Bartholet, *Nobody's Children*, p. 170.

22. Children's Defense Fund, *The State of America's Children 2005*, pp. 66–67 at 65 (2004; Washington, DC: Children's Defense Fund).

23. Ibid., p. 69.

24. Robert D. Putnam, *Bowling Alone: The Collapse and Revival of American Community*, p. 25 (emphasis in original) (2000; New York: Simon & Schuster).

25. See www.aecf.org/initiatives/familytofamily.

26. Gary B. Melton, *Strong Communities for Children in the Golden Strip, Laying the Foundation for Stronger Communities for Children in Southern Greenville County: First Semi-Annual Report*, p. 5 (2002; Greenville, SC: Clemson University). Available: www.clemson.edu/strongcommunities.

27. See Special Issue: Community Building and 21st Century Child Welfare, 84 *Child Welfare* 101–336 (2005).

28. See Irving Browne, *Elements of the Law of Domestic Relations and of Employer and Employed*, 2nd ed., p. 17 (1890; Boston: The Boston Book Co.); James Schouler, *A Treatise on the Law of Domestic Relations*, 5th ed. (1895; Boston: Little, Brown):

> Though either spouse may be the more dangerous companion, because of greater physique, daring, recklessness, or depravity, nature gives to the husband the usual advantage. In a ruder state of society the husband frequently maintained his authority by force. The old common law recognized the right of moderate correction. . . . The civil law went still further, permitting, in certain gross misdemeanors, violent flogging with whips and rods. But since the time of Charles II, the wife has been regarded more as the companion of her husband; and this right of chastisement may be regarded as exceedingly questionable at the present day. The rule of persuasion has superseded the rule of force. (p. 75)

29. See Mary Keegan Eamon, Antecedents and Socioemotional Consequences of Physical Punishment on Children in Two-Parent Families, 25 *Child Abuse & Neglect* 787–802 (2001): "Children who are spanked more frequently exhibit more socioemotional problems" (p. 787); Clifton P. Flynn, Regional Differences in Spanking Experiences and Attitudes: A Comparison of Northeastern and Southern College Students, 11 *Journal of Family Violence* 59–80, pp. 59–60 (1996); Eric P. Slade & Lawrence S. Wissow, Spanking in Early Childhood

and Later Behaviors: A Prospective Study of Infants and Young Toddlers, 113 *Pediatrics* 1321–1330 (2004); Murray A. Straus & Glenda Kaufman Kantor, Corporal Punishment of Adolescents by Parents: A Risk Factor in the Epidemiology of Depression, Suicide, Alcohol Abuse, Child Abuse, and Wife Beating, 29 *Adolescence* 543–561 (1994); Thomas Styron & Ronnie Janoff-Bulman, Child Attachment and Abuse: Long-Term Effects on Adult Attachment, Depression, and Conflict Resolution, 21 *Child Abuse & Neglect* 1015–1023 (1997).

30. Flynn, Regional Differences, pp. 59–60; Eamon, Antecedents and Socioemotional Consequences, p. 798. Straus & Kantor, Corporal Punishment, pp. 550–551.

31. Benjamin M. Spock & Michael B. Rothberg, *Dr. Spock's Baby & Child Care*, 40th ed., p. 359 (1985; Bristol, PA: Pocket Books).

32. American Academy of Pediatrics, Committee on Psychosocial Aspects of Child and Family Health, Guidance for Effective Discipline, 101 *Pediatrics* 723–728, p. 726 (1998); T. Berry Brazelton & Stanley I. Greenspan, *The Irreducible Needs of Children* 146 (2000; Cambridge, MA: Perseus).

33. Elizabeth Thompson Gershoff, Corporal Punishment, Physical Abuse, and the Burden of Proof: Reply to Baumrind, Larzelere, and Cowan, 128 *Psychological Bulletin* 602–611, p. 609 (2002).

34. See Joan E. Durrant, Evaluating the Success of Sweden's Corporal Punishment Ban, 23 *Child Abuse & Neglect* 435–448 (1999); Julian V. Roberts, Changing Public Attitudes Toward Corporal Punishment: The Effects of Statutory Reform in Sweden, 24 *Child Abuse & Neglect* 1027–1035, p. 1028 (2000).

35. Belsky, Etiology of Child Maltreatment, p. 423; David J. Kolko, Child Physical Abuse. In John E. B. Myers, Lucy Berliner, John Briere, C. Terry Hendrix, Carole Jenny, & Theresa A. Reid (Eds.), *The APSAC Handbook on Child Maltreatment*, 2nd ed., pp. 21–54 (2002; Thousand Oaks, CA: Sage).

36. *People v. Smith*, 678, p.2d 886 (Cal. 1984).

37. See Michelle D. DiLauro, Psychosocial Factors Associated with Types of Child Maltreatment, 83 *Child Welfare* 69–96 (2004). DiLauro wrote: "The abuser's expectations are often unrealistic, and he or she expects children to fulfill maternal, paternal, or spousal functions that are inappropriate for their age or relationship with the abuser. These unrealistic expectations increase the likelihood of the child being noncompliant. The parent may then perceive the child's behavior as defiant, resulting in the parent's maltreating behavior" (p. 73).

38. Verna Hildebrand, *Parenting: Rewards and Responsibilities*, p. 512 (2000); Holly Brisbane, *The Developing Child: Understanding Children and Parenting*, p. 239 (1997).

39. Verdene Ryder & Celia Decker, *Parents and Their Children*, p. 56 (1995).

40. Brisbane, *Developing Child*, p. 239.

Chapter 8

1. See Cynthia Andrews Scarcella, Roseanna Bess, Erica Hecht Zielewski, Lindsay Warner, & Rob Green, *The Cost of Protecting Vulnerable Children IV* (2004; Washington, DC: The Urban Institute). The authors wrote, "Federal funds make up more than half of the expenditures for child welfare activities" (p. vi).

2. See Pew Commission on Children in Foster Care, *Fostering the Future: Safety: Permanence and Well-Being for Children in Foster Care*, p. 13 (2004; Washington, DC: Pew Charitable Trusts): "Title IV-E is the largest source of federal funding for child welfare, accounting for 48 percent of federal child welfare spending in state fiscal year (SFY) 2000. Title IV-E is a permanently authorized and open-ended entitlement program that guarantees federal reimbursement to states for a portion of the cost of maintaining an eligible child in foster care. Specifically, states may claim a federal reimbursement on behalf of every income-eligible child they place in a licensed foster home or institution. In FY 2004, federal IV-E foster care expenditures are estimated to be $4.8 billion" (p.13).

3. Ibid.

4. Scarcella et al., *Cost of Protecting*.

5. Duncan Lindsey, *The Welfare of Children*, 2nd ed., pp. 26–27 (2003; New York: Oxford University Press).

6. Ibid., pp. 189–190.

7. Ibid., p. 190.

8. In the colonial period, the term "dependent child" was used to describe children who were neglected, abused, homeless, or simply poor. The lines separating poverty from maltreatment were blurred. Over time, professionals increasingly recognized that it is important to distinguish poverty from maltreatment. The gradual process in which poverty was distinguished from maltreatment is discussed in some detail in John E. B. Myers, *A History of Child Protection in America* (2004; Philadelphia: Xlibris).

9. Leroy H. Pelton, *For Reasons of Poverty: A Critical Analysis of the Public Child Welfare System in the United States* (1989; New York: Praeger); Pelton, Child Welfare Policy and Practice: The Myth of Family Preservation, 67(4) *American Journal of Orthopsychiatry* 545–553 (1997).

10. Leroy H. Pelton, personal communication, April 4, 2005.

11. Pelton, *For Reasons of Poverty*, pp. 142, 158.

12. Elizabeth Bartholet, *Nobody's Children: Abuse and Neglect, Foster Drift, and the Adoption Alternative*, pp. 109, 177 (1999; Boston: Beacon Press).

13. Ibid., p. 239.

14. Ibid., p. 68.

15. Dorothy Roberts, *Shattered Bonds: The Color of Child Welfare*, p. 147 (2002; New York: Basic Books); Martin Guggenheim, Somebody's Children: Sustaining the Family's Place in Child Welfare Policy, Book Review of Elizabeth Bartholet. (1999). Nobody's Children: Abuse and Neglect, Foster Drift, and the Adoption Alternative, 113 *Harvard Law Review* 1716–1750 (2000).

16. Bartholet, *Nobody's Children*, pp. 178–182 (emphasis in original).

17. The U.S. Advisory Board on Child Abuse and Neglect was housed in the U.S. Department of Health and Human Services, Office of Human Development Services, Washington, DC. The titles of the reports are *Child Abuse and Neglect: Critical First Steps in Response to a National Emergency* (1990); *Creating Caring Communities: Blueprint for an Effective Federal Policy on Child Abuse and Neglect* (1991); *The Continuing Child Protection Emergency: A Challenge to the Nation* (1993); and *Neighbors Helping Neighbors: A New National Strategy for the Protection of Children* (1993).

18. Gary B. Melton, Chronic Neglect of Family Violence: More than a Decade of Reports to Guide US Policy, 22(6/7) *Child Abuse & Neglect* 569–586, p. 571 (2002) (emphasis in original).

19. U.S. Advisory Board on Child Abuse and Neglect, *Neighbors Helping Neighbors*, p. 11 (1993).

20. U.S. Advisory Board on Child Abuse and Neglect, *Child Abuse and Neglect*, p. 80 (emphasis in original).

21. See Gary B. Melton, Ross A. Thompson, & Mark A. Small (Eds.), *Toward a Child-Centered, Neighborhood-Based Child Protection System* (2002; Westport, CT: Praeger).

22. Gary Melton and his colleagues at Clemson University are presently conducting a major research project, in which they are attempting to build stronger communities in an area of South Carolina. Melton's project is described in Chapter 7.

23. See Roberts, *Shattered Bonds*; Myers, *History of Child Protection*.

24. Roberts, *Shattered Bonds*, p. 47. See also U.S. Children's Bureau, *Child Maltreatment 2002* (2004; Washington, DC: U.S. Department of Health and Human Services). The Children's Bureau report states, "African-American child victims were 51 percent more likely to be placed in foster care than White child victims" (p. 70).

25. Roberts, *Shattered Bonds*, p. 268.

26. Richard J. Gelles, *The Book of David: How Preserving Families Can Cost Children's Lives* (1996; New York: Basic Books).

27. Harry Specht & Mark E. Courtney, *Unfaithful Angels: How Social Work has Abandoned Its Mission*, pp. 4, 8 (1994; New York: The Free Press).

28. See Senate Bill 409, 108th Congress, 1st Session, 2003, and House Resolution 734, 108th Congress, 1st Session, 2003.

29. U.S. General Accounting Office, *Child Welfare: HHS Could Play a Greater Role in Helping Child Welfare Agencies Recruit and Retain Staff.* GAO Report 03-357 (March 2003; Washington, DC: U.S. GAO).

30. See American Public Human Services Association, *Report from the 2004 Child Welfare Workforce Survey: State Agency Findings* (2005; Washington, D.C.: APHSA): "the average tenure for workers leaving due to preventable turnover was five years for CPS and in-home protective service workers" (p. 8).

31. U.S. General Accounting Office, *Child Welfare*, p. 5.

32. Brenda D. Smith, Job Retention in Child Welfare: Effects of Perceived Organizational Support, Supervisor Support, and Intrinsic Job Value, 27 *Children and Youth Services Review* 153–169, p. 154 (2005).

33. See American Public Human Services Association, *Report from the 2004 Child Welfare Workforce Survey*. The average salaries for CPS social workers "are markedly lower than salaries for nurses, public school teachers, police officers, and firefighters" (p. 8).

34. Jane Waldfogel, *The Future of Child Protection: How to Break the Cycle of Abuse and Neglect*, p. 138 (1998; Cambridge, MA: Harvard University Press).

35. Leroy Pelton, Book Review of Jane Waldfogel, *The Future of Child Protection*, 27 *Journal of Sociology and Social Welfare* 184–187, p. 185 (2000).

36. In Missouri, "the family assessment approach began in selected counties in 1995. By June 1999 all counties had implemented the family assessment approach." Missouri

Department of Social Services, Division of Family Services, *Child Abuse and Neglect: Calendar Year 2001: Annual Report* (July 2002). See Minnesota Code Annotated § 626.5551; Missouri Code Annotated § 210.145.

37. Gary L. Siegel & L. Anthony Loman, *The Missouri Family Assessment and Response Demonstration Impact Evaluation*, p. 2 (2000; St. Louis, MO: Institute of Applied Research). Available online at www.iarstl.org.).

38. Siegel and Loman (ibid.) describe the methodology of their research as follows:

> A quasi-experimental research design was utilized consisting of two basic parameters. The first was an analysis of baseline versus demonstration-period data, in which outcomes during the two years prior to the demonstration were compared with outcomes during the first two years following its implementation. The second involved pilot versus comparison site analysis, in which outcomes from pilot areas were compared to outcomes in a set of sites designated as the comparison area. (p. 3)

39. Missouri Department of Social Services, Division of Family Services, *Child Abuse and Neglect*, p. 21 (July 2002).

40. Minnesota Department of Human Services, DHS Issues Amended Guidance on Alternative Response to Reports of Child Maltreatment, *Bulletin* no. 03-68-02, p. 2 (March 14, 2003).

41. Minnesota Department of Human Services, *Minnesota Alternative Response, Second Annual Report*, pp. 23, 33, 53 (February 2003). Evaluation conducted by the Institute of Applied Research, St. Louis, Missouri. The Minnesota evaluation employs an experimental design in which counties using alternative response are compared with a control group of counties using the traditional approach.

42. L. Anthony Loman & Gary L. Siegel, *Minnesota Alternative Response Evaluation*, p. vi (2004; St. Louis, MO: Institute of Applied Research).

43. Gary B. Melton, Mandated Reporting: A Policy Without Reason, 29 *Child Abuse & Neglect* 9–18, pp. 10, 14 (2005).

44. See David Finkelhor & Gail L. Zellman, Flexible Reporting Options for Skilled Child Abuse Professionals, 15 *Child Abuse & Neglect* 335–341, p. 335 (1991).

45. Ibid., pp. 337–338.

46. Ibid., pp. 335, 337–338.

47. See Marshall B. Jones, Decline of the American Orphanage, 1941–1980, 67 *Social Service Review* 459–480 (1993); Myers, *History of Child Protection*.

48. See Bilha Davidson-Arad, Fifteen-Month Follow-Up of Children at Risk: Comparison of the Quality of Life of Children Removed from Home and Children Remaining at Home, 27 *Children and Youth Services Review* 1–20, pp. 2–3 (2005). Davidson-Arad concluded, "These findings suggest that removing children at risk from abusive or neglectful homes can improve their quality of life, while leaving them in such homes does not" (p. 14).

49. Joseph H. Reid, Next Steps: Action Called For—Recommendations. In Henry S. Maas & Richard E. Engler, Jr., *Children in Need of Parents*, pp. 378–397, at 388–389 (1959; New York: Columbia University Press).

50. Henry S. Maas & Richard E. Engler, Jr., *Children in Need of Parents*, p. 356 (1959; New York: Columbia University Press).

51. David Fanshel & Eugene B. Shinn, *Children in Foster Care: A Longitudinal Investigation*, p. 491 (1978; New York: Columbia University Press).

51. *Code of Federal Regulations*, Title 45, Section 57 (2004) defines foster care as "24-hour substitute care for children outside their own homes. . . . The foster care settings include, but are not limited to family foster homes, relative foster homes (whether payments are being made or not), group homes, emergency shelters, residential facilities, childcare institutions, and pre-adoptive homes." In 2001, "of the estimated 542,000 children in foster care . . . , 48 percent were in foster family homes (non-relative), 24 percent were in relative foster homes, 18 percent were in group homes or institutions, 4 percent were in pre-adoptive homes, and 6 percent were in other placement types." Quote taken from Foster Care National Statistics, June 2003, at www.calib.com/research.

52. During the Great Depression of the 1930s, approximately 250,000 children were in some form of foster care. That was between 1 and 2 percent of the total child population. In 1965, approximately 300,000 children were in foster care, roughly 1.8 percent of the total child population. During the 1980s, the number of children in foster care expanded, due in part to the crack cocaine epidemic. In 2000, the foster care population topped 500,000. Yet, because the total child population had grown, the percentage of children in foster care remained less than 2 percent.

53. Leroy H. Pelton, personal communication, April 4, 2005.

54. See U.S. Children's Bureau, Administration for Children and Families, *Safety, Permanency, Well-Being: Child Welfare Outcomes 2000: Annual Report* (2001; Washington, DC: U.S. Department of Health and Human Services).

55. See Mark E. Courtney, Amy Dworsky, Gretchen Ruth, Tom Keller, Judy Havicek, & Noel Bost, *Midwest Evaluation of the Adult Functioning of Former Foster Youth: Outcomes at Age 19*, p. 3 (May 2005; Chapin Hall Working Paper, University of Chicago).

56. Andrea G. Zetlin & Lois A. Weinberg, Understanding the Plight of Foster Youth and Improving Their Educational Opportunities, 28 *Child Abuse & Neglect* 917–923, at 918 (2004).

57. Courtney et al., *Midwest Evaluation*, p. 3; Gloria Hochman, Anndee Hochman, & Jennifer Miller, *Foster Care: Voices from the Inside*, p. 8 (Commissioned by the Pew Commission on Children in Foster Care).

58. Courtney et al., *Midwest Evaluation*, p. 71.

59. Ibid., p. 3.

60. "The time children spent in foster care remained relatively unchanged between 1988 and 2001." Quote taken from Foster Care National Statistics, June 2003, p. 4, at www.calib.com/research. See Pew Commission on Children in Foster Care, *Fostering the Future*: "Almost half of these children spend at least two years in care, waiting for the safe, permanent family that should be their birthright. Almost 20 percent wait five or more years. In fiscal year (FY) 2001, nearly 39,000 infants under the age of one entered foster care, where they may lack the stability that promotes attachment and early brain development. That same year, about 19,000 older youth 'aged out' of foster care without a permanent family to support them in the transition to adulthood. On average, children have three different foster care placements" (p. 9).

61. U.S. Children's Bureau, *Safety, Permanency*.

62. See Duncan Lindsey & Ira M. Schwartz, Advances in Child Welfare: Innovations in Child Protection, Adoptions, and Foster Care, 26 *Children and Youth Services Review*

999–1005 (2004). Lindsey and Schwartz wrote, "The number of children leaving foster care for adoption increased from 27,600 in 1996 to more than 50,000 in 2001, and the number of adoptions has continued to increase" (p. 1000).

63. Cornelia M. Ashby, Director of Education, Workforce, and Income Security Issues with the U.S. General Accounting Office, *Testimony Before the Subcommittee on Human Resources Committee on Ways and Means, House of Representatives*. GAO-03-626T, p. 2. April 8, 2003.

64. The Pew Charitable Trusts, *Fostering Results, Nation Doubles Adoptions from Foster Care*, p. 1 (October 9, 2003), Washington, D.C.

65. Mark Testa, Nancy Sidote Salyers, Mike Shaver, & Jennifer Miller, *Family Ties: Supporting Permanence for Children in Safe and Stable Foster Care with Relatives and Other Caregivers*, p. 1 (2004; School of Social Work, University of Illinois at Urbana-Champaign).

66. Mary Bissell & Jennifer L. Miller (Eds.), *Using Subsidized Guardianship to Improve Outcomes for Children* (2004; Washington, DC: Children's Defense Fund).

67. Gloria Hochman, Anndee Hochman, & Jennifer Miller, *Foster Care: Voices from the Inside*, p. 5 (2004; Commissioned by the Pew Commission on Children in Foster Care).

68. Sigrid James, Why Do Foster Care Placements Disrupt? An Investigation of Reasons for Placement Change in Foster Care, 78(4) *Social Service Review* 601–625, p. 601 (December 2004).

69. Ibid. James studied foster care in San Diego, California. She found that "approximately seven out of ten placement changes for this cohort of children occurred for system or policy reasons," not because the foster parents desired a change.

70. See Hochman, Hochman, & Miller, *Foster Care*, p. 5; Massachusetts Society for the Prevention of Cruelty to Children, *Fifth Annual Report for 1885* (1886; Boston: Wright & Potter).

71. Massachusetts Society for the Prevention of Cruelty to Children, *Fifth Annual Report*, p. 20.

72. Ray S. Hubbard, *Crusading for Children, 1878–1943: The Massachusetts Society for the Prevention of Cruelty to Children*, p. 43 (no date, probably 1943; Boston: MSPCC).

73. A. Fox, K. Frasch, & J. D. Berrick, *Listening to Children in Foster Care: An Empirically Based Curriculum* (2000; Child Welfare Research Center, University of California, Berkeley).

74. *In re Gault*, 387 U.S. 1 (1967).

75. Sarah H. Ramsey, Representation of the Child in Protective Proceedings: The Determination of Decision-Making Capacity, 17 *Family Law Quarterly* 287 (1983).

76. Thomas Grisso, What We Know about Youth's Capacities as Trial Defendants. In Thomas Grisso & Robert G. Schwartz (Eds.), *Youth on Trial: A Developmental Perspective on Juvenile Justice*, pp. 139–171, at 162, 163 (2000; Chicago: University of Chicago Press).

77. Rona K. Abramovitch, Michele Peterson-Badali, & M. Rohan, Young People's Understanding and Assertion of Their Rights to Silence and Legal Counsel, 37 *Canadian Journal of Criminology* 1–18 (1995).

78. Melinda G. Schmidt, N. Dickon Reppucci, & Jennifer L. Woolard, Effectiveness of Participation as a Defendant: The Attorney-Juvenile Client Relationship, 21 *Behavioral Sciences and the Law* 175–198, p. 181 (2003).

79. Ethical Issues in the Legal Representation of Children, 64 *Fordham Law Review* 1279–2132, pp. 1294–1295 (1996).

80. Martin Guggenheim, A Paradigm for Determining the Role of Counsel for Children, 64 *Fordham Law Review* 1399–1433, p. 1431 (1966).

81. Peter Margulies, The Lawyer as Caregiver: Child Clients Competence in Context, 64 *Fordham Law Review* 1473–1504, p. 1497 (1996).

82. American Bar Association. *Standards of Practice for Lawyers Who Represent Children in Abuse and Neglect Cases.* Standard B-4. (1996; Washington, DC: ABA).

83. National Association of Counsel for Children, NACC Recommendations for Representation of Children in Abuse and Neglect Cases. Standard IV-B (2001; Denver, CO: NACC).

84. Martin Guggenheim, Counseling Counsel for Children, 97 *Michigan Law Review* 1488–1511, p. 1508 (1999).

85. Jean Koh Peters, *Representing Children in Child Protective Proceedings: Ethical and Practical Dimensions* (1997; Charlottesville, VA: Lexis).

86. Donald N. Duquette, Legal Representation for Children in Protection Proceedings: Two Distinct Lawyer Roles Are Required, 34 *Family Law Quarterly* 441 (2000).

87. Emily Buss, Confronting Developmental Barriers to the Empowerment of Child Clients, 84 *Cornell Law Review* 896–966 (1999).

88. Several animal species abandon their young at birth. Such behavior only occurs, however, when the newborn is precocious and able to fend for itself. When a species produces offspring that are unable to survive on their own, lengthy and devoted parenting is the norm.

89. *Prince v. Massachusetts,* 321 U.S. 158, 166 (1944).

90. *Santosky v. Kramer,* 455 U.S. 745 (1982).

91. *Proceedings of the Conference on the Care of Dependent Children.* 60th Congress, 2nd Session, vol. 13, S.D. 721 (1909). Child welfare professionals had reached consensus on the benefits of family life long before the 1909 White House Conference. See, e.g., Charles Richmond Henderson, The Relief and Care of Dependent Children. In Charles R. Henderson, *Introduction to the Study of the Dependent, Defective, and Delinquent Classes and of Their Social Treatment* (1901; Boston: D.C. Heath). Henderson wrote, "It is a first principle of charity to avoid breaking up the natural relations of the family so long as the interests of the children are not in jeopardy, parental responsibility must not be weakened, and the affections which cling to offspring and parents must not be lightly destroyed" (p. 98).

92. *White House Conference on Child Health and Protection.* Section IV–The Handicapped: Prevention, Maintenance, Protection. Carl C. Carstens, Chair. Committee on Socially Handicapped-Dependency and Neglect. Homer Folks, Chair. J. Prentice Murphy, Vice-Chair, p. 8 (1933; New York: Appleton-Century).

93. See Myers, *History of Child Protection,* pp. 124–125 (2004; Philadelphia: Xlibris).

94. *Prince v. Massachusetts,* 321 U.S. 158, 166 (1944).

95. *Hodgson v. Minnesota,* 497 U.S. 417, 446 (1990).

96. *In re Gault,* 387 U.S. 1 (1967).

97. See Mark Hardin, *Family Group Conferences in Child Abuse and Neglect Cases: Learning from the Experience of New Zealand* (1996; Washington, DC: American Bar Association).

98. See *Washington Revised Code* § 13.34.062(5), 2006. Washington law provides that when a child is placed in shelter care, parents must receive notice of the proceedings,

including notice of their right to "request that a multidiciplinary team, family group conference, prognostic staffing, or case conference be convened." See also *Montana Code Annotated* § 41-3-422(12), 2006. Montana law states that "at any stage of the proceedings considered appropriate by the court, the court may order an alternative dispute resolution proceeding or the parties may voluntarily participate in an alternative dispute proceeding. An alternative dispute resolution proceeding under this chapter may include family group conference, mediation, or a settlement conference." See also *Oregon Revised Statutes* §§ 417.365 and 417.368, 2006. Section 417.368 provides: "(1) The Department of Human Services shall consider the use of a family decision-making meeting in each case in which a child is placed in substitute care for more than 30 days. (2) When the department determines that the use of a family decision-making meeting is appropriate, the meeting shall be held, whenever possible, before the child has been in substitute care for 60 days." See also *Kansas Statutes Annotated* § 38-1559(a), 2006; *Montana Code Annotated* §§ 41-3-102, 41-3-205(3; k), 2006; *Oregon Revised Statutes* §§ 417.365, 417.368, 2006; *South Carolina Code* §§ 20-7-545, 20-7-690, 2006; *Washington Code Annotated* §§ 13.34.063(5), 13-34.094, 2006.

99. See Knut Sundell & Bo Vinnerljung, Outcomes of Family Group Conferencing in Sweden: A 3-Year Follow-Up, 28 *Child Abuse & Neglect* 267–287 (2004).

100. National Council of Juvenile and Family Court Judges, *Essex County Child Welfare Mediation Program.* Available online at www.ncjfcj.org.

101. See Burton J. Cohen, Reform the Child Welfare System: Competing Paradigms of Change, 27 *Children and Youth Services Review* 653–666 (2005). Cohen described a conference he attended titled "Reinventing Child Welfare." "The one thing that everyone could agree on was that the child welfare system was not working and needed fundamental reform" (p. 653).

102. Leroy H. Pelton, Resolving the Crisis in Child Welfare: Simply Expanding the Present System Is Not Enough, 48(4) *Public Welfare* 19–25, at 19 (1990).

103. Alvin L. Schorr, Comment on Policy: The Bleak Prospect for Public Child Welfare, 74 *Social Service Review* 124–135 (2000).

104. Theodore A. Lothrop, Correction and Prevention of Neglect of Children. In *White House Conference on Child Health and Protection.* Section IV–The Handicapped: Prevention, Maintenance, Protection. Carl C. Carstens, Chair. Committee on Socially Handicapped–Dependency and Neglect. Homer Folks, Chair. J. Prentice Murphy, Vice-Chair, pp. 353–389 at 386 (New York: Appleton-Century); Carl C. Carstens, Children's Protective Work in a Community's Programs, Child Welfare League of America, 18(2) *Bulletin* 4 (February 1939); Claire R. Hancock, *A Study of Protective Services and the Problem of Neglect of Children in New Jersey*, p. 4 (1958; Trenton, NJ: Department of Institutions and Agencies, State Board of Child Welfare); Vincent De Francis, *Child Protective Services: A National Survey*, p. vii (1967; Denver, CO: American Humane Association); U.S. Advisory Board on Child Abuse and Neglect, *Neighbors Helping Neighbors*, p. 34.

INDEX